A SIKH DIPLOMAT

G. J. MALIK

A SIKH DIPLOMAT

From childhood in India,
through Cambridge University,
as a scientist in war time England,
the Royal Air Force, then around the
world in the Indian Foreign Service.

by

Gunwant Malik

First published in Great Britain 2008 by WritersPrintShop

ISBN 9781904623694

Clothbound edition ISBN 9781904623687

Designed by e-BookServices.com

Dedicated to my farsighted
and
loving parents

TABLE OF CONTENTS

LIST OF ILLUSTRATIONS

FOREWORD

This is my father's autobiography, covering the origins of the family through to the end of his career in the Indian Foreign Service, with observations on the people, politics and events he encountered from 1921 to 1979.

He was born the son of a Sikh Civil Engineer in Karachi (now in Pakistan) and toured the assigned districts with his parents on various modes of transport including camels. Because they were always on the move, he was initially educated by his mother, who had also had to educate herself.

Later on he went to study in universities in Europe including Cambridge, at the same college his father had attended. He experienced the changes in Europe as war loomed, joined the Officers Training Corps, and also worked as a scientist with colleagues involved in developing advanced materials for the war effort. During the war, he served as a Royal Air Force Officer, supporting aircrews from bases in Norfolk, and after the war, because of his facility with languages, he was sent with the interrogation teams to Germany.

After the war ended, came the trauma of India's partition and the family's forced emigration to Delhi. Around the same time his marriage was arranged to the beautiful daughter of a Sikh Conservator of Forests, with whom he subsequently raised my brother and me.

My father joined the Indian Foreign Service in the new India, so beginning a career which took him to Belgium, Ethiopia, Argentina, Japan, Singapore, Philippines, French West Africa, Chile, Thailand and finally back to Europe. Along the way he encountered interesting and important persons, and dealt with the effects of Latin American coups d'etat , in particular the tragic end of President Allende in Chile, receiving what was probably The President's last phone call before he died. He retired from the service at the statutory age of 58, as the Indian Ambassador in Madrid.

— Kiran Malik

THE BHAGATS

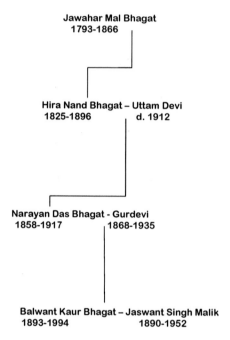

Jawahar Mal Bhagat
1793-1866

Hira Nand Bhagat – Uttam Devi
1825-1896   **d. 1912**

Narayan Das Bhagat - Gurdevi
1858-1917   **1868-1935**

Balwant Kaur Bhagat – Jaswant Singh Malik
1893-1994   **1890-1952**

THE MALIKS

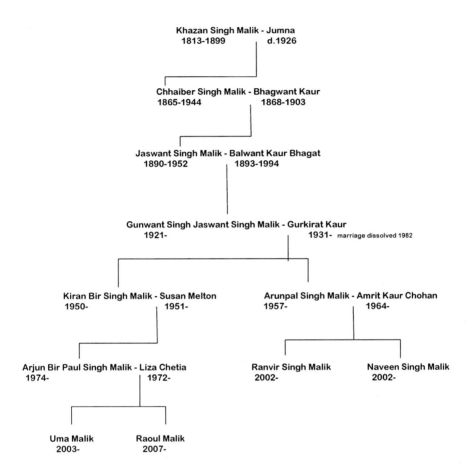

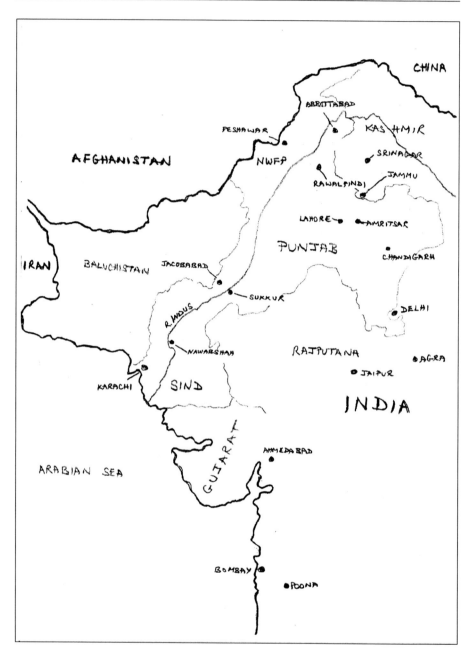

PUNJAB & SIND BEFORE 1947 PARTITION

THE MALIK NAME

The name MALIK is well known in all countries where Semitic languages are in use. Depending upon the pronunciation and the country it can mean anything from OWNER to KING. In Northern India it usually means the headman of a village. The theory in India is that all land belongs to the Raja. Of course, today that means the State. Consequently the occupant has to pay rent (known as LAND REVENUE) to the State. This revenue may be paid to a Zamindar or directly to an official appointed by the State. The two systems are known respectively as ZAMINDARI and RYOTWARI. Some political scientists refer to the Zamindar as an INTERMEDIARY.

In other parts of India people refer to the headman by another title. In Gujrat he is called the PATEL; in Maharashtra and neighbouring states, he is called PATIL. There are, therefore, hundreds of thousands of persons entitled to call themselves by these titles because, as in Germany, all the descendants in the tail male of the awardee use the title. Furthermore, under the present legislation, it is open to everyone to change his or her name as often as they please by signing an affidavit on a ten-rupee stamped paper and having it notarised. If they cannot find an obliging notary they can put an advertisement in two newspapers to say they have changed their name and what they wish to be known as in future. Copies of newspapers are accepted by all authorities. I must admit I have not seen any one calling themselves Maharaja of Siberia or Whisky Soda in consequence of this facility.

The reason for using titles as surnames is that surnames were not common in India and, in legal documents, a man was referred to as 'A, son of B, caste C, sub-caste D'. Of course, this refers to Hindus and those covered by Hindu Law. With the advent of English education, many men wanted to have surnames. High-caste persons were happy to use their castes or sub-castes as surnames and others resorted to other ways. Many Jains, generally belonging to trading castes, called themselves simply by their religion.

Yes, caste fortunately or unfortunately, is not restricted to Hindus. I have a friend belonging to a nationally known Roman Catholic family who once said to me, 'We are five brothers and sisters and if any one of us were to marry a non-Brahmin our mother would die.' A Pakistani Muslim woman I met at a party in Bangkok many years ago said, 'Of course, we have the four castes, Syeds, Sheikhs, Kureishis and Weavers.'

Foreigners find all this very confusing. A visitor to Gujrat remarked, 'Yesterday I saw a sign-board which read PATEL MANUFACTURING COMPANY. Is that why I have met so many Patels since I came to Gujrat?'

My cousin Bhupinder Singh Malik (born 1918) has done some research into our family history and he tells me that some five hundred years ago a great landowner in Patohar (the present Rawalpindi division of Punjab in Pakistan) married an heiress from another part of Punjab. In those days, such a great lady naturally came with a train of servants which included a secretary. Her husband found this secretary very useful and finally awarded him 1600 acres of land. It was thus that our ancestor became a minor landowner and built a village which he called Dera Khalsa – a camp paying revenue directly to the Raja , i.e. not through an intermediary. This village and this land remained with the family till Partition in 1947.

Of course, these sixteen hundred acres could not feed the hundreds of descendants who constituted the family four or more centuries later. The official designation of the head of the family was Lambardar – the official who collected the revenue, remitted it to the government and was paid a nominal salary. The village land was equally divided among all males and only the office of Lambardar was governed by primogeniture. Many members of the family saw no future in cultivating a couple of acres of land, sold it to a relative, and left the village to seek some other occupation elsewhere.

Bhupinder, before Independence, searched the revenue records of Dera Khalsa and found the names of all our ancestors from the foundation of the village and compiled a linear family tree. I have only taken interest in our great-grandfather Khazan Singh Malik (1813-1899) of whom my father Jaswant Singh Malik (1890-1952) had fond memories.

As a young man, Khazan Singh served in the cavalry of Maharaja Ranjit Singh (reigned 1800-1839) as a trooper. When the Sikh state collapsed in 1848, he returned to Dera Khalsa with his horse and the clothes he wore. He was already a widower and a family council decided that since he had seen the outside world and appeared big, strong and enterprising he should go and seek a fortune in the nearby city of Rawalpindi which the

1895 Lahore   Khazan Singh Malik in formal dress (Choga)

British-Indian army had chosen to make the headquarters of its Northern Command. But how to set out without a penny? A search found a girl in the family who was wearing a rupee coin as a hair ornament. Khazan Singh left the village on horseback with that rupee in his pocket.

It is nearly a day's journey on horseback from Dera Khalsa to Rawalpindi and on the way Khazan Singh saw a country fair in progress. One of the attractions of the fair was a wrestling contest with money prizes so he joined in. As I have said he was big and strong. The result was that he arrived in Rawalpindi with seven rupees in his pocket.

This was enough to enable him to rent a room from the Chaudhry of Rawalpindi. Chaudhry is a title like Malik but of higher rank. The successor of this wealthy property owner today in the twenty-first century is Tariq Azam Chaudhry and he is an advocate in Islamabad. I know him and he was my house-guest in my flat in New Delhi a few years ago.

I do not know how Khazan Singh started earning a living but it is likely that he started by buying and selling liquor which was in great demand among the sepoys. Our caste is known as KALAL throughout Northern India. The kalal makes and sells alcoholic drinks of all kinds. In popular speech no distinction is made between brewed, fermented and distilled – all are known as SHARAAB. If one wants to be technical, sharaab 'of the oven' (still) is considered more potent than other kinds. Distilling is an honourable profession in Scotland but in India a kalal works with his hands so he is a shudra caste; besides his activity ruins families and is particularly hated by women because a popular proverb says that 'if a man drinks sharaab, his wife drinks tears all her life.'

Fortunately for us, in the eighteenth century two Sikh kalals became great soldiers; the first was Kapur Singh who founded the city and erstwhile princely State of Kapurthala and commanded one of the twelve independent armed groups of Sikh barons/ chieftains who were united by Maharaja Ranjit Singh at the end of the century. He was childless and was succeeded by Jassa Singh who was recognised by the Mughal court as the Commander-in-Chief (Sultan-al-kaum) of the Sikhs after he sacked Delhi. Of course all kalals from all parts of Punjab now call themselves

Ahluwalias instead of kalals – from the name of the missal which Jassa Singh commanded.

I do not know what other business Khazan Singh did but he must have supplied much more than liquor to the Army because we know that in the Second Afghan War he was able to make three lakhs of rupees (Rs.300,000). The family fortune had been made.

In the meantime Khazan Singh had remarried. His wife's name was Jumna; she had only one eye and was a strong-minded woman. She survived till 1926 and I remember making obeisance to her in the town-house which her husband had built in what was known as the Street of the Maliks in the old walled city. This was the second house which Khazan Singh built. The first was a single storey house in the same street and he donated it for conversion into a Gurdwara (Sikh temple) which continued in existence till the time of Partition.

The second house had three storeys. It was never provided with electricity and I remember that there was no banister or even a hand-rail in the staircase which was always dark. Instead one had to hold on to a rope which was greasy and, to me, quite disgusting. I was glad I never had to stay in this house.

There were four sons of this marriage and I saw them all. My grand-father Chhaiber Singh (1865-1944) was the second son. The two elder sons only went to school for eight years after which they were absorbed in the various family businesses. The two younger sons finished their schooling (10 years) and went on to study at Gordon College in Rawalpindi where they got their B.A. degrees. This college was run by American Protestant missionaries and is probably still operating.

My grand-father's elder brother was called Mohan Singh (1863-1931) and I am told that one day his father said to him, 'I have to go on a business trip which will take me over a month. In the meantime, the Excise Commissioner will come to Rawalpindi and that is when our liquor licence, which is running out, has to be renewed so you will have to go and see him about it. Liquor is no longer our principal business but it is the oldest and we must not lose it.'

Mohan Singh did go to see the Excise Commissioner who was, of course, an Englishman. However, he was kept waiting a long time and, being the son of a wealthy businessman, he felt offended and left. When the father returned, Mohan Singh duly told him what had happened. The father was furious, 'Idiot,' he said, 'That is not how business is done and you should know better; now I will show you how I am going to undo the damage you have done to the family's fortunes.'

Since the Excise Comissioner had moved on to another District, Khazan Singh got the best horse he could find and caught up with him in Jehlum. However, the Officer refused to see him so Khazan Singh got a carpet, spread it on the footpath beside the road from the Circuit House to the Camp Office and made repeated bows every time the Englishman went past – all to no purpose because the Officer pretended not to see him. Khazan Singh followed him to all the towns where he went in the course of his duties but met with no success. Finally, having done his work, the Commissioner decided to enjoy some shikar in the company of his acquaintances. In the course of this exercise he found that his good horse had taken him away from his companions so he called out like the traditional burra sahib, 'koi hai?' (Anybody there?).

Khazan Singh's horse was, if anything, better than the Excise Commissioner's and he had never let him get out of his sight but without causing the burra sahib any embarrassment so he cantered up and responded in Urdu, 'At your orders, Sir!' The Excise Commissioner answered him also in Urdu, 'Khazan Singh, I think you will pursue me to my grave' and gave him the licence which he had been carrying in his pocket. This was the lesson which the father taught his son. I am afraid none of his descendants learnt the lesson and I, as a First Secretary in the Indian Embassy in Buenos Aires in 1953, had to learn it all over again from my Ambassador, Nawab Ali Yavar Jung.

After the death of the patriarch, business did not do so well and the sons became rentiers. They no longer wanted to live together so they decided to dissolve the Joint Family. To divide the property, the two younger sons made four lots and offered the choice to the two elder brothers and agreed on the left-overs. The two elder brothers got the urban property, the third Harnam Singh (1875-1945) got orchards and Dogar Singh (1878-1946) got the farm land.

1903 Lahore My Dadiji (paternal grandmother) with her two sons Mukhbain Singh and Jaswant Singh (two smaller children not identified).

The two elder brothers thought of sending their sons abroad to study when cholera broke out in Rawalpindi. My father's elder brother – I always called him TAYAJI – Mukhbain Singh (1884-1989) and he, arrived together at Downing College, Cambridge, in 1908. Tayaji wanted to be a barrister and chose to study history. He thought his younger brother should prepare for the Indian Forest Service (I.F.S.) so he had to enrol for the Natural Sciences Tripos.

Downing, being the latest college to be founded (1800) had difficulty in attracting students – strange as it may seem to us today – so it set up a Chemistry laboratory. At Trinity, there was no such new-fangled facility and an undergraduate there who wanted to study Natural Sciences before becoming a barrister had to come to Downing for his Chemistry practicals. It was thus that my father met Jawaharlal Nehru whom Pitaji knew to be much richer and, therefore, avoided cultivating.

Pitaji – that is how I addressed my father in Punjabi – felt that there was no assurance of his getting into the I.F.S. and that, if he did not, there were no family forests for him to look after. He felt he would have a better chance as an engineer. Apart from the Indian

Service of Engineers, various railway companies were recruiting engineers and offering better salaries than the Government. He moved therefore to London where he felt he could live better on what his elder brother allowed him as a stipend. He joined University College in London and found lodgings in Gower Street nearby. He finished his studies in 1911 and worked for some time as an apprentice in the London and North Eastern railway at Sheringham in Norfolk. I met his landlord there in 1944.

After all this, he could not find a job and returned home where his father had married Gurdevi Bhagat (1888-1965) after the death in 1903 of his first wife Bhagwanti (born 1868). Bhagwanti had developed cancer and was operated on in Lahore but this did not help so she knew she was going to die and was keen to 'fix up' her two sons before she passed away. This she did and her husband respected her wishes so my father married my mother Balwant Kaur Bhagat on 12th October 1912. Of course, arranged marriages are still the rule in India, and a hundred years ago, there was no resriction on child marriages. Bhagwanti's own marriage provides an interesting illustration of how marriages were arranged in the nineteenth century.

One fine morning the municipal vaccinator of Rawalpindi woke up to find his wife smiling and looking very happy.

'What makes you so happy, my good woman?'

'Sir, I dreamt that the child in my belly is going to be a girl and that she is going to marry the son of so-and-so born last year. Would it not be wonderful if that could happen?'

The husband did not say a word but put on his turban and shoes and picked up his stick.

'Where are you going , Sir?'

'My good woman, since you have spoken, I have to fulfil your wishes.'

We are all – Bhupinder, his three brothers and I and our progeny – descended from this marriage. I remember Bhagwanti's mother. When I saw her she was reputed to be a hundred years old (which I doubt now) – having long survived her husband Kishan Dayal and, of course, her daughter Bhagwanti. She was blind but loved by everybody; she lived in the Malik house with Pitaji's other grandmother.

1920 Ahmedabad   On stools: Bhupinder, Gajinder, Jagjit. Seated: Mata-ji, Tayiji (Balwant), Dadiji, Mohinder. Standing: Pitaji, Dadaji, Tayaji.

1925 Rawalpindi   Malik men at the wedding of Dr. Gurdit Singh Malik to Abnash Kaur.

THE BHAGATS

The family of my mother were, of course, kalals like the Maliks. It appears that, at the beginning of the eighteenth century, they were Hindus and one of my ancestors, whose name I have not been able to find out, became a devotee of one of the godesses in the Hindu pantheon. Devotion in Hindi is *bhakti* and a devotee is known as a bhagat. Of course, there is no shortage of families in India calling themselves Bhagat. In this particular Bhagat family there are both Hindus and Sikhs. The best known person in this family was Bhagat Jawahar Mal (1793-1866). He was what is known in India as a god-man – the word exists in the 1998 New Oxford Dictionary of English. Probably the earlier English word was THAUMATURGIST. He is better known by his respectful nick-name of Sain Sahib. Even today he is remembered by Patoharis scattered all over the world. The tradition in India is that religious leaders should earn their living by work. Sain Sahib, therefore, made and sold liquor which he did not drink himself. He had a shop in the bazaar in Rawalpindi.

The story goes that he went to see a neighbour in the latter's shop. This shop-keeper went on attending to his clients while talking to his friend. Sain Sahib noticed that he kept a set of weights on the counter which he used for weighing the merchandise he sold. However, when a wholesaler came to supply him, he produced and used another set from under the counter. When he did not have a customer, the shopkeeper turned to his friend and asked him,

'You know, Jawahar, I perform all my religious duties but I do not find inner peace.'

The latter put his hand under the counter, took a weight in his right hand, then he took the corresponding weight from the counter in his other hand and said,

'My friend, this is what deprives you of inner peace.'

I think I have read about Epictetus that when he was banished to Cheronea by Augustus Caesar, he asked a pupil,

'Thou sayest that Caesar hath given thee peace; can he give thee peace of mind also?'

Sain Sahib's son Hira Nand (1825-96) took to business but he did not succeed although he made the difficult and dangerous journey to Bokhara. His contemporary Khazan Singh Malik had found this journey very profitable.

Fortunately, his sons turned out to be very good students. My maternal grandfather (*nana* in Hindi and Punjabi) named Narain Das (1858-1917) was the third son. Rawalpindi in those days only had a middle school, that is to say up to the eighth class. To go to college, he had to join a high school and take the matriculation examination which meant moving to Lahore. One month before the matriculation examination he got a letter from his father ordering him to return to Rawalpindi to get married and he had to obey. The marriage took place in a village. At that time there was no railway line between Rawalpindi and Lahore and the practical way to travel was to join a caravan which would provide protection from robbers. These caravans left at regular intervals. Unfortunately the marriage ceremonies took longer than he had anticipated and he missed the caravan by which he had planned to return to Lahore. He got back the day before the examination and rushed to see his Headmaster.

The Headmaster was furious, 'You were always my favourite pupil and I was expecting you to get a gold medal. If you sit for the exam tomorrow after missing a fortnight's classes and without having prepared at all for the exam, you cannot but fail and disgrace me. I cannot possibly allow it.'

The unhappy student wept, touched his teacher's feet and was finally allowed to take the examination. Not only did he get the gold medal but he also won a Fuller exhibition which paid for the four years he took to get his B.A.

There was no University in Punjab and the B.A. exam had to be written in Calcutta (now Kolkata). Fortunately there was a railway line and so he was able to go to Calcutta in a third class compartment. The journey was well worth it. Not only did he get a gold medal but the examiners were so impressed by his performance that they advised him to stay on, study for a month and take the M.A. examination scheduled for that year which normally requires two years' study. He got a gold medal for the M.A. also.

He went on to become an advocate like his elder brother Ishwar Das (1856-1952) who was making a great success in the profession – he too had won a Fuller exhibition. However, Narain Das was different. One day when he was pleading before an English judge, the latter said to him,

'Mr. Bhagat you are arguing like a judge rather than like an advocate; I advise you to become a judge.'

He took the advice and had no difficulty in getting into the judicial service in view of his brilliant academic record. It was thus that my mother Balwant Kaur was born on 14th December 1893 in Hoshiarpur where her father was District and Sessions judge. He was a very successful judge – his judgements were seldom reversed – the next step should have been the High Court but, at that time, Indians could only be appointed to the High Court if they were members of the Indian Civil Service.

Unfortunately, I never knew this grandfather because he died four years before I was born. Some of his letters still exist and everybody admires the fluency and eloquence of his English which is all the more admirable as he learnt it from teachers who were all Indians. Apart from his professional ability he was remarkable for his erudition and honesty which was above all suspicion. With all that, he was very human. My mother used to relate how the first time she visited him after her marriage, she said to him,

'Father, your way of lacing your boots is very old fashioned. Let me show you the modern way.'

'Why are you telling me? Tell my valet.'

This from a man who had been travelling third class!

At the time of my mother's marriage, Narain Das Bhagat was Minister of Justice in Alwar State. Earlier, he had been Law Member of the Council of the Maharaja of Kashmir. These two positions and his earlier reputation as one of the few Indian District and Sessions Judges had made him well-known throughout Punjab and he counted many of the top personalities, both Indian and British, as his friends. The largest princely state in Punjab was Patiala, and Maharaja Bhupinder Singh had a towering personality which made him the most influential person in Punjab. In particular the Government of India considered him as the leader of the Sikhs. My Nanaji went to see him and requested him to recommend his son Surinder Singh Bhagat (1889-1938) as well as his new son-in-law (my father) to the Secretary of State for India for appointment to the Indian Service of Engineers. My father left immediately for England to make his application. However, the Secretary of State only accepted one recommendation and it was only Surinder Singh Bhagat who was appointed.

Pitaji returned to Rawalpindi and was unemployed till the outbreak of the Great War in August 1914.

1912 Murree, Punjab Murree. My Nanaji (maternal grandfather) with wife and some of his children. Mataji is the girl with glasses behind him.

THE SIKHS

In the United Kingdom today, most people have probably seen a Sikh. In fact many people know a Sikh. Of course the first question which arises is, 'What is a Sikh?' and the answer would be 'a man with a turban and beard.' However this is not a satisfactory answer primarily because a woman is as much a Sikh as a man! Apart from that, in the first years of the twenty-first century a lot of men are wearing beards all over the world. More to the point, some Muslim men are wearing turbans and beards; in fact, in some countries in Europe and North America there have been cases of Sikhs having been assaulted and even killed in the mistaken belief that they were Muslims.

The word in Punjabi means 'disciple' and the disciples of a succession of ten gurus (teachers) who flourished in the sixteenth, seventeenth and eighteenth centuries were so known for their devotion to their teachers. The Sikh as described in the previous paragraph is more strictly classified as a 'keshadhari Sikh' and came into existence on Vaisakhi day in 1699. Vaisakhi is a Hindu harvest festival and its date falls on either 13th or 14th April of the Christian calendar. Making allowance for the Gregorian reform in the latter, some scholars have stated that the *khalsa* (the army of the pure) was inaugurated on 30th March 1699.

Sikhs who are not *keshadharis* (do not wear their hair unshorn) are described as *sehjdharis*. Guru Gobind Singh (1666-1708), the last Sikh Guru, prescribed that a khalsa must:

(i) wear all his or her hair *(kesha)* unshorn,

(ii) carry or wear a comb *(kangha)*,

(iii) a sword *(kirpan)*,

(iv) wear boxer shorts *(kachha)* and

(v) an iron bracelet *(kadha)*.

In the Punjabi language all these five items begin with the letter K *(kakka)*. I wear as a symbolic sword a piece of metal incrusted in the comb I wear in my hair. The shorts are my underpants and the bracelet is of stainless steel. I always wear a turban during waking hours to hide my increasing baldness although the hair I have is long and untrimmed. My beard is rolled up so that I don't trip over it when I get up. I do look like a keshadhari Sikh. A woman normally dressed in any traditional Indian dress can be recognised as a Sikh only by her iron kadha because few women would want to wear an iron bracelet unless they are practising Sikhs. Some years ago a rumour went round that Sikhs are immune to arthritis – totally incorrect because I have arthritis - and one would see men and women who were obviously not Sikhs wearing a kadha!

The first Sikh guru was Nanak Dev (1469-1539). He had Hindu and Muslim disciples whose religions he respected. He started the tradition that the guru on his deathbed nominated his successor. The guru became for the Sikhs much more than a teacher – for instance God is described as *satguru* (true teacher) and the ten gurus were often referred to in their lifetimes as *sacha patsha* – the True King. However, the gurus did not claim to be avatars of any Hindu god or claim to be other than mortal human teachers.

As I have mentioned, Guru Nanak did not start a new religion. When he died the Hindu disciples wanted to cremate the body and the Muslims to bury it. The argument went on till nightfall when they agreed to postpone the decision till the morrow, leaving the corpse covered by a sheet. Next morning, the body had disappeared so they cut the sheet in two. One half was buried and the other cremated.

It can be said that the theology of Sikhism is of Islamic-Christian-Jewish inspiration – one God who is invisible and has no physical form so that there are no idols in Sikhism. However, the majority of disciples were probably Hindus who celebrated Hindu festivals. On Vaisakhi day 1699, the names of the five disciples - the five beloved ones - which have come down to us, were all Hindu names, belonging to five different castes and from different parts of India. On the other hand, when the fifth Guru Arjun Dev (1564-1606) started building the Golden Temple in Amritsar, he asked a respected Muslim to lay the foundation stone. Hindu friends have told me that the Upanishads accept the idea of a single God and that Sikh theology is perfectly compatible with these sacred Hindu scriptures. I have also been told that Hinduism is not a religion but a culture in which there are various philosophical schools one of which appears to accept atheism.

Why did Guru Gobind Singh decide to create the khalsa? I am sure there are many answers to this question. My mother told me this story. I do not claim to be an authority on Sikh history or doctrine much less to enter into any controversy but since I am writing this I prefer to state what I was brought up to believe. The ninth Guru Teg Bahadur (1621-75) was a peace-loving and modest man. His predecessor was a child who died before the age of ten years. Asked to nominate his successor as he lay on his deathbed, all he said was, 'Guru at Baba Bakala'. Immediately twenty-two relations proceeded to this small town to set themselves up in the style of earlier gurus.

In the meantime, a rich drover who was transporting his cattle on a ship on the high seas met with a storm and apprehended that the ship would sink. He happened to be a Sikh and he prayed that his ship might be saved and promised to give the Guru a thousand ashrafis (gold coins). The storm abated and he arrived safely at his destination with his cattle.

The sea is a long way from Punjab and when he got there he was told to go to Baba Bakala where he found the situation which I have described. He also learnt that the eighth guru had already passed away on the day on which he had made his vow. He was advised to go to the shop of the principal claimant. He went there, prostrated himself and put down ten ashrafis. The offering was acknowledged but that was all. He had no better luck with the other twenty-one 'gurus' – of course, the offerings kept diminishing. On making further enquiries, he was told that there was a member of the extended family but he was only a shopkeeper who had always lived at Baba Bakala and had made no claim to being the Guru or set up a *gaddi* (throne). There, when he put down his ashrafi, the shopkeeper remarked, 'I am not greedy for your gold but a Sikh should keep his word.'

In northern India, middle class homes are built with flat roofs (for sleeping on during hot summer nights) which are accessible by an internal staircase. The drover rushed on to the roof and shouted,

'Guru's found.'

With this witness, Teg Bahadur was immediately accepted as the ninth Guru.

Some years later, the Guru's son noticed that his father appeared sad and preoccupied. On being asked by the child, he answered,

'Some Brahmins from Kashmir came to see me. The Emperor Aurangzeb (1658-1707) has asked them to choose between Islam and death. I am afraid that to save them some very good man will have to sacrifice his life.'

'But, Father, there is no better man than you.'

This settled the father's fate and he was executed at Delhi in 1675. The sentence was carried out in the main square of the commercial centre and a guard was put on the body and the head to make sure that they rotted there. Sikhs had already acquired a reputation for courage and one who had a good horse galloped it across the square, picked up the head and disappeared. The guard was doubled. A rich drover had a brilliant idea. He drove his large herd through the square and, when the dust settled, the headless corpse had disappeared. The guard troop followed the cloud of dust. Finally they saw the drover sobbing beside a house (*bangla* in Punjabi) in flames. He had made his own substantial villa into a funeral pyre for his Guru.

When the rider with the head arrived at Anandpur – the last residence of the Guru in the Shivalik hills nearly two hundred miles from Delhi – he laid it before the Guru's son and told him what had happened. After thanking him appropriately, Gobind Ram said, 'Why did they have to hide? I shall make a Sikh who will never be able to hide.' He achieved this on Vaisakhi day 1699. After having baptised the five new khalsas, he made them baptise *him* with the name of Gobind Singh. Till then, only Kshatriyas (the Hindu warrior caste) used to use the title Singh meaning tiger. There is a magnificent gurdwara at Anandpur called Keshgarh to commemorate the creation of the keshadhari Sikh. In old Delhi, there is an equally imposing gurdwara in Chandni Chowk – the main square of the old walled city – called Sisganj from *sees* meaning head. Another great Gurdwara in New Delhi is called Bangla Sahib where the disguised cremation of the ninth Guru took place.

IV

SIND 1921-30

L a Rochefoucauld says in his maxim No.342 that the accent of the place in which one is born remains in the mind and in the heart as it does in one's speech. However, I can not speak Sindhi although I was born at five minutes past noon on 29th May 1921 in Karachi. Some people claim that I speak Patohari with a Sindhi accent.

After having served the Government of Bombay Presidency for seven years, my father's reputation for honesty, hard work and professional competence had been rewarded by his being appointed to the Indian Service of Engineers which he had failed to enter in 1912. Sind, in those days, was a Division (headed by a Commissioner) of Bombay Presidency. The three coastal provinces of British India which were also the oldest were called Presidency because the Governor – usually a British politician – was the President of the Governor's Council. Today Sind is a Pakistani province and the population of Karachi, the commercial capital of Pakistan, is probably a hundred times what it was in 1921.

My mother (called Mataji by me and later by my children) had given birth in 1918, in Rawalpindi, to a little girl with the assistance of a midwife. This had happened in my Dadaji's (my paternal grandfather's) house according to tradition. The baby only lived a fortnight. The midwife had been consulted and she had said, 'This baby lacks an intestine.' When my mother rejoined my father in Malsiras in what is today Maharashtra, she told him that for any future baby, he would have to be present. It was for this reason that I was born in the Lady Dufferin Hospital in Karachi far away from my grandparents.

My father was, at this time, Assistant Executive Engineer (Roads and Buildings) and reported to the Executive Engineer who was in charge of all the public works of the District of Karachi. Sind is an arid region (like Egypt) whose population depends for its agriculture on irrigation and the water comes from the Indus which is one of the World's great rivers. Looking after the canals is, therefore, a matter of life and death. My earliest memories go back to the age of three when Pitaji was Executive Engineer in Nawabshah responsible for its canals. There was another set of government engineers in Nawabshah who were building new canals which would be fed by the Lloyd Barrage. This was under construction at Sukkur and, when completed, would enable Sind to have two crops a year because the existing canals could only get water when the river was in spate, either from the melting of the glaciers in the high Himalayas, or a little later, from rains in Punjab or occasionally in the North West Frontier Province (N.W.F.P.). This was roughly from April to October – a season known locally as *abkilani*, the season of the water.

From my point of view the house in which we lived – the official residence of the Executive Engineer, Nawabshah - was huge and its grounds covered ten acres. I remember this figure very well because it has served me all my life to estimate land areas. The garden was large, there were two tennis courts, a water course, fountains and a cistern. For all this my father paid a rent equal to 10% of his salary which was, I think, about Rs.800/- per month. Of course money did not mean anything to me at the time. I had to learn to count and when I got to a hundred I was rewarded with a bugle. The bugle I got in Rawalpindi where we used to go on Pitaji's annual leave. In Nawabshah where imported items like bugles were not available, Pitaji brought a hundred silver rupees in a cloth-lined envelope on his pay day to give me an idea of what a hundred of anything looked and felt like.

I have mentioned the garden and its fountains but I think I only saw them play on my fifth birthday. There was no electricity or municipal piped water in Nawabshah. As far as I can remember there was a well with a Persian wheel but I don't recall any bullocks. I think we depended on a rope and buckets from

1919   Bombay, My parents   A wise and farsighted choice of parents helps to provide a good start in life!

which the *bhishtee* (a servant who carries water) used to fill his buffalo skin and bring it to the house where the water was kept in various receptacles. In the bathroom there was a galvanised iron tub which used to be filled by the bhishtee and Mataji would put some alum crystals in it to settle the mud and I could take water from the top in a jug for washing.

One of my earliest recollections is of sitting in my mother's lap on a camel when we were leaving the house for Pitaji to 'go on tour'. Pitaji had to go on tour for a specific number of days every month. For this, he was required to maintain tents – he was paid 'tentage'. It was quite a caravan which used to go because it was not only the family – my mother used to wear salwar-kameez to sit astride the camel behind the driver from whom we were separated by the hump of the camel - which was moving, but a whole office comprising my father's Personal Assistant *chaprassi*s (office boys) etc. I have found a press cutting in which a 'camelman' (actually a woodcutter with a string of camels) had hurled his axe at my mother's back when he was told to get out of the way of the Burra Sahib's caravan. It hit my mother on the

1926 Nawabshah, Sind.   On my fifth birthday

joodha (chignon) in which she had done up her hair so she was only bruised. The woodcutter was tried and sent to jail for six months. The camels were only for going on tour. For getting about Nawabshah, Pitaji had a motorcycle (a Harley Davidson, I think) and a sidecar for my mother and me – in her lap, of course. This motor cycle had been bought second hand I am sure, because we had a large wooden box which contained tools the like of which I have not seen since. The box and tools were kept long after the motor cycle had been disposed of. There was a tool for cutting washers and gaskets from a sheet which looked like leather but must have been some fireproof material.

On the tours, we lived in Inspection Bungalows or rest houses – the former were the more austere. Worse still were Dak Bungalows set up to represent the Post Houses of Europe but providing only minimum furniture. One was lucky if the Dak Bungalow had a *khansama* (cook). Even today, guidebooks contain the notation DBK (Dak Bungalow with Khansama).

I think we were camped in an Inspection Bungalow one summer when I had an unforgettable experience which illustrates how arid Sind was. We all used to sleep out of doors under the open skies on *charpoys* (light string beds) equipped with mosquito nets. That night I had a terrifying experience when my beautiful moon was suddenly swallowed up and I ran screaming to the beds of my parents – I had seen my first cloud!

Another memory I have of Nawabshah is of the visit my Naniji (Mataji's mother) accompanied by her two youngest daughters, my aunts Bansi (born 1898) and Jeet (born 1905). Aunt Jeet cut out the letters of the Gurmukhi alphabet from cartridge paper for me to learn them. In this way I am told I had mastered the Gurmukhi alphabet before I was three but, of course, dates did not mean anything to me at that time. Gurmukhi is the script invented by Guru Arjun (the fifth Guru) when he wanted to compile a book (the Granth Sahib) of his own and his predecessors' teachings and he found the Persian and Devnagri scripts (used for writing Urdu and Hindi respectively) unsuited to his needs. Today Punjabi writing, both religious and secular, is in this script. I think in Pakistan Punjabi is written in the Urdu script.

From subsequent inquiries I have found that it was in 1924 that Pitaji took two months' leave and we went to Kashmir. I have a faint recollection that we lived in a houseboat on the Jehlum in Srinagar. Houseboats in Kashmir were, of course, copied from the ones on the Thames. The difference was that, on the Thames, the occupant was left to his own devices. In Srinagar the houseboat was and still is connected by a plank to a much more austere and primitive vessel occupied by the owner who waits, hand and foot, on the tenant of the houseboat. Srinagar is and was then the summer capital of the 'native state' of Jammu and Kashmir. Pitaji had visited it with his parents as a child and Mataji had lived there for some summers when her father was a member of the Maharaja's council. Mataji used to relate that when my Nanaji (maternal grandfather) got his first salary for this job he brought the whole amount of eleven hundred in silver rupees to show his children how much he was getting. She was about six years old at the time and had difficulty in carrying the bag, which must have weighed about twenty-five pounds, across the room.

There is in Srinagar a hill which is a thousand feet higher than the Valley of Kashmir. Hindus call this hill Shankaracharya because there is a temple of that name on its summit whereas Muslims call it *koh-i-Suleiman* (Hill of Solomon). In 1924, the hill could only be climbed by a footpath and I think I was carried up by a Kashmiri porter. In 1956, I went there again and my son Kiran (born 1950) was carried up by Bharat Singh who is still my butler. In 1980, Kiran's son Arjun (born 1974) made it up all the way on his own, encouraged by his mother Susan who would, every few minutes, give him a sip of water or retie his shoelaces! On my next visit in 1999, I found a good motorable road to take me to the top.

To get to Srinagar we had taken a taxi which had carried us all the two hundred miles from Rawalpindi. We came back a different way via Abbotabad where we stayed for a few days. It was very hot and I remember both Mataji and I were very sick in the car. It was my first experience of motion sickness. Mataji's elder sister, Kundan Kaur lived in Abbotabad where her husband was a lawyer. I met their three sons for the first time. The middle one Bhuvan Jeet Singh had a mechanical, battery operated toy which made me very envious. From Abbotabad we went to Peshawar, the capital of the North West Frontier Province. There I saw my first cinema and wanted to get on to the bus on the screen.

From Abbotabad we went to Allahabad which was the capital of India's most populous province – the United Provinces of Agra and Oudh – then and still known as 'U.P.' – now standing for Uttar Pradesh (Northern State). In Allahabad the elder of Mataji's two brothers, Surinder Singh Bhagat (1889-1938) was Executive Engineer. As Allahabad was the capital of a province, his house was much more sumptuous and lavishly furnished than the one in Nawabshah. Of course, the downside was that the compound of the house was very much smaller. To get to Allahabad we had to change trains at Delhi; to get to the refreshment room at Delhi junction we had to take a lift – I was astounded to find the whole room rise into the air. In fact, when Mataji and Pitaji moved toward the lift, I thought we were going into an Indian style dining hall and had started to unlace my shoes preparatory to sitting on the ground!

It was at Allahabad that I met my three cousins Tony (Nripendra Singh 1914-2003), Tutu (Brijendra Singh 1915-99) and Prem (Premindra Singh 1918-76). Since Prem was the closest to me in age, he was the one I got to know best. Little did I guess that he was going to be a world beater!

Uncle Surinder had had a turban and a beard when he joined

1936 Mussoorie Surinder Singh Bhagat and his third son, Prem, playing a table game at his rented house, 'Clovelly'.

the Indian Service of Engineers in 1912 – otherwise Maharaja Bhupinder Singh would never have given him a recommendation to the Secretary of State for India – but he abandoned all that probably under the influence of his wife Surinder Kaur (1892-1927) and because he thought that it would help in his career to be more anglicised. For the same reason, the two elder sons had English-sounding nicknames, their Sikh names not being easy to pronounce in English. There were other Sikhs who did the same in those days.

I was not unaffected by this atmosphere. Prem had an intermittent fever (probably some form of malaria) which made it necessary for his temperature to be taken every evening and he would be walking around the house for several minutes with a thermometer in his mouth. I thought this very glamorous because it reminded me of a cigarette which Sikhs are strictly forbidden to smoke! As an adult, Prem did become a smoker but I have never smoked.

All this was in 1924 and I have already mentioned my fifth birthday party in 1926. It must have been shortly after this that Pitaji sold the motor-cycle and bought a car. It was bought second hand and had probably belonged to a British Officer earlier. It was a Willys Knight coupe. The arrangement of seats was most unusual. The driver's seat was placed more than a foot further forward than the bench-seat for the passengers. This left a space behind the driver's seat for a luggage compartment or tool-box which was provided with a lid. The car was from then on used for touring instead of the camels. Two servants (and occasionally I for the lark of travelling in the open) could be accommodated in the 'dicky'. This word is today commonly used in India for the boot of a car. Pitaji had a kidney problem so his drinking water had to be filtered. The filter was a stoneware cylinder about twenty inches high with a diameter of a foot. This was firmly fastened down on the lid of the luggage compartment where it was safe from the jolts and bumps which we all had to suffer on the unpaved roads. Normally, I sat on the bench seat along with Mataji. The thermometer which indicated the temperature of the water in the radiator was mounted on the radiator cap where it could always be seen by the driver before the water came to the boil and blew the cap off!

In those days it was unusual to see an Indian gentleman driving his own car. In fact many professional drivers considered it beneath their dignity to clean a car and the owner had to employ another servant as a 'cleaner'. Pitaji drove and maintained his car himself and trained one of the chaprassis to clean it.

I think it was shortly after acquiring the car that Pitaji was transferred to Jacobabad as Executive Engineer (Shikarpur Canals). Jacobabad was a relatively new town founded by an English Collector (the District Magistrate in most parts of India is known by this designation because he collects the Land Revenue) named Jacob or Jacobs who had had the hobby of building clocks including grandfather clocks. I remember Pitaji took me along once when he visited the Collector and I saw a grandfather clock for the first time in my life. It must have been left there by the founder of the town. Jacobabad had a cantonment where the Upper Sind Frontier Force was stationed. The next big city to the North West was Quetta, the capital of Baluchistan, a tribal territory ruled (like the North West Frontier Province) by an entirely different kind of administration from 'settled' India.

Shikarpur, the big city to the South of Jacobabad is an ancient commercial and banking centre well supplied with water from old canals and I could never understand why Pitaji was stationed in Jacobabad which was, in those days, the hottest district town in India. I remember one day the temperature reached 128 Degees Fahrenheit. Since it is surrounded by desert, it is correspondingly cold in winter and I saw natural ice for the first time when Mataji deliberately left out a dish filled with water on a winter night. I must explain that there was no electricity in Jacobabad and I had never seen a refrigerator.

Of course, I knew nothing of administrative arrangements but I was very much aware that the house was not built of bricks, like all the houses I had known until then, but of mud with walls a yard thick and plastered over. It also contained some unusual furniture and lots of books and magazines. I was told that the previous occupant had been an Englishman who had gone home on leave in a hurry leaving all these things behind. However, we stayed there for nearly two years and all the furnishings remained. I learnt to read English magazines. Up to that time Mataji had taught me Punjabi and I could only read the Gurmukhi script. We subscribed to STRAND magazine and other Indian magazines in English and Hindi - Mataji could read Hindi - which my parents read. We also had several hundred English books which only Mataji had time to read. Pitaji read professional journals and the magazines in English and the Punjabi newspaper. I remember several other details about this house. It had a smaller compound than the house in Nawabshah and no fountains. However, there was a huge lawn in front of the house and flowerbeds around this lawn. In winter, the flowerbeds bloomed with English flowers. One end of the house was my father's office with a room for his P.A. There was a verandah in front of the house and on the side where the office was. The verandah was usually occupied by the six chaprassis which my father was entitled to. One of them was available to me to entertain me and to serve me as a valet. All these chaprassis and our own six servants lived, most of them with their families, in servants' quarters situated in the compound well away from the eyes of visitors to the office and the house. There was also a clerical staff which worked in a separate building near Pitaji's office. They all lived outside the compound, as did the P.A.

I never went to school in Sind because such schools as there were in those district towns functioned in Sindhi which would not have been of any use to me in any foreseeable future. I was taught by Mataji. Had she been to school? No, for much the same sort of reason. She had been taught Punjabi, Hindi and arithmetic by her mother. When she was sixteen, Irish nuns opened a convent school for girls in Lahore but it was considered inappropriate for a 'young lady' of that age to go to school! There were several other girls in the same situation in Lahore whose parents wanted them to have an English education so the nuns opened a 'ladies' class' for them which she attended for two years.

After marriage, particularly when she was living in her own house well away from an extended family, Pitaji wanted her to learn English, among other reasons to be able to converse with the wives of his English and Indian colleagues most of whom did not know Hindustani or Punjabi. In a newspaper he found that a bookseller was having a sale of English novels in Bombay at one rupee a volume. I still have in my possession a few nineteenth century English novels bound in leather! Mataji particularly enjoyed Dickens, Trollope and Mrs. Henry Wood. In this way, she acquired a knowledge of English literature such as a B.A. in English would have had in those days. There were already women graduates in the Presidency capitals. In fact I have read that when the first medical school for women was opened in U.S.A. after the American Civil War, there was an Indian woman from Calcutta in the class.

Why did we have six servants in Jacobabad? There was a butler, a cook, a driver, a *dhobi* (servant who washes and irons clothes), a sweeper and a servant for cleaning the house. What was a sweeper needed for if there was someone to clean the house? He cleaned the bathrooms which included the 'thunderboxes' – yes, the word exists in my dictionary – a work which only an Untouchable (the lowest Hindu caste) person would do. Fortunately, this work has since been declared illegal. All the chaprassis were Muslims but our own servants were Sikhs or Hindus. In addition, there were gardeners and a bhishti to provide water for the garden and the house and they must have been paid by the government. I remember there was a well in the compound but no Persian wheel as there had been in Nawabshah. Times have changed since then. I read in the papers in 2005 that the Chief Minister of Bihar ran a dairy farm in her official residence which has enabled her to accumulate a fortune of fifteen million rupees which she has declared to her income tax officer.

Since there was neither electricity nor gas in Jacobabad, light was provided at night by half a dozen kerosene lamps of Austrian manufacture. There were fireplaces in all the rooms. In the summer, we slept on string beds placed on the lawn which was a couple of degrees cooler after it had been watered. I remember some nights when there was no breeze and we tried sleeping on the roof (accessible only by a ladder) but it did not help much. To operate the punkah (a large fan consisting of a frame covered with canvas, suspended from the ceiling and pulled by a rope) which kept rooms bearable in the daytime, a punkah-boy was employed for the summer. He was generally a teenager liable to fall asleep in the afternoon. I have heard that there were people who slept indoors at night and employed another punkah-boy at night but we never did that.

I have mentioned that in Nawabshah we were visited by my maternal grandmother and her daughters. In Jacobabad, we were visited by my paternal grandfather and his wife and children. They stayed with us in Shikarpur where there was a luxurious Circuit House – some of the rooms were actually panelled with teakwood - in which Pitaji rented two suites. For the first time Dadaji saw in what sort of luxury his second son lived and in what style – all those servants and chaprassis! Tayaji had visited us earlier with all his family and I had got to know Bhupinder who was a favourite of my mother's. He was a very good-looking little boy with his curly hair; unfortunately he knew he was good looking.

I recall an interesting conversation with 'my' chaprassi. He mentioned that something was very expensive so I asked him what that meant. He said it cost a lot of money to buy in a shop. 'But surely, when one buys something in a shop, the shopkeeper gives money with the purchase?' I did not realise that little bits of paper were more valuable then coins and had not noticed that Pitaji gave notes to the shopkeeper and he only gave the change back in coins! Indeed, I had seldom been to a shop in Nawabshah or Jacobabad. Food shopping was done by the cook. Any other necessities were also bought by one of the servants because the congested streets in the bazaar were unsuitable for a car. Luxuries (this included clothes and shoes of a type bought only by the British and the very few Indians who lived in 'European' style) were usually purchased during our visits to Rawalpindi where there were 'Civil Lines' i.e. an area of the city where Europeans and Indians like us lived so that there were appropriate wide streets and shops. On the way to Rawalpindi we would generally stay with Mataji's uncle Govind Das Bhagat who was a prosperous advocate at the Lahore High Court. Lahore was the capital and largest city of Punjab so there were plenty of shops selling imported goods and all sorts of luxuries including the toys that I loved. I never carried any money because I never went out of the house alone. One can say that at the age of seven years I did not know what money was. Sometimes I wonder if I understand it today!

Early in 1928, Pitaji told us that we would be going on a long holiday in England. I was tremendously excited and delighted at this prospect. I liked all sorts of imported things, particularly mechanical toys and MECCANO. I thought of England as a paradise of toys. Mataji was also very pleased because she had heard so much from Pitaji about his stay in England. Being more realistic than I she also wanted to see how much the war had changed the England that Pitaji had known or that she had read about in Dickens. The first requisite was that I should learn to speak and read English. There was also the question of knives and forks and table manners. Fortunately, Pitaji was the senior Indian Officer in Jacobabad and he had had to give a dinner the previous winter for the Commissioner of Sind who had come on tour from Karachi. At home we used to eat Indian food at a dining table out of thalis (metal trays made of steel, brass, silver, or gold) with our fingers; some of Pitaji's Indian colleagues preferred, in their own homes, to eat seated on the ground in their spacious kitchens where the food could be served piping hot. In government bungalows the kitchen was built in a separate block from the main house because British families did not like the smell of 'curry'!

So, for this dinner, candelabras, crockery and cutlery had been acquired. A new English Assistant Executive Engineer named Phillips had arrived to work with my father. He was a friendly soul, frequently visited us and was always looking for ways to entertain and amuse me. He taught me a lot about life in England. We started to speak English at home so that I would learn the language. I became quite good at this and read more and more English magazines. Every time we went to the railway station, Pitaji would buy me one or other of the English children's' weeklies available at the bookstall. I would also try to make sense of the newspapers and magazines with varying degrees of success.

However, this English holiday was not to be; tickets for the ship had already been bought when Pitaji got a letter from his elder brother (Tayaji) that he was seriously ill with a lung ailment, was short of money and was unable to borrow any and wanted his brother to go to his aid. The ship tickets were returned and we left for Rawalpindi where we were to stay for two months in Tayaji's house. I think I have mentioned that we used to go to Rawalpindi at least once a year. There we would live in the villa (*kothi*) of Pitaji's father (Dadaji). This was situated in a one acre plot and was quite spacious. We always had a bedroom, a dressing room and a bathroom for ourselves. I used to sleep in the dressing room; later I was given a room for myself, but shared the bathroom and dressing room with my parents.

Once or twice I had gone to Rawalpindi with Mataji without Pitaji and then we had stayed in the *makaan* (townhouse) of her mother (my Naniji) in the walled city. This had been built by Narain Das Bhagat but I think he never really lived in it because he was always employed outside Rawalpindi. It had two and a half storeys. One of its peculiarities was a tubewell equipped with a hand pump which filled an overhead tank - I think there had been no piped water in Rawalpindi when the house was built - the pump was worked morning and evening by the *chowkidar* (watchman) who was employed by the family for over forty years. I never got to see the ground floor rooms of this house; I was told they were store rooms – I never found out what was stored in them. We all lived on the first floor with minimum furniture, a dining table, some chairs, one or two wardrobes and string beds. Some meals were eaten in the kitchen in traditional style or, when there was company, at the dining table. Actually, my maternal grandfather had built and furnished a luxurious drawing room in European style in which he expected to entertain his English friends but he did not live to do so. I think there were a couple of maids in addition to the chowkidar.

But this time we were staying with Tayaji. He really had a first floor flat although it was always referred to as 'Ajanti wala makaan' (the house of the Ajanti, the Indianised version for an Agent which was an English term for a senior manager such as a Bank Manager). It was situated on the wide fairly new Nehru Road in a new development just outside the walled city - opposite it was the modern villa of Tayaji's uncle Dogar Singh Malik. I think the building must have been designed as the office of the company operating transportation for goods and passengers to Srinagar. This company was known as the North West Railway Out Agency – hence Ajanti – and had long since disappeared being replaced by competing truck, bus and taxi operators who had taken over from the bullock carts on which Pitaji had travelled to Srinagar as a child. This building had a high plinth with a verandah onto which opened a dozen rooms, but in the middle there was a carriage entrance beyond which there was a courtyard giving access to stables. In one of these stables Tayaji

kept his Victoria – a one horse, four-wheeled carriage.
he also had a horse to draw the carriage. Tayaji had
polio in infancy and had developed very strong hands so ɪɪᴇ ᴄ◡◡.._
hobble around the house with just a stick. However, out of doors
he always wore a calliper and a boot on his left leg. He also used
the stick for walking but then everybody, men and women of the
upper classes, carried a stick. He was able to climb into the driving
seat of the Victoria and drive it. A bell which he operated with his
good right foot gave the pedestrians warning of his approach.

Above the carriage entrance and the ground floor rooms I
have described was Tayaji's spacious flat. I think it must have
been designed for the manager (known at that time as 'Agent') of
the Out Agency. It had no electricity and the thunderboxes were
in a room above the flat. Pitaji got electricity installed in the flat.
Mataji took over the supervision of the care of her brother-in-law.
There was a problem because there was a custom that a wife had
to draw a veil over her face when she saw any of her husband's
elders (father, uncles, elder brothers, male cousins older than her
husband) and conversations with such men took place through
a third party, usually a child. Tayaji and Pitaji agreed that this
custom had to be abandoned. The reasons for Mataji's taking over
the care of her brother-in-law (she would not touch him) were her
general competence – (Pitaji left the running and accounts of our
house including the payment of salaries to the servants entirely
to her) and her knowledge of English which enabled her to speak
to doctors, an Anglo-Indian nurse, read prescriptions and so on
– all of which were beyond my Tayiji's capabilities. Pitaji took
over the finances – he had saved up money for the very expensive
planned long holiday in England.

I found this flat fascinating. I had always lived in government
bungalows situated in large compounds behind high walls where
I saw nobody but the servants and their children. Here, out of the
drawing room window, I could see passers-by *below* me in the
street. If I recognised someone I knew I could talk to them. Then
again, everybody entering or leaving the house was below my
feet. This was all incredible and fascinating. I also had playmates
– my cousins and their friends - who were my equals and not the
children of servants. These were all new social experiences from
which I learnt a lot while my studies were abandoned because

Mataji was fully occupied with the sick-room. Tayaji had few visitors at this time because it was feared that he had tuberculosis which scared away most people. In fact this was not the case; he was suffering from pleurisy. This was one of the reasons why my Dadaji and his family appeared to take very little interest in his sick eldest son and Tayaji felt abandoned. My parents gave him invaluable moral support at this time which he and his sons never forgot.

After a couple of months, the Doctors decided that Rawalpindi had become too hot and the patient should be moved to Murree. This is a hill station about seven thousand feet above sea-level and forty-five miles from Rawalpindi (altitude 1700 feet above sea level). Temperatures there are similar to England but it receives much more rain – most of it during the monsoon. Since it was used mostly by English families during the hot weather the bourgeois of Rawalpindi had built, equipped and furnished dozens of English or Scottish-style wooden houses to let out – mostly to European families – it was a good investment. Tayaji had the gift of making friends and one of these, Sardar Sohan Singh, had over forty such houses of which he placed one, 'St. Helens', at our disposal. This was my first experience of a Hill Station and I thoroughly enjoyed it. I was given a raincoat, a shower cap and a child's set of garden tools with which to amuse myself and my cousins in the garden.

However this was not to last long because the monsoon arrived and the medical advice was to move to Gulmarg in Kashmir where the monsoon cannot reach because of the intervening Pir Panjal range. Gulmarg is a large saddle of land on the North side of this range overlooking the main valley. On a clear day one can see the beautiful Nanga Perbat peak which is one of the highest in the world. The name Gulmarg means 'valley of flowers' and there is enough undulating land for two 18-hole golf courses. Of course, there was a British golf club, membership of which was accessible to Indian Officers of the Secretary of State's services. Pitaji was not a golfer and did not try to join the club but one of his cousins – Hardit Singh Malik of the Indian Civil Service - had won a half-blue in golf at Oxford, played county cricket in England and made friends with the Prince of Wales so the family was known to many club members and we were able to look round the club house and do some shopping there – such clubs still sell eatables to members.

Gulmarg is eight thousand feet a.s.l. so it was slightly cooler than Murree. Pitaji was able to rent a 'hut' (that is what houses for the summer are called in Gulmarg) which must have been very spacious because the two families were accommodated in it and the servants' quarters sheltered six servants of whom Pitaji took a photograph which I still have. Only two of these were our own, if I remember right, the rest being Kashmiris hired locally. Two of them were porters needed in Gulmarg because no vehicles were allowed. We walked everywhere and everything which was purchased had to be head carried from the shop to the hut. Tayaji was in no condition to walk so he was taken out every evening in a 'dandi'. This is a kind of chair with long arms in front and behind to be carried by two porters. It had a hood to protect the passenger from rain and sun. Many otherwise healthy persons used to be transported in dandis when they arrived till they could get acclimatised to the rarefied air at that altitude and walk without getting out of breath.

Gulmarg must have suited Tayaji because, in a few weeks, he was able to get out of bed and start walking. Soon the dandi was dispensed with and he would go out for a walk in the evening. He was declared convalescent by the doctor.

Pitaji decided therefore to make arrangements for the further stay of Tayaji and his family in Gulmarg and to have a proper holiday of our own in Kashmir for the weeks of leave which still remained to him. All this leave was a holiday for me because no textbooks had been brought away from Jacobabad and Mataji had had no time to teach me. However, my spoken English had progressed greatly because I was spending much more time in the company of Tayaji and Pitaji who spoke to each other in English. The downside was that Pitaji had more time to instil some discipline into me which I did not appreciate at the time. Of course, what I learned above all else was from the social experience of living with my four cousins.

We left Gulmarg and shifted to a houseboat in Srinagar. Pitaji was of an adventurous disposition and wanted to explore more of the State of Jammu and Kashmir. In particular he wanted to see the Zojila pass which gives access to the region of Ladakh also known as 'Greater Tibet' where the population is mostly Buddhist and there are a number of monasteries. The Zojila pass is generally snowbound and is open only for a few weeks beginning in August. This was the time to see it. The first step was to have the houseboat moved to Ganderbal further down the Jehlum where the Wular lake – the largest in India – begins. This was done by hiring labourers to punt the houseboat down the river.

Ganderbal turned out to be an uninteresting place but ponies could be hired along with the men to look after them. There were ponies for the three of us and our two servants. I think our luggage and bedding were loaded on to mules. The owner of all these animals was our guide and he and his assistants walked. Our little caravan moved up the valley of the Sind Nullah. This was a little stream which, for most of the year, could be forded at several points. There was a sort of road – a little better than a bridle path - up which we went. There were dak bungalows at every day's march where we stayed. I remember particularly one at Sonamarg (the golden meadow) where there was a snow bridge which was a unique experience. The next stop was at Baltal the last village before the Zojila pass.

That year it rained a lot. I have mentioned that the monsoon does not reach Kashmir but the valley does receive rain all through the year rather like conditions in England which is one of the reasons for which English people love it. At Baltal we were informed that the unusual downpour had damaged the road through the Zojila pass making it inaccessible. That morning – the day after we arrived from Sonamarg – it was still raining so Pitaji decided, with a heavy heart, to turn back.

On the way back, some three miles from Baltal, we saw that a little fast-flowing stream had formed across our path. Our guide borrowed Pitaji's walking stick to test the force of the water but suddenly Mataji shouted 'Back'. I looked to the right – up the mountain – and saw an advancing wall of water. We moved quickly enough to avoid the water and went back to Baltal in the pouring rain.

In Baltal we noticed that the dak bungalow in which we had spent the previous night was only accessible from the village and the road by a path which crossed a stream by a small wooden bridge. Pitaji said that the little stream was now quite full and might destroy the bridge considering how hard it was raining.

It would be wiser to stay in the village, but where? There was a *dharamsala* in the village in which travellers stayed. On inspection, the only available room appeared to have been shared by the travellers with their animals! There was, of course, no furniture. Our men cleaned it up and we slept on the floor.

Next morning dawned bright and sunny and Pitaji declared that such clouds as there were were not rain clouds at all. We resumed our journey. At the place where we had turned back the previous day a canal, now dry, six feet deep and twenty feet wide seemed to have been neatly dug. The only way to get across was to follow it downhill for a hundred yards where it ended at the Sind river and to cross it there. Proceeding further we found that some bridges on the road had been washed away. Our guide was helpless. Fortunately some shepherds turned up and we accompanied them by bridle paths on the side of the steep mountain. In this way we were able to reach a dak bungalow before nightfall. The provisions usually available there were not to be seen because of the interrupted communications. Fortunately, Pitaji had planned for this and we were carrying some tins of imported food. I tasted Swiss cheese and Wall's Oxford sausages for the first time in my life. I did not relish the cheese but the sausages were delicious; unfortunately I cannot find them anywhere today.

I tried to retrace this Sind valley trip by air-conditioned and heated car along an asphalted road in May 1999 but the time was ill-chosen because the Pakistani army decided to launch a spring-time offensive in the Kargil area – near the Zojila pass - and we (I was accompanied by a guide and two lady friends) were not allowed by the Army to go beyond Sonamarg where the snow bridge had disappeared and there was quite a pleasant, warm, hotel where we were able to have our mid-morning coffee.

After this six-month holiday the government of Bombay decided to post Pitaji to the newly-created post of Executive Engineer in Dadu in the Division of Sind. The job was new because it was to look after a new canal resulting from the Lloyd Barrage, mentioned earlier, and now operational. The bungalow was also new and had no garden at all. It was built of brick but was half the size of the old bungalows in Nawabshah or Jacobabad. It had no character and Dadu was a non-descript town with nothing attractive about it.

The new thing in the house was the telegraph room in addition to Pitaji's office. This was a medium-sized room which held a table and chair for the telegraph operator and a number of shelves full of rather large Leclanche cells which the operator had to maintain by topping them up with distilled water. The operator was named Mehar Chand Neela and he had learnt this job after passing his matriculation examination. He was also appointed my tutor because Mataji had decided that she could no longer teach me all the subjects that I needed to learn. Because he taught me, Mr. Neela was called 'Masterji' by everybody.

Pitaji decided that because the house was new it should have running water in our bathroom. For this, he built a platform outside the bathroom with steps leading up to it. On this a one cubic-yard steel tank was installed with a cover. It was the bhishti's job to take water from the well in his buffalo-skin and fill the tank. A pipe led from the bottom of the tank to a tap in the bathroom so we had running water! Instead of Mataji putting alum crystals in a tin tub, the mud accumulated at the bottom of the tank. In the winter of 1928-29, one fine morning there was no water in the tap – the water in the pipeline had frozen! It was quite a job to thaw it.

It was soon after the cold weather that Pitaji was appointed Executive Engineer in Sukkur. This was a much bigger city – the

1928 Dadu. Sind   The House at Dadu.

third in Sind – and had electricity and municipal piped water which I regarded as great luxuries such as I had only seen in my uncle's house in Allahabad. Among other things it meant electric fans, so we no longer needed the services of a punkah-boy and could keep cool day and night. Another feature of the house was that it was situated on a hill and had a fine view of the city across a large playground. One could almost see the mighty Indus river beyond the city.

Another luxury in Sukkur was the telephone. I had never lived in a house with a phone. Of course, even in Sukkur there were very few phones and I remember that our telephone number was 10. The only instrument was in Pitaji's office and, indeed, we had no need for it anywhere else. I have mentioned the telegraph room in Dadu. This was to provide immediate communications between the barrage at Sukkur and the various engineers on the network. The older canal administration depended on the normal civil postal and telegraph connections. Pitaji had nothing to do in Sukkur with Lloyd's barrage although it was situated within a couple of miles of his office.

Pitaji's main concern in Sukkur was with the old canals above the barrage and with the right bank of the Indus. I should explain that most of Sind is the flood plain of the Indus. For thousands of years the Indus has been bringing down silt all the way from the Himalayas and the Hindu Kush – the Kabul river is a tributary of the Indus. After running fast through the mountains and the relatively high gradients of Punjab it slows down in the flat plain of Sind and deposits its huge load of silt thereby obstructing itself. For this reason, it changes course every so often and meanders through Sind like the smaller river of that name in Turkey. The canals which have been built in Sind are all irrigation canals and therefore *built* above ground level instead of being *dug* like the navigation canals in England. Both banks of the canal are of earth dug out of burrow pits in the adjoining fields. This earth is consolidated using heavy rollers and as the banks are over twelve feet wide they are used as roads by the officials travelling in that area where any other roads are only fit for bullock carts. I am writing about the situation in 1929. I do not know what it is like in the twenty-first century.

Obviously, the canals can only function if the river maintains its course and, for that reason, it has to be kept in place by building *bunds* (dykes) like the banks of the canals. On the integrity of these bunds depends the safety of the cultivated and inhabited area. The bunds are inspected and maintained during the dry season. This was Pitaji's responsibility for scores of miles North of Sukkur starting above Lloyd's barrage. During the dry season the river runs far from the bund and the water only reaches the bund during the abkilani season. Normally, this is not a problem but some years the flow is more than usual. In those days, there was a phenomenon known as 'Shyock dam burst.' In an uninhabited part of Kashmir there were glaciers which were slowly melting every summer. The moraine from these glaciers had accumulated in a gorge and formed a natural dam – the Shyock dam - creating a lake. Every few years the water in the lake would get too high, the pressure would be too great for the dam and it would give way causing floods all down the Indus. The telegraph and weather station highest up the Indus was at a place called Attock where there was a natural gorge over which a rail bridge (for the line connecting Rawalpindi to Peshawar) had been built. It was from here that a telegram would be sent to the Executive Engineer in Sukkur and he then knew how many hours he had to prepare for the emergency. Since the existence of so many villages depended on the integrity of the dam, it was not only the officials but the villagers themselves who were aware of the procedure to be followed. The whole process was like a well-organised fire drill where everybody knows exactly what he has to do.

In 1929 the telegram arrived and Pitaji drove to the office of the Collector who, of course, had also received a copy of the telegram and had called a meeting of all the concerned officials. When Pitaji asked for *begar* (statute labour) he was told. 'It has already been ordered; the police is in the villages rounding up the men. I am doing more. I am giving you my new Assistant Collector, H.M.Patel, who has just arrived from England. He has already been sworn in as a Magistrate so he will be able to give orders to all the police officers.' Indeed, the villagers were only too willing to proceed to the dam where they were carried in all the means of transport available including trucks and bullock carts. They expected to be there for several days and nights and were provided with rations, bottles of kerosene oil – to have wicks inserted in them to serve as flaming torches to enable them to look for rat-holes and other leaks in the bund – and other necessities.

When Pitaji got back to the house, he found H.M.Patel having tea with Mataji. He was telling her that he had seen this tall and handsome Sikh the previous day, ascertained his identity and decided to call on him but had been overtaken by events. Little did I know that this delightful 'Uncle' was going to be my friend and benefactor all his life, much less that he would one day be Finance Minister of India. He had read Modern Greats at Oxford and knew French and German.

The immediate task was to prepare to spend the night on the bund and to tell the driver to carry food and prepare to go without sleep. A number of the most powerful electric torches had been purchased; for me the great treat was that I was going to be allowed to travel in the car at night with my parents and H.M.Patel. We drove off to the bund after a hurried dinner. The peasants were already there and were delighted to find the *sahib log* joining them in their vigil. Other subordinate officials were there as well, and command posts had been set up at regular intervals to look for defects in the bund. Snakes and rats were coming out of their holes; they had to be dispatched and the holes filled with earth and tamped down. It is of the utmost importance to stop the smallest possible leak quickly and thoroughly because if the water finds its way through the bund, it breaks it up very effectively indeed and such a breach is very difficult – nay often impossible - to repair. The consequences can be catastrophic.

By midnight I had fallen asleep in the car and woke up next morning in my bed but my parents patrolled the bund for three successive nights. Conditions were much better in the daytime when damages were easily visible and could be managed by junior officials who were on duty in shifts. At that time there were still relatively few Indian District Officers and it was a great relief and reassurance for the villagers to see Officers of their own race being so dedicated and vigilant. In today's conditions the politicians would probably object to government servants becoming so popular and thus endangering the position of the 'elected representatives of the people'.

The bungalow next to ours was occupied by the District Forest Officer who was a Roman Catholic and had a Portuguese name. There were a number of such persons in Bombay Presidency. Most of them were domestic servants of British Officers and businessmen some of whom preferred to have Christian servants who they felt were closer to them in habits than Hindus or Muslims. Such servants were called Goanese. However, Government Officers and professionals or businessman objected to this word and insisted on being called Goans. This D.F.O. had a large family including some girls of near about my age. I played with them and they taught me to keep and breed butterflies. We had no pets in the house and this was, for me, a first lesson in biology. It was also the first time I saw children wearing skirts and realised that girls might play with boys but had to be treated differently. In fact, it was my first encounter with children who were not my relations but were social equals unlike the servants' children I usually played with.

We spent that winter in Sukkur in this large and luxurious house – the last government bungalow of the old style that I was destined to live in. Of course, I did not know this at the time. Much less did I know that the Montague-Chelmsford reforms had been approved by the U.K. Government in 1919 – they were known by the names of the Secretary of State for India (the Honourable Edwin Montague) and the Viceroy (the Marquis of Chelmsford) who had jointly recommended them – and would change the nature of government. According to these reforms, the I.C.S. and the I.P. (Indian Police) were to be the only Secretary of State's services and even for these services limited recruitment would take place in India. Indians had always been able to compete for the Secretary of State's services in England but relatively few could afford to go to England for the purpose.

All the other services, health, public works, medical, forest, education, etc. were to be recruited in India so that they would be staffed entirely by Indians – the Universities and other higher educational institutes were producing enough qualified graduates for the purpose. Indians would cheerfully accept lower salaries than Englishmen and live more simply in smaller and less grandiose houses. It was for this reason that the bungalow in Dadu had appeared so austere to me.

I have mentioned that canals were constructed by digging 'burrow pits' and using the soil for building the bund (dyke). The contractor was paid after measuring the burrow pit. If the dimensions of the burrow pit were not entered correctly in the registers or were wrong, the overseer would hear all about it from Pitaji. One day wandering around in the compound of the bungalow, I saw an obviously well-to-do visitor slip two rupees into the hands of the Jemadar (Head Chaprassi). As soon as I knew that Pitaji was alone, I went into his office and told him what I had seen. He smiled and said he was not going to do anything about it.

'But Daddy, you are so hard on the overseers when you find something wrong.'

'I want to stop and even punish the fifty rupees of the overseer, not the two rupees of the chaprassi.'

I found this incomprehensible but I knew Pitaji had a reputation for being terribly honest and strict.

In the meantime, H.M.Patel's family consisting of his wife Savita and his new-born daughter Usha had joined him in Sukkur and were frequent visitors at our house.

Reginald Heber (1783-1826) who was appointed Anglican Bishop of Calcutta in 1823 and had travelled in 'the interior' was convinced that without the caste system Hindu civilisation would have perished like the Egyptian or the Sumerian. However, in the twentieth century it was causing real problems. This became obvious to us all from the case of the Patel family. H.M.Patel's father was an incurable gambler (I do not know if it was on the stock exchange or in commodities) and had ruined himself so there was not enough money for his brilliant son's higher education. I had occasion to meet the old gentleman later and found him quick-witted but rather eccentric and knowing very little English. He expressed himself well in Hindustani in addition, of course, to Gujrati which our family had no difficulty with. Anyway, H.M. Patel, as a schoolboy, attracted the attention of a young Gujrati who had made a fortune as a trader in East Africa. He decided that this boy was brilliant, should be educated in England and would make a good husband for his younger sister, Savita. He paid for

H.M.'s education with the result which we saw. However, he did not think of educating his sister to be the wife of an Officer. She knew no English and had all the prejudices of a high-born Gujrati village girl. Readers of Mahatma Gandhi's autobiography will have some idea of what this meant.

H.M. tried very hard to complete his wife's education. She learnt to express herself in English but could not get rid of her prejudices. There is a hierarchy of villages in the Patel community and H.M.'s village was lower down than Sojhitra, Savita's village. She felt that her friends and relations were taunting her behind her back on this account. No one could find fault with her husband because no one from her village had got into the I.C.S. She refused to give up her vegetarianism because she was convinced that, in her next life this would have dire consequences. Obviously, she did not want to be married to H.M. in her next life as Hindu wives generally do.

Many years later, this was to have consequences for Usha who was brought up partly abroad and thought she could choose her own husband from among the numerous suitable and enthusiastic boys that she kept meeting. She was married off to a young man from a village *higher* than Sojhitra; this marriage was not a success. She is now happily married to a Parsi. In the summer of 1929, Usha Patel was the first baby I, at the ripe old age of eight years, was allowed to carry in my arms. I have often teased her about this.

This was not to last long. Pitaji received an offer of the post of Municipal Engineer of Ahmedabad. Apart from nearly doubling his salary he was thinking of my education. He had been Municipal Engineer in Ahmedabad in 1920-21 and had left and accepted a much lower salary as Assistant Executive Engineer in the Public Works Department of Bombay Presidency because the Indian Service of Engineers offered him a permanent job with prospects of promotion. On that occasion, the President of Ahmedabad Municipality had been Vallabhai Patel later Deputy Prime Minister of India (1947-50). In 1920 he had been looking for an honest and competent Indian engineer who would keep away from local politics which in the Municipality were dominated by the Chief Officer (equivalent to Town Clerk in England) named Bhagat who belonged to a very prominent local bourgeois family.

A Punjabi who was a Sikh could not possibly get involved in town politics especially if he was made independent of the Chief Officer and directly responsible to the President. These factors were again important in 1929 as they had been in 1920 so Vallabhai Patel recommended the name of J.S.Malik to the new strongman of the Municipality – Ganesh Vasudev Mavalankar who ended his political carrier more than thirty years later as Speaker of the Indian Parliament.

V

AHMEDABAD 1930-38

Ahmedabad, at that time, had a population of half a million, much larger than any town in Sind. It was an old city having been the capital of the Mughal province of Gujrat. In 1929, it had a hundred cotton textile mills, the majority of them owned by local Hindus. It also had a government college of good national reputation, Gujrat College, with a Scottish principal. The Professor of Physics was a Cambridge man whom Pitaji had known for many years.

On previous transfers, there had always been a large crowd to welcome Pitaji. Apart from the engineers and clerks who would be working with him, there would be the chaprassis who would be directly in contact with the family because the office was in the same compound as the residence. There was none of this in Ahmedabad because there was no official residence for the municipal engineer. He had to look for a place to live in like any other common mortal instead of being a Government Officer feared and respected by everyone in the town. The personal assistant was at the station to receive us and we went and lodged for a few days in a dak bungalow. Obviously, in these circumstances we could not even unpack our luggage!

Pitaji found a bungalow in the cantonment area which he rented. Yes, Ahmedabad was a garrison town and there was a cantonment subject not to municipal but to military control. At that time, all the army officers were British and lodged in the cantonment area. The commercial or industrial British community – there were a score or so of British owned textile mills – preferred to live in the cantonment also so as to be near the Army Officers and the Gymkhana which was the whites-only club in Ahmedabad. In fact, Indian Officers of the Secretary of States services could be members of the Gymkhana. Apart from tennis, billiards, bridge, etc. the Gymkhana also offered golf on a miserable course interspersed with roads where instead of greens there were 'browns' – carefully raked sand surrounded the holes.

All this was new to me. In Sukkur, Dadoo and Jacobabad I am sure there were clubs but we did not go to them because they were essentially for the British Officers and there were not enough Indian Officers or others accustomed to the European way of life to form a club. Ahmedabad was a very big city. In the city there was a prestigeous club known as the Reform Club which had been entirely taken over by Indians – professionals, industrialists, and officers of the municipality. The only white man I used to see there was the 'Agent' (Manager) of the Imperial Bank of India; I dare say he wanted to keep in touch with his Indian clients – probably the European community were looked after by some other bank.

In the same area of the city there were other clubs – the Parsi Gymkhana for Ahmedabad's large and prosperous Parsi community; the Gujrat Club, full of lawyers and other clubs that I do not remember. The Reform Club had members of all religions – generally known in India as 'communities' even today. Why am I talking of clubs; was I, a little boy, a member of a club? Of course not, but my parents had a habit of going for a walk as soon as the evening got cooler, after Pitaji returned from his office. His practice was to visit ongoing works, etc. in the morning from about 8 A.M., come home in time for a light lunch just before 1, have a short nap immediately after and go to the office at 2 P.M. He would normally be back for tea at about 5 P.M. unless he had to be present at a committee meeting which could go on till even 7 P.M.

After tea, my parents and I would go for a walk and from there proceed to the Club where they would talk to other members or play a rubber of bridge. At the Club, membership was usually for husbands and wives; unmarried men or the very few unmarried women (I remember a Doctor) were not made to feel very welcome. Some of the members had small children like me who would accompany them and play among ourselves in a corner where we were not too obtrusive and could be supervised by one of the members' drivers. When I was a little older, I was allowed to go into the billiard room which was usually empty and take lessons from the 'Marker'.

The Reform Club and the Town Hall were a long way from the cantonment. Moreover, Pitaji felt that it was inappropriate for him not to live in the municipal area for which he himself was partly responsible. He therefore found a suitable bungalow in an area called Khanpur. There was no strict zoning law in Ahmedabad. The bungalow had a compound of about an acre which was triangular in shape. The apex of the triangle faced a crossroads. The road on the right separated us from an old, smoky and noisy textile mill – Pitaji as an engineer said that a mill whose chimney emitted so much black smoke must be inefficient and must necessarily go bankrupt. On that side the compound had a high wall to shut out these unwelcome sights and sounds. Against a part of this wall was the garden but the rest was the back of our servants' quarters. The other side of the triangle had no wall but a fence because on that side of the street we faced two

1935-A Ahmedabad.   The house.

huge mansions with large gardens and high walls belonging to wealthy mill owners. The base of the triangle was separated by a fence from a large compound in which there was one very big house and a small one.

I must go back to important events which happened before we moved to Khanpur from Camp – as the cantonment area was called. I think we had arrived there in the month of February and I remember feeling very hot in the clothes I had been wearing a few days earlier in Sukkur, where the weather was still cold as we call it in India although by European standards it was only cool. In fact it was the season for the English cricket team's tour of India. They were to play a Test Match in Bombay and Pitaji decided that we should go to see it. Arriving at the since disappeared Colaba railway station, Pitaji decided to engage a taxi for the whole day for the sum of rupees ten, petrol included! I don't think I had seen a taxi before. We had always used *tongas* (horse drawn carriages) in towns we had visited. This car was American, bigger than the Ford Model A which Pitaji had bought after the Willys Knight. We stayed at the Taj hotel which I think also charged ten rupees per person, all meals included. They must have charged half-rate

1932 Ahmedabad,   Servants. Kanhaya Singh (driver) , Ghela (butler). Cook, Odd job man, Devji (chaprasi), Gardener.

for me! Anyway, apart from the luxury of the holiday, the match was very exciting. A complete newcomer was Amarnath who made history by making a century. For me, all these players were superior beings. I did not know that I would have Yadvinder Singh – son of Maharaja Bhupinder Singh of Patiala – then Yuvraj (heir apparent to his father) playing the first Test Match of his long and glorious cricketing career, as a guest at my table twenty-nine years later.

Ahmedabad was a larger city than Lahore and had a sewage system. I had not seen flush toilets till then except in railway trains. However, even the richest citizens were not interested in imported luxury goods other than American cars. Even the bookshops only stocked school and college textbooks. No English novels could be found except occasionally at the railway station. I could not find a meccano set or any of the toys I was so keen on. In Punjab there was a popular saying, 'What you can eat and drink is yours; Ahmed Shah (Abdali, an Afghan warlord who made several successful raids on India in the eighteenth century) will take the rest.' In Ahmedabad, parents used to tell their children, 'If you spend a pie, your grandson will be poorer by a rupee.' There were 16 annas to a rupee and 12 pies to an anna.

In Ahmedabad, Pitaji made a point of driving once a month to the Sabarmati ashram (the term for a Hindu monastery) of Mahatma Gandhi. The Mahatma used to have hymns sung in the evening – hymns which had been rewritten so as to be acceptable to all religions. After this, all present were able to talk to him. Pitaji was introduced and suggested that, for hygienic reasons, the well in the ashram should be covered and equipped with an electric pump – a proposition which Gandhiji immediately accepted in spite of his known opposition to machinery. In May Gandhiji decided to resort to civil disobedience against the newly-imposed Salt Tax. To do this, he had to march all the way to the nearest coastal village, Dandi, where he would make salt from sea water and refuse to pay the tax. Of course, he was accompanied by hundreds of persons including several who were to play an important part in the freedom struggle and later in free India. Pitaji decided to be present at this departure from the ashram. This was not strictly correct because he continued to be a servant of the Government of Bombay and could have been disciplined for taking part in 'an anti-government demonstration'. However, he decided he could argue that he had been formally allowed by the government to serve the Municipality of Ahmedabad and the Congress flag flew over the Town Hall. So Mataji and I were able to claim afterwards that we had walked a few steps in the Dandi Salt March.

Do I need to say anything about Mahatma Gandhi? Albert Einstein said that generations yet unborn would hardly believe that such a one had walked this earth in flesh and blood. Many people disagreed with his economic theories – individual production, minimisation of wants, labour intensive technologies, prohibition of alcoholic drinks (tried unsuccessfully in U.S.A.) and so on – but about the moral stature and charisma of the man there can be no doubt. All this meant very little to a boy of nine taught by my parents to tell the truth. This teaching had a curious result some months later.

The English judge who tried the Mahatma for the crime of refusing to pay the salt tax appreciated his non-violent nature and the nobility of his character and said so when sending him to prison 'because I have to uphold the law.' The result was widespread non-cooperation which made the country ungovernable.

The Viceroy of India was Charles Wood, Viscount Irwin – this was his courtesy title as eldest son of the Earl of Halifax. 'Viceroy' meant that he represented King George V and did not give him more powers other than those of the Sovereign who reigns but does not rule. However, he wore other hats one of which was 'Governor General-in-Council' whose powers were unlimited except by his own conscience – the members of the Council, except the Commander-in Chief were all appointed by him - fortunately for both the United Kingdom and India, his conscience was very strong. The Viscount was a deeply religious man like the Mahatma and I am convinced that all religions teach the same thing to a sincere believer. To the horror of Winston Churchill, 'This ...seditious fakir striding half naked up to the steps of the Viceroy's Palace' was released from prison.

We had no radio but we knew all this from the newspapers. One evening in March 1931, Naeem Tyabji, Assistant Traffic Superintendent of the Bombay Baroda and Central India Railway in Ahmedabad rushed to the Town Hall and told my father, 'There is a crowd of over a hundred thousand at the Railway Station and the police have said they cannot manage it. We are disembarking Mahatmaji at Shahibag level crossing. You can be there to receive him if you hurry.'

Pitaji hurried home, picked up his little family, and we were driven to the indicated spot. The train arrived, the Mahatma got out on the other side, the train moved off and he crossed the track in the gathering dusk. However, there was enough light for him to see the little boy in the white turban. The only other turban was Pitaji's a few places down – I had already mastered the art of finding a good vantage point. He stopped and addressed me in English,

'Little boy, why aren't you wearing khadi?'

'I don't like it, Sir!' was my immediate, truthful and formal reply – a Gujrati boy or even an adult would have addressed him as 'Bapu' (Father).

A couple of days later, Pitaji brought us a Gujrati paper which related the event, identified the little boy as the son of Engineer Malik, but quoted me as saying, 'I shall wear it from tomorrow, Sir'. Thus I was first misquoted in the Press at the age of nine. An older colleague in the Indian Foreign Service, to whom I related this sixty years later, said, 'You have not changed.'

I have mentioned Mr. H.M.Patel's father. The University of Bombay used to insist that all candidates for the Matriculation Examination should fill the form with their given name, the father's name and the family name – even if the last is invented for the occasion. Thus, H.M.Patel is short for Hiralal Mooljibhai Patel. So this gentleman was Mr. Mooljibhai Patel. One evening I was given the car and the driver, and told to fetch Mr. Mooljibhai Patel – he would recognise the boy with the turban – from the railway station. In the evening the driver had instructions to take down the hood of the car – it was what was called a tourer model in those days. On the way back from the station I noticed the old gentleman, turning his head left and right all the time. I asked him,

'Sir, what are you looking at?'

'My boy, in the old days I could identify every man's village by the shape, colour and design of his turban. Today, everybody is so casual; hardly anybody is wearing a turban!'

Indeed, the only Gujratis wearing turbans in Ahmedabad were boorish villagers with untidy, dirty pieces of cloth round their heads – so different from the spotless white, starched turbans which Mataji used to wind lovingly round my hair. Most Gujrati men were bareheaded unless they wanted to display their attachment to the Indian National Congress Party by wearing a white, Gandhi cap. Gandhiji, or someone on his behalf, had designed this so as to make Muslims and Hindus of different castes and social classes indistinguishable. Muslims and Sikhs, of course, have to cover their heads and touch the ground with the forehead at some stage during prayers. This is only possible with a turban or a soft cloth headgear.

I have mentioned that Mooljibhai – all Gujratis are formally addressed at least in Gujrat by their given names adding the termination bhai (brother) – had ruined himself. There was no legal obligation for the son to pay off these debts but Hiralal insisted on doing so. This was what the Chinese call an act of filial piety. However, the public did not know this and thought that this munificently-paid I.C.S Officer was a miser who did not live in accordance with his station..

Returning to the subject of names, the Bombay University rule is responsible for my being known as G.(Gunwantsingh) J.(Jaswantsingh) Malik. This is very confusing for people from other parts of India where my name as a Sikh would be written as G.(Gunwant) S.(Singh) Malik. Having lived most of my life far from Sikh societies, I am familiarly known as Gunwant Malik. Have I explained that my given name is more usual in Gujrat than in Punjab and means AMPLY ENDOWED WITH VIRTUES? One day I explained all this to a Turkish colleague whose comment was, 'There is no accounting for what fond parents will call their children; my name is the Turkish for INTELLIGENT'.

I always spoke to people who did not know Punjabi or English, in Hindustani. This name for the *lingua franca* of Northern India has all but disappeared. It was a word favoured by Mahatma Gandhi because it was accepted by Hindus and Muslims and in fact the language is widely understood. However, after independence, Pakistan adopted Urdu as its official language. Urdu is Hindustani written in the Prersian script with some Persian words thrown in. The Indian Constituent Assembly refused to accept Roman script for India's national language although both Indonesia and Malaysia have since adopted it as the script for their languages. In India the Constituent Assembly chose the Devnagri script in which Sanskrit is written and there was a move to banish English and Persian words from Hindustani. I would say that, by and large, this move has failed. However, native speakers of Hindi in the area between Delhi and Agra tell me they have had to learn afresh the language taught to their children in schools and used on television and radio. This move has, by and large, succeeded. Some thirty years ago there was a slogan, 'Angrezi Hatao' – Away with English. The success of Call Centres and Information Technology has dampened the enthusiasm of the Hindi fanatics.

How did Ahmedabad, under British rule, have a Municipality dominated by a political party opposed to British rule? Lord Mayo had introduced local self government in 1870. This was, naturally, on British lines and once established, the Government of Bombay accepted it. In fact it was in this way that the concept of representative government with all the democratic apparatus that goes with it was introduced to India. Of course, there was no universal suffrage any more than there was in Britain. Only persons with property or income or educational qualifications were allowed to vote. The amazing thing was that women were not excluded. Thus, as soon as women got higher education they were allowed to vote – long before they could do so in Britain or in U.S.A.!

To return to the house in Khanpur, Ahmedabad. Both our bungalow and the equally large compound adjoining it belonged to the Chinubhai family. The curious fact is that I only saw one or two female members of this family – never the head of the family. An ancestor named Chinubhai must have been amazingly important in Ahmedabad in the nineteenth century because Queen Victoria had made him a Baronet, the only one in Ahmedabad. Five other Indians became baronets, all in Bombay and, with one other exception, all Parsis. The family had a large compound overlooking the river near the Shahibag level crossing mentioned earlier. I never managed to get into that compound. I do not know to whom Pitaji paid his monthly rent cheque.

I am mentioning all this because, in addition to our bungalow the same family owned the large compound containing two

houses which adjoined ours. I think the occupants did not pay
rent. The smaller house had a little vegetable garden and was
occupied by a well-known Gujrati writer, Professor Joshi, who
wrote under the pen-name of 'Dhumketu' (Comet). He had four
or five children, two of them boys close to me in age with whom
I played. The house was a 'grace and favour' residence for an old
family tutor.

The other house was two-storied, a veritable mansion, which
had obviously seen better days. The principal occupant was
a retired headmaster named Contractor, whom Pitaji treated
with respect because of his age and eminence. He was indeed a
remarkable man who gave me some lessons in English poetry and
syntax. He spoke beautiful English although he had never been
out of India. He had two sons, presumably also retired because
they were always there and seemed to have no work. I never saw
a woman; were they all widowers? The other remarkable thing
about the house was that the compound was barren land except
for the Joshi vegetable garden.

The contrast with our house was startling. When we moved
in, we could see that the garden had been neglected at least for
several months. Between the front of the house – it had a high
plinth so there were a dozen steps down to the drive-way – and
the gate at the apex of the triangle, there was a circular lawn with a
diameter of sixty feet around which was the driveway so a vehicle
could come in and go out without having to reverse. To make sure
that the lawn was watered, Pitaji had a fountain installed with
a circular cement concrete cistern which would be filled by the
fountain so the gardener could fill his watering cans and sprinkle
the lawn. The problem of water was serious. My father did not
want the piped municipal water meant for drinking (for which
he was responsible) to be used for gardening. The gardener came
one day saying he had found a set of planks in the undergrowth
near the high wall. The planks were removed and revealed a
well! An overhead tank and an electric pump solved the problem
of water for the garden. There were, of course, hedges, flowering
shrubs, and flower beds in the compound so when we left the
house it looked vastly better than when we had entered it. When
I went there again forty-two years later, I had difficulty locating
the spot and could only recognise it by its triangular shape. The

house and the garden had disappeared to make way for blocks of flats. Even the footpath had vanished, having been built over.

I have mentioned that my education was one reason for Pitaji accepting the job in Ahmedabad. I have also said that the difficulty about sending me to school was the question of language. The Doon School in Dehradun was just being opened and Pitaji was asked why he did not send me there where English was the medium of instruction and there was provision for Sikh religious training as well as for studying Punjabi. He replied that he intended to send me to England for higher studies and did not want his only son to go to a boarding school a thousand miles away at the age of ten. In Ahmedabad, the practice was to send children to a Gujrati medium school at the age of 5 for four years after which they were sent to a government school with English medium of education for seven years to take the matriculation examination of Bombay University. The problem was that Gujrati was a compulsory subject until Standard V after which the student could choose Sanskrit or French as the second language.

In the meantime, Masterji who had accompanied us to Ahmedabad had declared that he could not teach me physics or chemistry which would be necessary for the Ranchhodlal Chhotalal High School. This was the name of the government High School in Ahmedabad which had been founded by Sir Chinubhai's father. Pitaji found a tutor Mr. Jagannath D. Trivedi who was a science master at another high school. He was good not only for science and mathematics but for other subjects as well. Considering everything and after a conversation with Mr.B.V.Dalal (Headmaster of the R.C. High School) it was decided that I should sit for a special examination and join the school in Standard VI. There was the problem about French. Other students would have had two years of French by Standard VI and J.D.Trivedi did not know French.

Trivedi is a Brahmin name and means literally a person who (in practice whose ancestor) had learnt three vedas by heart! The French teacher was named D.C. Trivedi. I do not remember what the initials stood for but the two tutors were not related. French proved to be a difficult subject for me which is strange considering that today I read and speak French almost as well as English. Mr.B.V.Dalal who had learnt to teach French in France gave me some special lessons and I managed to scrape through the entrance examination.

I entered the school in 1932, at the age of 11 so I was three years younger than my class-fellows because I had not had to learn everything twice, once in Gujrati and again in English. I had other advantages also. I had the opportunity to speak English at home and had access to the parental library of several hundred books on all sorts of subjects. Probably the most useful of these was THE BOOK OF KNOWLEDGE in twelve volumes which Pitaji had bought a few months after I was born. Another advantage was that Pitaji had taken a subscription for an American magazine POPULAR SCIENCE MONTHLY which had a couple of pages every month about a home laboratory. Reading from this, Mr.J.D.Trivedi had ordered a complete chemical laboratory for me and a cabinet-maker had built a laboratory table. Offsetting these advantages was the fact that none of my class fellows believed that I had given the right age. The ambition of thousands of middle class boys in those days was to appear for the I.C.S. examination which meant prestige, power and a fabulous salary if one was successful. To write the examination one had to be between 21 and 24 years old so obviously understating one's age was an advantage.

It was easy to believe that I was older than I said because I was taller. Most Gujrati Hindus are vegetarians which may be one reason why Punjabis are taller than Gujratis. Today I have the height of the average Englishman - 1.76 meters but am perhaps three inches taller than the average Indian adult male. This problem of looking older than I was persisted for a long time. In Hamburg, before my eighteenth brthday, some one who saw me on the skating rink told H.M.Patel that he thought I was forty-six years old. My having a little bit of beard and looking dignified in a turban misled the man completely. Things seem to have changed now when I am in my eighties and am told I am too active and neatly-dressed to be so old!

School was, of course, a new experience for me and not altogether pleasant but I realised that I had to make a success of it, that I could not change things to suit me but had to accept the new situation and adapt myself to it. Most people go through this experience between the ages of 3 (nursery school or kindergarten) and 6 (Elementary school) but a change at 11 is a horse of another colour. Most of the teachers realised this and treated me kindly, especially the teacher of history who was uncomfortable with the English language and would lapse into his mother tongue soon after starting in English – the language he should have taught in all the time. Then, he would ask me if I could follow what he was saying and I was happy to be able to answer in the affirmative although I never ventured to speak to anybody in Gujrati. I was quite happy to speak Hindustani but I think the others liked to speak English to a class-fellow who spoke English better than they did. I must explain that there were no English boys in the school and no opportunity to speak to an Englishman. During my two years in the school, the only Englishman I saw there was one School Inspector. Later when I lived in Senegal I realised how thin on the ground British rule had been in India compared to French rule in West Africa.

Having little social experience, it was difficult for me to make friends with my class fellows with vast differences in religion, in dress, in appearance, in food and in styles of living; however I did succeed in overcoming my natural shyness and reserve to make a few friends.

Fees in a government school were, of course, low but even so there were boys who had to have scholarships to survive. One of these was the prefect of the class. His name was Vyas which revealed that he was a Brahmin. He always wore a dhoti and a kurta and it was obvious that they had been washed at home rather than by a dhobi, because the dhoti was less white than the dhotis of the other boys. I knew that there were rich boys in the school especially the nephew of one of the richest mill owners who had no son and had named his textile mill 'Arvind' after this nephew. However, these rich boys did not try to show off their wealth except that some of them had a car and driver parked outside the school all day. I, like many of the other boys, went to school on a bicycle.

There were other ways also which indicated the variety of the boys' backgrounds. The majority were Hindus but in my class there was one Parsi and at least one Muslim named Chhipa (textile printer) who was a very good cricketer. Today in the early years of the twenty-first century we read and hear a good deal about

Muslms not wanting their children to go to state schools which, in India, are necessarily secular. Indeed there was a Muslim High School, not far from the Town Hall, the Anjuman-i-Islam where my tutor J.D.Trivedi was the Science Master! The Headmaster of this school was a Muslim; I suppose they appointed a Hindu to the post of science master because they could not find an equally good Muslim. For his part, J.D.Trivedi made it quite clear to me that he did not have a high opinion of his Headmaster or the students. However, the school appeared to have a laboratory just as good as the one in R.C.High. There were wealthy Muslims in Ahmedabad, mostly traders.

Another way in which the diversity of Indian society was brought home to me was the 'water room'. This was a room where we could get water to drink. A man whom I took to be Brahmin – he wore only a dhoti – poured water out of a pot to the boys who put forward metal cups to him. These cups were kept on shelves and each cup bore the name of a caste or sub-caste. Presumably some member of that 'community' had donated the cup and it was meant for the exclusive use of boys of that community. Obviously there was no cup for a Sikh and I think I used a cup meant for Muslims or perhaps there was one without a name – I do not remember. In any case I went to the water room as little as possible.

The boy I admired the most was Vyas because he cheerfully performed his various duties as prefect and still always stood first in almost all the examinations. He had a physical peculiarity – both his thumbs were forked. There was an examination every Saturday in one subject of which I was always scared out of my wits although I must confess I did not do badly in examinations. Probably I was unduly sensitive to criticism either by my teachers or by my class fellows, howsoever well meant it might be. I think I was aware of all the advantages I enjoyed and felt that I should stand first instead of boys who had no private tutors and no libraries in their homes. Apart from French, my other weak subject was history. This again is curious because today half the books in my library relate to history. My own explanation is that at the age of eleven or twelve I had too little experience of human nature to be able to understand history.

The Parsi in my class was named Pistakia. He was the son of the Assistant Manager of the Imperial Bank of India. Of all my class fellows he was the only one whose father was known to Pitaji. One day I missed a class and wanted to see the notes of a class fellow. The only one whose home address could be found was Pistakia. His family lived over the office of the bank. I met him and was amazed to find that he had not taken any notes!

The following year, in Standard VII. I found several new faces. One was Ramnik Parikh who was one of the several sons of the owner of the Proprietary High School. As the name indicates, this was a business venture entirely owned and managed by a schoolmaster. I think he had one son every year and they had all topped the matriculation examination every year and Ramnik was confident he would do so in 1934. Of course, our headmaster was delighted to recruit such a star performer but why would the father not want to have him in his own school? The reason was that R.C.High was the most prestigious school in all Gujrat and all parents thought that their son would do better in life if he could claim to be an alumnus of this school.

Ramnik Parikh did not become a friend of mine but his academic performance was as expected. Much later, I saw him in Cambridge where he got admission as a non-collegiate student. After that he became Principal of a college but his ambition was great and I heard that he became Manager of a textile mill which, of course, was much better paid than any teaching job.

Other new faces were not in the same category academically. There were several Parsis who could be easily distinguished because they wore European clothes (like me) instead of kurtas and dhotis and were non-vegetarians. With one exception, they resembled Pistakia – they were not interested in studying. I think two were there because they had failed the previous year. They were obviously well-to-do, bigger and older than the others and interested in extra-mural activities like scouting and sport.

The exceptional Parsi was the one I liked. Unfortunately I have forgotten his name and I never saw him after leaving school. He was interested in reading other than school-books so we could discuss novels and other subjects which were not taught in the school. He was considerably older than me but much more of a kindred soul than anybody else in the class.

I got on well with the teachers except the science teacher who seemed to take a dislike to me. I think I was showing off what I had learnt from J.D.Trivedi and my home laboratory and this must have annoyed him. When the matriculation results came in I had done only moderately well but had stood first in Ahmedabad in English – hardly surprising in view of my advantages.

As it happened, a prize of Rs.10 was to be awarded to the boy who stood first in English from the school. The teacher in charge of this award was precisely Mr. Shah, the science master, so I had to go to see him. He admitted rather grudgingly that I had done better than 'we expected'. He explained to me that the prize had to be a book and I could leave the choice of the book to him or, 'If you have book, give it to me, I will put the ten-rupee note in it, wrap it up and it will be given to you at the prize ceremony.' The man who wanted to choose a book for me was weak in English grammar.

Of course, by this time the subject of the prize had been fully discussed with my parents and their friends. Finally, the package I received contained the ten-rupee note, a new leather-bound volume of Sir Walter Scott's poetical works and an equally new 'Life of Thomas Alva Edison'.

In 1934, my Naniji was no more and Aunt Bansi was spending several months every year with us in Ahmedabad. She was, of course, accompanied by her nurse. With his adventurous nature Pitaji decided that this was the appropriate time to visit Southern India, and that too by car! This was quite an adventure because although he had the right vehicle for the job – a FORD V8 tourer, there were very few motorable roads. To begin with, there were two large rivers, the Tapti and the Narmada, without bridges for cars in the 320 miles to Bombay. The car was therefore taken to Bombay by rail and we all travelled by train. All meant, the three of us, Aunt Bansi, her nurse nicknamed 'Plaza' and a driver.

The car had no boot but an open carrier which unfolded at the back. We were going to stay in the stops on the way either with Pitaji's colleagues or in rest houses arranged by them. We would have furnished rooms but would have to carry our bedding and towels. The problem was going to be with the bed for Aunt Bansi who could not sleep on a string or webbing bed which was what was commonly in use. So Pitaji got some five-ply wood of sufficient size to make a bed, had it cut into four equal strips cross-wise and hinged them so a to make a large wooden box which would, when folded, contain the folding steel trestles on which the plywood sheet would rest to make a bed. It was large enough to contain the beddings for all of us. On the carrier, this wooden container would be placed first, our suitcases on top of it, the whole being fastened with ropes.

In Bombay the Western India Automobile Association gave us maps, route notes and good advice. The first stop was Poona (now PUNE) which was the monsoon capital of Bombay Presidency and all sorts of facilities were available. The next stop was going to be Belgaum which was the Headquarters of a Division and the Superintending Engineer was an old friend of Pitaji's. His name was Salman Tyabji and he had arranged comparatively luxurious accommodation for us in the Circuit House.

Salman Tyabji was the uncle of Naeem Tyabji, the Assistant Traffic Superintendent in Ahmedabad. In fact, Naeem was a friend because his uncle had written to tell him that on arrival in Ahmedabad he should call on the Municipal Engineer and identify himself by name and relationship. This is the occasion to mention the Tyabji family. They are all Muslim Shia Bohras and one of the most distinguished Muslim families in India and Pakistan. Their traceable ancestor had migrated from Yemen to Bombay in the eighteenth century and Badr-ud-Din Tyabji had made a vast fortune in trade in the nineteenth century. He had twenty-two children by one wife and they had survived to adulthood – practically a miracle in India at that time. The children had benefited by English education and the men had done well in various professions. They were staunch nationalists and some had participated in politics. Abbas Tyabji had presided over one of the annual Congress sessions. This can be considered membership of the Indian National Congress aristocracy!

Salman Tyabji had a large villa of the old type. In addition to his ample salary as a Superintending Engineer he was quite rich and lived in great style. He gave a lunch on the occasion of our visit to which he invited the important officers, British and Indian, of Belgaum. It was cooked and served in European style and made a great impression on me because I had never sat and eaten at such a large table or a meal of such formality.

From Belgaum we went to see Jog falls. This place was only accessible by a gravel road and as the gravel was of laterite – the prevailing stone in that area – Pitaji's beard turned a reddish brown instead of being predominantly black with streaks of grey. Mataji and aunty Bansi found this very amusing.

I think not many foreign tourists visited Jog in a year – the three rooms in the rest house were the only tourist accommodation in the village - and Indians travelled round the country either to visit relations or on pilgrimage which did not apply to Jog. The spectacle was magnificent as the monsoon had just ended and there was plenty of water in all the four falls. We were told that during the monsoon they became one sheet of water and, in the hot weather only one waterfall functioned. I took a photograph which I still use as a bookplate.

Our host in Bangalore, the next important town on our route, was very different. He was also a P.W.D. engineer but an orthodox South Indian Brahmin. The whole family were strict vegetarians and ate their meals in their kitchen. It was a singular honour for us to be invited to lunch by them as we were not Brahmins, much less of the same caste. It was explained to us that when Brahmins

1934-B Kohlapur Hunting Cheetahs of the Chhatrapati (Maharaja of Kohlapur) out for exercise.

1934-A Jog Falls at that time constituting the border between the Princely State of Mysore and Bombay Presidency. This picture used by me as bookplate ever since.

of another caste were invited they sat in a different row from the family but the kitchen was too narrow for that so we were being seated in a row across – the foot of the letter L! We were of course accustomed to eating in kitchens but things were different here from Northern India. To begin with, there was a Hindu idol on a wall at head level before which each of us had to bow as a sign of respect. In the late nineteenth century, Swami Vivekanand had said, 'Our God is in our kitchen' and the reason is obvious. Sweepers and low caste servants are not allowed to enter the kitchen which is both ritually and hygienically clean and besides one has to take off one's footwear to step in. In Punjab or Gujrat we sat on a mat and the thali was placed on a board a couple of inches higher up. Here it was the other way around.

All this did not surprise because I reflected that when a non-Sikh enters a gurudwara, or the prayer-room in our own house, he has to kneel and touch the ground with his forehead. Some religions object to this and their adherents choose not to enter a gurudwara on that account.

Our host had arranged for us to be State guests in Mysore city – the capital of the State – which was our next stop. Many Indian states were badly run in those days but Mysore had an administration equal to any province of British India; the Maharaja was very responsible, had chosen excellent Ministers and built up a civil service based on merit and competitive examinations. As I have mentioned many important roads over which we had driven were only covered with gravel. This was so also for the Bangalore-Mysore road which went over some hilly areas. However, to make life easier for motor vehicles, long slabs of stone about a foot wide had been dug into the road to make a sort of railway track for motor vehicles. Pitaji was a skilful driver and managed to drive on this unusual surface. The problem was when there was an oncoming bus or truck – cars were quite scarce there.

The Maharaja of Mysore had several guesthouses and we were accommodated in one meant for Europeans. The butler welcomed us and told us that we could order food and drink of our choice and there would be no bill to pay. When we left, he commented on Pitaji's moderation because he said most guests asked for Scotch whisky and chicken at every meal even though he could see that they were not of a class or status to have such luxuries in their own homes. It is amazing how sensitive servants are to class distinctions.

The objective of this whole trip was to spend a month in the hill station commonly known as Ooty (at that time Ootacamund, now Udagamandalam) in the Nilgiri Mountains in Madras Presidency but for which we had taken the most direct route. Pitaji had rented a house for a month which was fully furnished and had competent servants. The arrival of a tenant by car from a place as far as Ahmedabad created a great sensation. An Englishman who had built a large house in Ooty thought he could sell it to Pitaji! The Sindhi merchant who ran a small department store, mainly for European customers, said, 'Sardar sahib, you have come by car but next time you will fly here in your own plane!' Pitaji never got to Ooty again but I drove there in an 800 CC Maruti car some seventy years later and found the place much less prosperous or so it seemed to me.

In June 1934 I entered Gujrat College which was also a government college and its Principal was a Scottish economist named G.Findlay Shirras who belonged to the Indian Educational Service (I.E.S.), one of the Secretary of State's services doomed to disappear by the MONTAGUE-CHELMSFORD reforms. The Principal was the only European in the faculty. Again, there were no European students. Some of the older professors also belonged to the I.E.S.; I was particularly happy that the professor of physics, V.B.Divatia, was an old friend of Pitaji's whom he had known since Cambridge. He belonged to a well-known Gujrati Brahmin family. He had several children, one of them a son who became my class mate. Unlike my school, this was a co-educational institution but the women sat on separate benches from the men and there was little social contact. In fact, the only place one could meet was in the library (necessarily silent) and the laboratory for science students – very few women studied science. Of course, there were sisters of some of the men among the women so contact could not be avoided. However, flirtations could only be conducted outside the college.

At college, I lost touch with my schoolmates of whom only Ramnik Parikh chose to read natural sciences. As a science student, my afternoons were taken up in the laboratories so there was no time for sports. This suited me because I had neither aptitude nor inclination for sports. College was a four-year affair, the first year being common to both science and art streams. I intended to take Chemistry for my principal subject and Physics as subsidiary. In addition to these I had to take French and Mathematics in my first year, dropping the French for my second year and mathematics after that. As French was my weak subject and I had difficulties with solid geometry and spherical trigonometry, the services of D.C.Trivedi were continued for one year and of Jagannath Trivedi for two years by which time I regarded him more as a friend.

The year I entered college, a Sikh graduated brilliantly in economics. His name was Tarlok Singh and he won several prizes along the way. I knew him; he was one of the several sons of Mr. Gurmukh Singh, Income Tax Officer. One of his brothers had been a year junior to me in school. His father was a widower, rather parsimonious and not very sociable probably because he had so many sons to educate. Tarlok Singh went on to join the I.C.S. in which he carved out a magnificent career, ending up as a Member of the Planning Commission. Today (2005), aged over ninety he continues to write on economics.

I think it is time to deal with the word BARADRI which is bound to appear in any discussion or account of Indian society. I have been for the last twenty-five years one of the trustees of the Ahluwalia Baradri Trusts. This is a charitable organisation which receives the income from six trusts all created by wills of childless persons who died in the first half of the twentieth century. I understand from my second cousin Vinoo Bhagat, a lawyer, who has been the Secretary of the Trusts for over thirty years that such trusts are known in English law as 'poor relations charities'. The intention of all these wills was to give financial assistance to relations of the testators who might fall on hard times in future. As the laws stand at present, the tax and other benefits of charities are lost if the beneficiaries are limited to members of one social, religious or linguistic group. Therefore we do give aid to some members of the general public.

However, we also have to respect the wishes of the testators and we endeavour to give preference to members of the Ahluwalia Baradri of Rawalpindi. The word Rawalpindi needs no definition but, in fact, nothing has been given to any one in Rawalpindi since Independence! I have explained the word Ahluwalia previously. The Secretary told us that there is no definition of the word 'baradri'. This was some fifteen years ago when my mother was chairing our meetings. She was asked how she would like to define the word and her answer was, 'There were thirty houses of Ahluwalias in Rawalpindi before Independence and I knew all those who lived in them.'

We have interpreted this to mean that the baradri was an endogamous group of thirty extended families who were living in 1947 in perhaps fifty or more houses or apartments. As I have explained, no member of the baradri has lived in Rawalpindi since Independence. At first most of them lived in Delhi or New Delhi but today the few survivors and their many descendants can be found not only all over India but in North America, Europe, the Persian Gulf and other Asian countries.

Is that a sufficient explanation of 'baradri'? Of course, 'endogamous group' has little meaning today but, those who live in India do very often seek a 'partner from within the baradri'. In this respect, the baradri does not have a geographical constraint. Traditionally, a family used to seek a partner for its son or daughter from outside the village. In fact, the children in the village belonging to any particular sub-caste were told to regard each other as brothers and sisters. Again, this concept is weakened when the village is replaced by a much larger urban unit. My nani – not the bride Narain Das Bhagat had married while at school: she had died leaving one daughter – was from the prosperous and influential Ahluwalia Hoon family of Amritsar.

All this, of course, is connected with the caste system which prohibited the sharing of 'bread and daughter' with other castes. Today restrictions on eating with other castes have practically disappeared from cities and towns of Northern India. One does not know the caste of the neighbour in the factory canteen, the dining car of the train or the restaurant. However arranged marriages are still more numerous than what are called 'love marriages'. The results can be absurd. A friend suggested to a servant in the house she was visiting that the son of an employee in her office – of the same caste and dialect – might be suitable for his granddaughter. 'Madam,' he replied, 'That is not done among us.' A few months later, he had to celebrate the girl's marriage to a boy from the neighbourhood with whom she had been playing since childhood and who was of a different caste and language – they speak Hindi to each other!

Of course, a small endogamous group can lead to problems of inbreeding – the original reason for seeking a bride from another village. To prevent this, there exists the concept of the gotra. This was supposed to be trans-caste and is said to have been the name of the *'gurukul'* (school) in which an ancestor in the paternal line had been educated. I am told that in those (mythical) days, many gurus chose pupils according to their potential and not their caste. The gotra is an exogamous group which necessarily includes all those who claim a common ancestry in the tail male. *Reductio ad absurdum*, a man may marry his mother's brother's daughter but not his father's brother's daughter! I understand that among the Nairs of Kerala a man usually does marry his mother's brother's daughter. Of course none of this applies to Muslims, Christians or Parsis and , in many aristocratic Muslim families it is customary to marry the father's brother's daughter. Tariq Azam Chaudhry has told me that he prefers endogamous marriages for his own five children. Obviously he does not see any harm in inbreeding.

Today most men and women that I meet do not know what their gotra is. They have to ask their family priest. I have mentioned the problems in connection with the 'water room' in my school. At that time, in the 1930's, at railway stations, vendors used to shout 'Hindu water' and 'Muslim water'. Fortunately, this practice disappeared some years before Independence.

This is a good occasion to explain the word 'community' which is widely used in India even by people who do not speak English. Depending on the context, it can mean a baradri or a whole religion even one as numerous and as varied as Hinduism. Thus the press and politicians will not refer to Hindu-Muslim riots but to 'communal riots'. Marxists explain these in their usual way. Others attribute them to the failure of the monsoon, the electricity shortage or any other event that they can think of.

I have mentioned that the Principal of the College was G.Findlay Shirras. I did not see much of him because he was not interested in the Natural Sciences. In fact, he knew so little about them that when a demonstrator in an English University (C.T.R.Wilson) won the Nobel Prize in Physics, he wanted to know why neither the Professor nor the Lecturers in Gujrat College – to say nothing of mere demonstrators – could do the same! It did not occur to him that they had hardly any more equipment than I in my home laboratory.

As a Scotsman and a loyal subject of the King-Emperor, he was disgusted that so many of his students were sympathetic to a subversive movement – the freedom struggle. He was always looking for 'loyal' young men and women of whom there were few. He may have been happy that I was not politically active. But he would have liked the son of a senior Indian Officer to take an active part in the debating society and other similar bodies in the College and oppose the 'subversives'. I think finally he understood that science students do not have time for such extra-curricular activities.

I have mentioned that in Sind we slept out of doors during the hot weather, generally on the lawn on light string-beds with mosquito nets. In Ahmedabad the hot weather was longer than in Sind but interrupted by the monsoon (June to September). Perhaps this was the reason that the custom of sleeping out of doors did not appear to be known in Ahmedabad. There was another factor. I have said earlier that middle class houses in Northern India are built with flat roofs meant for sleeping on. This will not work in the peninsula where roofs have to be sloping and generally tiled on account of the heavy rain during the monsoon. Today with air conditioning the rich sleep very comfortably indoors throughout the year. The poor, of course, sleep on the footpath or any other place they can find. I have seen fairly well-paid workers sleeping on the footpath in Mumbai – they have to send the bulk of their earnings to the village where an extended family depends on one bread-winner in the distant big city.

In the thirties, there were hardly any air conditioners because they had to be imported which put them beyond the reach of any one I knew. Ahmedabad was a big city and many well-to-do people lived in the walled city in houses which had no gardens and only small courtyards. We were not on visiting terms with such people but once I had occasion to visit such a family in the company of an eye surgeon. I was horrified to find that there were no beds in the house! The owner was to be operated on for cataract lying on a thick mattress on the floor. I could not understand how any one could sleep on a thick mattress in the hot weather. It only goes to show that one can get used to anything.

For ourselves, we found that sleeping in the garden was only possible on a few nights in the year. Even then, the beds could only be brought out after dark after making sure that the light from the street lamps or from our own house did not illuminate the lawn. Fortunately the front part of the house had a wide verandah protected by a grill. This made it very convenient for sleeping in the verandah even during the monsoon. We were protected by the grill from stray dogs which were numerous in a city where animal life is considered sacred and there were no municipal or other dog-catchers.

The driveway into the compound was from the left, from the road where there were the mansions of the two rich mill-owners. The other gate at the apex of the triangle facing a large square was kept locked and I never saw it open. Thus our own car and any visitors had to stop at the foot of the dozen wide steps at the front of the house. Here the driveway was wide because the distance between the steps and the circular lawn was over twenty feet. Adjoining the lawn a durri (cotton carpet) was laid out in the evenings. Two easy chairs with cane seats and backs were placed for my parents facing the house with a small tea table between them. Facing them across the durri were two smaller easy chairs, one of which was usually occupied by me and the other by any informal visitor who might turn up unexpectedly.

The house was different in design and construction from houses in Sind and Punjab. It was pentagonal with the front facing the apex of the compound. This front verandah was open, i.e. it had no grill. Two sides were slightly inclined on the right and left of the front and could be isolated by doors in the grill. The left verandah bow was where we sat most of the day using the furniture which was taken out in the evening. It could not be used during the hottest months because it was too warm. The left side facing the road with the mansions was used for the siesta during the cool months.

The right side bow accommodated my laboratory. The right side verandah faced the servants' quarters, the garage and the kitchen. It was used as a store room because there was no loft or basement for the purpose. The house had only one storey but looked high because of the high plinth. The roof was gabled and tiled. The tiles were supported on a wooden frame and hidden from the interior by a ceiling of hessian coated on both sides with white paint which made it practically waterproof. It also created a problem because vermin of various kinds would infest it which necessitated frequent fumigation. The main part of the house was a large central room divided by an arch leaving the drawing room in front and the dining room behind. We arranged for a curtain in the arch.

Originally there had been two huge bedrooms each with its own dressing room and bathroom at the back. However, they were too big and had been divided by screens of the painted hessian referred to above with a door connecting the two parts. On the left, I had the rear bedroom and my parents had the front one. We shared the dressing room and the bath. The front room was accessible from the drawing room and the rear one from the dining room. On the other side the rear room and its dressing room and bathroom were reserved for guests. The front room was divided in two. One portion was my study, accessible both from the laboratory and the drawing room. The other was a kind of store room which I also used as a dark room when I took up photography and wanted to process my own pictures – unsuccessfully because of the heat.

There were ceiling fans in the bedrooms and the drawing and dining rooms. There were also table fans for use in the verandahs and one with a very long lead for use out of doors. Half way through our stay in the house a refrigerator was acquired and kept in the dining room as still happens in middle-class homes in India – it is usually the most valuable item of furniture in the house!

We had plenty of furniture. The dining table was for six but could be extended to 12. I used to do my homework on one end under the large ceiling fan. There was an overstuffed sofa set and other chairs with cane backs and sides. Also in the drawing room there were two glazed bookshelves (to protect the more valuable books from the dust), a roll-top desk, a revolving bookshelf and two open bookshelves. The drawing room was used during the 'cold weather' and when we had more formal visitors.

Behind the dining room there was a small verandah half of which had been converted into the butler's pantry. This contained a 'hot case' because the kitchen was forty feet away at the end of the row which contained the garage and the servants' quarters.

I have mentioned that my mother had two younger sisters, Aunts Bansi and Jeet born in 1898 and 1905 respectively. The latter married a cousin of my father's Iqbal Singh Malik (1902-1977). This was an important event because it was the first marriage of a close relation which I attended. Mataji and I used to spend roughly a month with my Naniji every year, usually at Mussoorie in the hot weather where her elder son, Surinder Singh would rent a house for the season. This time Naniji rented a house for a month in Lahore for the wedding. As an Indian marriage costs a lot in time and effort, she wanted all her four daughters to be present and this was, of course, done. Her two sons and the sons-in-law came when they could spare the time for two or three days.

Iqbal Singh Malik was an engineer working for the Bengal Nagpur Railway. But he was much better known as a golfer – at that time I don't think there were a hundred Indians playing golf. It is an expensive game and the princes who were very much addicted to cricket, horseracing and polo had not taken it up. Many golf clubs did not accept Indian members but when a player was very good, he could not be refused membership. Sport is wonderful at overcoming racial and class barriers! As it was, he devoted all his spare time to golf and the railways have always favoured sports. Even today in the sports pages of newspapers one finds railway teams for different sports playing a prominent role. Sometimes, a railway administration will employ a well-known sportsman in a non-existent job or a job for which he has no qualification. Sportsmen are often very good as administrators, especially at very high levels where technical skills are not a pre-requisite.

As it was, I.S.Malik took premature retirement from the railways and joined a multi-national firm in which he proved himself a successful businessman. He was three times National Golf Champion of India and was playing golf a few days before he died. His son, Ashok Singh Malik has been five times golf champion of India. In fact Ashok, became All-India Golf Champion (necessarily Amateur because at that time the only golf professionals were caddies – a situation which has changed drastically now) before his father.

To do this he had to beat his father in the finals. Before sinking that putt, he went over, bent down and touched his father's foot with his own forehead – the traditional way of greeting a father by a son or by a daughter-in-law. This scene has become a part of Indian golf folk-lore.

It is not usual for a girl to get married before her elder sister but my aunt Bansi had a spinal problem which was finally diagnosed as tuberculosis of the spine. As a result she spent three years flat on her back wearing a plaster cast round her thorax. She was in this condition in 1930. Later, she was able to get up and move about wearing an elaborate metal corset. She could only take it off to lie down flat on her back on a hard wooden bed without a mattress with just a blanket beneath her. All this meant having a practical nurse to look after her, dress her, put her to bed etc. all her life. She lived with her mother in the house in Rawalpindi but they both used to move for several months to either of the two brothers. When her mother and elder brother passed away and the other lost his job, she moved in with us.

In 1927, Surinder Singh Bhagat had lost his first wife (Sunder) leaving him with the three sons mentioned in an earlier chapter. Next year he married an eighteen-year-old girl called Mohinder Kaur (daughter of Sher Amir Singh) but nick-named Shiela who was a great beauty except that her face was slightly marked by smallpox. Obviously, she had not had a college education but she was very quick to learn and was soon able to hold her own in both Indian and European society. She became quite proficient at ballroom dancing. Her step-children called her 'Aunty' and so did all their cousins including me. She kept her slim figure and her beauty all her life.

I had gone with my mother to Kashmir to stay with my mother's other brother, Satinder Singh Bhagat in, I think, 1931. He was at that time Conservator of Forests in Kashmir, keeping up the link his father had established with the State of Jammu and Kashmir. Good at studies, like his brother, he had gone to Pembroke College, Oxford and graduated in Natural Sciences before becoming a forest officer – as my Tayaji had wanted my father to do! Unfortunately, his career in the J. & K. Forest Service was cut short when he was accused of corruption. This happened at about the same time as his elder brother died in a riding accident in Benares (now Varanasi) in 1938, shortly after he was promoted to be Superintending Engineer.

Fortunately, by this time, his two elder sons, Tony and Tutu were army officers and Prem was due to follow in their footsteps. Shiela and her children were able to manage with their father's savings and investments.

The situation of the younger brother Satinder Singh was not so good. He had seven minor children, and no house. He was able to scrape together enough from his savings and his inheritance – the house in Rawalpindi had had to be sold - to build a house in Model Town near Lahore and to buy shares in Bengal Potteries.

This company had been started in Calcutta by some Bengali businessmen some years earlier and was the largest pottery in the British Empire. It had not done well.

My great uncle Govind Das Bhagat, had decided that his three sons by his first wife (Rukmini, a cousin of my father's) would not go to England to become lawyers, doctors or engineers or to compete for the I.C.S. but would acquire more specialised qualifications to start new independent activities. Pitaji was closer to him than to his two elder brothers because of the relationship through Rukmini. His eldest son Madan Gopal Bhagat (1894-1962) had trained in France as a potter and returned to India to become Manager of Gwalior Potteries in Delhi. This was one of several industrial and commercial ventures started in the twenties and thirties by the then Maharaja Scindia of Gwalior who turned out to be a very successful entrepreneur.

Govind Das Bhagat suggested to Sir Shri Ram, the very successful Delhi industrialist that Bengal Potteries should be taken over and that his son, who had been so successful in Gwalior Potteries, should be the Chief Executive of the revived enterprise. This worked out very well till after Independence when the Communist Party of India came to power in the trade unions in Bengal and practically destroyed its industries.

The second son of Govind Das Bhagat, Har Gopal (1899-1963) went to U.S.A. and became a radio engineer. He started selling these new-fangled gadgets in PARCO RADIO in Lahore. This was a great success.

The third son Harbans Lal (1902-1938) trained in the United States also, as a sugar technologist. Until about 1930, India with its vast sugar cane output had not produced any white sugar which had to be imported from the Dutch East Indies (specifically Java) and was a great luxury. Harbans Lal's arrival was therefore very timely and he had no difficulty in finding a job in spite of the Depression. Sher Amir Singh, mentioned on the previous page, was very desirous that Harbans Lal should marry his younger daughter Raj (1911-67). He was told that Harbans Lal had an incurable kidney problem and was not expected to live long. Raj was as beautiful as Shiela, in fact more so as she did not have small-pox marks. On the other hand, she did not have Shiela's personality or wit. The marriage took place, and Harbans Lal died in 1938 leaving an infant daughter.

The fame of Raj's beauty had spread far and wide. It had reached the very wealthy Sardar Sohan Singh mentioned previously as being a good friend of Tayaji's; he had recently lost his wife. The latter therefore came as an emissary, to his cousin-in-law (Govind Das Bhagat) to ask for the latter's newly widowed daughter-in-law's hand in marriage. That gentleman was horrified that 'the ashes of his son being hardly cold' he should be asked to give away his daughter-in-law. He asked his second son Har Gopal who lived with him to handle the situation. Har Gopal was very close to my parents. As I have mentioned, whenever we went to Lahore we stayed with Govind Das Bhagat who, a widower for the second time, always had Har Gopal, his wife Lachhmi and children with him in the house. In 1931, we had taken a large hut in Gulmarg and Har Gopal Bhagat and all his family had stayed with us for some days. They had brought a large radio which could receive transmissions from many countries in the world and entertain us all in the evenings.

I am told that, thinking far ahead, Pitaji and Tayaji had been contemplating alliances between their sons and two of Har Gopal's daughters. With all this background, Har Gopal Bhagat expressed surprise that Mukhbain Singh Malik (Tayaji) should come as an emissary for a totally unrelated person. The latter was prepared to sacrifice relationships to friendship for Sohan Singh who was, in the circumstances then prevailing, a very powerful person. He said that Sohan Singh could easily take away any women he wanted from the Bhagat family.

Sardar Sohan Singh married Raj and had two sons by the marriage. But relations between my Tayaji and Har Gopal Bhagat were never the same again.

To return to Ahmedabad and my studies, let me complete the story of my academic career. I did pass my B.Sc. in Chemistry and Physics in time for my seventeenth birthday but I only got a second class as I had done in all previous examinations. This was enough to get me into Cambridge where Downing College had promised me a place but they would only have me after my eighteenth birthday.

At that time, the two most prominent mill owners in Ahmedabad were Ambalal Sarabhai and Kasturbhai Lalbhai, whose nephew Arvind had been a year junior to me at school. These two industrialists did not use surnames – they probably never had to fill the forms of Bombay University but Sarabhai and Lalbhai are recognised today in Gujrat as surnames of wealthy and important families. I have mentioned that Kasturbhai Lalbhai had no sons and, as far as I could make out devoted all his time, energy and wealth to his industries. Many years later I found that he had paid for the construction of the Jain temple at Ranakpura in Rajasthan which is probably the most beautiful Jain temple built in the twentieth century.

Ambalal Sarabhai was very different. He had three sons and five daughters. Some of them were very talented and he was keen that they should have all the scope for their talents that his money and energy could provide. He decided that the schools in Ahmedabad were inappropriate for the needs of his children and set up a school in the ample compound of his own magnificent mansion. Not only did he get the best teachers but he also provided laboratories and even workshops should any of his children be interested in engineering.

The first I saw of any of the Sarabhai children was the second daughter Bharti. This must have been when I was about ten and had accompanied my parents to a sari shop. This was the time when the Congress Party was organising a boycott of foreign goods. Bharti was picketing the shop, recognised my father, and came in to request my mother not to buy anything imported. My mother assured her that she had no such intention. I was dumbstruck by her beauty.

Of course, at the time I did not understand that the boycott served Ambalal Sarabhai's interests very well. He owned CALICO MILLS! Recently, the wife of a Gujrati colleague has told me that the dowry of a middle class bride necessarily had to contain shares of Calico Mills. The company no longer exists. Later, when Mahatma Gandhi extended the boycott to mill-made cloth, the Sarabhai family tactfully gave up its support. In fact Bharti did not look for a career and married an Englishman.

The eldest sister Mridula was very different. She never married and was a political activist all her life. Mridula was totally without fear. She made her name after partition when she took charge of the Abducted Persons recovery organisation. The problem was that during partition some Muslims in Pakistan abducted Hindu and Sikh women and Hindus and Sikhs in India abducted Muslim women. There was therefore a need to trace these women, and take them back across the frontier to their own families. This had to be done in both countries and was obviously very dangerous work. The abductors could often find support among their neighbours for holding on to their prey. I do not know what happened if the woman refused to leave the man she had come to accept as her common-law husband!

Mridula's work necessarily brought her to Delhi quite a lot and she heard that my father was here and came to see him in 1952 during his terminal illness. Having seen the more dreadful results of Partition at first hand in both countries, she told my father that she was full of admiration for the Sikh masses but not for the Sikh classes.

I have mentioned that Ambalal Sarabhai was a man of wide vision who wanted his children to have all possible opportunities. It became his custom to go to Europe every year with all his family for several months. In those days, this necessarily had to be done by ship. I think it was in 1934 that he met a German nobleman on the ship who was able to tell him a lot about world affairs which did not appear in the Indian press; I must explain that the biggest newspapers were British owned as were the wire services. The Indian owned papers could not afford to have correspondents abroad. Ambalal decided, on his return – probably in the month of October - to invite the German to be his house guest, and to give a tea party for some of his friends to meet him.

Mrs. Sarabhai put me at a table with her fourth daughter Gita who, she said, 'is the same age as you, but not a prodigy.' Gita said to me that although she did not go to school, she had heard that children of our age enjoyed school. I had passed my matric some months before this and was very proud of being the youngest student at Gujrat College, so I replied that some of them liked it so much that they stayed on for extra years! The fact was that I was stunned by her beauty. Twelve years later my opinion was confirmed by the Cambridge landlady of her brother Vikram who said to me, 'They are a very good looking family. I think Gita could melt any man's heart.' I never saw her after 1934.

On an earlier European trip, probably before he had children, Ambalal Sarabhai had met a young Indian on the ship who appeared very depressed. He engaged him in conversation and learnt that he had gone to study in England in order to appear for the I.C.S. competitive examination, but had failed – which explained his depression. Ambalal was very impressed by the young man – in fact not much younger than him – and employed him immediately. He was a Sindhi named Gidwani who became Ambalal Sarabhai's right hand man. In Ahmedabad, the Gidwanis became the closest friends of my parents. They had a son named Narain who was a year younger than me; they engaged Jagannath Trivedi as a tutor for him.

I lost touch with the Gidwani family after Independence.
They belonged to the Amil community like many of my father's
Sindhi colleagues. The majority Muslim community (they were
almost three quarters of the population) were either landowners
or agricultural labourers. There were very few middle class
Muslims in Sind. The Hindus were more literate than the
Muslims, particularly the women. I think Mrs. Gidwani was a
graduate. The Hindus considered the cities of Haiderabad and
Shikarpur as their home. This was a custom in India at the time.
Government forms asked for 'native place'. Strictly, this should
mean birthplace but most Indians mentioned the village in which
their families originated. Similarly, the Hindu bourgeois of Karachi
(the provincial capital) generally claimed that their homes were
in Haiderabad or Shikarpur. They divided themselves into three
'communities'. The Amils were landowners and government
servants. They had probably been in the service of the Khairpur
Mirs from whom Napier had conquered Sind – *peccavi* – (I have
Sin(ne)d) had been his Latin message after his victory. Anyway,
after the arrival of English education in India they had gone for
it in a big way and they constituted the majority of the *Macaulay
Indians* in Sind.

The other rich Hindus who regarded Haiderabad as their
home were the Bhaibands. They were shopkeepers. With the
arrival of British rule they had decided that they could have
access to the whole of the British Empire for trading. In this they
were entirely successful. They established Sindhi communities in
Shanghai, Hong Kong, Singapore, Colombo, and set up a large
network of retail shops in West Africa, particularly Nigeria.
Later, they extended their network outside the Empire to some
French colonies. In my service life, I have seen large networks of
their shops in the Canary Islands, in South America and I am told
they are well established in Panama. They are not very interested
in formal education; usually they go to work immediately after
finishing school, acquiring trading and linguistic skills on the job.
I shall never forget meeting the Chairman of one of the largest
Sindhi firms in 1970 in Bathurst (now Banjul), Gambia. He had
twenty outlets in Nigeria, an office in New York and shops in
several other countries. He told me that his father had paid Rs.500
to a Professor at Sydenham College of Commerce in Bombay to

go through the Indian Contract Act with him. After that, he had hired another professor to go through the Income Tax Act in the same way. A man employing hundreds of persons in three continents had had no other education after school!

Equally contemptuous of Higher education are the Shikarpuris. For centuries they were bankers (better known as moneylenders). With the arrival of more formal modern banking, this had proved unrewarding and they had gone into trading like the Bhaibands, concentrating their activities in the Persian Gulf which has proved a gold mine with its oil wealth.

The census statistics of 1931 (the last census before the World War) mention Muslims, Hindus, Anglo Indians, Europeans and Christians in Sind. This is somewhat misleading. Sind was the first part of India to be conquered by Muslims. These Muslims were in fact Arabs led by the brilliant seventeen-year-old Muhammed *bin* Qasim who conquered Sind between 710 and 713 A.D. Although Hinduism was not abolished, it seems that in the course of centuries the training of purohits (Brahmin priests) came to an end.

At the time of Partition, Sindhi Hindus were known as *daryapanthis* or *Nanakpanthis.* Daryapanthis had a ceremony of floating paper boats down the river Indus with lights in them on certain days of the year. Nanakpanthis were followers of Guru Nanak and, as such, recognised by other Sikhs as Sahajdharis. I have worshipped in several Sindhi gurudwaras where the discipline and devotion of the public were always exemplary.

The Gurdwara in Ahmedabad when we arrived was in a crowded locality. Pitaji was elected the President of the Gurdwara committee. He managed to get a plot of land for constructing a new Gurdwara. I think Mr. Gidwani was the largest contributor to the building fund.

When I entered my second year in College, Vikram Sarabhai (the third and youngest son of Ambalal Sarabhai) joined the college in the First Year (Science) class. He was the first member of the family to read natural sciences. He was two years older than me which made him 16 years old – the normal age for entering college. He had taken his matriculation examination as a private student – unconnected with any school. Two years later, in 1936, he passed his Intermediate Science examination in the first division.

He was then eighteen years old and with his good marks he was admitted to Cambridge (I think at St. John's College). I was to join Downing in 1939. Like other very rich students, he used to return home to Ahmedabad in the long vacations, a time-consuming and expensive process by sea.

In 1939, Vikram Sarabhai was in India when the war broke out and he chose not to return to Cambridge. I was surprised to meet him in the street in Cambridge towards the end of 1945 when I was there on leave from my posting in the Royal Air Force in Germany. He had, since I had last seen him, married the famous dancer Mrinalini and acquired a reputation for his knowledge of nuclear physics. He was doing research in Cambridge in, I think, photons. In the altered post-war situation, we were soon on first-name terms.

Before finishing with Ahmedabad, I must mention the loss of two important close relations. I think I have mentioned the Indian custom whereby married women return to their paternal home for a month every year, at least by the references to visits to my Naniji and one or other of my two Mamajis in the company of Mataji. The last visit to her mother's home was done by my mother without me in 1935 because it was term time for me in

1935-B Ahmedabad crayon sketch by Boris Georgiev from Bulgaria.

College and Mataji had gone for Naniji's terminal illness. She had cancer and four of her daughters were at her bedside when she expired. Mataji always said very proudly that, in the last days, her mother was looked after round the clock not by nurses but by her daughters.

This was the first time I had been separated from my mother for so long. As it happened, a foreigner had arrived at our house with a letter of introduction from Abbas Tyabji in Baroda. He was a Bulgarian artist named Boris Georgiev and he was going round the country in a three-ton truck which he had had fitted out as a mobile home. He had employed an Indian servant to clean his vehicle and cook food of his liking. He spoke English and I learnt a lot from him about Eastern Europe of which I knew hardly anything. He made a portrait of Pitaji which is hanging in my library (see photos). He taught me how to mount it between two sheets of glass to protect it

1935-C Ahmedabad H.M. and Savita Patel on steps of house.

from humidity and insects. It is still in mint condition. He had some meals with us but his truck was parked in our garden for a month.

It was three years later that Pitaji came back from his office in the middle of the afternoon and Mataji knew by his face that he had had bad news. A telegram had come to the office announcing the death of her elder brother Surinder Singh. He was Superintending Engineer in Benares at a time when most Superintending Engineers were British. His daily exercise was to ride his horse early in the morning before breakfast. He had gone out as usual trotting his horse on the unpaved berm of the road when he saw a nursery maid coming towards him with the children of one of his friends. To avoid inconveniencing them, he had crossed the road, his horse had slipped on the asphalt and he had broken his neck and died immediately leaving his thirty-year-old widow, a son Hari (Harinder Singh b.1930, and three daughters Piki (Pamela b.1931), Sarla (1933-2004) and Baby (Indira b.1934). Of course the sons of his first marriage mentioned earlier were all employed or in the way to being so by this time. It says much for them that they looked after their stepmother and the relations between the first and second families continued excellent as long as they lived.

While in Ahmedabad, we got to know H.M.Patel and his growing family much better. He continued to serve in Sind till about 1935 when he was transferred to the provincial secretariat in Bombay. As they were Gujratis, he and his family had to pass through Ahmedabad every time they went to their ancestral homes and they would break journey and stay with us. When he was transferred to Bombay he became Resident Under Secretary and had a magnificent flat in the beautiful Secretariat building and we stayed with him whenever we went there. He had given me a book FIRST OVER EVEREST when I passed my matric which contains a stereo-photograph of the peak taken by the Marquess of Douglas and Clydesdale from his plane, which I still have. Later, he gave me his own copies of Moliere's LE BOURGEOIS GENTILHOMME and Voltaire's SIECLE DE LOUIS XIV. This was my introduction to French literature which I have enjoyed ever since.

In 1938, Pitaji applied for eight months' leave at the end of his contract with the Municipality. Leave was very generous for the

1938-A Ahmedabad At the gurudwara when I assured the gathering that I would come back from England with turban and beard.

Secretary of State's services because British officers had to return frequently to Britain otherwise they might *go native* – a fate worse than death. The leave was granted and Pitaji booked passages for the three of us on the 'City of Benares' from Karachi via Bombay to Marseilles. The choice of a ship of the 'City and Hall' line rather than the 'P&O' was because the former were one-class ships. The P&O ships had First, Second and Steerage 'for Asiatics only'. The word 'Asiatic' in this context upset Pandit Nehru so much that he banished it from the bureaucratic vocabulary when he became Prime Minister. He tried to persuade the French government to do the same but they replied that in French there was no choice. In the P&O ships, wealthy British and Indian businessmen and Maharajas travelled first class as did all those who could persuade their employers to pay first class passages. Pitaji did not want to spend so much and he did not want to be literally looked down upon by his British colleagues. There was no such problem on the CITY OF BENARES.

My parents had a cabin to themselves while I shared one with two other students, one going out for the first time like me and a slightly older Bengali who had been studying at Dresden and spoke German. I was not quite clear why he had returned to India or why he chose to go to Germany in June many weeks before the winter term was due to start. He liked to be mysterious and there was nothing I could do about it.

The choice of the time for us was dictated by two factors. The fares were reduced in June because it was the start of the off season. The other was that we could not start till my results had been published and this happened on the 31st May two days after my seventeenth birthday.

We had chosen to embark from Karachi because it cost no more and Pitaji was determined to visit Rawalpindi before going away from India for so many months. We took the metre-guage train as usual from Ahmedabad to Delhi where we changed to the broad-gauge which took us all the way to Rawalpindi. After Rawalpindi there was a train to take us all the way to Karachi where we embarked.

Usually, the monsoon hits Cochin on 1st June, and gets to Bombay on the 6th. The voyage to Bombay from Karachi took three days and the monsoon hit us in the middle of the Arabian Sea. This was the reason for the 'off-season'! Pitaji was not affected by the monsoon but Mataji and I were miserable. I was able to recover by the time we got to Suez but Mataji was only happy when we disembarked at Marseilles on the 15th June.

VI

EUROPE 1938-39

Having arrived in Marseilles in the middle of June, I was exposed as soon as the S.S. City of Benares had docked, to the French porters who swarmed on board. To my horror, I found that I could not understand what they were saying! The fact was that I had never heard a Frenchman speaking and nor had the teachers from whom I had learnt my French. The situation was complicated by their *Provencal* accent. It took me a few days to get my ears used to this situation. The receptionist at the Grand Hotel de Geneve where we put up was very good. She spoke slowly and with exaggerated clarity to me when I persisted in speaking to her in French although she and most of the staff could converse perfectly easily with my parents in English.

My mother mentioned to us that the lift operator looked like an Indian. When Pitaji put the question to the receptionist, she replied, 'Oh, no, he has been here for many years and is perfectly French now.' This, of course, convinced us that Mataji's feeling had been correct so Pitaji spoke to him and found that he was not only an Indian but came from Rawalpindi! He sounded rather embarrassed by the situation and we guessed that he was in the same situation as one of Pitaji's cousins, named Ujagar Singh Malik. This man had gone to England to study but had failed in his examinations and never returned. On another cousin making enquiries, it was found that he had secretly married an English bank clerk and they were living on the wife's earnings. I said 'secretly' because in those days an English bank clerk marrying a 'black man' – yes, even in my time, Indians were considered 'black' in common English parlance even if they had light skins and blue eyes, like me – would have been against the bank's rules and they would both have starved because, in the early twenties there was no dole.

Some Indian students married English girls and took them home. This was commonly called returning with an 'Ll.D.' The letters did not mean a Doctorate in Laws but a 'landlady's daughter.' At least the lift operator was earning an honest living in Marseilles although his presumably middle-class family in Rawalpindi would never have admitted that their son was doing such work since manual labour is not well looked upon in India.

We stayed some days in Marseilles. All three of us had read 'The Count of Monte Cristo' in an English translation and we were delighted to visit the Chateau d'If which had rooms marked as in the novel, knowing full well that it was all fictitious.

Another visit was to the large church on a hill called, 'Notre Dame de la Garde'. We had been seeing this from our hotel which was situated overlooking the old port. Mataji had been shocked by the skimpy clothes of many girls we saw on the street. This was the first summer of the paid holidays introduced by the Leon Blum government and young people of both sexes were exploiting it to the full by wearing leisure clothes. Pitaji was also surprised because the situation had been very different in 1912 when he had last visited Europe. So they were both very pleased when I translated a notice on a board outside the church ordering everybody 'including little girls' to be adequately dressed in the 'House of God'. Pitaji and I were wearing three piece suits and Mataji was wearing full-sleeved silk blouses in weather as hot as June in Bombay!

After a few days in Marseilles, we left for Paris by train. It was probably the day a P&O. liner had arrived, because an Englishman said to Pitaji that the train was noisier and shakier than the Frontier Mail train in India. It certainly was no better, but to me the scenery was stupendous. The Rhone Valley was green all over, there was no dust to be seen; even the traffic on the road raised no dust. In fact the whole landscape was clean and delightful to behold. Some years later, I met a young Englishwoman in Cambridge who had been brought up as a child in India and had seen the same scene for the first time in her life as as a teenager. She told me she had asked herself, 'How many *malis* (gardeners) must they be employing to maintain this unending garden!' I have often asked myself why India always looks so dusty and dirty. Part of it is poverty but the main reason is undoubtedly the climate – the heat and lack of rain for many months at a time. The dust of India is unique. I have lived in other poor and relatively arid countries in Africa and in South America but the dust in the Sahel and the Sahara and on the Andean Altiplano is much more coarse so that it does not remain so long suspended in the air. The only explanation I can find is that the Indo-Gangetic basin is full of alluvium and has been ploughed and cultivated for thousands of years which has ground the particles to a fineness not found anywhere else.

We were travelling with the help of Thomas Cook whom Pitaji must have told how much he was prepared to pay for hotel rooms. It had worked out very well in Marseilles but in Paris the Grand Hotel du Globe was horrible; we arrived there late in the evening, there was no restaurant and we had to walk to the Boulevard des Italiens to have a bad meal at 11 P.M. Throughout the night the antiquated plumbing system made gurgling noises which kept us awake.

Fortunately, we had got a copy of EUROPA TOURING from the Western India Automobile Association and that gave us the OXFORD AND CAMBRIDGE Hotel which suited us perfectly. We went to Versailles, the Eiffel Tower and to the Folies Bergeres as also to a Cinema (Courcelles) where we saw an old silent film with sub-titles in Danish based on an Emile Zola novel.

Pitaji had professional interests as well. In Marseilles the British Consul General had given him an assistant recently arrived from Spain – Britain had just refused to recognise Franco's government and withdrawn its Ambassador from Madrid – to show us the drainage system. Unfortunately this assistant, probably of a family of British descent long settled in Spain, did not speak very much French and could not translate Pitaji's technical questions. We were very lucky in Paris because the engineer we were introduced to was married to a White Russian woman whose father had settled down in London and become quite rich. This lady was perfectly bilingual so that the visit was a great success and we all had a meal together. I was very impressed with this couple and sought them out when I visited Paris in the summer of 1945. He had given up his government job and joined the private sector where he was obviously well paid. He invited me to lunch in their apartment. Rationing was not noticeable in the meal I ate and I told them so. They said they were lucky to be well off and they sometimes saw men searching in the dustbins for food because even the garbage of rich people contained edible items!

Several of the engineers and consuls Pitaji met in Europe during this holiday expressed their surprise and admiration that an Indian engineer would spend his own hard-earned money to interrupt his holiday and study matters from which only his employer could benefit. It gives an idea of Pitaji's character.

For me Paris was a great and wonderful city where I would have liked to stay longer but the language was a problem for my parents and Pitaji was impatient to get to the London where he had lived so happily a quarter of a century earlier. So we got to London where we were welcomed by uncle Jit. Jagjit Singh Malik (1913- 2004) was the youngest of the three sons of my Dadaji by his second marriage. The eldest, Mohinder Singh, had gone to England to study veterinary science, had returned during the long vacation and died in a car crash. He had been driving the car and had crashed into the car of a relation – they were all going together for a picnic. That crash took three lives. Jit had also been in the car and had suffered head injuries, remaining concussed for several days. He was lucky to survive without any long-term damage. In fact, of the three brothers, he turned out to be the best student, specialising in mathematics. He had taken his B.A. in Rawalpindi, then gone to Bombay for his M.A. There he had been advised that there was a demand for actuaries and that he should study in London which is what he was doing when we arrived. Let me continue the story of his studies. He did not qualify as an actuary and thought he would become a statistician. Ten years later I was told that there were Indian professors of statistics in most American universities. The best-known statistician in England at the time was called Hammond who was a fellow of Downing College Cambridge. The result was that there came a day in 1941 when there were only two Sikhs in Cambridge – my uncle and I.

There were other people in London that my parents were anxious to meet. I have mentioned Hardit Singh Malik previously. Although he was only four years younger than Pitaji and they had been born in the same house, they were not particularly close because he was the favourite son of his father, Mohan Singh Malik (1863-1931) and had been sent to Public School in England - the only member of the clan to do so. Subsequently he had gone to Balliol College, Oxford, joined the Royal Air Force as a pilot in the Great War and then the Indian Civil Service. Anyway, he had been designated the first Indian Trade Commissioner in New York. At that time there were Indian Trade Commissioners in Europe in London, Hamburg and Milan. He was being briefed for his new job in London and had managed to get his passage changed from an ordinary Cunard liner to the new QUEEN MARY which was classified as a luxury liner so the passages were more expensive. 'H.S.' as he was familiarly known was quite a figure in England. Apart from having gone to Public School and Balliol, he had played cricket for Sussex scoring a century and got a golf half-blue at Oxford. He had many friends in the English nobility (including the Prince of Wales) and gentry. He had also been some years earlier the Assistant Trade Commissioner in London.

I have mentioned Sardar Sohan Singh earlier more than once as a friend of Tayaji's. His younger brother Mohan Singh had been selected by the British government as one of the Advisers to the Secretary of State for India. This was a position of considerable prestige and was only given to very wealthy men. I have mentioned that Sohan Singh had over forty houses in Murree - the family was really very rich. The grandfather of these two, Sujan Singh, had made five lakhs in the Afghan War of 1878 in which Khazan Singh Malik had made three lakhs. Moreover, Mohan Singh was very different in personality and character from his elder brother and took good care of his money. When we arrived in 1938, we found he had rented a large house standing in its ow[illegible]unds in Putney. He dressed in Indian style in achkan and ch[illegible] often served Indian dishes; the dessert was generally c[illegible] gold or silver foil - rather like that which was used [illegible] those days for gilding. His English guests were ve[illegible] by being served 'gold to eat.'

LONDON, JUNE 1938

1938-B London Tea party at the Mayfair hotel given by Sardar Mohan Singh in honour of H.S. Malik going to the U.S.A. to be India's first Trade Commissioner in New York. The host is at the central table with Sir Zafrullah Khan and Sir Feroze Khan Noon (the High Commissioner) at his left. H.S. Malik and Aunty Prakash are opposite with an unidentified white man between them. Pitaji is visible in the right foreground and Khushwant Singh in the left foreground. Find me!

Sardar Mohan Singh gave a tea party for Mr. and Mrs. H.S.Malik at the Mayfair Hotel. A professional photographer was engaged to take a photograph of this event. I have a copy of this picture which is the largest photograph I possess; in fact I had to have a special album made to accommodate this photograph. It contains many persons, mostly Indians but also some English, who have since played important roles in history.

Pitaji rented a two-room service flat for us in 'Kensington Palace Mansions' which faced Kensington Gardens. I visited the place some sixty years later. It is now a hotel and I had lunch in its restaurant. In 1938 it had a TV room where we saw the rather flickery black and white television pictures of those days. This persuaded the other residents that we knew English and they started speaking to my parents! The conversation of what I considered 'old people' did not interest me.

Pitaji took us to an expensive restaurant for dinner and to a theatre but what impressed me most was a visit to Brooklands where I saw racing cars for the first time.

The London that Pitaji had known from 1908 to 1912 had largely disappeared but there were still Lyons Corner Houses where we had most of our meals – they were good and cheaper than the meals in the restaurant of Kensington Palace Mansions. He was able to trace his landlady's daughter who had got married and had children but he learnt that her marriage had broken down; however, what she told him was that her 'husband had gone to his club'.

Pitaji had planned his trip carefully and, from Ahmedabad had ordered a Studebaker convertible. Such cars were not available in India where we had always owned 'tourers'. The difference was that a tourer had four doors and its top could be taken down quite easily, but it had no windows, and when it rained, curtains had to be put up. These curtains had mica panels so one had a rather hazy view of the outside world and some of the monsoon rain generally managed to find its way inside. A convertible was usually a two-door model, had windows like a saloon car and a very elaborate roof which fitted hermetically with the window frames. When we saw a convertible in Ahmedabad, we knew that the owner had been to Europe and had brought the car back with him as 'accompanied luggage'. The Sarabhais had two of them and the second son Gautam had told me that one of the strips of the roof usually broke every time the chauffeur took the roof down.

A yellow six-cylinder Studebaker convertible had been ordered after Pitaji had considered every aspect of the specification of the available competition in spite of the fact that Dadaji had decided never to buy a Studebaker because his favourite son had been killed driving one.

We were delighted with the car when we saw it. Of course, mechanically the six-cylinder engine was a come-down after the Ford V8s that we had had since 1932 but the Studebaker engine proved quite adequate for all that it was asked to do. My sons have often asked me how Pitaji, a government servant, could afford to have an eight cylinder car as they see today's highest Indian officials in four cylinder cars. The answer is that cars have become

more complicated and much better in the last seventy years. At
the same time, civil service salaries in India in the highest ranks
are a fraction of what they were before Independence.

Let me explain the political background to this decline. The
Secretary of State's services were recruited in England; therefore
they had to be related to British civil service salaries. Why would
an Englishman in the nineteenth century leave his own country
and risk being buried abroad – Anglican cemeteries in India are full
of the graves of Englishmen who died at an early age of tropical
diseases - unless he was paid more? One of the major complaints of
the nationalist movement was that millions of rupees in pensions
and leave salaries were going out of the country every year on this
account. Those Indians who got the same salaries as the British
were envied by everybody and hated by political activists on
this account. Why should Indians be paid such 'princely salaries'
when compared with salaries paid to civil servants in other
countries – mostly much richer than India? After Independence,
new salaries were fixed for the new civil servants a little lower
than the old ones which did not look 'princely' any more because
they had not been increased since 1890 and inflation particularly
during and after the second World War had diminished their
value considerably. I noticed the difference myself in my own
service career. When I joined the Indian Foreign Service in 1947,
my salary was about the same as that of my British colleagues.
In 1979, when I retired, I was earning a fifth of what they were
getting. Even so, a report published in 2005 showed that, in terms
of national per capita income, top Indian civil servants were
being paid three times as much as their colleagues in O.E.C.D.
countries.

To return to the Studebaker, Pitaji was the only one to drive
it because Mataji had never learned to drive and I was too young
to have a driving licence. From the Automobile Association in
London we got all the documents and advice we needed for
taking the car out of the country and around Europe. The most
important document was a sort of exercise book with very broad
pages perforated so as to form three identical forms. They had all
to be filled up and the right-hand one was torn off by the customs
officer when we entered a country; at the same time, he rubber-
stamped the left-hand document or stub. The central portion was

detached by the customs officer at the exit-post who also rubber-stamped the stub. The whole exercise book went by the French name 'carnet de passage en douanes.'

Of course, Mataji sat in the passenger seat alongside Pitaji.. She had to get up every time I got in and out of the car because it was a two-door. I shared the back seat with a suitcase as the boot was not big enough to hold all the luggage we felt we needed for the long trip which we had planned.

In London, this car made us very noticeable because most cars were saloons and black or dark-coloured. A yellow convertible was very striking. Even on the Continent where cars were rarer and more varied than in England, the impression created was that Pitaji was a Maharaja! Thousands of Indians came to Europe every year but relatively few bought cars because they were afraid to drive in a foreign country – particularly on the wrong side of the road - and very few could afford to pay the salary and expenses of a chauffeur or want him to sit at table with them.

Equipped with EUROPA TOURING and Michelin road maps, I became the navigator especially as I could read French and claimed to be able to speak it too! Pitaji had been on the Continent in 1912 when he was asked to escort a wealthy Sikh lady who had come to England and wanted to join her husband in Budapest. From that brief experience he had become convinced that French was the language to speak on the Continent.

We crossed the channel by a Dover-Ostende ferry which was cheaper than the one to Calais altough the voyage was longer. On the ferry, there was a set meal at lunch and I ate beef for the first time in my life because Pitaji said we should not starve. Mataji had taken to her bed as soon as the ferry cast off.

At Ostende, I saw a European seaside resort for the first time. As a non-swimmer (which I still am) I had no interest in the beach but I was looking for a Congolese because I knew that Belgium had a colony with a much larger area and population than that of Belgium. I expected therefore that Africans would be as numerous there as Indians were in England. I finally saw a black man in the hotel so I asked the receptionist if he was a Congolese. 'No,' he replied, 'He is an American musician who will perform here tonight.'

After the tarred roads of England, the cobbled roads of Belgium were a come-down but we noticed that the smaller cars of Europe seemed to tackle them better than our large Studebaker. Pitaji managed to drive very well on the wrong side of the road. Mataji gave hand signals when we had to make a left turn. Having always had tourers, we usually drove with the windows open. However we never took down the roof. In fact, I don't think the car ever had its roof taken down in all the years that Pitaji owned it!

At Brussels we stayed at the Grand Hotel Cosmopolite and were delighted to find that everything appeared to be cheaper than in England. The head waiter not only spoke English but recognised us as Indians and said, 'You will not want to eat beef or pork.'

We took a bus tour of war cemeteries which were numerous and separate for the British, Canadians, Belgians and French. We were surprised to find that there were fewer French cemeteries but that was because they were huge. There were no cemeteries for Indian soldiers because, on the Western front, the Indian troops only fought in France and that too for one season after which they were transferred to Iraq.

European countries seemed small to us when we got to Amsterdam from Brussels in a few hours. However, the difference was noticeable when, in Amsterdam, we saw men and women wearing clogs which we had never seen. They were also wearing their national costumes. It did not occur to us that this might be for the benefit of tourists like us. We had our first linguistic surprise when we went into a shop to buy film. The shop assistant addressed us in Dutch so I stepped forward asking, 'parlez-vous francais?' She made a gesture asking us to wait and brought the manager from the back of the shop who was able to speak some French. When I translated his answer into English for Pitaji, they both laughed and said, 'Oh, you speak English. That is much easier for us.' I had no occasion to speak French in Germany, Denmark, Sweden or Norway.

I was very much impressed by the greenery and beauty of Holland. I had always thought that a flat country could not be beautiful because flat Sind and Punjab as I knew them were brown earth and dust most of the year. Here was a country flat as a pancake which was green and where no dust was to be seen anywhere. The neatness of their houses and other buildings including the famous windmills was eye-catching. I learnt that

Dutch housewives were very proud of their housekeeping and would not allow a speck of dirt to be visible anywhere. In most cities in India you can dust the dining table after breakfast and in the evening it is dusty again. Since then I have known many Dutch diplomats and one of them – married to an Englishwoman – said that earlier he had 'belonged to the Amsterdam school of hygiene which meant having a bath every Saturday whether it was needed or not.' In India everybody I knew had a bath every day – some had baths twice a day, the second before sitting down to the evening meal – but the Dutch looked as clean as anyone could wish.

It was a new experience that the principal streets of Amsterdam were in fact canals on which the biggest and most opulent homes were situated. I was reminded of Srinagar where Mataji had pointed out to me the mansion on the Jehlum which my Nanaji had rented when he first got there. It had a watergate although I think there was a back door on a street which I could not see from the shikara (boat paddled by one or two watermen for the use of tourists) in which we were travelling.

I had seen few bicycles in Europe compared to India. We had seen the young holidaymakers riding them in Marseilles and again in Cambridge where under-graduates were not allowed to have cars; Pitaji said that at least had not changed since his days. In Amsterdam people of all ages and both sexes were riding bicycles and, for the first time I saw a tandem. The man riding it was alone and everybody was teasing him about it. The reason for all these cycles was the narrowness of the streets and the amount of traffic which meant that Pitaji had difficulty in finding parking places in the street and the car remained in the garage of the Krasnopolsky hotel. This old building which I understand has survived into the twenty-first century had a 'winter garden' which served as the breakfast room – an arrangement I had not seen in any other hotel.

From Amsterdam we arrived in a single day at Osnabruck in Germany. The difference between the two countries was noticeable right at the frontier where the beautiful and picturesque Dutch houses gave way to utilitarian brick structures rather like India. However the hotel was situated in its own grounds and we could walk around the garden rather as we did in the bungalows in India in which we were accustomed to living. This was a welcome change from all the hotels we had stayed in in Europe where one stepped out of the hotel on to the footpath of a crowded city street. I next saw Osnabruck in May 1945 from an Air Force vehicle I was driving. It came into view as my convoy crossed a hill. It had been completely destroyed by bombing and shelling. I could not see any building standing.

In 1938 we drove in one day from Osnabruck to Hanover. Part of this journey was on the newly built *Autobahn*. This appeared to us to be a motorist's paradise. We had never seen anything like it. No oncoming traffic, separate lanes for vehicles travelling at different speeds and no crossroads. What more could anyone desire? Until then we had looked down on European roads many of which had been cobbled while even the smallest village roads in England were tarred. Of course, on the Continent the highways were generally straight whereas many English roads lived upto G.K.Chesterton's description, 'The rolling English drunkard made the rolling English road.' The Studebaker was large, heavy, powerful and comfortable but on cobbles it became noisy and shaky which shocked us. Later I was to hear complaints from my European friends that the autobahns were boring, they had no character, etc. But even in the twenty-first century, when I have a choice I prefer to drive on a motorway by whatever name it my be called in different European countries. I regret that there is not a single kilometre of motorway in India. However the six-lane highways now being built are quite good. I only wish they could be built faster.

In Hanover, I saw for the first time that the most important and beautiful buildings had green domes whereas I had only seen gilded or marble domes in India and England. Pitaji explained to me that the weather in Northern Europe is very severe with sleet, snow and hail in winter. Gold or even marble would not be able to stand up to it. Domes and sloping roofs of important buildings are therefore covered with copper plate which is turned into green patina by acid smoke. This patina protects the copper from pollutants in the air and the copper protects the building underneath from the elements.

We only stayed one night in Hanover and drove the next day to Hamburg where we were put up by H.M.Patel in his large third floor flat in a street called Fernsicht. The building had no lift but its location was superb. The drawing room had large windows with a magnificent view of the lake called ALSTER.

H.M.Patel was the Indian Trade Commissioner in Hamburg with jurisdiction over the whole of Northern Europe extending south as far as Switzerland. This post was very coveted because it was the nearest thing to a diplomatic one that an Indian could aspire to. One of the qualifications which H.M. had for this post was his knowledge of German as I have mentioned earlier. One of his predecessors several years earlier had been H.S.Malik who had come for a few months while he was Assistant Trade Commissioner in London to hold the fort during the incumbent's unforeseen absence.

Of course, I knew Mrs. Patel (Savita) and the daughter Usha. Since then two more daughters, Uma and Nisha had arrived. This was, of course, the result of the usual desire for a son to carry on the family line. He still had the problem of his father's debts and had not bought a car. His office was situated in the building of the Vier Jahreszeiten hotel, one of the two best in Hamburg. It was located near the other end of the Alster and he commuted by the very punctual and pleasant ferry service. It was, in fact more practical than going by car because it avoided the parking problem.

I have mentioned that the University of Cambridge would not accept me before the age of eighteen. I felt that I had a talent for European languages so I had enquired which language would be useful and I was told that for a chemist the most useful language was German. Of course, Hamburg was not the most prestigious German university but its comparative mediocrity was more than offset by the presence of H.M. He enquired from the university authorities what I had to do to get admission. The answer was that whatever was sufficient to enter a university in my own country would do. I discovered later that there was a tradition of 'migration' among European universities and many better-off students would attend two or three universities in order to learn several languages and familiarise themselves with the customs and traditions of several countries. This was an old tradition dating back to the time when college and university education was all in Latin so that migration presented no linguistic problem. In fact for the aristocracy and those who aspired to be diplomats, it was almost essential in an age when all the 'powers' were European.

We had been given a long list of things to buy by friends and relations in India who wanted imported items not available in India. Hamburg was the obvious place to do this because the contacts and knowledge of German of H.M. were available and there was a very favourable rate of exchange for tourists with sterling to buy Reichsmark.

After a few days with the Patels we moved on to Denmark. The weather was good, the roads had very little traffic and travelling was very pleasant. Oh, yes, we had to have trafficators installed because we were so advised. It was not very difficult or very expensive. As it was summer, the days were very long which was a novel experience for Mataji and me. We learned to draw the curtains of our hotel rooms before going to bed so as not to be woken up by the sun at four in the morning.

The first stop in Denmark was at Kolding where the hotel was old, in the middle of the town in a rather narrow street. We had to park the car in the courtyard which needed rather complicated manoeuvring because the car was so big. When Pitaji had completed this exercise, we were told we had to go into the street to get to the hotel entrance. This took a long time because the news of the arrival of these strange creatures in the little town had attracted the whole population and they had packed the street. It seemed that Pitaji's turban and beard were attracting a lot of attention. It was our introduction to Scandinavia and we found it rather amusing and not unpleasant. After dinner we did not go for our usual walk because we felt that the entire village would follow us.

There was nothing interesting to see in Kolding so we left early the next morning for Copenhagen. The first remarkable event was the crossing of what is known in Danish as LILLE BAELT. This was done across a large bridge where we did not even have to pay a road toll. I found the bridge remarkable not only because of its length but even more its height. Ocean-going ships had to pass beneath it. The next hurdle was the STORE BAELT. There was no bridge and we had to take a ferry; the whole procedure was very efficiently carried out and we were at the hotel in Copenhagen in time for lunch.

Denmark was much more expensive than Belgium or Germany but everybody spoke English and people did not appear surprised by our appearance. I think Indian tourists travelled around Europe by train or by ship and they got to the capitals and big cities but in villages and small towns no one had ever seen a Sikh. The Tivoli garden was wonderful and we spent so much time there that we got back to the hotel after midnight – something we had never done anywhere.

We had the choice of taking a boat or a bus tour of the city. We chose the boat and then did the rest in our own car. Pitaji had no difficulty in finding places to park the car. We were very impressed by the statue of the mermaid.

There were several ferries for crossing the ORESUND which separates Denmark from Sweden and we chose the ferry from Elseneur to Helsingberg. The reason was the history of Elseneur which is the Elsinore of Shakespeare's HAMLET. To get there, we had the choice of two roads and we chose the coast road which was about twenty-five miles long. However, we never saw the coast! The explanation was that the villas of the rich had monopolised the entire coast and the road was the back entrance to their estates. The population of Denmark was less than five million but so many of them appeared to be rich to judge by the mansions which we had seen all over the country. Other signs of their wealth were not noticeable. In England we had seen Rolls Royces, Daimlers and Bentleys. There were no such cars to be seen in Denmark. At the same time there were no poor people such as we had seen in England and France visible in Denmark either. It appeared that there was greater economic equality than in the bigger, richer and more powerful nations of Europe. The wealth of the very numerous rich was only noticeable in their mansions.

We were not able to enter Elsinore castle, contenting ourselves with a walk on the *glacis*. It was obvious that the castle had nothing to do with Shakespeare's play because it was certainly built no earlier than the seventeenth century.

When we arrived in Sweden we saw at once that traffic was on the right of the road whereas EUROPA TOURING had said that Sweden was the only country in Scandinavia which adhered to the British rule. Obviously, the Swedes had only recently decided to conform to the Continental decision first imposed by Napoleon. Apart from that, the weather was fine and the warmth of the sun had induced people to open their windows. I remember taking a photograph of a whole street of houses with open windows – the first time I had seen such a scene in Northern Europe. Mataji had been afraid that the North would be cold and was very relieved to find it was not so. The bright sunshine and the many hours it lasted ensured that it did not get cold even at night.

In Sweden we saw for the first time, some large American cars like our own. As I have mentioned, we had seen large English cars in England and after that only small European ones on the Continent. We knew from pictures in the newspapers that there were large German Mercedes and Auto-Unions (some even with six wheels) but they seemed to be reserved for the Fuehrer and his Ministers and we never saw any. Of course, Sweden is a large country and, at that time, it seemed to be the wealthiest country in Europe. Pitaji explained it by saying that Sweden had kept out of the Great War. There was a more practical reason for using large American cars. I learnt later that, at that time, the vast territory of the United States had very few tarred or cement concrete roads. The other roads were no better than roads in India – either water-bound macadam or earth roads - which was what made American cars so popular in India. Only the British or those particularly anxious to please them, the Princes and the landed aristocracy, bought English cars. In Sweden also, once one got away from the coastal arterial highways, the roads were mostly gravel. We were travelling in a bright sunny dry summer and I shudder to think what happened to the roads in conditions of rain, snow and frost. In such conditions, I suppose only large American cars would do. Some weeks later, as we were leaving Germany, on a motorway, Pitaji pointed out a large car to me saying, 'That is a Maybach with a twelve-cylinder Zeppelin engine. It is the German answer to the Rolls Royce.'

After crossing over into Sweden, we stopped for lunch at Goteberg, on the terrace of a hotel in full view of the street. Reports of our presence must have reached the local newspaper and an English-speaking reporter came to interview Pitaji. When his questions took a political turn, Pitaji said that as a government servant, he could not have political views, and advised the reporter to talk to me. However, I did not want to express anti-British views either so he got nothing out of me about British colonialism. I cannot recall any further experience of this kind. We found that a lot of Swedes spoke very good English; we were told that this was because many of them had lived in the United States where there were large Swedish populations in the mid-western states.

We crossed the next day into Norway and we noticed that the distance between the customs posts of the two countries was over a kilometer whereas at all the previous frontiers we had crossed, the customs posts were next to each other. We attributed this to the low population density of the two countries and the relaxed good relations between them.

No hotel had been booked for us in Oslo. Europa Touring indicated a hotel at Holmenkollen with magnificent views. When we got there after driving ten kilometres, mostly uphill, we found that the hotel not only overlooked Oslo but also lake Tyrifjorden on the other side. I cannot recall another hotel with such views in the whole of the trip. Unfortunately the hotel did not have a single bathroom! Back in Oslo, we found the hotel Regina with ample facilities but no restaurant! They only served tea or coffee for breakfast with a large buffet of cold cuts with which we could make our own sandwiches or *smoargasbrod*. Fortunately there were several satisfactory restaurants in the neighbourhood.

In the course of our after dinner walk, we encountered an Indian girl and two young men – obviously students. We stopped to chat with them and found that they had come from London on a holiday. They said they were travelling on a low budget and staying in a youth hostel. We had never heard of such an institution. They explained that they slept in small dormitories and were expected to make their own beds; I was horrified at the idea. They went on to explain that the janitor had realised that this was a new experience for them and offered to make their beds.

The conversation had by now lasted several minutes during which we had paid no attention to what was going on around us. We were standing on the footpath of a road which traversed a public park. Imagine our surprise, when a policeman came up to us and very politely indicated to us that we should move on. We had never had occasion to speak to a Norwegian policeman but we had noticed that instead of being equipped with a truncheon or baton like policemen in England and France, these men wore swords. I have since reflected that the Metropolitan Police in London claims to be a force entirely of Officers – a view difficult to accept when one finds a man wearing a Sergeant's stripes (like a Head Constable in India) who obviously had authority over others. By wearing swords, the policemen in Oslo were telling the public in no uncertain terms that they were Officers.

The reason for police intervention was that a crowd – curious, but not unfriendly – had formed around us and was not only blocking the footpath but also the road. We had unknowingly created a traffic obstruction. We were amused and also impressed by the exquisite manners of the police officer who spoke some English. Throughout our few days in Norway we found crowds gathering around us. They had obviously never seen a Sikh.

The main sight in Norway, according to the information we could gather, were the fjords and it appeared that they were only accessible by ship – the roads leading to them we were told were very poor – we had not been impressed by the road into Oslo from Halden at the Swedish frontier. So we decided not to explore the country but to take the shortest road to Uppsala in Sweden.

On the way to Uppsala we stopped for the night in Karlstad and I remember very clearly the hotel in which we stayed. For once I had a bathroom all to myself. In most of the hotels, only my parents had a room with an attached bath and I had to wait my turn. To go to the toilet, I would have to put on my dressing gown and find the common toilet. In Ostende, the hotel did not have a room with an attached bath and a tub was carried into my parents' room, hidden behind portable screens and I was given buckets of hot and cold water. The advancement of Sweden in so many respects was attributed to the U.S. connection.

The main attraction in Uppsala for me was that I had read Voltaire's 'Charles XII' in addition to his 'Age of Louis XIV' and wanted to see if I could find any connection with Swedish history in the Cathedral – Uppsala is the ecclesiastical capital of Sweden. Indeed the tomb of general Lennart Torstenssen (1603-1651) was there in addition to that of Swedenborg and several Swedish kings and I felt I was touching history. Then again Uppsala is a university city and in the long warm summer evenings many people were in shirt sleeves. In fact I saw Swedish men whose faces were so tanned by the month of August that they could have been mistaken for Indian professors!

It did not take two hours to drive from Uppsala to Stockholm but the two cities were very different. Uppsala was obviously an ancient city and the hotel was like hotels we had stayed in when touring Belgium and Germany. The Strand hotel in Stockholm looked very modern and had no restaurant. It was explained to us that most of the clients were businessmen from the provinces who had work in the neighbourhood and were happy to eat in one of the many good restaurants there.

I knew very well that Stockholm had been the capital of Sweden for centuries but most of the buildings in our neighbourhood looked quite new and, except for the Royal Palace and a few other historic buildings, the city looked as if it had been built in the twentieth century. Apparently, the exploitation of hydro-electricity, the growing importance of aluminium and newsprint had created new industries which had brought about the renovation of the capital. It was true that water was everywhere but it looked different from Amsterdam because the buildings were new and the streets had ample room for cars.

We were convinced that we had arrived in the richest country we had seen so far. Pitaji explained it, as I have mentioned earlier, by the fact that it had remained neutral during the war while Germany and France had been devastated. However, I was unconvinced because of the difference between Norway (which had also been neutral) and Sweden.

Pitaji wanted to see workers' apartments. We were taken to one of these and were delighted to find the family all speaking English and living like the middle classes in England. In fact I felt that the apartment would be acceptable for us! Sweden appeared to be a country where there were no poor people.

Of course, we had seen Sweden during the summer when the days appeared to be endless and everything looked bright and cheerful. The beauty of the country was even more striking when we got to our last stop in the country. This was at Granna on lake Wetter where the hotel was a series of little self-contained cottages in a wood around a main building which housed the reception, the restaurant and the other amenities. Of course, I have seen a number of hotels on this pattern in recent years but, in 1938 it was the only one we encountered.

To cross over to Germany we had to take the ferry at Tralleborg on the southern tip of Sweden and it took about four hours for the crossing to Sassnitz on the island of Ruegen which is connected by a bridge to the German mainland. The difference between Germany and Sweden became apparent as soon as we got off the ferry. In Sweden everybody we had to deal with spoke English and we never had any difficulty. At Sassnitz, we were given to understand that we did not have a visa. Finally an official appeared who spoke a little English and he pointed out that the visas in the two passports (my parents had one passport between them) were for a single entry. The visas had been obtained by Thomas Cook and were in German so we were quite unaware of this. He offered to give us visas on the spot but he insisted that we pay for them in Sterling. This was very much more expensive than if we had paid for them in German currency which we had bought at the much cheaper tourist rate in London. We expressed our surprise that in German territory a German official should refuse to accept his own national currency but there was nothing for it and we ended up by paying in sterling.

At the Kaiser Hotel in Berlin, we appreciated the benefit of the difference in exchange rates. The official rate was about Rm11 to the Pound whereas we had got our Reischmarks at the rate of 24 to the Pound. The hotel was comfortable without beng modern just like several hotels we had been staying at in other countries but very much cheaper than the hotels in Scandinavia. Then again, in Berlin everybody appeared to be familiar with Indian tourists – no one looked surprised at seeing a Sikh – and we could forget about Nazi-ism except for the flags hanging in the streets.

Next day in the big department stores there was no language problem, the prices were lower than in England and the quality of the goods appeared excellent. Mataji bought a Siemens hair dryer and other items which she used all the rest of her life – 56 years. What was not of good quality was woollen clothing – wool was in short supply in the Third Reich. Of course German resourcefulness was excellent. We heard plenty of jokes about comedians patting each other on the back and saying 'Come in' because the clothes were made of wood fibre or 'Cheers' because glass fibre had been used.

From Berlin we took the road for Dresden. I knew from the guide book that there was an area known as 'Saxon Switzerland' but Pitaji said there would be enough time to see the real Switzerland. I was particularly interested in seeing the IHAGEE works because I had a vest pocket EXAKTA reflex camera which had interchangeable lenses and I had managed to damage the mount of my 250 millimetre telephoto lens. We got to the reception desk on a Saturday morning and I explained my problem to a man who spoke excellent English. He said the factory was about to close and he would have the problem attended to before showing us around and he did. I was most impressed by the service. It explained why German products were so highly appreciated and Germany is always able to live by exporting.

We drove from Dresden to Karlsbad or Karlovy Vary as the Czechs called it. The crossing of the frontier was quite something. The two customs houses adjoined each other and there were soldiers at the Czech post in addition to the customs and immigration staff. Moreover, anti-tank barriers had been built across the road on the Czech side. I could not understand the point of this because I knew that tanks are designed as off-the-road vehicles and there were no trenches in sight a hundred yards away. However, it was obvious that the Czechs wanted tourists like us to know that they felt threatened by their German neighbours. On seeing our British Indian passports, we were welcomed and treated very politely by the Czech officials and we reciprocated by expressing our sympathy for their plight in having as neighbours a country which was traditionally hostile to Czechoslovak independence.

In Karlsbad we found that the hotels and restaurants were well organised for receiving tourists and everybody we had to deal with spoke English. We were offered all kinds of baths but since we had no rheumatic or arthritic pains or digestive problems we took no interest in this facility. However, the local craftsmen were making all kinds of glasses and cups of bone china or glass which were beautiful and even fantastic. Mataji found these hand-crafted articles irresistible and bought several of them. In spite of their fragility some have survived the transport back to India and the dozen or more changes of residence which have taken place in the last 66 years.

When we set off on our *post-prandial* promenade, a man who appeared quite European except that he might have been a little darker-skinned than a northern European addressed Pitaji in Punjabi. He turned out to belong to a princely Punjabi Sikh family but he was not a keshadhari. He explained that since he was fond of good food and drink, he had to have recourse to the waters of Karlsbad from time to time to undo the damage to his system caused by good living. Pitaji told him that since we drank only water, we had no need of the curative waters of Karlsbad and that we had come to see the fate of those whose life styles exposed them to these problems. I had the feeling that our encounters with our compatriots in Europe tended to be unfortunate.

We had another such experience when we got to Prague because we had not made an advance reservation and, at the height of the tourist season, rooms were scarce. At the second hotel we went to we were told there was no room but because it was around our usual teatime, we sat down in the lounge for afternoon tea. Great was our surprise when we saw Pandit Jawaharlal Nehru arrive accompanied by half-a-dozen other men to do the same. Soon, one of his acolytes came over and said to Pitaji,

'Panditji says that he thinks he has met you before but he would like to know where and when it was.'

'The first time was in the Chemistry laboratory of Downing College, Cambridge in 1908.'

'No, no, it must have been more recently than that!'

'Well, last year he came to Ahmedabad where I was the municipal engineer and I was introduced to him at a function in the municipal garden.'

We found accommodation in the Hotel Alcron which was satisfactory but had a rather depressing atmosphere. There were interesting things to see in Prague such as the ghetto which showed in what miserable conditions Jews had had to live in Central Europe in the middle ages. We knew of course that Hitler was persecuting Jews in Germany and Pitaji knew that Jews had been a despised minority in Europe for centuries. Mataji knew from her reading of nineteenth century English and French (in translation) fiction that Jews were regarded mainly as moneylenders who are not highly thought of in India either, but I was perplexed. I remembered first meeting a Jew (I think he was a medical man) in Ahmedabad when he came to the house. I was informed of his forthcoming visit by one of the servants so I asked him,

'What is a Jew?'

'Oh! They are like Muslims; they don't eat pork,' came the answer. Verily our God is in our kitchen, as Swami Vivekanand said.

Prague was quite a picturesque city. We visited the Castle and were told about 'defenestration' - Austrian Roman Catholic plenipotentiaries had been thrown out of the window by Bohemian protestant noblemen in 1618. From the centre of the city, the way to the Castle lay over the Charles bridge which was adorned with a number of religious statues. We were shown that one of these was decorated with gold because 'a Jew had damaged it and been made to pay a fine of his own weight in gold'. This sounded far-fetched. The amount of gold in sight did not look as if it would weigh a hundredweight. Besides, how would so much gold survive centuries, unguarded through wars, occupations and revolutions?

In Prague we also met a fellow countryman who said that he had come to see the city before German guns and planes flattened it to the ground. Many Indians loved and admired Hitler because they thought that he would free them from the British yoke. We did not share this view.

Going from Prague to Vienna we found another world. We had no problem finding rooms in the Imperial hotel which was obviously one of the best in this great city and very inexpensive because we were paying with our cheap German currency whose value *vis-à-vis* the now defunct Austrian Schilling had been fixed to favour the German occupants. What Hitler called the *Anschluss* had taken place in the month of May. Goods in the shops were inexpensive and there was a greater variety than in Germany where shortage of foreign currency since some years had made imported goods very scarce indeed.

Vienna had been for centuries the capital of a great empire so it had beautiful buildings, parks and statues. Reduced since the Great War, twenty years earlier, to being the capital of a country with less than ten million inhabitants without major industries – they had been in what had become the Czechoslovak Republic – it could only maintain itself by tourism and, in spite of the political transformation, it did have a large number of tourists that summer.

In Vienna, as in Stockholm, Pitaji wanted to see workers' housing; he had read that the previous (Dollfuss) regime had been innovative about this. I was terribly disappointed. There were common bathrooms and laundries and they did not look clean. I felt that, allowing for the difference in climate, the Viennese worker was no better off than his counterpart in Ahmedabad.

From Vienna we arrived in a few hours at Budapest. Half-way there, we saw a sign which read AMPHITHEATRE so Pitaji stopped the car and we walked over an embankment to see what appeared to be a Roman amphitheatre – the first I had ever seen. It looked quite small with a capacity for between two and three hundred persons. It must have been restored because it looked new and there was no habitation within sight. Otherwise, the country was flat and featureless.

The Hotel Bristol was as luxurious and as cheap as the Imperial in Vienna. In the street, we met Madan Gopal Bhagat. As a successful manager knowing French, he travelled to Euope quite often looking for new designs and trends in pottery; he was staying at the Dunapalota Ritz hotel which was considered the best in the city. His visit to Budapest was for sightseeing because he had never been in Hungary. Pitaji had been there, as I have mentioned, in 1912. He had told us that Hungary had the most beautiful girls in Europe and I could well believe it by the evidence of my own eyes. We went to see an open-air opera on an island in the Danube. Of course, we could not make out a word of Magyar but the bright costumes, the music and the animated acting made it quite spectacular. It appeared to deal with a war and the men seemed to be cavalry officers. Later I learnt that the Magyars were proud of their equestrian skills and that the best *sabreurs* in Europe were Magyars but I also learnt that Hungary had not won a war for four hundred years! Budapest was a beautiful city and there were plenty of handicrafts in the shops for Mataji to buy as presents for all the relations who were following our travels through picture postcards that summer.

Apart from Budapest the country appeared uninteresting as we drove back into Austria by a different route via Semmering, a ski and summer resort within a couple of hours drive from Vienna. It was a warm day, there was no air conditioning - the hotel was equipped for the winter with double windows and padded doors - and we were glad to find what felt like iced water in the bathroom tap. We were told that Vienna got its water from Semmering.

Next day we went to Graz and were able to appreciate the beauty of the Austrian Alps on the way. The intention was to drive from there to Munich and as we looked at the map and worked out the distance, we wondered if such a long trip could be completed in one day because as we set out torrential rain (as severe as the monsoon) started to fall. We were all the more amazed when we were overtaken by an American coupe with its hood down! The young couple in it were wearing raincoats and seemed to enjoy getting drenched. We were quite apprehensive of the car skidding on a steep decline where the road surface was water-bound nacadam. However, we noticed that steel strips had been set across the road precisely to eliminate such a risk.

Conditions changed dramatically as we crossed what had been the old frontier between Austria and Germany – the abandoned customs posts were still standing. For one thing, the summer storm ended as suddenly as it had begun, giving way to bright sunshine on the beautiful mountains. Then, even more to our pleased surprise, a new kind of motorway emerged. Europa Touring had told us nothing about this. Its German name was Bergautobahn. It was slightly narrower than the normal autobahn but each track was wide enough for safe overtaking. The curves had half the radius of the curves on the normal autobahn but the system had been so well planned and executed that it was possible to drive at sixty miles per hour - Pitaji did not want to drive any faster. There were few vehicles on the road. As I have mentioned, cars were much less numerous than in England or Sweden and the road was not much used by trucks – it may have been that truck drivers like our guidebook were not aware of the existence of this magnificent road. We arrived at our hotel in Munich much earlier than we had expected. We went to see a musical show. It was suggested that we might visit one of the city's famous breweries but this did not interest us.

Munich is a large and ancient city. We consulted our Europa Touring and decided to take a bus tour with an English-speaking guide and this enabled us to see all that appeared of interest to us.

From Munich we took an autobahn going west – this was when we saw the Maybach mentioned earlier. This connected with an autobahn going north and brought us to Heidelberg which we had chosen as our next stop. Heidelberg has one of the oldest and most famous universities in the world and Pitaji was expecting to see magnificent buildings like the colleges of Cambridge – even something like 'the most beautiful mile of scenery in England' – the Backs. There was indeed a river very much broader, deeper and faster than the Cam but the city looked rather ordinary built of brick or stone of a colour much like the brick. I did not know then that brick is known in German as *Beckstein* (literally baked stone). To Pitaji's question to apparent faculty members, 'Where are your colleges?' or even, 'Why don't you have colleges?' the reaction was total incomprehension. Old university buildings, when these were pointed out to us, looked functional and undistinguished. There were some large churches which did not interest us and Pitaji did not feel like driving up the narrow and winding road to see the remains of the castle which had been taken and destroyed by the troops of Louis XIV nearly three hundred years earlier, even when we were told that it contained 'the largest barrel in the world'. In those days students in Oxford and Cambridge could not attend classes unless they wore gowns and the college of each student could be identified by the distinctive shape of the gown. In Heidlberg students looked like anybody else. Some even carried battered brief cases like commercial travellers! Pitaji was terribly disappointed.

However, the hotel was to our satisfaction and we decided to use it as a base for exploring the cities along or near the Rhine. Baden-Baden appeared to be a nice place and we happened to meet a German who spoke very good English and offered to show us around. He took us to a cigarette factory where he spoke to the manager who was delighted to show his establishment to an 'Indian Maharaja' or so it sounded to me – by now I was able to understand a few words of German. Neither the manager nor the guide could know that tobacco is forbidden to Sikhs. The guide benefited by receiving a couple of hundred cigarettes (Turkish tobacco) intended for Pitaji! He also benefited because Pitaji took us (and him, of course) to a luxury hotel – the Stefani. I think that was the only occasion when we ate fruit at a restaurant table.

After visiting a couple of uninteresting cities, we decided to shift base to Cologne. The road alongside the right bank of the Rhine was fantastic. The high hills on both sides had many castles on top which could be seen from the road. Then there were romantic places like Lorelei which we could read about in Europa Touring. For once we were happy not to have an autobahn to drive on because we could only appreciate the scenery from a slow road on which we could stop whenever we wanted to. There were many hotels and restaurants on the way, the food was inexpensive and good and the scenery was beautiful. I even made plans for visiting the Rhineland during future vacations from Cambridge – all totally unrealisable, as it turned out.

Cologne turned out to be a beautiful city with a famous cathedral and many other fine buildings. It also had a Hoehe Strasse leading to one of its bridges. This was essentially a narrow shopping street and it was closed to wheeled traffic in the evenings. We entered one of the shops (it was selling optical goods) where we found interesting merchandise. We were looking around when we observed that the shopkeeper was locking the door of the shop! We asked him if it was closing time and we should leave. He appeared rather embarrassed and explained that too many inquisitive people had entered the shop just to look at us. We observed then that in addition to the crowd in the shop there was another crowd outside who were impeding the flow of pedestrians – just like Oslo. I think we ended up buying a pair of Zeiss Opera glasses.

The time was coming to start studying German and mineralogy if I was going to be able to follow classes in a few weeks' time so my parents drove to Hamburg to leave me with the Patel family while they drove off to England. Mr. Patel had already found a German family near his flat which agreed to accept me as a paying guest (bed and board, all meals). This family was obviously an upper middle class one headed by a widow. There was a schoolboy son of about my age and a younger daughter. The person I had to deal with was a young friend of the family in his twenties who was to teach me German.

This was the first occasion for me to live in a family which was not my own or with close friends or relations and I felt quite unhappy. I had read a lot of English magazines and novels and thought I knew all about the European family. These German bourgeois were very different from the English gentry that I had read about. On top of it all, the young man who was to teach me German seemed more interested in learning English from me and was telling me about his views on sexual morality which were very different from what I had been taught.

The political situation came to my rescue. Hitler threatened to make war on Czechoslovakia to 'liberate' the Sudeten Germans. I knew all this from the English newspapers to which I had access in Mr. Patel's office, from our own recent visit to Czechoslovakia – Carlsbad was in the heart of the 'Sudetengebiet' – and because everybody kept talking about it. I had never thought that Britain and France would allow things to get to such a point that Czechoslovakia could be threatened – obviously Adolf Hitler understood international affairs better than I did! For the first time the Prime Ministers of Britain and France took aeroplanes for international meetings. Mr. Patel consulted the British Consul General and decided that British Indian subjects (his family and I) should leave Germany in view of the impending threat of war. The Government of India accepted his advice and we all took the train for London.

In London I was happy to see my parents who had taken a service flat in Bayswater. Of course, I stayed with them sleeping on a sofa-bed in their sitting room.

The Czechoslovak crisis was on the front page of all the English newspapers. The political parties were not in agreement about the action to be taken. Britain had made no preparation for a war. There was no compulsory military service as there was in the continental countries. The British Army was meant to maintain order in the Empire – especially India and Egypt. There was a Territorial Army and a Reserve of Army Officers but the former was under no obligation to serve abroad and the reserve of officers was small. I knew nothing of all this. I thought that Great

Britain was the greatest power on earth which had won the Great War twenty years earlier and would have no difficulty in doing so again! I learnt something of the reality from the newspapers but even my parents were quite unable to understand the decision of Chamberlain and Daladier to let Hitler have his way with Czechoslovakia. We felt that the great western powers had betrayed their little friend.

After a pleasant and interesting fortnight in England which included Pitaji driving the Patels to Badminton school where Usha and Uma had been admitted, I had to go back to Hamburg. There I found the situation had changed. The family in which I had been living did not want me; they said someone else had come to occupy my room – perhaps they liked me no more than I liked them. I found a boarding house in a part of Hamburg called Schlump. There was a family there which took in foreign students on board and lodging terms. The man appeared to be in his sixties; he had been a prosperous cattle dealer who had been ruined by the Depression. We were supposed to call him 'Onkel Willie'. He had a wife and a daughter aged about forty who had lived in the United States for ten or twelve years and spoke American English fluently. Willie did nothing at all but to look after his collection of a hundred and eighty cigar holders which had survived the crash. He had rented this huge apartment – the whole of the sixth floor of a large block of flats to serve as a boarding house for young people who were the children of businessmen in their own countries. They were serving as 'volunteer workers' in the offices of the German correspondents of their fathers with the intention of learning German and the business office practices of this great port. I remember an Italian, a Swede, a Norwegian and a Swedish girl. No one was studying at the university. In fact, they would go to their offices when they felt like it, were not paid – as far as I could make out – and seemed only interested in having a good time. I quite liked the Swede and the Norwegian but I was delighted when I was told a Frenchman was coming and I decided to use the occasion to improve my French even if this prevented him from learning German!

I was not impressed by Willie or his collection of cigar-holders. I had been brought up to think of smoking as a vice. I had seen lots of men and even women smoking but I had never seen a cigar-holder. The idea of a collection of objects to support a vice appeared bizarre to me. Then again the fact that he did nothing while his wife and daughter looked after this huge flat with only a part-time maid to help did not give me a good opinion of him. Of course, I understood later that the collection could be a very valuable asset and that his position was not very different from that of H.M.Patel's father.

The difference between Indian and German societies became very clear to me. I never found out if Willie had a son or if the son had died during the Great War. Again I never knew what the daughter had been doing in America. Had she been married to an American? If so, had her marriage ended in death or in divorce? I realised that I should not ask questions but I was surprised that any one should come back from America. Anyway she was more than paying for her keep by doing housework.

The case of H.M.Patel was very different. He had a job which most Indians could only dream of, but he did not live like his colleagues; for instance, he did not have a car. The reason was that he was still paying off his father's debts and that was quite expensive. This was something that I knew but not many others did. It is something for which I have admired him all my life.

Joining the University was a new experience. I had to buy a registration book, stick my photograph in it, then fill in the details of the courses I had to take, get it stamped and wait for a bill to arrive by the post. I was not in when the bill arrived and Willie thought he was doing me a great favour by filling a post office form for paying the bill. All this seemed very strange to me. In Ahmedabad, I used to collect my bill from the College office and pay it in cash. Mataji kept cash in the house. Pitaji had made me open an account with the Imperial Bank of India in London which he used to feed every month. I had opened a Reichsmark account in Hamburg with the Imperial Bank's correspondent bank in Hamburg. I paid the few bills I got by cheque. Mostly I collected cash Reichsmark (which I got at the tourist rate of exchange) for my monthly expenditure including rent. Apparently, in Germany students did not have bank accounts. Anyway, I still have this registration book with a photograph of me at the age of seventeen.

Even more surprising was the reaction of Germans to my appearance. I have already mentioned how an acquaintance of

H.M.Patel's guessed my age at forty-five years. A turban, the beginnings of a little beard, my English suits and my dignified behaviour which I had been taught in India to correspond to a child of good family caused me to be mistaken for a middle-aged man.

For exercise I had found an ice-skating rink accessible by tram from my lodgings, bought a pair of skating boots and skates and used to skate generally with my French friend Jean-Charles Lussat.

For learning German I used to go once a week to a Dr. Buck who was a professor of languages. He was the only German I could respect and like during this stay in Germany; he was also the only adult I could converse with about current affairs, cultural differences between India, England and Germany and so on. From a bookshop he ordered for me a copy of Wilhelm Ostwald's 'Die Schule der Chimie'. I had never seen this book but from my chemistry studies in India I knew that the author had won the Nobel Prize in chemistry and that this book was a literary and scientific classic. He also lent me some German literary works so that I would learn that the Germans could do more than impose discipline – the word *verboten* was visible everywhere – and torture Jews. Dr. Buck lived in a comfortable flat with his family and employed one maid who was expected to open the door for me when I rang the bell. As I am punctual by nature, everybody knew that I would arrive at 2.30 P.M. on Wednesday. One day it took some time for the door to open and I was surprised to see that Dr.Buck opened it himself with an apology for the delay. The following week he told me that he had dismissed the maid because she had refused to open the door for 'this strange man' whom she was afraid of.

'Torturing Jews'? Apart from what I read in the English papers, H.M.Patel had lent me a book by William Shirer which described what had been happening in Hitler's Third Reich including the names and locations of concentration camps in which the British and American governments and public refused to believe. On 11th November 1938, walking about in the fashionable shopping area around the Vier Jahreszeiten Hotel where the Indian Trade Commission was situated I saw the smashed windows of showrooms and shops which are known in German history books as 'Kristallnacht' – the night of the broken windows.

The excuse for this organised vandalism – nothing was stolen from any of the shops – was the murder in the German Embassy in Paris by a Jew named Grynspan of a Second Secretary of the name of vom Rath. In addition to the humiliation and damage, the Jews of Germany had to pay a collective fine of a billion Reichsmark. I had noticed that at various prominent places in Hamburg – crossroads, small parks – notice boards had been put up on which the posters were changed every week. I made a point of reading these notices assiduously. They were all anti-Semitic, often accompanied by disgusting cartoons. For me it was an occasion to learn official or bureaucratic German.

In the meantime I had decided that the boarding house where I was living had too many foreigners in it and was not the place where I would learn German. I found a large house at 15 Goethestrasse where there were some paying guests but all German. Of course, my arrival changed that specially as my friend Lussat soon followed me. The owner was an old German widow of over eighty years. She spoke a few words of French but her son, in his fifties, spoke it fluently. He looked after the coal-fired central heating and any other work which was too heavy for the maid and the *haustochter* (daughter of the house). I was given to understand that in some lower middle class families, daughters were sent to other families of similar status in other towns so as to learn housework instead of being spoilt by doting parents. This did not seem to be the case at 15 Goethestrasse. This woman who appeared to be about forty years old was treated the same way as the maid. Her education appeared to have stopped at the primary school. She was good natured and quite good looking. She wanted to work as a stewardess on a passenger ship which would require her to know English. She asked me to help but she soon realised that her even her German was not good enough.

I had a first floor room and Lussat soon joined me on the same landing. The third room was occupied by a fat blonde woman who said she was engaged to a sea captain. I never saw this sea captain. She was the secretary of an advocate. On the ground floor lived the owner, her son and a pretty young German woman named Erika Dach with her one-year-old son whom we all called

'Alexandre le Petit'. Her husband was said to be abroad and I never got to see him. We all ate together and we ate well. On the second floor were a dentist named Schneeroff and his wife. On the same floor lived his unmarried sister. They were Jews and had their own kitchen but there was no discrimination in this house and they would some times come down and talk to us after dinner when some of us would play ludo. I never went up to the second floor or down to the basement. Somewhere in the house lived an actress but Lussat and I could only see her if we happened to be looking out of the window as she was entering or leaving.

I became quite friendly with Dr. Schneeroff. His sister was able to get an entry visa for the United States which certainly saved her life. To leave the country she had to have customs inspection of her luggage. When she had chosen the objects she wanted to export, she informed the authorities and a customs inspector came to see her pack her bags after which he sealed them. The inspector was polite and helpful so she had nothing to complain about on that score. I got the impression that many officers and lesser officials were polite and helpful in dealing with the Jews but the police were tough. I never had occasion to speak to members of the S.S. who wore black uniforms or the S.A. who wore a slightly lighter shade than the khaki of the British Army. My landlady – I do not remember her name – did not like the Nazi regime and she took advantage of her great age to say things for which a young man would certainly have been punished. One day in the tram she asked for a ticket to go to 'Rathausplatz' (Town Hall Square). The conductor corrected her,

'You mean Adolf Hitler Platz?'

'Has the Town Hall fallen down?'

That did not stop the Gentile residents of the house from making traditional jokes about the Jews. 'She calls her husband Heinrich, shouldn't she call him Joseph?' Apparently the Minister of Propaganda, Goebbels had decreed that Jews must make themselves conspicuous by the men putting Joseph somewhere in their names and the women Sarah; I don't remember anyone paying any attention to this 'ruling' – Goebbels's first name was Joseph!

Dr. Schneeroff told me that he had applied for a visa for Palestine but that the British Consulate General had been very difficult and he feared that he would die in Germany probably in a concentration camp even though he had served in the German Army during the Great War. When I finally 'migrated' to Switzerland to join the University of Zurich he asked me to take his gold pocket-watch and chain as well as his diamond ring and give them to a person he named in Zurich. For the first and last time in my life I wore a diamond ring – while travelling third class – and I felt very relieved when I handed it over to the designated lady.

I had no difficulty with the lectures in the University. I had no intention of sitting for an examination in Germany but I was keen to learn some mineralogy because I knew absolutely nothing of this subject and I apprehended that at Cambridge I would be competing with men who had studied it intensively for a year. I did not find the subject very interesting but I attended all the lectures and practicals and they did not take too much of my time. On the other hand, I hardly went to the chemistry lab and one of the lecturers spoke to me about it. I told him I was studying German and he had to admit that I had made good progress in that.

I was conscious of increasing tension and rather fed up with seeing the word 'verboten' everywhere. I was a frequent visitor to the Patel household which increased that winter with the birth of his daughter Sharad. Many years later an English friend asked me if I had known her very long to which I replied,

'Oh no! She was already thirty-six hours old when I first saw her.'

The winter of 1938-39 was my first winter in a cold country and it was a wonderful experience as the winter was unusually severe. One day I was told that the temperature was lower than at Cape North, Norway. Women were wearing fur hats and men put on earmuffs. I was well protected by my turban but I took full advantage of my tropical background to bag the warmest seats available in classrooms, trams and so on. It snowed on Christmas Eve and I slipped and fell in Goethestrasse!

The Alster froze over and the ferryboats stopped. I noticed signboards at various places where steps led to the landing stages warning of the danger of stepping on the ice, but a couple of days later I saw that snow had fallen on the ice and footprints on the snow. I took my friend Lussat to one of the landing stages and we decided to risk crossing the ice to the next landing stage. We were pleased with our adventure.

Christmas brought a new revelation to me. I had always wondered if the son of my landlady had ever had a profession or trade. One evening I saw him in full evening dress! He went out and came back an hour later in a furious temper. He said at the Uehlenhorster Faehrhaus he had only been given one table with four diners; his tip would hardly justify his going out of the house! At the major landing stages there were restaurants and the one nearest Goethestrasse had laid on a gala Christmas Dinner Dance. The man spoke fluent French because he had been a headwaiter and his coming out of retirement had not been up to expectations.

I had been discussing with H.M. my increasing dissatisfaction with Hitler's Germany and he suggested my moving to Zurich which had a prestigious University. I would continue improving my German and my studies in mineralogy and live in a democratic atmosphere. So it was decided that I should leave as soon as the winter semester was over, have a skiing holiday in Chamonix, and join the summer semester in Zurich.

Chamonix was not a success. Skiing was different from skating, I entirely lacked a sense of rhythm and had no aptitude for sports. I ended up with a torn ligament in an ankle and 'housemaid's knee' which caused much hilarity when mentioned to English-speaking acquaintances.

The train journey from Chamonix via Geneva to Zurich was memorable in that I met a man who gave me his card 'Dr. Lucien BERNHEIM-BORNET, vice-versa uebersetzungen'. He explained that he was a language teacher and also did translations. Looking out of the window, at the scenery of Lake Leman, he said that I was looking at western Switzerland but that all the beauty of the country was in the south. I was amazed by this remark because my own view of the scene was that the setting of Geneva was the most beautiful I had seen of any city and sixty-six years later I do not think very differently. Of course, I did not argue the point but asked him what languages he talked and worked in. The conversation was in French and he mentioned that Switzerland had four official languages, German, French, Italian and Romansch; in addition to these he knew English. I had never heard of Romansch and he explained that it is spoken by less than one per cent of the population living in high mountains in the south-east. I told him that I knew English rather well and he soon found that I did when we discussed the English newspaper I was carrying. I said I was interested in learning Italian; perhaps I could help him with translations into English and he could teach me some Italian?

He accepted this suggestion and some weeks later I took my first Italian lesson. The first hurdle was that, in Zurich I could not find an English-Italian dictionary, and had to buy a French-Italian one with which I made do for the next twenty years. I had wanted to learn Italian in order to read Macchiavelli in the original but when I did I came to the conclusion that he wrote well but that what he advised did not make much sense to me. Still, I have since read most of the Italian classics and enjoyed many of them as well as the English and French ones. I have never written Italian and cannot converse easily in it.

It proved easy to find a boarding house in Zurich within ten minutes walk of the University. When I presented myself at the university and enquired about the classes I could take, I learnt that as a student at the University I could also attend classes or do practicals at the better known Eidgenoessische Technische Hochschule (Federal Polytechnic). Wolfgang Pauli (who was to get the Nobel Prize in Physics in 1945) was on sabbatical leave that year but I was able to attend lectures by Paul Karrer who had got the Nobel Prize in Chemistry in 1937 and by P. Scherrer who had worked closely with the Dutch Chemist P.J.W.Debye who got the Nobel Prize in Chemistry in 1936. I never had another opportunity to study under such illustrious professors.

Of course, such great teachers were wasted on me. I did learn a little Mineralogy but have no recollection of the other studies except for Scherrer's lectures which were accompanied by spectacular electrical experiments on the table behind which he stood to speak. What I did learn was how the Helvetic Confederation worked – I had no earlier experience of a federal state. I also met men and women of my own age who knew much more about Europe and European politics than I did. In Hamburg, I had made one friend, Lussat, with whom I am still in touch. I do not remember the names of any of my class-fellows in Germany.

The other residents in the boarding house were mostly students and interesting for various reasons. One was a German Jew studying engineering named Thomas Traube who became a life-long friend and whom I specially went to visit in the clinic in Locarno, Switzerland a few weeks before he died some fifty years later. There was an Englishman named Derek van Abbe who was reading German. I met his parents when they came to see him. I think they were artists. Ten years later I read his name in an Australian paper to which he had written criticising some aspect of Indian foreign policy.

There was a German Jewish girl called Trudi (Gertrude) who became the envy of the others when she got a U.S. immigrant visa and immediately departed for her new home. There was a very vocal young half-Jewish German named Hans-Hartmut Weil who managed to get into France and join the French foreign legion. There was his sister named Brigitte who joined her father in England a few months later. I saw her once or twice in London during the war.

My appearance still caused some surprise. One day Trudi told me that she had been sitting on one of the front upstairs seat of a bus in the Bahnhofstrasse (the High street of Zurich) when the unknown middle-aged woman sitting on the next seat suddenly exclaimed,

'Oh, look! A Chinaman.'

'Madam, that is no Chinaman, that is an Indian you are looking at.'

'How can you know?'

'I know him, he is a student a the University.'

All the persons I have mentioned in the pension were foreigners. The only Swiss in the house were the landlady , a widow named Schiesser and her daughter. Although German is the official language of the canton of Zurich, the natives all speak a dialect called Zueri-Deutsch. In the same way the other German-speaking cantons have their own dialects. I soon learned to understand Swiss German dialects. The German of the newspapers and formal speech (lectures I attended) they call Schrift-Deutsch (written German). Every Zuricher I met would speak to me in proper German but with a Zurich accent which I could immediately recognise and which I did *not* want to learn.

The only place I could hear German spoken without an accent was the theatre which mostly produced translations of contemporary British dramatists such as George Berrnard Shaw.

I found this situation fascinating. I learnt for the first time that the study of (written) languages is called PHILOLOGY but that speech comes under LINGUISTICS. I heard good German in class because the Zurichers were a minority in the faculty. One of the lecturers in mineralogy was named Parker. I found that he was an Englishman married to a Swiss woman. Pauli whom I have mentioned was Italian by birth; Karrer was born in Moscow. I do not remember the name of any student of Swiss nationality. At the Polytechnic, I saw a number of Dutch students. They seemed to be very rich; some of them drove large cars. When I spoke to a couple of them they said their fathers had made their money in 'the Indies' and that a Swiss diploma in engineering required one year less study than in Leyden and was equally acceptable in Holland.

I also learnt the difference between British (Indian, U.S.) educational qualifications and those on the Continent. Today, in India, one has to pass the 'Higher Secondary' to get into College. One comes out of College with a Bachelor's degree. (In French and Spanish, college or colegio means a boarding school.) Diplomas can be got in certain professional studies from non-university institutions. In those days, one could practice medicine or surgery in India with an L.M.S. (licentiate in medicine and surgery) or an L.C.P.S. (licentiate of the college of physicians and surgeons). An M.B.B.S. (Bachelor of Medicine and Surgery in Latin) which is the minimum qualification of any medical practitioner I have met in India in the last fifty years was considered 'a high qualification' seventy years ago.

In Switzerland I was told by my friends that they got a 'bachot'French (baccalaureat) or 'maturitaet' in German when they left school. Today my French friends in Delhi tell me that they don't consider an Indian B.A. or B.Sc. any better than their bachot.

My friend Thomas Traube ended up with the 'title' of DIPLOM INGENIEUR and worked as an engineer for many years. I have since met Doctor Ingenieurs from Zurich. In South America I learnt that 'graduarse' meant getting a doctorate.

As I have suggested, some of my friends were German Jews. They faced another linguistic problem. I remember one day listening to a conversation between two of them. They were saying that when they entered a shop, the shopkeeper or salesman's attitude changed for the worse as soon as they spoke because they spoke 'schriftdeutsch'. Obviously, the salesman could not know from their appearance that they were foreigners much less that they were Germans. Some Germans had been heard to say that the Fuehrer would soon incorporate Switzerland into the Third Reich which naturally made *all* Germans unpopular. My response was, 'Why on earth do you speak German in shops? I always speak French when I go into a shop.' They had no answer to this one because they could speak French better than I.

Altogether I enjoyed my stay in Zurich enormously. I think one reason was that for the first time I was entirely alone with no one to turn to for advice or guidance. I could only consult H.M.Patel by letter. This developed my spirit of independence which has stood me in good stead all my life and often been commented on – In India these comments are usually adverse. This, I have been told, is because 'In India the son is protected'. I am not quite sure what this expression means. All I know is that I was never the victim of this sort of 'protection' and I am sure my sons are as independent as I. Perhaps it is because none of us ever had a sister.

There was a Whitsun holiday of four days and Thomas Traube suggested that I go with him to Geneva where his mother was living in a cottage in a pension. Board and lodging in the pension would not be expensive and we would travel in the large French car of a rich student who was also going to Geneva. We would share the cost of petrol with him and travel at night when there would be less traffic. This worked out very well. I learnt that Thomas's parents were divorced and his father who had been an Officer in the Prussian Imperial Guard – exceptional for a person of Jewish race even under the Kaiser - was now the Kodak distributor in Johannesburg, South Africa. I loved Geneva and bought some French books.

The summer term was only three months and the Michaelmas term in Cambridge was not due to start till October so I had plenty of time to have a good holiday. I had heard a lot of praise from Thomas Traube of the Upper Engadine valley including a cheap hotel in a place called Sils. I had been walking a good

deal in Zurich because the weather was ideal, there were hardly
any hedges or fences and no one objected to my walking. One
Sunday I had walked to Rapperswill, a distance of twenty miles
carrying a small rucksack with a water bottle and sandwiches. I
put this experience to good use in the Engadine Valley which is
surrounded by snow-covered peaks. Sometimes I would take a
bus to some distant point and walk back or the other way around.
Large scale maps were available and I even climbed mountains
where there were no footpaths. Once I found I could not climb a
rock either up or down but I managed to find my way down the
side of a waterfall which was nearly dry in the summer.

After a fortnight in Sils I shifted by bus to Lugano which I
found somewhat cheaper but it was hot and I did not feel up
to walking very much. I found I could get guided tour buses to
various beautiful parts of these lower Alps. One day I took a trip to
Milan where I visited the Cathedral. I was admiring a magnificent
but horrific statue of St. Bartholomew – he had been flayed alive
and was standing looking like an anatomical picture with his skin
draped over his left arm – when a priest came and ordered me take
off my turban because it was disrespectful. The guide who was
accompanying the tourists argued with him but I had to leave the
cathedral. My next stop was Nice where one of my German Jewish
friends from Zurich was spending the summer with his family. In
Nice I found that the season had been a failure probably because the
political situation had scared the rich British from taking Continental
holidays. Several large hotels of the highest class were half-empty.
My friend's sister who lived permanently in Nice took me to the
Hotel Ruhl and negotiated very advantageous bed and continental
breakfast terms for a vast room with attached bath.

Everything else seemed cheap after Switzerland. At a café
on the Promenade des Anglais – the main road on the sea-front
on which my hotel was situated – I had a seven-course set meal
for twelve francs. I was getting 176 French francs for my pound
Sterling. Of course, the restaurants were offering these cheap
meals in the hope that the clients would pay the full price for
expensive wines. I had to pay for my refusal to drink wine. Some
guided bus-tours that I took were also cheaper than in Lugano.
All this was very well but I was feeling the heat and missing my
mountain walks in the Engadine. Enquiries about the French

Alps indicated that if I went to the Departement of Hautes Alpes I could find villages like Sils.

In the meantime, I had been keeping in touch with European politics in the local newspaper and, when I could read them free, in day-old English newspapers and it soon became clear that the situation was deteriorating rapidly. Hitler had invaded and occupied Czechoslovakia in the Spring after having said at the annexation of the Sudetengebiet that it was his last territorial demand in Europe. Since then, Britain and France had issued guarantees to Poland and Germany had remained heavily armed. I felt that war was imminent and that I should return to England.

My heavy luggage I had handed over to a transport company in Zurich. It contained a lot of books both scientific and literary, my portable typewriter which Pitaji had bought for me while I was still at school, and my winter clothes. It was to travel slowly when I sent my instructions about the destination address in England. In fact, the war interrupted communications and I only got my things after the fall of France and then damaged by water.

I took the train from Nice to Marseilles with my suitcase and attache case, booked in at the Grand Hotel de Geneve and spent the day watching the newsreels in the cinema halls until I could take a seat in the night train to Paris. The trains were crowded and seats were hard to find. Travel to England was somewhat more comfortable and I arrived in London a week before war was to break out.

The morning after my arrival in London I went to India House, the Office of the Indian High Commissioner. If I recollect right, the High Commissioner was a politician, Sir Feroze Khan Noon. I never met him; I only dealt with Mr. S.Lall, the Deputy High Commissioner who was an I.C.S. Officer and an important landowner in the then province of Bihar and Orissa. I found that H.M.Patel had already arrived from Hamburg with his family. He said that there was nothing for him to do in London. I think he also felt that with the risk of impending war, London was an obvious target for the Luftwaffe. In any case, he decided that he was going down to Bournemouth and invited me to join him which I did. This was how I came to be sitting with the Patel family in a café in Bournemouth at 11 A.M. on 3rd September 1939 when the manager turned on the B.B.C. and we heard Neville Chamberlain's declaration of war against Germany

VII

THE WAR – CAMBRIDGE 1939-41

I had thought that the war would start with major air raids between Britain and Germany and fighting on the 'Maginot line'. There was a token R.A.F. raid on, I think, Kiel but it soon became obvious that the Western Allies could do nothing to avert the conquest of Poland by the Wehrmacht.

Everybody, not only in England and France but also in Italy and Japan, had been shocked by the Ribbentrop-Molotov pact. To me it meant nothing because I could see no difference between Hitler's National Socialism and Stalin's Soviet Socialism. That, before long the egoes of the two men would result in a war costing tens of millions of lives which would save the West at great cost to Eastern Europe, I could not imagine.

In practical terms there was not much that I could do. I returned to London, found a bed-sitting room not far from Paddington station and settled down to wait till I could go to Cambridge. There was a notice asking all men to go and register and I did but nothing came of it except that I got a gas mask.

In Cambridge, at Downing College in K staircase, I was allotted a set of rooms – the bedroom was across the corridor from the sitting room – which I had to share with a Christian Tamil of Ceylonese ancestry from Malaya named Robert Chelliah. All this was a complete surprise, not to say a mystery to me. I knew that Ceylon was a British Colony which was not a part of India; I also thought that the Isthmus of Malaya was a British Colony. I had no idea that people in 'South India' spoke four different languages; much less did I know that Tamils had emigrated to Ceylon a thousand or more years ago and settled down in the North and East of the country and continued speaking Tamil. Nor did I know that the majority population of Ceylon was Buddhist and spoke Singhalese. Slowly I learnt that Christian missionaries had had little success with Buddhists but had been able to convert some of the Hindu Tamils – Chelliah was descended from one of these.

It was much later that I learnt of the emigration of Tamils, both from India and from Sri Lanka, to rubber plantations in Malaya and of the complicated political structure of that country. There were three British colonies, the islands of Singapore and Penang and the tiny enclave of Malacca which had been a Portuguese possesion for centuries; the rest of the territory consisted of princely states, on the Indian model but some were federated and some were not. To this day, I do not know what difference it made to the inhabitants whether the state was federated or not. It is possible that whereas I was a British Indian subject of the King-Emperor, Chelliah was a 'British Protected person'. Anyway, we were treated equally by everybody; he went to Church and I did not. He wanted to be a barrister-at-law like my Tayaji. He was a hard-working and diligent student and he ended up as a barrister in Kuala Lumpur where I met him many years later.

One of the first friends I made was a student of biological sciences, John Chandos Bewley Fenton, who was really reading to be a medical practitioner like some other undergraduates I got to know. He ended up as Pathologist at St. Bartholomew's. We kept up correspondence for a few years but we have not been in touch for decades.

There was another Indian student at Downing, C.Raja Raman. He was a year senior to me and I do not know what he was reading at the time. Later, we became friends and he took to the law. His father was Justice Kunhi Raman of the Madras High Court and Raja ended up as Dean of the Law School in Madras. I never had much occasion of going to Madras but I always looked him up when I did. One day about fifteen or twenty years ago, a Tamil visitor told me that my friend had passed away.

There was an older Indian named S.K.Chowdhary who had been to school in the Channel Islands. His accent when he spoke

English was unlike that of any Indian I have ever met. His French was not fluent but he seemed very confident about it. He claimed to have been a 'Vice-Consul in the Levant' and to speak Turkish which I found quite incredible; probably, he had a vacation job as a clerk. Later, he joined the Indian Foreign Service but he was a misfit and left.

One immediate problem was what my course of studies was to be. It had already been decided that I would read Chemistry, Physics and Mineralogy for Part I of the Natural Sciences Tripos. At that time, one could get an honours degree with just Part I of the Natural Sciences Tripos. I could take two years to take the exam and get away with a good degree. Alternatively, I could write the Part I exam after one year, and go on to take Part II in Chemistry specialising in a branch of my choice. If I succeeded there would be a possibility of getting a research job as a Chemist in Industry or in a government laboratory. I was brimming with confidence and took the second, more difficult alternative.

I have often been asked in subsequent years if I regret any of the choices I have made in my life and, with hindsight, would make a different choice. My answer is a firm and clear NO. I am not of a contemplative nature and do not spend time or effort in speculation.

At the time, my interests were different. The 'phoney war' had started; I expected it to 'hot up' at any moment and I was anxious to join. There was a University Recruitment Office but I was told there that Freshmen were not accepted. Part of Downing College had been handed over to the Royal Air Force and young men in uniform were to be seen walking in and out. Apparently, this was a kind of waiting room to give them an idea of wearing uniform and service life till they could be shipped off to Canada for flying training. I walked into an Air Force recruiting office. The officer was delighted to see me especially when I told him that an 'uncle' had served as a pilot in the Great War. I was even more happy with the idea of being a pilot but felt I should point out that I was wearing glasses. That terminated that interview.

The only choice left was to join the Officers Training Corps. I went and was interviewed by a young 'don' in uniform, Major Taylor, who was the Adjutant of the Corps. He had never spoken to a Sikh and decided that I must be a Prince.

'How do I address you? I have never met any one like you.'

'Sir, you call me by my surname Malik like you address everybody else.'

Since I was a student of Physical Sciences, it was decided that I should serve in the Artillery.

I had not foreseen the problems I would face. For some years there had been great keenness in India to study at Cambridge; many well-to-do families had decided that it was a good investment. In England, there was a feeling that poorer students shold not be kept out of Universities by lack of funds. Of course, scholarships had always existed but they were few and far between. Local government bodies had started giving 'council grants' for boys and girls to go up to Cambridge. Unlike 1908 when Pitaji went there, there was now considerable competition to enter Cambridge. It was decided that Indians should be subjected to a quota system. In 1939, thirty-five Indians could get admission; of which Downing could have 2. In fact, the other man did not show up. His place was taken by a Muslim who had failed at Oxford! I do not remember his name but I know he joined the Pakistani Foreign Service and failed there also.

Of the 105 Indian undergraduates who should have been there, several were missing. Those who were present had no interest in participating in the war. In India there was not much enthusiasm for fighting Hitler. Churchill, who was no friend of India or Indians had many years earlier described the Indian Army as the 'greatest scheme of outdoor relief in the world.' In fact, during the Great War the British government had very much appreciated the contribution of the Indian Army to the war effort. The Minister in charge of the India Office, Montague, had been sent to India in 1917 specifically to persuade Indians to join up; for this he offered the famous Montague-Chelmsford reforms as the reward they would get after the war for their services. Landlords were given knighthoods if they could induce their tenants or labourers to join up in sufficiently large numbers.

The attitude of Indians to the Indian Army was complicated. The larger part of the population could not think of joining the armed forces because they 'did not belong to martial races'. Nationalists claimed that this was a concept invented by an alien government to divide the people. This was not true. Fifty-eight years after independence the Indian Army will not enrol any man into an infantry or cavalry unit if he can not claim to have had a relation in that unit at some time. This only applies to 'other ranks'. Officers can be of any religion, language or caste if they are successful in competition. The other services, the Indian Navy and the Indian Air Force are not so fussy.

Lieutenant General Harbaksh Singh, the 'Hero of Khemkaran' (India – Pakistan War in 1965) , told me shortly before he died that when he joined the Indian army before Independence he considered himself a 'mercenary'. I have mentioned that my uncle Surinder Singh Bhagat got all his three sons admitted into the Royal Indian Military College, Dehra Dun. They were among the first Indians to become K.C.I.O.s (King's Commissioned Indian Officers) without the trouble and expense of going to England to take their chance for Sandhurst. K.C.I.O.s were paid almost as well as I.C.S. officers and were admitted to Clubs, etc. like Officers of the Secretary of Sate's services. There was less competition for these jobs because they were considered to be 'dangerous'. Moreover, the chances of promotion over the heads of British Officers were unknown and their work would be less appreciated by the general public which saw the army mainly as an instrument of repression rather than defence.

Against this background, I was, for many months, the only Indian in the Cambridge University O.T.C. When a Bengali joined a little later, he was not a success and resigned.

Even among my British colleagues, I saw a difference. The men and women whom I saw every day in the laboratories were mainly 'council grant boys and girls'. They came from municipal schools or grammar schools. I would say nearly half the undergraduates at Downing also belonged to this social class. The men in the O.T.C. were mostly from public schools. They did not read Natural Sciences. They had been Boy Scouts and had nearly all belonged to the junior O.T.C.; they knew all about drill, army routines and so on. I had no such background. There was a similar organisation in India but not in Ahmedabad. Gujratis are not a 'martial race'. My fellow students at Ahmedabad would have laughed at the idea of being soldiers – they would have preferred to be shopkeepers! In fact some of them joined the armed forces during the World War in administrative or technical capacities because they could not find other equally well-paid jobs.

I was devoting a lot of time to the O.T.C. For political reasons or should I say appearances, its name was changed to S.T.C. (Senior Training Corps). We should not think that because we were undergraduates at Cambridge we were guaranteed Commissions in the Army.

Immediately, the Officers saw that I was willing and enthusiastic but not able to keep up with my colleagues because of my lack of background. I was told to transfer to the Infantry and come back after passing my 'A' certificate examination. In the event I got the 'A' and 'B' certificates in Infantry and the 'B' certificate in Cavalry. I had been reading more French and English novels and history books and had decided that cavalry was aristocratic and artillery was bourgeois. A second cousin who had passed out of Cambridge the year I went up had told me that for him Cambridge had meant sport, 'I know a man I go to history classes with but my real friends are the men who play tennis and cricket.'

Reading Natural Sciences is different from reading History. Apart from not being a sportsman, I spent much more time in laboratories than in classes and in the labs one could talk to one's neighbours and make friends.

The O.T.C. was also an opportunity for socialising and I met many interesting men, whom I became friendly with. Some of them did not survive the war. Others I lost touch with because they joined the Army and I did not. Two whom I met but did not make friends with became famous afterwards. One was later Sir Alistair Pilkington the inventor of float glass which is now used all over the world. His family had been making glass for two hundred years so he was able to make a fortune out of his invention. He acquired fame as a philanthropist and gave a lot of money to Cambridge University.

Another in the same category was Lord Andrew Cavendish who later became Duke of Devonshire as a result of the death in action of his elder brother, the Marquis of Hartington, who had married Ambassador Kennedy's daughter and whose father was at that time Under Secretary of State for India; Of course, I did not know all this at the time; he only mentioned to me that he had visited Canada.

The O.T.C. gave me an unexpected experience when the Germans invaded Belgium and France. When the real war started in Belgium, the British Expeditionary Force found itself facing new and unexpected tactics. The Wehrmacht was not looking for a conventional battle. It was reaching all parts of the country by landing troops from the air in addition to outflanking British troops it encountered and the situation became very fluid. The Allies were unable to cope with this situation. In the meantime, a few German air raids were taking place over England. The danger of German landings in England was envisaged and the question of opposing them came up. There were hardly any fighting troops available to defend the country. Hastily, a Home Guard was organised and its kernel in Cambridge was the O.T.C. Work had been started on building new airfields in various part of East Anglia with the intention of using them as bases for the foreseeable air war against Germany. Two or three were under construction in Cambridgeshire and it was feared that the Germans might try to land their gliders and even some aeroplanes on the cleared ground. We were to be used to protect them.

One fine day I found myself at Oakington - where work had been started on a new airfield - with a company of my colleagues, living in tents, 'standing to' at dawn and dusk and whenever the sirens sounded an 'alert' to shoot down any Germans we might see. Of course, we had not done any musketry practice and had no idea of shooting at moving targets. Our weapons were 303 rifles left over from the Great War. We got good rations but hardly any one knew how to cook. Toilet facilities were improvised. The 'cook' would give everyone enough hot water for shaving which was of no use to me. I could wash with cold water under a hand pump. Even in College, baths had been a problem. There was one bathroom for eight men. At Oakington, there was no possibility of a bath. Finally, a local squire heard of our plight and invited some of us over for baths. This was a wonderful treat. This was the time of Dunkirk. After, I think, three weeks, regular troops became available and we were released. It gave me some idea of what I would have to deal with if and when I succeeded in my ambition of joining the Army.

Actually, I had opted to move out of College after the Michaelmas term. Sharing a bedroom had not appealed to me. I found very good digs at 39, Parkside on the other side of Parker's Piece. Owing to rationing, the arrangement was that I would have all three meals in Hall which was a brisk five minute walk from my digs. I had a sitting room on the second floor with two windows overlooking the Park. Up a narrow flight of stairs, under the sloping roof was my little bedroom in which I was provided with a stoneware basin and an ewer filled with cold water. I don't remember ever using them.

Apart from its location near the College, 39, Parkside had another asset. There was a telephone in the house. This was quite rare in 1939. Even in College, the only telephone available to me had been a Public Call Box (PCB) near the Library. Of course, a telephone was not as useful as it is today when everybody has a mobile and easy access to a landline. Still, if a friend wanted to communicate with me, he could go to a PCB and call me. It was easier and quicker than writing me a letter or coming to see me when I might not be at home.

The biggest advantage of my digs were Mr. & Mrs. Chapman. They were friendly and helpful. After he had heard the 9 P.M. B.B.C. news, Mr. Chapman would bring me a glass of warm milk – milk was not rationed. We would then converse for ten or fifteen minutes about everything from the news to Mr. Chapman's life. He told me that he had served in the Army during the Great War, driving trucks. When he joined, he had been asked whether he had been driving cars or transport vehicles. He had lied, he said because car drivers had to drive senior Officers to the Front whereas truck drivers would only be asked to deliver supplies to rear areas which was obviously safer.

In fact, he had been driving cars. Among the employers he had worked for was an Indian gentleman named Basheshwar Singh. I was stunned by this information because I knew Basheshwar Singh. The name is unusual and I have only known one person of this name and he was a friend of Pitaji's and, even more, of Tayaji's. He was from Patiala and I had known him as Collector of Rewari district in Patiala State.

Later, when I mentioned this matter to Pitaji he said that, at Cambridge, Basheshwar had lived in style, much more so than my Tayaji. He remembered asking his brother how this son of a salaried man – his father had also been a Collector in his time – could spend so much more money. The answer was,

'Our father is a businessman whose income is variable and uncertain; Basheshwar's father gets a thousand rupees on the first of every month, rain or shine. That is why he can live like that.'

This was incomprehensible. Pitaji's future brother-in-law Satinder Singh Bhagat, whom he knew, was an undergraduate at Pembroke College, Oxford. There was no question of his having a car and driver. Of course, *his* father's salary was eleven hundred rupees but he was known to be a terribly honest person.

Mrs. Chapman solved my problem of having an early morning bath every day. The house had a W.C. in the entrance hall near where they lived and a full bathroom opposite my sitting room. At 7 A.M. I would find the bathtub full of hot water. This was in spite of how many other lodgers there might be in the house. I was not expected to clean up the bathtub after my bath. It was many years before I realised that I should have learned to do that.

The details above relate to the Lent term of 1940. Before that, in the Michaelmas term I had made a few friends thanks to living in College. I discovered that several European Jews had got into Downing. Two of them were freshmen like me; one was named Peter Egon Lax. He was of Czechoslovak nationality and had managed to get to England with his parents to whom he introduced me in London. Another with whom I became friendly was, in fact, two years senior to me. He was an Austrian and was reading Engineering. I realised that he was very bright; later on our tutor William Cuttle confirmed this and told me that he was expected to get a First. His name was Heinrich Stefan Marmorek. I mention these two names because I was still corresponding with them till they passed away many decades later.

The Lent term saw cataclysmic events. The Germans invaded Western Europe as I have mentioned and Holland and Belgium were quickly overwhelmed. I was surprised when I found that Marmorek was no longer in our midst. The Government had decided that all German males of military age living within fifty miles of the sea should be interned. Marmorek, having arrived in England two or thee years earlier with an Austrian passport had been classified as a German and arrested at dawn! I relate his story now although it unfolded slowly during the war.

He and several hundred other 'Germans' were put behind barbed wire dressed in POW (Prisoner of War) uniform. This consisted of overalls with round patches of a different colour on the front and back 'so that our hearts would make good targets if needed' as he told me later. After some weeks they were shipped off to Canada where they continued to be POWs but got better food. All this sounds idiotic. Knowing the attitude of Hitler to Jews, why should they not be utilised for the war effort? Why risk British seamen and ships urgently required to bring essential supplies for ferrying these unfortunates across an Atlantic ocean infested with U-boats?

These questions remained unanswered for some time. The only sensible British person Marmorek encountered during his internment was an Officer who happened to be a classics scholar with whom he could discuss Greek literature. I learnt all this when I found him, nearly a year later, looking into a bookshop in King's Parade in civilian clothes. I immediately recognised him, expressed my happiness at seeing him free and well, and asked him where he was staying. He said he had still to tackle that problem. I told him term had just ended and Mrs. Chapman had a vacant room. So he had a roof over his head; he stayed there for about a week during which he told me his story.

He said that his father had been a prosperous merchant in Vienna and had sent him to read Mechanical Sciences at Downing in 1936. He was, of course, like me, receiving adequate funds for his studies and living expenses. Suddenly, in May 1938, his father had to get himself and his family out of the Greater Germany in which he unexpectedly found himself and he stopped receiving money. The College, appreciated this situation, and gave him a stipend to allow him to continue his studies. He had performed well and when he was arrested, the University gave him an *aegrotat*. This is an honours degree without a class given to an undergraduate who, for reasons beyond his control – usually illness – is unable to write a final examination.

The military authorities had released him on condition that he joined the Pioneer Corps which was really a body of unskilled labourers subject to military discipline. This happened shortly afterwards and he went through a course of military training. However, his qualifications and ability were recognised and he became an Officer. After the war, he obtained British citizenship, emigrated to America and made his fortune as an industrialist in Canada, becoming Chairman of his own medium sized company.

During his war service, he faced a problem with the Army authorities. While he was serving in North Africa he got engaged to a girl he had known in Cambridge. To marry her, he had to get permission from the Army. To his surprise, this was refused. When he asked for the reason, he was told, 'Too many Officers are marrying Arab women and our experience is that such marriages are seldom successful. Besides there is the security angle to marrying a foreigner.'

'But she is not an Arab! She is a Polish Jewess just as I am an Austrian Jew. Besides, she is a Nursing Officer in the American Army.'

He finally got the permission and the marriage lasted all his life.

The winter of 1939-40 was not a severe one but for me, and everybody else in the United Kingdom, it was the first winter of blackout. This was very disagreeable and Winston Churchill appreciated this and he decided that the blackout would be made less rigorous. At its peak, we were ony allowed to use electric torches if we put two sheets of tissue paper behind the glass. The winter seemed a very long one.

In these conditions, I was walking across Parker's Piece at five minutes to eight every morning. One day I met a middle-aged gentleman at a party in the Master's Lodge. The Master was Admiral Sir Herbert William Richmond, Professor of Naval History. Why should a freshman get invited to the Master's Lodge? Perhaps because Sir Herbert claimed that he was 'the father of the Royal Indian Marine' 'Does Lady Richmond know?' , had asked a wag.

Anyway this gentleman was a Hungarian. He said to me that I resembled a picture he had seen in a newspaper of an Indian also called Malik. I told him he was probably referring to a relation of mine who had been known in England as a cricketer and a golfer and was now the Indian Trade Commissioner in New York – H.S.Malik, whom I have mentioned earlier. This started the conversation. He said his name was Lengyel and that he was a refugee in England. He had earlier been a judge in Budapest. Well, he was a refugee *de luxe* because he was living in the University

Arms hotel – the most expensive in Cambridge at that time. He told me he could set his watch by me when, at breakfast, he saw me walking past the dining room every morning.

Since I wanted to participate in as many activities of my English colleagues as possible – except pub crawling – I had taken up fencing and was getting lessons at Fenners' from the French 'Professeur Dap'. I had been reading too much Alexandre Dumas and had visions of duelling. In this activity, I got to know a Hungarian, George Winter, who was President of the Downing College Fencing Club. When other members went down, he made me captain of the D.C. Fencing Club! I asked him about Judge Lengyel. He replied,

'Oh yes, he is very famous. One day he was taking evidence from a woman witness. The clerk of the court asked her name, then age, when he came to profession, she replied, 'registered lady of leisure.' Judge Lengyel immediately intervened, 'write down, common whore.'''

In the College I was becoming known for my interest in the O.T.C. Few Downing men had such an interest. They were quite content to pursue their studies, sports and other activities and wait to be called up. There were also men who had a conscientious objection, of the Gandhian type, to war. I learnt that in the Great War conscription had been introduced rather late and then pursued with excessive vigour. A man of the moral, social and intellectual stature of Bertrand Russell (Earl Russell of Kingston Russell) had spent several months in jail. There was some surprise at seeing robust young men not in uniform but it soon came to be understood that they could be in 'reserved occupations' – doing important war work. One Downing undergraduate was a conscientious objector on religious grounds. His name was Baker and he was a Quaker. Of course, he was known as 'Baker the Quaker' and, to this day, I do not know his first name. We were on opposite sides of an ideological chasm.

I mention his name because I have met few Downing men of my generation outside the College in the world in which I have moved. In 1947, holidaying with my parents in Mussoorie, I was walking along the main road – in which cars were not allowed at the time – I saw Baker coming towards me in a rickshaw. His face and figure were distinctive and I immediately shouted 'Baker!'

He stopped the rickshaw and I discovered that he was the head of the Quaker operation in Delhi. I saw him once in Delhi after that. Years later I discovered that he had died rather young working for 'Amnesty International'. I was reminded of that on 27th February 2005 when I saw on a B.B.C. television programme that the founder of this world famous organisation had passed away.

I should mention at this stage that communication with my parents had become a problem at the outbreak of war. In the nineteen-thirties an Empire flying-boat service had been set up between England and Australia. It did not fly at night and the passengers had to be accommodated in hotels. In India, there were stops at Jodhpur and Agra. At Agra, the river Jumna and world-class hotels provided hospitality for the flying boat and its score of passengers and crew but at Jodhpur in the middle of the Thar desert, the Maharaja had to provide an artificial lake and a guest house. This service was more expensive than travel by sea so it was used only by those who were in a hurry or who wanted the thrill of air travel and who could afford it. Most Indians considered air travel dangerous and would only risk it in a grave emergency. It was therefore used mainly for carrying mail, what was known as the 'all-up empire air mail'. This service was relatively cheap. I think the postage was sixpence from England to India for a letter written on air mail paper in an appropriate envelope. I was able to correspond with my parents by this weekly service from Germany, Switzerland and from France during the weeks I had spent there in 1939 just before the outbreak of war.

As soon as war started, this service was terminated. I kept on writing my weekly letters but they travelled, if at all, by sea. Our communication was effectively terminated. I may mention that, on his return from leave in January 1939, Pitaji was posted as Executive Engineer in Mirpur Khas in Sind. Mirpur Khas was a small town in Eastern Sind not far from Haiderabad but east of the Indus. It was much less important than Sukkur and his salary was probably not much more than a thousand rupees instead of the fifteen hundred he had been drawing 'on foreign service' with Ahmedabad Municipality. Mataji always said that this salary was 'blessed' because 'we were able to pay off the debt we had incurred with a friend for the customs duty on the car on arrival in Karachi and send you money too'. It was not till late in 1941 that Pitaji was promoted to Superintending Engineer with a salary of seventeen hundred and the designation of 'Special Road Engineer' (S.R.E.) in Sind to build roads and aerodromes against the possibility of the Germans reaching the frontiers of India as they had managed to get through to Southern Russia! This involved his moving from Mirpur Khas to Karachi. He then decided that his beautiful yellow Studebaker was inappropriate for driving on non-existent roads in the desert and bought a second hand Model A Ford tourer for that purpose.

From Mirpur Khas Pitaji sent a telegram in September 1939 to Thomas Cook asking about my whereabouts. They knew nothing of me after Nice. Anyhow H.M. Patel provided the communication and for some weeks I had to put stamps of half a crown on my letters till a new service by 'aerogramme' was provided. I think I used to buy the forms at the Post Office of about quarto size for three pence, type my letter and post them after which they were micro-photographed and sent in the form of a spool of film containing hundreds of letters and they reached their destination when they were enlarged to about the size of a postcard and could be read, if need be, through a magnifying glass. This service was quick and inexpensive. I think I used to write two letters a week. Communication by sea was very slow – British merchant ships stopped going through the Mediterranean as soon as Italy entered the war – and problematical because of U-boat activity in the Atlantic. I was pleasantly surprised and amused when, one day in 1941 I received a parcel neatly stitched inside a piece of cloth containing two printed georgette silk turbans and a jar of Chivers strawberry jam made at Histon, Cambs. Maternal love is a remarkable thing. I have been told that a Hindu preacher has explained the difference between 'Himsa' and 'Ahimsa' (non-violence as preached by Mahatma Gandhi) by saying that a spanking from a mother is ahimsa but the same by a father is himsa (violence?). Of course, I do not share this view.

It was during my first term that I was charged with an offence under the Emergency Powers Act. I was caught by the police getting onto my bicycle in King's Parade *before* switching on the lights after blackout time. I was tried at the Guildhall and fined forty shillings. This is the only time I have been the accused in a trial.

I got my money back in an unusual way a year later, and with interest. I learnt that the Advisor to Indian Students wanted to see me. I knew that there was such a person, paid for by the Indian taxpayer. but I had never needed to get in touch with him. He was, of course, an Englishman and a retired Indian Government servant and he was looking for someone who could interpret between Punjabi and English.

Before the World War there used to be what the students and the Sikh gentry in England called 'the East End Sikhs'. They were usually illiterate in English and earned their livelihood by hawking collars and ties. With the progress of the war, they had found that jobs as unskilled labourers were more remunerative than hawking. Perhaps a dozen or a score of them were doing this, digging ditches in Cambridgeshire, when a fight had broken out between them. One of them was being tried in court by a bench of Justices of the Peace and my services were required as an interpreter. I was to go to an O.T.C. 'parade'that afternoon so I wore uniform in the Court. The presiding magistrate asked a witness, of course, through me,

'Had you been drinking at the time you are relating?' The man's answer shocked me, as coming from a Sikh, but I translated literally,

' We had been drinking cigarettes.'

'I was not asking about smoking but drinking.' I took it upon myself to answer,

'Your honour, this is a language in which cigarettes are drunk.'

'Thank heavens we have an interpreter like you to explain things to us.' The accused was let off with a warning – because he had engaged a good solicitor whereas the prosecution was handled by a Sub Inspector of police. At this stage, he requested the court to pay me two guineas for my services to which the presiding officer replied,

'No, no, you will never find such a good interpreter again; he deserves three guineas.'

An important war-time activity was fire-watching. Incendiary bombing from the air by whichever side it had been carried out had been disastrous for the victims. After the Battle of Britain there were not many air raids in daylight but night air raids continued culminating in the bombing of the City of London on, I think, the night of 10th May 1941, which did not damage St. Paul's but burnt down Paternoster Row and the adjoining bookshops. There was never a serious air raid over Cambridge but the authorities could not afford to take any chances. Fire watchers were trained and appointed from the civilian population. Of course, I volunteered and was assigned the Cavendish Laboratory. There were always two, sometimes three, of us on any night and we were supposed to be on duty for the same night every week – of course the rule about being in College or in one's digs was waived for that night. My regular companion was Dr. Clement Henry Bamford, a research fellow of Trinity College. The third, occasional, member of the team was Daphne Patricia McKay Ohm of Girton who had attended Chemistry classes with me in my first year.

The training had included fire fighting when we were addressed by fire brigade officers. They explained that fires are easily spread even when the building contains little or no timber in its construction because curtains, wooden furniture, clothing and papers burn easily.

The joke was that Dr.Bamford, who was a chemist, was leading a small team of scientists who were trying to invent new incendiary materials and this was not easy. Clement Bamford soon became a friend and would invite me to his house where I met his wife Daphne, a New Zealander and also a chemist working with Norman Adrian De Bruyne the designer of the Mosquito aircraft. 'Bam' as he was called by his friends explained to me that it is very difficult to set fire to furniture. One day he invented a powder which could be easily ignited and would then burn briskly on its own *but on its lower surface.* He put it on a wooden table and lit it with a match. It burnt brightly on its lower side where it was in contact with the table. When the powder was consumed, the fire went out leaving the tabletop barely charred. It takes skill to set fire to furniture!

A quarter of a century later, I became interested in fires when I was serving in Manila. I found that large fires were frighteningly common and were often accompanied by fatalities. I attributed it to the cheapness of wood in the Philippines where most houses and even some public buildings contain floors and beams of the beautiful Philippine mahogany. I requested the fire department to send some one to the Chancery (Embassy office) to advise us what to do to prevent or, the worst coming to the worst, deal with fires. The Officer came, saw the office and our fire extinguishers. He said that was all very well but if there is what he called a 'conflagration' (a big fire embracing several buildings) the only course is evacuation. Then he said,

'I don't see why you are worried. This seems to be an Indian establishment. In my experience, fires occur in Chinese establishments!' His opinion was confirmed to me a few years later in Thailand by the visiting Managing Director of an Indian insurance company. He said,

'This is not my first visit to Thailand. I come here every two years because it is an important market for us. I have paid for the building of several office blocks because the numerous Chinese businessmen here insure their buildings only with us. British and American insurance companies will not touch Chinese business but we have found it profitable. I know most of these businessmen by their first names.'

After the Lent term, I went to London for a short visit mainly to see 'GONE WITH THE WIND'. I called on H.M.Patel at India House where he had been assigned an office while waiting for the orders which would take him back to India when space could be found on a ship. He invited me to spend the night in his guest room. He had rented a house in one of the northern suburbs.

My guest for the film show – I had had to book it weeks in advance from Cambridge – was Brigitte Weil. She had a German passport but only men had been arrested and shipped off to Canada so she was working as a sales girl in a shop but living in the large house of a wealthy ex-German Jew. I met her at Leicester Square, we had a snack, and went to the cinema. Half-way through the film she announced that the rules for 'enemy aliens' required her to be home at 10 P.M. I also realised that I could not reasonably expect to knock on the door of the Patel residence after that time. To this day I have not seen the rest of this classic film.

I had bought a second-hand bicycle for twenty-five shillings as soon as I arrived in Cambridge. When the long vacation started I decided to make full use of my investment and make a bicycle tour. The bike had a carrier and a basket affixed to the handlebar to hold books. I purchased a pair of pannier bags and set off for Oxford where I knew a man whom I had met in Zurich. He took me to the 'cafeteria' whch was my first experience of self-service catering. He also found me a room in a private house. Otherwise I stayed in good hotels on the trip. There was a look of surprise on everybody's face when I got off my bicycle and asked for a room. I was carrying ties and shirts in my pannier bags and did *not* wear shorts. This turned out just as well because the season was not warm and there were spells of rain for which I had equipped myself by having a raincoat designed for cycling. One day in Buckinghamshire I was sheltering under a tree from the rain when a friendly gentleman came and chatted to me. He had obviously had a public school education but when I told him I was reading chemistry he thought that I was going to be a pharmacist. I did not disabuse him.

The object of my tour was to see Stonehenge for which I stayed at the County hotel in Salisbury. Stonehenge was impressive but incomprehensible. What I did admire was a 'white horse' I saw from a hill when I crossed the Great West Road. In Salisbury, near the Cathedral, I saw a second hand bookstall where I was able to pick up a couple of odd volumes in the 16* of the Memoires de Grammont – a set I was not destined to complete.

On the return journey which altogether lasted a fortnight I spent a night in Hertford where I had a political discussion with some of the residents in the hotel - it was only when the Battle of Britain took place the following month that I realised that what I had been saying in the hotel lounge in Hertford had been completely wrong!

By this time, H.M.Patel and his family had departed for India and I was not to see them again for six years. However, I was keen to go to London to see some plays and films. I found a room and decided to go and see a French film at Studio Two. When I came out I found an air raid in progress and the sky all red from the fires which had been started by the incendiary bombs. It was the beginning of September and I had seen the start of the Battle of Britain. I stayed the full fortnight in London; it was the most exciting fortnight of my life. One bright sunny afternoon I stood on Westminster Bridge and counted 72 Stukas overhead flying in perfect formation. To my great surprise they did not drop any bombs. I was waiting to see them attacked by Hurricanes when an older man pulled me away saying, 'Are you mad; standing on Westminster Bridge with German bombers overhead?' It had not occurred to me that I could be a legitimate target for German bombers. I left London on 15th September which has ever since been commemorated as Battle of Britain Sunday.

Of course long before this the class lists had come out. I had got a II,2 which rather disappointed me as I had been hoping for a II,1. However, discreet enquiries from senior friends elicited the information that I had only got the second class by a hair. Anyway, it was good enough to enable me to proceed to part II where I would be free of Physics (there was too much higher mathematics in it for my liking) and Mineralogy (which I had never been happy with). I could choose any one of six specialties and opted for the 'physics and chemistry of surfaces' which included colloids, the pet subject of Professor Sir Eric Rideal who had acquired a great reputation. This brought me into contact with a new Downing friend, Ronald Arthur Blease who was nearly three years older than me and was working in Rideal's laboratory for his Ph.D. We remained in contact all his life and I saw him a few months before he died early in the twenty-first century.

After the excitement of the Battle of Britain, nothing that happened during the academic year 1940-41 could be as sensational. The work in the laboratories and classes seemed dull compared with the war. However, when the year ended I was told that as a qualified chemist I could not join the Army because chemists were more valuable than army officers. I got a third class in Part II; again my senior friends told me that I would have failed but that I was rather popular. I had to look for a job.

VIII

BIRMINGHAM 1941-42

The University Appointments Board, after several unsuccessful attempts, found me a job as 'physicist' with British Industrial Plastics at Oldbury in Worcestershire. I understand that the whole system of counties and boroughs has changed since those days. Anyway, Oldbury was near Birmingham in what was known as the 'black country' because it was an industrial area and, at some time, must have been full of what William Blake called 'dark Satanic mills'. A chemical factory can not be called a mill but the area was depressing, the houses looked grimy and uninviting and the people on the footpaths were badly dressed.

I was told there must be a residential area of Oldbury but I chose to live in Edgbaston, the most upmarket area of Birmingham. The Midland Red Bus service was quite good and the working hours were not too long. I found that the Chairman and Managing Director of the Company was Kenneth M.Chance generally known as 'K.M.C.'. He must have been a Cambridge man because most of the senior positions were held by Cantabridgeans. The Chief Chemist was a Dr. Blakey; there was another senior chemist, a Scotsman also from Cambridge and the Labour Manager was a soccer blue. The atmosphere was rather secretive. I was told I could not go into the 'works' as the factory was called. I never knew what work the Scotsman was doing. I was told that the factory at Oldbury produced 'Beetle' resins. Moulding tools were made at another factory in Aston several miles away which I never saw. The main entrance was into the Office block where

K.M.C. had an office on the ground floor. The Chief Chemist had an office on the first floor adjoining the laboratory where I was to work. The Scotsman had another laboratory at the other end of the building.

After some time I found out that the Chance family had been glass makers for two centuries – in competition with the Pilkingtons – and they had decided two or three decades earlier that they should go in for this new material, plastics. An American company was making phenol formaldehyde resins under the trade name of 'Bakelite'. The Chance family had bought an Austrian patent for urea formaldehyde which can be made in any shade whereas phenolic plastics tended to be black or dark brown. The new product was given the trade name 'Beetle' but was not nearly as popular as Bakelite.

K.M.C.'s ambition had been to make unbreakable plastic gramophone records for which he saw a great future. Much money had been spent on research but without positive results when suddenly 'the bottom fell out of the shellac market' and the scheme was abandoned. The company was saved by the invention by Alfred Brookes, a lab assistant, of 'melamine' a plastic from which vessels could be made in which food could be boiled – oven-proof but not flame-proof and much less fragile than Chance's 'Hysil' glass. Later on Alfred Brookes' invention was used for making 'Tupperware' which has been a great commercial success.

I was to work under Alfred Brookes whom I found to be a pleasant and sincere person without much sense of humour and with few interests outside his work. He must have attended a grammar school but had never been to college. I respected his common sense and his dedication to his work. He read scientific papers relating to plastics but was not well-read in other aspects of Chemistry. His invention had been brilliant and I attributed that to hard work, perseverance and chance like the synthesis of indigo which gave birth to the great German synthetic dye industry.

The problem I was set was to try and find a paper-based plastic for making aeroplanes. Aeroplanes were made of an alloy based on aluminium which was not being made in the United Kingdom. Before the war it had been imported from France and

Norway. Whereas Bauxite, the ore from which aluminium is made is comparatively cheap and widely found, the main cost is of electricity which is required in vast quantities to produce and refine the metal. This problem had been tackled in Canada which had created huge hydroelectric capacity for this purpose. The problem was that bringing aluminium from Canada was expensive in ships and the lives of seamen.

Plastics for domestic use were being made by mixing beetle resin with paper pulp, heating and moulding. Such plastics are called thermo-setting plastics because the moulding powder undergoes chemical change during heating and moulding and cannot then be reshaped. Other plastics which can be used over and over again like metals were known as thermoplastics which, in 1941, were in their infancy. Stronger, more reliable plastic articles like switchboards could be made by laminating stout paper or cloth sheets with moulding powders. Wood, in physical terms is a 'colloid' consisting of a disperse phase of cellulose fibres in a continuous phase of lignin. In a tree, the fibres are aligned so that the tree grows mainly in length. In wood pulp, this alignment is lost and so is the colloidal nature of the product. When paper is made, the colloidal form is recreated and in the milling process the fibres are realigned but, of course, there is no growth factor.

We tried to make a strong plastic by laminating sheets of paper. Its tensile strength had to be measured by using an Avery testing machine. This proved unsatisfactory because the grips being used to hold the two ends of the sample were damaging it. To my great surprise a superior Swiss machine was imported via Germany and Finland but the material we were making was just not good enough. We found that the strongest paper was of the type known as Manila which contains some Philippine hemp and we tried it, but even that did not meet the specifications laid down by the Aircraft Inspection Directorate (A.I.D.). The project had to be abandoned.

The next problem was that wooden aeroplanes (light aircraft used for initial training) were breaking up in India. They were breaking apart at the joints where they had been glued together – with Beetle glue! Before the advent of plastics, most glue was of animal origin. This meant that the quality was variable. Moreover, it had to be applied hot and took time to dry and set. Urea formaldehyde had produced a glue which was applied to one surface, 'cold hardener' to the other surface and, hey presto!, after a few minutes of clamping, the joint was hard. 'Cold hardener white' was essentially hydrochloric acid. Since hydrochloric acid is inconvenient and dangerous to work with, an unstable chloride salt was used which would hydrolyse on wetting and release the acid. The amount of acid involved was small and would evaporate or be consumed during the process. The problem was that, in a hot, damp climate the remaining salt left over in the joint would hydrolyse and release acid which would eat away the adjoining wood with disastrous, even fatal, results.

The first step was to build a hot/damp chamber for testing joints in the laboratory. The workshop soon produced an appropriate glazed-in box connected to the mains with a receptacle containing a measured amount of water so that the right temperature and humidity could be maintained. This provided and confirmed the information (which we had suspected) in the preceding paragraph. It was obvious that hydrochloric acid would have to be eliminated.

Experiments I had done in Cambridge with thiocyanic acid made me think that it would provide the acidity required in the hardener and break up in a few minutes unlike hydrochloric acid which is a stable and durable compound. When I mentioned this to Blakey and Brookes, they were sceptical and rather frightened of the syllable 'cyanic'. However, the published literature on this relatively little-known chemical convinced them that working with it would not be life-threatening. A few weeks work produced the desired result. The hardener was red not white and it was named accordingly, but jokingly it was called 'cold hardener wine' This led my colleagues in the laboratory to coin a doggerel,

Hail to thee blithe spirit
Burgundy thou never wert.

To test the hardener's effectiveness, it was necessary to cut pieces of wood to a uniform size, then stick them together, let the glue harden and finally test their breaking strength on the Swiss tensometer mentioned earlier. We had to have a machine to cut the wood. A plane table with a circular saw and a planer were soon procured and a skilled workman to maintain and operate it was found in the works. His name was Bill Knowles and Brookes told me to call him 'Bill' and every one in the laboratory called him that. Of course, with this new facility, one or two assistants wanted to use the machine also. Bill got quite worried about these men not trained for machines using it and this caused problems between them. I got on very well with Bill. Everybody remarked on the good relations between me and Bill which nobody else in the laboratory enjoyed.

The work in the laboratory was interesting, challenging and appreciated but I was not happy.

I was boarding with a widowed lady, Mrs. Boyd. Her husband had been a professional working for a major firm which had transferred him from London to Birmingham when their business grew. He had bought this house in Edgbaston, fallen ill shortly thereafter and died. There was another boarder named Samuel Brand, an economist working for, I think, British Steel Tubes. He appeared very well read in his own subject and I learnt something of economics from him. It was a subject of which I, till then, had known nothing. He even told me of a magazine called THE ECONOMIST of which and its founder, Bagehot, he thought very highly. It never occurred to me that a time would come when my son Kiran would be a Director in this magazine group and that it would be the only magazine I would read every week!

Brand was like me a person of a studious and serious nature. We used to be together at dinner time and neither of us went out much in the evenings. Mrs. Boyd would serve us dinner sitting with us while she ate. Our breakfasts were eaten at different times. However, we seldom sat together after dinner and I never regarded either Brand or Mrs. Boyd as a friend. I may mention that Mrs. Boyd was a singer who used her maiden name of Hilary Pay in that capacity. At the time when I knew her she used to sing in Church on Sunday.

I used to have the one course lunch served to every one in the office block. It could not be called satisfying but, with rationing, we realised that nothing more could be expected – and it was free. At about 5 P.M. a cup of tea was served and one could buy a pastry when it was available.

What I found surprising and disagreeable was the lack of social relations between fellow workers. While there was plenty of conversation between us at work on all kinds of subjects, there was very little mention of families and never the possibility of meeting outside the laboratory or office. The lunch was quickly gulped down and the rest of the lunch hour was spent in the billiard room where there were two billiard tables, one of which was for the Chairman and those he chose to play with him. One man would race everybody else from the lunch room to the billiard room, grab a cue and stand menacingly by the other billiard table – it was quite comic to see this man behave like a schoolboy.

In my father's life his closest friends were his professional colleagues – their wives were my mother's friends. At Cambridge I had made friends with the men in the laboratories or those I ate with in Hall. At Hamburg and Zurich two of the men I boarded with had become life-long friends.

I joined the Home Guard but I found that I was in a position to teach the men there who were of a different class, occupation and education to those I was used to. Moreover, the bus connections were inconvenient so I came to an agreement with the Officer that I would be available in case of need and gave it up.

I found a skating rink to get some exercise but again the crowd there was uncongenial. In the Spring I decided to buy a bicycle and to go to work by bike instead of relying on a bus which was becoming overcrowded. On leaving Cambridge I had given away my old bike to the Chapmans' son. By this time, the war with Japan had broken out and the government had decided that the war-effort had to be geared up. We were told we would have to work a forty-eight hour week and salaries went up more than proportionately. I think I found myself earning four hundred and fifty pounds a year. Income tax increases were also decreed but I was told I did not have to pay any tax in my first working year. Suddenly, for the first time in my life, I was saving money. Indeed, owing to clothes rationing I could not buy many more clothes. I never thought of going to a restaurant since the three and a half guineas a week I was paying Mrs. Boyd covered all the meals when I was not at work. If I could get to the centre of Birmingham before the shops closed on Saturday, I could buy books. In Cambridge I had acquired a taste for bindings and old books; in short I had become a bibliophile and old books were available quite cheaply; when a bibliophile died his heirs would sell his books because they had no place to keep them as they had moved to smaller flats owing to the lack of servants. In Birmingham I could only buy new books which were not well bound. I found myself contributing to National Savings.

There was a news item that the India and Burma Office was asking for applicants for the Indian Civil Service and I was now old enough at twenty-one to apply. I was placed fourth after a short interview and only two were appointed. Later, one of these two opted for the Indian Foreign Service and I succeeded him as Ambassador in Madrid but I was promoted to a higher grade there than he had retired in.

In spite of my success in the laboratory I could see no future in my job. I did not consider settling down in England since my family was in India. In any case, the lack of any social life made a future in Birmingham not to be thought of. It was suggested that, when the war ended, British Industrial Plastics might want to set up a factory in India and I could aspire to be the head of the Indian operation but I found life in industry unattractive. I could only think of government service with its generous leave and the prospect of a change of scene every three years or so.

To return to the bicycle, I bought a new Royal Enfield for eight guineas. It looked very impressive but it was a wartime product and a few minutes after I got onto it, the seat slid down which, apart from being uncomfortable, made all the spectators laugh at me. The metal of the screw was inferior and it would not hold. It took over a week to rectify the defect. Since both Blakey and Brookes wore three-piece suits, I did the same. It seemed strange to work in a laboratory wearing a suit and even more so riding a bicycle but custom is king.

With the end of the academic year in Cambridge, two new Cantabridgean chemists turned up at B.I.P. (British Industrial Plastics). One was Corwyn Philip Vale who worked in the same laboratory as I. He was small, thin, quite good-looking and competent. Talking to him I found that he lived not very far away with his parents who appeared to belong to the lower middle class. He had, he said, a retarded brother so he was regarded as the great hope of the family with his Cambridge degree. Seven years later, happening to meet some one from B.I.P. in the street in Brussels, I found he was still working there and had married one of the lab assistants, a red-headed rather ladylike Jewess.

The other new chemist was a woman who worked in some other laboratory in the premises. She had been employed at her father's suggestion because, as she told me, she wanted to get away from her mother at least part of the day. Her father was a prosperous businessman and had been honorary Consul for Austria before that country was annexed by Hitler. The family lived in Edgbaston like me and she also rode a bicycle so we often rode side by side. This was the subject of jokes in the laboratory.

There were one or two opportunities to see my colleagues away from the workplace. One such occurred when we went to attend a discussion in London on a subject related to my work on glue. Scientists fom other companies who were doing similar work read papers. I find it very difficult to keep awake when people hold forth on subjects about which I think I know as much as or more than they do. Later one man who had read such a paper met my friend R.A.Blease who asked him if he had come across me describing my appearance. He said, 'Yes, I saw him at a meeting; he seemed to be sleeping through it.'

'He is really quite bright.'

'Now that you mention it; he did ask quite an intelligent question afterwards.'

More than sixty years later, I still have this problem and have to explain to my acquaintances that I do not suffer from narcolepsy. What I did learn from this trip was that in the business world one can legitimately go to expensive shows and restaurants at the expense of one's employer. This is not possible in government service.

At a meeting in Birmingham followed by a fork lunch, I was able to meet K.M.C.'s wife and son, a Cambridge undergraduate. Mrs. Chance said to me,

'When I saw you I did not know that you worked for us.'

'Yes, I do work for British Industrial Plastics.'

As I said I had a feeling of being socially isolated throughout my stay in Birmingham. The Luftwaffe came to my assistance. I think it was in July that year that some air raids took place on Birmingham. Generally, I used to sleep through these raids. But one night the planes seemed to be very close and Mrs. Boyd called me down to the kitchen in which she had taken shelter. I went down in a bad temper – I do like my sleep – and soon after a plane came down very low and dropped some incendiary bombs. One fell on the hedge of the back garden and I went out to investigate but it did not explode or light up. However, another went through the tiled roof, the ceiling and exploded on my bed which was soon smouldering. I went up with the stirrup pump and a bucket of water, opened the door slightly and tried to spray the bed but the fumes from the burning feathers were too much for me. Fortunately, the fire brigade arrived quite quickly; I explained to them that I could not do much more to help them because I had donated blood earlier that day. It did not take them long to put out the fire before the bomb could burn its way through the floor of my room and set fire to the dining table in the room below.

I was in my pyjamas and dressing gown. The fire was out but it would be some hours before anybody could enter the room. I fell asleep on a sofa in the sitting room. When I woke up, I went upstairs to see the state of my belongings. Two empty suitcases I had stored under the bed were no more. The bed was reduced to an iron frame and parts of a burnt out smelly mattress which I threw out of the window on to the back lawn. There was one wardrobe in which I kept not only my clothes but also my beloved books. Fortunately, neither my clothes nor my books had caught fire but some items had got charred and had to be thrown away. Others were covered in soot. I was able to retrieve enough clothes to get dressed and take the bus to Popes Lane, Oldbury where B.I.P. was located.

At the laboratory, word had got round of the fire-bombing of Edgbaston and everybody realised when I did not arrive on time that the house I lived in must have been involved. When I was seen two hours late walking at my usual fast pace, they came out and applauded. Later I learnt that a Malay Tunku (prince) who had also been an undergraduate at Cambridge had gone to visit his English girl friend in Birmingham. In those days, among the people I knew, a girl friend was not someone one went to bed with. The girl friend's family gave him the guest room and he had been the only person in the house to burn to death when an incendiary bomb fell on the bed. Mrs. Boyd's waking me up had saved my life.

Of course, I had to move out of the house into a guest house for a couple of weeks till Mrs. Boyd's house could be repaired and my bedroom refurnished. The Home Ministry had made elaborate arrangements for rehabilitating victims of air raids. I got clothing coupons to enable me to buy new clothes and money to make good my losses but the correspondence went on for months. Finally, all I can claim to have lost were some books and papers. Mrs. Boyd was even able to find my watch which I had taken off and kept by my pillow. Of course, like my Exakta camera it had to be repaired all of which took time – the Ministry paid for all the repairs.

The bombing had scared me. For weeks afterwards, I felt that the sound of an air raid warning siren was like the sound of a dive bomber. Even a bus or a truck starting up sounded to me like a dive bomber. I became convinced that life was not safe for a civilian in England. As it happened, there were no more serious air raids until the Germans invented the V-1, commonly known as a buzz bomb which started falling over South East England in 1944.

As I have mentioned earlier, I was not happy in Birmingham and had used every opportunity to visit Cambridge. One such visit had taken place on the occasion of my 21st birthday - 29th May 1942. I had held a dinner party in a small room at the Red Lion to which I had invited the Bamfords, Bill Blease and his then girl-friend Margot Bent who was a physical training instructress and three other people whose names I no longer remember. To supplement the rather dismal war-time fare I had served a bottle of Sauternes wine.

I have mentioned earlier that Blease's names were Ronald Arthur but at this time he was known as Bill for no reason that I know. My other friends had either been called up, completed their studies or, in the case of medical students, were at London hospitals. Blease had got a first class in Part II of the Natural Sciences Tripos and was working for a Ph.D. under Professor Rideal.

These visits to Cambridge had enabled me to find out how I could join the Armed Forces in spite of being in the reserved occupation of research chemist. I could acquire a new qualification of electronics specialist and join any of the forces – preferably the

Royal Air Force - as a Radar Officer. I decided to do this after the fire-raid. I had to say good-bye to K.M.C. and Mrs. Boyd. I told Dr. Blakey that I wanted to resign from my job to prepare for the I.C.S. competition and he arranged an appointment with the Chairman and Managing Director. When I saw K.M.C., he said he was sorry to see me go because there were very few men in England who knew as much about aircraft glues as I did. The farewell to Mrs. Boyd was very simple. We had very little in common.

CAMBRIDGE AGAIN 1942-43

My life in Cambridge in the Michaelmas term of 1942 was rather different from what it had been the previous year. I was a graduate and was treated differently by the 'dons' and the staff. Of my friends only Blease and Raja Raman remained. I have mentioned Raja Raman earlier but I had not seen much of him in my undergraduate years; our subjects of study were different. He had not joined the O.T.C. which had taken up much of my time. I think he played tennis while I fenced. I do not remember what he had been reading but he had decided – or his father had decided - that he should read law which he was doing. All this was quite usual at Cambridge. Tayaji had read history before joining the Middle Temple. Pandit Nehru had read Natural Sciences at Trinity before becoming a barrister. So, Raja was following in the right footsteps.

In my undergraduate years, I had spent a lot of time and energy with the S.T.C. This was no longer relevant. I had got two 'B' certificates and there was nothing more to work for. I diligently followed the classes for electronics and spent three afternoons every week in the laboratory. I had bought the relevant books and gone through them. The best written was the Royal Navy's HANDBOOK OF WIRELESS TELEGRAPHY. It was a massive tome and we all knew it had been written by Lord Louis Mountbatten who was making a name for himself as a war hero; it was remarkable that a Naval Officer of the Executive Branch should write a technical handbook. Some of the material I was familiar with from my Physics; the rest related to telegraphy in which I was not interested. In fact, I had never been a 'ham' or tried to build myself a radio set, being quite content to depend on the available material. I was only interested in passing my examination which I did to the satisfaction of all concerned. In fact one of the men who had given me mineralogy supervisions said that if I had taken two years instead of just one over my Part I, I would probably have got a First.

In my second year I had realised that I was not going to succeed with the foil at fencing and I decided to try the sabre. Monsieur Dap the fencing instructor said this was appropriate for a cavalry Officer as it was the traditional cavalry officer's weapon. Of course this made no sense because I was not aspiring to be riding a horse but commanding a tank in which there would be no room for any weapon bigger than a pistol! I think the point was that I am rather ham-handed and not able to execute the delicate movements of the fleurettiste. However my reactions are quite fast so I can respond to the cut and thrust of the sabre.

I have already mentioned that the President of the Downing College Fencing Club was a Hungarian named George Winter who was a wizard with the sabre which is a favourite weapon with Magyars. As we were, by 1942-43, the only fencers left in Downing, he was happy to appoint me the Captain of the Downing College Fencing Club. This was to stand me in good stead in interviews whenever I was asked the question,

'Mr. Malik, what games do you play?' I could truthfully answer,

'Er....I was Captain of Fencing at my College in Cambridge.'

After this, I never fenced and was never asked to prove my prowess as a sabreur.

Kenneth Chance had said that there were few men who knew as much about aircraft glue as I. He may have been right but obviously he had not thought of women. By the time I got back to Cambridge everyone was talking about the MOSQUITO. This remarkable twin-engined two seater was made of wood. One big advantage was that it could be made in furniture workshops without disturbing the aircraft factories which were working all out to make the existing planes. Before the war a company called Harris Lebus had set up factories for the series production of household furniture which they manufactured in large quantities of uniform quality. They now started making planes quickly and efficiently. The second advantage was that it was much lighter so it could carry more fuel or bombs and fly faster. In fact it was, for quite some time, the fastest warplane in use. Everybody knew that it had been designed by de Bruyne who, was the employer of Daphne Bamford, a Chemist from New Zealand and the wife of Dr. Clement Bamford.

When I went to see the Bamfords, I learnt that the Mosquito was held together with ARALDITE, a new glue invented by Daphne. 'The first batch was all mixed with these hands', she told me. Later she invented another glue which could bond wood to metal and enabled the HORNET to be designed. I have no knowledge of the composition or method of use of these glues.

At the outbreak of war, many institutions had been evacuated from London. One of these was the London School of Economics or at least a part of it. There were some activities which they shared with Cambridge University. I found that there had come into existence the 'Universities Liberal Club.' In India I had read John Stuart Mills's ON LIBERTY and found that it expressed my political views perfectly. Up to that time I had not joined any of the political clubs which were active in Cambridge. The Pitt Club was Conservative and, of course, opposed to Indian political aspirations; besides, in my mind, the Conservative party was associated with the sell-out of Munich which I despised and detested. The Labour party was socialist and I had no use for socialist views which I have been opposed to all my life because I consider them to be expressed by the phrase 'What is yours is mine; what is mine is my own.'

I joined the Universities Liberal Club where I met a number of L.S.E. students. One was David Mann who later joined the British Civil Service. I still correspond regularly with him and meet him and his wife Daphne whenever I go to London. At one of the meetings I offered to look after the printing of posters because I was interested in printing as a bibliophile. I became a frequent visitor to Foster and Jagg who had a printing press near the Downing Site.

One of the L.S.E. men offered to find a Polish student to recruit as a member – after all Britain had entered the war on account of Poland. It was thus that I met Barbara Morawska, the daughter of a Polish diplomat. She was a blonde, one month and a day younger than I and one centimetre shorter. We got on very well and she soon became President of the Universities Liberal Club. She told me that her father had been a Polish delegate to the League of Nations in Geneva where he had met the Maharaja of Patiala (Bhupinder Singh) who was in the Indian delegation. The Maharaja had a problem. He had brought some of his wives with him and they were getting bored in Geneva. Mr.Morawski suggested that he send them on a European tour by special train. The suggestion was accepted with alacrity. Later, when they had come back, Mr. Morawski asked his Indian acquaintance how his spouses had enjoyed their trip.

'Very well,' came the answer, 'Of course, they only saw Europe out of the train windows. They observe strict purdah, so they never got out of the train.'

Anyway, Barbara was not surprised at meeting a Sikh although she must have realised that I had very little in common with the gallant Maharaja whose role in the Great War had earned him the right to prefix the title SHRI one hundred and eight times before his name.

The end of our relationship came when we organised a ball with a four-man dance band to raise funds for the Club. The Ball was a great success – over a hundred tickets were sold - and the Club became solvent but I do not know how to dance.

What did I get out of British Liberalism? I managed to get into the National Liberal Club in Whitehall Place. This was very convenient because I could stay at the Club whenever I came to London. I could also entertain much more economically than in a hotel or restaurant and at a very prestigious address. Historically the Liberal Party had been favourable to India and its aspirations. In the nineteenth century, Dadabhoy Naoroji had got elected to the House of Commons on a Liberal ticket. Very prominent Indians had been members of the National Liberal Club and I met men who would not normally have been accessible to a student. Later, as an Air Force Officer, I often stayed at the Club for fairly long periods, thus enjoying the benefits of civilian company instead of putting up at the new service clubs which had sprung up and where the life style was 'animated' not to say rowdy.

At the N.L.C. I met an African who was the Counsellor of the Ethiopian Embassy which had recently been re-opened after the defeat of the Italians in East Africa. His name was Abebe Retta and I was to meet him again as Minister of Education in Addis Ababa in 1950.

The defeat of the Italian Army in Eritrea had brought great prestige to India. The advance on Keren had been along a heavily mined road which had to be cleared. This operation was entrusted to Second Lieutenant Premindra Singh Bhagat – my cousin Prem – who got the Victoria Cross for it. This decoration was created by Queen Victoria at the time of the Crimean War and many Indian soldiers had earned it during the Great War and other conflicts but never an Indian *Officer*, the implication being that Indians of 'warlike races' made first class fighters when led by British Officers but were not really expected to be leaders of men in battle. A Downing man named Sidebotham – one of the few members of the gentry that I met at Downing – had joined the Royal Navy as soon as the war started; he came back shortly after this time, invalided out of the service. He maintained that Prem would only have got the George Cross if that decoration had existed in 1940 because his role of removing mines had been passive rather than active. Prem had had three vehicles blown up under him, had an ear drum blown out and had worked continuously for over twenty-four hours. He was offered a replacement but had refused, saying, ' I have learnt how to defuse these mines and the next chap may get blown up while he is uncovering their secret.'

I was, of course, still at Downing and, once again, I was invited to the Master's Lodge. The Master, Admiral Sir Herbert William Richmond, was Professor of Naval History and was very intrigued by what I had been doing in Birmingham at British Industrial Plastics. He thought I must have been a worker in the factory. I did not attempt to disabuse him. One evening, another guest, a middle aged woman came up to me and said, 'You are not English, are you?' This remark spread round the College very fast. It had many interpretations from, 'She was impressed by your very good teeth' to, 'She was trying to say that since you live in England you should conform to English men's hairstyles.' In fact my front upper teeth are rather too large.

Much of the attitude to Indians has changed in the United Kingdom in the last sixty years. In 2004, I was driving in Northern Ireland and stopped to ask the way from a middle-aged man on the footpath. His instructions were very detailed and I invited him to get into the car and direct me till we got out of the village.

'But I am going for a walk; I have to take exercise.'

'I know, the same applies to me in Delhi where I live. I will drop you at the point you indicate so that you can walk the number of miles you need to.'

'You live in Delhi? I thought you were from here.'

'Well, I do come to England quite often. I am a retired diplomat and have progeny in England'

'I am a retired Police Officer. You should not be offering rides to strangers. It can be quite dangerous.'

THE ROYAL AIR FORCE 1943-46

In October I got my call-up for the Royal Air Force. I had to report to a depot near Cambridge where I received my 'kit' as an airman. I would have to dress as an airman and go to the Officer Cadet course at Cosford (not far from Birmingham) to be trained as an Officer. Most of my companions were eighteen-year-olds straight from school who had served in the Officers' Training Corps or its R.A.F. equivalent and were therefore going to be commissioned without having to serve in the ranks like normal conscripts.

A couple of days later, I was in Cosford. The first problem was my turban. The other cadets were given little strips of white cloth which fitted in their forage caps and distinguished them from 'other ranks' as cadets. I treated my turban as a 'hat' and pinned an R.A.F. brass badge on the front of it. One Officer seeing me in a corridor asked me if I intended to keep my turban and beard. My answer was,

'Yes, Sir.'

After which I heard no more about it.

During my service in the Royal Air Force, I seldom heard a good word about Cosford. The usual comment was, 'A place of long queues'. I was not happy about the drill sessions but I was used to them from my experience with the Cambridge O.T.C. The problem was that having no ear for music I could only keep in step with myself which is guaranteed to drive a drill sergeant up the wall.

1944 London R.A.F. uniform.

The object of Cosford was to teach us to look and behave like Officers. This meant learning various rules, getting used to a multiplicity of forms, customs in Officers' Messes and so on. Here I found myself more or less in my element. There was the mighty volume of 'King's Regulations and Air Council Instructions' for which amendment slips seemed to arrive every day. If any cadet had to be punished, he was allotted the task of pasting in the amendment slips. King's Regulations had originally been copied verbatim from those for the Army substituting the word AIRMAN for SOLDIER but then it was found that that would not work. The soldier is meant to fight whereas the airman has mainly to repair and maintain aircraft. Originally, all aircrew had been Officers but in the World War sergeants became pilots, air-gunners and so on. However, any one below the rank of sergeant could only be assigned ground duties and new King's Regulations had to be drawn up for airmen who were mostly mechanics.

It took me little or no time to learn that the Manual of Administration is AP (Air Publication) 837, that 'raising a form 252' means framing a charge against an airman and other jargon meaningless except to air force personnel. In the England of those days, language was an important indication of class and it was important to make men and women of different social classes and nationalities – there were large numbers of Canadians and Poles in the Service – feel completely at home. There were cases of Officers returning from leave saying, 'My family does not understand English any longer' because they themselves were speaking in jargon instead of the King's English.

When the course was over I was given a sum of money and clothing coupons to get an Officer's uniform. In 1938 H.S.Malik had introduced Pitaji and me to his tailor F.W.Hume in Princes Street, Hanover Square, London and the three suits I possessed had all been made by him. I had already told him that I would need an R.A.F. Officer's uniform and he had it ready for me with all the accessories when I got to London on 2nd December. The only problem was a turban of the appropriate colour to be my 'hat'. For many years I had been wearing turbans of silk chiffon. The usual material for a turban is cotton muslin which has to be starched and ironed every day. With a dhobi coming once a week, this means possessing at least 14 turbans. When we had been thinking of my living abroad, Mataji had found the solution of the silk chiffon turban which does not need to be starched and can be washed in a wash basin and dries quickly if held and waved by two persons. Of course, the resultant shape is different from the fashionable 'Patiala' turban. The latter is still fashionable today but many Sikhs wear turbans of other shapes. A few wear chiffon turbans. In 1943 French chiffon was not available but Liberty (the department store in Regent Street) produced crepe of the appropriate colour. There was the problem that my clothing coupons were for uniform but Mr. Hume was able to sort that out with Liberty. Hume had also procured the badge which goes on the front of an R.A.F. Officer's hat and fixed a safety pin behind it so it could be pinned securely to the turban after it was tied. I don't think any Air Force Officer was wearing such a headgear. Of course, earlier in the war several Sikhs in England had joined the R.A.F. but as soon as Japan entered the war they had been transferred to India where they wore a different kind of badge on their cotton muslin turbans.

I had a week's 'kitting leave'. In fact leave in the R.A.F. was quite generous and I generally spent it in Cambridge or London depending on where I was stationed. In London I could always find room at my Club which was good and economical. In Cambridge, I could not stay with the Chapmans because they were not organised for short lets. Finally I found the Garden House hotel comfortable and well situated.

I had been told to report to Sheringham in Norfolk after my leave. I had not had any training in radar although I was qualified in electronics. At Sheringham I found transport waiting for me. R.A.F. Sheringham was one of the oldest radar stations in the United Kingdom, perhaps in the world. It worked on medium waves – about six metres – and had antennas fixed to towers about thirty or more feet high. Of course, the East Coast of Norfolk is fairly windy and the antennas sometimes needed repairs but I was concerned with the transmitters and receivers. More modern radar has scanners which revolve or oscillate and the direction from which an 'echo' is received can be measured on the monitor. In these C.H.L. (Chain Home Long) stations the antennas were fixed and the direction could only be judged by the relative strength of the signal received by neighbouring antennae pointed in different directions. Since there were no computers like those available today, the signals passed through an elaborate system of electro-magnetic relays before they reached the electronic P.P.I. (Plan Position Indicator) monitors where the distance, direction and altitude of an aircraft could be read out. These monitors were in a dark room and 'manned' by Waafs (Women's Auxiliary Air Force personnel). The conditions were not good and many of these unfortunate girls developed squints so there was a large turnover.

All this was on the 'A' or technical site which had no civilian buildings near it. We all lived on the 'B' or domestic site which was five or more miles away. Since the station operated day and night, there was a shift system and transport was organised accordingly. The 'B' site was near the village of Bodham. The small town and resort of Sheringham was an hour's cycle ride away.

As I remember it, there were seven Officers in the Mess. The Commanding Officer was a middle-aged man who had served in the Great War and volunteered his services although he was well past military age. In peacetime he had worked in the entertainment business and was self-employed as a theatrical agent. He would represent entertainers (actors, jugglers, acrobats etc.), find them jobs, help to develop their talents and skills and get a percentage of their earnings. Of course, he did not have the bearing or style of an Officer but he was a competent administrator and I admired his patriotism. He had given up a lucrative business when he was under no obligation to join the armed Forces and he knew that he would have to take orders from men much younger than he was. He had the rank of Flight Lieutenant. There was one other man who was, like me a technical Officer but he had done a course of Ground Radar. He was still, like me, a Pilot officer. He was a Scotsman with a degree in Pure Science from Edinburgh University and was really responsible for the operation of the station. I cannot remember his surname but his first name was Nicholas. The other four were women. One was middle aged and responsible for the administration and welfare of the numerous Waafs on the station. Then there was an attractive young married woman named Rosemary Anne who was a technical officer. Her husband, a banker in peacetime was an Officer in the Army and, at that time, stationed in India – specifically in Karachi where my parents were. Then there were two teen-aged girls who were part of a scheme thought up by Lord Hankey for replacing male officers in non-combatant jobs by women. They shared watches with the rest of us but what they went on to do later I do not know.

On my very first leave, I brought over my bicycle from Cambridge. It was winter and, if I was on day shift, I was not seeing daylight at all because the working areas of 'A' site had no windows. However, when I was on one of the night shifts, I had free time even after my sleep and could explore the countryside on my bicycle. One of these trips took me to the house of the family with which Pitaji had boarded when he was an apprentice with the London and North Eastern Railway. I met the couple there and the man remembered my father very well. He was a retired estate agent and obviously well off. I was served tea and he apologised because he said the family silver had been buried at the time in 1940 when a German invasion had been feared.

He said he had, as a boy before the Great War, gone to live for a few months with a family in Germany; this had given him an enduring distaste for the Germans. Apparently his German host had found him undisciplined and told him that he would find life very different 'when you will be in the Army'. Of course, at the time, he had had no more intention of joining the Army than of becoming a polar explorer but the Great War brought conscription so the German 'had something there.'

On the whole, the posting at R.A.F. Sheringham was not very interesting. It was an R.A.F. station without aircraft and the war seemed very far away so I was glad when I was transferred to the 'Signals Training School' at South Kensington. This was the occasion for saying at the National Liberal Club and enjoying the delights of theatre-going, meals in good restaurants, and so on. By this time Daphne McKay Ohm was doing research in London in the laboratories of the Dutch division of Shell so I was able to invite her once a week to dinner at the Club or a theatre. There was a severe shortage of sugar and I found one lump quite inadequate with my after-dinner coffee. Daphne could drink her coffee without sugar so she was a very welcome dinner guest. Her father was Headmaster of a Public School in Devon. The family was armigerous (entitled to bear a coat of arms) claiming descent from a Danish Baron Ohm and Lord Reay. Her mother had been brought up in France and Daphne wrote as well in French as in English.

With all these diversions I was not paying too much attention to H2S and G, the two airborne devices I was supposed to be studying at the Natural Science Museum in South Kensington but I was still surprised when I, along with one of my colleagues, was 'recoursed' for a fortnight having failed the test at the end of the twelve week course. Of course a posting in London had its own advantages.

Finally I was told to report to a nineteenth century country house in Norfolk which was the headquarters of '100 Group' in Bomber Command. 100 Group was in Bomber Command but the planes of the squadron to which I was assigned, American Flying Fortresses, did not carry any bombs. Instead they carried RCMs (Radio Counter Measures) which were even more secret than warlike devices. Let me explain. At this time, Spring

1944, the Germans had excellent ground radar but hardly any airborne radar. British bombers at night were clearly visible to the Germans but they did not have good nightfighters to oppose them. However, bombing from heights of over ten thousand feet (the approximate range of anti-aircraft guns) could not be very accurate because of wind. To protect the bombers it was necessary to confuse German ground radar which controlled their Anti Aircraft Artillery. This had been done very effectively in October 1942 by the invention of 'window'. This was a collection of strips of paper painted black on one side and coated with aluminium on the other side. These strips were about an inch and a half wide and two feet long folded double. A batch of these strips suitably released would appear on a radar monitor as an aeroplane.

On the night on which they were first used, the weather was fine and the objective was Hamburg. The working class district of Barmbeck was set on fire. There was no wind, the flames rose high sucking in air from all around. The next four nights were also clear and windless and British bombers made full use of them. German anti-aircraft guns were going round in circles because the radars to which they were linked showed thousands of 'bombers' and the guns were using up all their ammunition and overheating shooting at inoffensive strips of paper. Fire brigades from other German cities were brought hundreds of miles but all the water in the Elbe river could not put out the conflagration. It is estimated that a quarter of a million people died, mostly choked to death in the basements of the houses where they had taken shelter because the oxygen in the air had been used up by the flames.

Two and a half years later I was able to talk to children who had survived the fire and were living fifty miles away in improvised camps. They called their October 1942 experience 'Die Terreur' and looked frightened when they mentioned it. It had, in effect, been more destructive than Hiroshima but because it happened in the middle of the war it has been largely forgotten.

The Germans are not less ingenious than the British and the Americans and, in a few months, their radar was able to distinguish 'window' from bomber aircraft. The answer thought up by the R.A.F. was what looked like a barrel of beer. It was prepared in the Special Effects section housed in a 'sekonic' (non-metallic and therefore not likely to disturb electro-magnetic devices) hut very much like the one in which the radar section nearby was housed. These 'beer barrels' prepared for the day emitted radio waves calculated to disrupt the radio waves on which German radar worked. The operational frequencies of radars are supposed to be reset every day and, correspondingly, R.A.F. Intelligence was supposed to provide the German frequencies for the following night to the Special Effects section. As far as I know only one squadron was using these 'radio counter measures' and it was the one to which I was assigned. These matters were not discussed in the Officers' Mess. The air crew who were risking their lives every night from German anti-aircraft guns did not have much idea of what they were doing it for.

The aircraft they were using were American 'Flying Fortresses'. They had been designed many years earlier for use in daytime in the Pacific. Daytime bombers were supposed to protect themselves with their own fire-power. The Flying Fortress had eleven heavy machine guns and a total crew of eleven including the pilot, the co-pilot, the navigator and the wireless operator. Training, maintaining and replacing so many air crew was impractical. As far as I know they were not used as bombers in the Pacific. They became 'surplus to requirement' and were handed over to the R.A.F. for the purpose which I have indicated. They were cold and very draughty because of the eleven machine gun ports.

The aerodrome to which I had been assigned was R.A.F. Oulton. It was a wartime station and the operational site was brand new, with camouflaged and dispersed buildings. The domestic site was the famous Blickling Castle in which Anne Boleyn had lived. The main rooms of the House had been locked up but we were allowed to use the second floor – earlier the servants' quarters - which had been cleared out for us. I quickly laid claim to a room there, on the grounds that a Nissen hut would be too cold for me, and furnished it with a camp cot.

The Officers' Mess had been set up in new temporary buildings which were quite comfortable. There were a number of Nissen huts in which Officers and men were accommodated in rather horrible conditions.

I was living in Blickling Castle but it was not the life P.G.Wodehouse describes his characters as leading in Blandings Castle. There were no servants except in the Officers Mess and bathing arrangements were a problem. However, the winter was over and the strong walls protected me and, of course several other Officers, from the rain and the wind. Colleagues sleeping in Nissen huts were kept awake when it rained by the noise of the drops on the corrugated iron hut. The WAAF Officers and other ground staff were contemptuous of the 'operations' of Squadron 214 which dropped no bombs but merely flew among or near the bombers to divert the attention of German anti-aircraft radar from its real objective. To the Radar Section all this made no difference because the G and H2S equipment we were servicing was essential for the Navigators to find their way to the target and back.

The Radar section was in the charge of Flying Officer Dear who was a science graduate and had some civilian experience of radios but the man who understood the equipment was the Flight Sergeant (I do not remember his name) who had owned and operated a radio repair workshop in Stoke on Trent in peace-time. Dear had to ensure that equipment was quickly available, that the mechanics were comfortable and that good relations were established and maintained with other sections. He said that his main work was done in the Officers' Mess where Navigators would pester him with questions about the operation and maintenance of the radar equipment in the aircraft. As a supernumerary Officer I was learning Dear's job preparatory to taking it over when he was absent on leave, and later having my own radar section at some other station. These situations soon arose.

The G equipment consisted of two boxes and fixed antenna. One of the boxes (the monitor) had a place for a smaller box which had to be changed for each operation. We would be told three hours before take-off which particular frequency box of half-a-dozen that we kept (for each aircraft) had to be installed on that particular day. Dear duly went on leave leaving me in charge and suddenly we received a new lot of frequency boxes for that night. Unfortunately, the operation was for ten aircraft and I had only received nine boxes! Immediately, I rang up my counterparts in other stations and found one who had received an extra frequency box. The transport section was only able to offer me a motor-cycle and sidecar (I did not have a driving licence) to go and collect the little box. It was raining hard and my mackintosh did not provide enough protection in the open sidecar. When, quite soaked, I got back the frequency box would not fit – it was a different model from the one supplied to Squadron 214. I felt very foolish and the pilot of the plane left unprovided spoke to me in appropriate terms. When Dear came back, I told him the story but his comment was,

'What on earth were you worried about? There was absolutely no need for you to go cavorting about the countryside in the rain. You should have told the Squadron Commander that you had only received nine boxes. Everybody understands that you cannot create equipment out of thin air.'

I felt that I should do everything because the lives of aircrew were involved.

A Canadian Radar Officer of a Mosquito squadron at R.A.F. station West Raynham (about thirty miles from Oulton) had to have an appendectomy which would involve ten days absence so I was detached to West Raynham for those days. When I got there I called on the Station Commander (a Group Captain) and the Squadron Commander (a Wing Commander) and found the latter very friendly. He had the habit of walking around the workshops before lunch and dropping in to various sections. One morning I met him on this walk and he burst in to roars of laughter on seeing me. He explained his hilarity,

'I dropped into your section just now when you were not there. Your sergeant said to me, 'You were quite right, Sir, P.O. Malik does have a turban and beard!' Some days before you arrived I had met him and told him an Indian Officer was coming and that he would have a turban and beard.'

When I spoke to my Sergeant, he explained,

'I thought the squadron Commander was joking because I had seen Indian Officers at Cranwell and none of them had turbans and beards.'

West Raynham was a Bomber Station and I saw and experienced the life of aircrew who risked their lives every night. A tour of operations for a bomber crew involved twenty-five operations after which they were rested. 28% survived the first tour. Only seven crew of the original hundred survived a second tour. I never saw the statistics for Fighter Command but

Churchill's personal physician, Lord Moran, wrote in his book *The Anatomy of Courage*, 'There are no years in the life of a fighter pilot.'

West Raynham was a long-established Royal Air Force Station with proper pre-war buildings. The Officers' Mess was beautiful and I was assigned a room to myself for the few days I was there. This did affect the attitude of the Officers who lived like civilised human beings instead of sleeping in a dormitory in a Nissen hut. One day the Station Commander invited some of us to his house for coffee in his substantial well-furnished house after dinner in the Mess. He seemed to be a rich man – he was a regular peacetime Officer – and I was amazed by the political and social views he expressed. He was clearly anti-Semitic and admired some aspects of Nazi policy. I had never heard such views expressed in England before. I soon found that there were such people in the English upper classes and there are people in India in the twenty-first century who admire Hitler and Stalin both of whom I have always detested. Even in other social classes in England there was a lack of interest in German Concentration Camps if not a categorical disbelief in their existence.

But to return to the joys of a proper R.A.F. station. The air crews were 'briefed' before their departure on an operation about the weather conditions they could meet, about their specific target, (Factory, Ammunition dump, Communication facility or whatever), about the opposition they should expect (Anti Aircraft batteries, Night Fighters in the area) or on the positive side about new radar equipment they might be carrying. They were also served a sumptuous meal which for some could be a final meal. If they were carrying new radar equipment (e.g. the frequency box mentioned above) an Officer or at least a Sergeant from the Radar Section had to be present. This Officer or N.C.O. would then smuggle himself into the Officers' Mess for the sumptuous meal.

At this stage of the war (1944-45) beef, pork, bacon, mutton, butter, eggs and many other items were rationed. I remember a month in which the civilian egg ration was one per month. Even in the Air Force mess we could not expect more than one egg per week. Once I was advised to cycle out along a certain road and to knock on the door of the fourth cottage. I did so and said to the middle-aged woman who opened the door,

'I was told you might have some eggs.'

'You can only have five and they will cost you sixpence each.'

I gave her half-a-crown and went off rejoicing; the official price of an egg was sixpence. The honesty of the common people in England during the World War was exemplary. I gave the eggs to the Mess steward and enjoyed good breakfasts for five days.

At the pre-operational meals I sometimes had three eggs and bacon.

While briefing was an occasional event for a Radar Officer de-briefing necessarily followed every operation to listen to the complaints about any dysfunctional piece of equipment. This would usually take place before dawn and be followed by another sumptuous meal. If I was really lucky I could eat four eggs and bacon in one night!

Our gastronomic ambitions did not go beyond eggs and bacon. R.A.F. messes at operational stations were large with up to a hundred Officers So it was unlikely that the Officers – of whom some would not be well off - would agree to pay for off-ration delicacies like poultry or fish as battalion messes in the Army or destroyer messes in the Royal Navy could. At Sheringham with a mess of seven members and a generous Commanding Officer we had been eating a lot of fish but, of course, there were complaints about that too! The fact was that very little beef, pork or lamb was available and that only out of rations.

My stay at West Raynham soon came to an end and I went back to Oulton where, by now a bomber squadron had arrived in addition to the Flying Fortress squadron carrying Radio Counter Measures. With this the importance of H2S increased. I have explained that the 'G' device consisted of two boxes and fixed antenna. Essentially it received signals from two transmitters in England and, by comparing their strength and direction indicated to the navigator where he was on the map. The accuracy which could be one nautical mile at the base airport diminished with distance so that, over the target it might be ten miles in longitude and three in latitude.

H2S worked on a different principle and was heavier, bulkier and much more elaborate. It consisted of eight boxes and a scanner which rotated inside a plastic 'bubble' beneath the aircraft. The

Navigator saw on his circular monitor a map of the country he was flying over in which he could distinguish water, open land and built-up areas. Another monitor gave him his altitude above the ground. He could vary the scale of the Plan Position Indicator (P.P.I.) from one mile to the inch to a hundred miles to the inch. It was quite independent of ground transmitters. With appropriate printed maps he could find his way to the targeted town and locate buildings, etc. within a tenth of a mile so it was useful to a bomb-aimer also. The radar section acquired a simulator – a kind of box replicating conditions inside the aircraft where the navigator could look at a radar screen and find himself looking at a picture of Berlin on his radar screen. Several navigators came to improve their skills using the simulator.

Canada had been chosen as the country where R.A.F. aircrew could be trained. It enjoyed much more sunshine than the United Kingdom and was beyond the reach of the Luftwaffe. The Royal Canadian Air Force became very closely associated with the R.A.F. At one stage, with the rapid increase in radar the Canadians were asked to train radar mechanics. They set up an assembly line and five thousand Canadian radar mechanics arrived in England. A Canadian Minister visiting England asked,

'How many of our boys are Officers?'

'Sir, none of them have the seniority to be Officers.'

'That is disgraceful; commission 10% of them immediately!'

This was done and soon half the radar Officers in England were Canadians. This caused much heart-burning among British radar N.C.O.s but I must say the Canadian radar Officers were as good as any of us.

At about this time the Allied Governments decided that they were winning the war against Germany and they should prepare for ruling the country after they had conquered it. As usual in such cases, they wanted to avoid making the mistakes after the Great War. At that time, Germany had made separate treaties with the Eastern and Western Powers and the situation had been sorted out to no one's satisfaction at Versailles. The overwhelming fear was that Germany would succeed in hiding its war machine and become a threat to Europe once again. The important decisions were that Germany should surrender unconditionally, that there should be no provisional German government and the country should be divided into four zones – Berlin should be a separate territory also divided into four sectors - where each of the major Allies, U.S.A., U.S.S.R., U.K. and France would exercise sovereignty.

Disarmament of Germany was all important and Officers were to be trained for that. A circular went out asking for volunteers to go to a disarmament school set up in London.

In the meantime, I had been transferred to a new bomber station belonging to 100 Group at Foulsham in Norfolk. This station had been built at a time when the major fear had been of Luftwaffe bombing raids so that all buildings were small, camouflaged and dispersed. We had to walk or cycle along muddy tracks for meals, for work, for recreation, for 'ablutions' and for sleeping. As most of the domestic buildings - toilets, mess halls, dormitories – were Nissen huts, it is hard to imagine more inconvenient or uncomfortable arrangements. There was a village in the middle all of these buildings. One sergeant found the answer. He rented rooms in in the village and installed his wife there, effectively creating peace-time conditions for himself because it was strictly forbidden to have wives on an R.A.F. station.

It was from here that I applied for the disarmament course. One evening in the mess, there was a discussion about Hitler's treatment of Jews and I was surprised to find the station Commander praising Hitler's policies. Unfortunately, I spoke up and learnt a couple of days later that my application had not been forwarded. Fortunately, I had got to know some of the Officers at Group Headquarters so I was selected for the course which was held in Regent's Park, London. Apart from impressing all concerned at the course with my knowledge of German and Germany I found my political views well received. Of course I was in London for about six weeks enjoying the facilities of the National Liberal Club and keeping in touch with my civilian friends.

After the course, in February 1945, I was posted to R.A.F. Ely, a bomber station under 3 Group. Here again, the station was a dispersed wartime one where there was one bathtub in the 'sick bay'! I was allowed to use that once a week. However it turned out to be the best posting I had in the Air Force during the war. I had one day off a week. Ely Railway Station was three miles from my Nissen hut and I covered that on my bicycle in a quarter of an hour and the train took me and my bicycle the eleven miles to Cambridge in another half-hour. Then I could pedal down to the Garden House hotel with my attaché-case and make myself comfortable.

I soon found that Bertrand Russell (Earl Russell of Kingston Russell) was giving a course of lectures on Nationalism and Nationality. With the end of the war in sight the subject was of all-consuming interest for politicians and diplomats of many nations and they would come all the way from London to attend these lectures. I arranged to time my off-day to attend these lectures where I was able to meet undergraduates who were reading history and political science. One of these was a German woman named Vera Heller who had arrived in England as a child with her parents who had left Germany with all their belongings as soon as Hitler appeared on the scene. They were among the lucky German Jews in England. Of course, having arrived in England so young she spoke English as well as any Englishwoman and no one would believe that she was an 'enemy alien'.

The spring of 1945 was bright and sunny. With the effective destruction of Germany's Bomber Command, the black-out was somewhat relaxed and everybody was more cheerful. My mechanics were also brighter and happier. I had mastered the problems of procuring spare parts and equipment in the right quantities at the right time so the radar section became more efficient.

One of the great things about the armed forces is that men and women in uniform treat complete strangers similarly dressed as friends. On my first evening in the mess I had been upset when an attractive young woman had approached me and said that that she hoped I would improve the 'ropey' radar section. She was a catering officer and I was sure she knew nothing about radar. Anyway her remark made me pay even more attention to my duties. One day I was appointed Orderly Officer which meant being on duty for twenty-four hours and carrying out inspections for which I had written instructions. In addition, I had to be available night and day. As I detested the Nissen hut which I had to share with others, I decided to take my typewriter and sleep in the heated workshop on a worktable under a blanket. In the morning, when I handed over charge, I was able to give a neatly typed report containing references to various rules and the A.P. 837 which had been infringed. The Station Commander had it framed and hung on his office wall. He would show it to visitors, saying,

'This was written by a colonial.'

At about this time, the Royal Air Force bombed Dresden concentrating on the railway station; the beautiful historic buildings in the centre of the city were reduced to rubble and ashes. It was the first time that this city had been bombed from England because it is so far from East Anglia where most of Bomber Command was stationed. The weather was fine, much of the ground overflown was in friendly hands (liberated areas of France) and casualties were relatively few on the British side. On the German side, they ran into thousands. Trainloads of demoralised German troops and civilian refugees were reaching Dresden railway station from areas further east where the Soviet Army was advancing. On the sixtieth anniversary of this massacre the British Government formally apologised for it.

However, at that time, I was complimented because the navigators of my squadron had achieved the longest and most accurate 'fixes' on their H2S equipment. In fact, the following day as I was walking to my section, a well-dressed civilian accosted me. He said he was a journalist who had come to do an article and the Station Commander had told him about me and advised him to speak to me. He said his item would be published all over the Empire within hours. What message did I have for my parents in Karachi? I told him my greatest joy was being so close to Cambridge which I regarded as my home in England. He said he could not publish that because my posting was 'classified information'. However, his article was very favourable to me; my parents and all their friends in Karachi read it and were overjoyed.

It was obvious that the War was coming to an end. Some of my colleagues were looking forward to being 'released' and going back to their families and the joys of civilian life. Many older men realised that the life they had known in 1939 could not come back; this was particularly the case of those who had enjoyed private means and had no qualification for earning a living. One such case was related to me five years later by a British diplomat in Addis Ababa. Alan Rowley's family had lived in Asia. He was about my age and had enlisted in the Army immediately after leaving college. He was delighted when his unit was posted to India and he was transferred to an Indian regiment. He had served in the Burma campaign as a result of which he had a very slight limp. Before the War ended he had applied for the British Foreign Service and was promptly selected after the end of the War. Apart from everything else, he had inherited tea estates in Ceylon as it was then called. In 1948, he happened to be in his home town in England when he was horrified to see one of his slightly older fellow officers, from the Indian regiment in which he had served, digging a ditch.

'George, what on earth are you doing?'

'Well, Alan, as you know I was a regular pre-war Indian Army Officer and expected to serve for at least twenty-two years. However, as a result of India's independence I was told six months ago that my services were no longer required and I was retired at the age of thirty-five and very generously given the full pension of a Major which is six hundred pounds a year although I would not have become entitled to it for another ten years. My problem is that I have two sons at boarding schools whose combined fees exceed my pension. I have no marketable skills but enjoy good health so I am earning five guineas a week as a navvy.'

In India people were complaining at having to pay 'millions of pounds every year, for all time to come, to British Officers who had only oppressed the Indian peasant during the Great Bengal Famine which had cost three million lives.' But, of course, I could sympathise with men like George whom I did not know but who was indistinguishable from my English friends and colleagues.

In 1944, it had been announced that the India and Burma Office had retained a number of vacancies in the Indian Civil Service (I.C.S.), the Indian Political Service (I.P.S.), the Indian Police (I.P.) and the Burma Civil Service Class I for British, British Indian and British Burmese male subjects who were serving with the Armed Forces and that interested persons could obtain the form IB2 and apply. I had immediately obtained the form, filled it up, attached the relevant documents and delivered it personally to a woman Officer at the India and Burma Office.

By March 1945 it was obvious that the War was coming to an end so I was not surprised when I received orders that I was to proceed to an R.A.F. station in Surrey for disarmament duties. What was even better, I was to be promoted to Acting Flight Lieutenant. In accordance with normal practice I had been commissioned as a probationary Pilot Officer but nothing in my uniform indicated that I was on probation and I do not think that I was ever informed that my probation had ended. A year after commissioning I was promoted to Flying Officer. One of the standing jokes was, 'Why is he a Flying Officer? He can't be bright.' The implication was that the R.A.F. was growing so fast that one should not serve in the same rank for as long as a year. Having got the station tailor to sew on the second stripe on my uniform, I rushed off to bid good-bye to the Station Commander who had been so good to me. He smiled and said he would have stopped my transfer but when he learnt that I was being promoted he had let it go through; he would miss me on the station. I don't recall any other Station Commander saying he was glad to have me there! Station Commanders were not fond of Officers doing ground duties.

The R.A.F.station in Surrey was Kenley, a pre-war station which had acquired fame as a Fighter Command Station during the Battle of Britain. Now that the threat to southern England was over, it no longer had aircraft but we were accommodated in proper pre-war buildings so I felt very comfortable. We were taught driving and self-defence - because it was feared that the Germans might try to kill off the occupying forces. I saw no point in this because I knew the German character. They do not make good guerrillas. They are very good soldiers but in the disciplined way. Once they are defeated they accept the situation and try to make the best of it. We were taught a good deal about the German Air Force – its organisation and the way it all works. We were also taught a good deal about German civil administration which we expected to find working and on which we would have to depend.

There was to be a new policy known as NON-FRATERNISATION. This meant that we were not to socialise with Germans. They must be made to understand that their behaviour through the war had been inhuman and they had become social pariahs. Only one exception was made. We could behave normally with children. My own knowledge of Germany was recognised and I gave a couple of lectures on German history. There were two or three interpreters recruited from central European refugees who had joined the R.A.F. in England. Their knowledge of both English and German was empirical – more or less what one might expect from a taxi driver.

We thought that our main duty would be to interrogate and cross-examine local officials about hoards of weapons concealed by soldiers and airmen. This was based on experience after the Great War when soldiers had taken off their uniforms, resumed their civilian work and concealed weapons – 'I am sorry but the key to this basement has been lost. No one has been there for years.' In actual practice, things were very different. Most soldiers had no clothes other than what they were wearing when they surrendered. They were forbidden to wear uniform after they were let out of the prison camps hastily built for them after surrender.

I remember some weeks later meeting a tall, handsome young man in a village. He knew no English at all and approached me when he learnt that there was a weird looking nigger – yes, I was once asked , 'Sind Sie Neger?' - in R.A.F. Officer's uniform who spoke fluent German. He was wearing what looked like R.A.F. battle dress but without any insignia of any kind – Luftwaffe blue was very much like R.A.F. blue. I asked him why he was not wearing his civilian clothes. He replied,

'Captain, I was sixteen years old when I was conscripted. I have grown ten centimetres since then and this uniform is the only garment I have which fits me.'

'Why have you come to see me? Do you have any information about concealed arms?'

'No, Captain. I am a qualified and experienced pilot. I would like to join the Royal Air Force; I will be happy to fight against Japan.'

The boy was unemployed and had to share his parents' rations. He very desperately needed a job even more than the Englishman, George, mentioned earlier. To us the idea of recruiting a German sounded insane.

Life at an airport in Surrey meant proximity to London which was less than an hour away by train and the railway station was easily accessible. On one of these journeys – always by first class – I met a man who belonged to a class I did not know. He had been a tea planter in Assam. Of course I knew that tea was grown in Assam but I was not aware that it was grown by Englishmen who became very rich in the process and were living like the great landowners of Bengal who enjoyed the title of Maharaja although they had no ruling powers and were not entitled to gun salutes. Yes, the major Indian princes were graded by guns from the 17 guns of Hyderabad and Kashmir to the 11 of medium states. Those with less than 11 guns were called 'non salute princes' but they all mentioned their guns to maintain their own table of precedence. This man whose name I have forgotten invited me to dinner at his house where I found that the women in the family had been to Roedean. I knew this was the feminine equivalent of Eton because Daphne McKay Ohm had been to Wellington and I knew that Roedean was considered higher in the pecking order.

It was on one of these trips to London where I always stayed at the N.L.C. (National Liberal Club) that I learnt that Germany had surrendered, walked out to the Mall and saw the whole of the Royal Family on the balcony of Buckingham Palace. A week later I was in Germany at the wheel of a fifteen hundred weight light truck.

If an Air Force Officer's uniform had given me a new social status in wartime England, it meant much more in the British Zone in Germany. I also enjoyed a special status in my unit by virtue of my ability to speak German. Our little unit was called a 'Squadron' although, of course, we had no planes. We spent about a week staying in tented accommodation or camping in school classrooms. We were about a dozen Officers. There were not many more airmen to look after our vehicles, maintain communications, cook and so on. What I missed most was the absence of a batman.

After that initial discomfort, we were accommodated at a pre-war German Air Force station. This was rather different from West Raynham. The Mess Hall had huge plate glass windows with a view of the wood in which the blocks of Officers quarters were located. The Hall could accommodate nearly a hundred Officers at a sitting. Adjoining it in the same building was the Anteroom which had a magnificent fireplace in one corner. This building and the residential blocks must have been centrally heated and there were radiators at all the appropriate places. However, the supply of coal had broken down at some stage and when the winter came there was no central heating. For the time being, in the late spring and early summer I was quite comfortable. Service in the Mess was by an adequate team of efficient German girls. We soon learnt that they were the wives, widows and daughters of Luftwaffe Officers who willingly accepted these posts because they had much better rations than they could hope to eat in civilian life. Because of non-fraternisation, they were not socially accessible to any of us, officers or men. Violation of the rule meant a court martial.

In the residential blocks there were more German maids to keep the premises clean, make beds and so on. These did not seem to be of the same social class as the waitresses but they were good at their work. I understand that their wages came out of 'occupation costs' which meant that they were paid by the German tax-payer. Occasionally, an R.A.F. batman would come in to polish buttons but mostly I had to do that myself. The maids did the polishing of shoes and there were good laundry arrangements.

The station was called R.A.F.Fassberg. Apparently a village of that name had been eliminated when the station was originally built. Since then, a new village – the name of which I do not remember – had grown up outside the guardroom of the station. The German civilian employees lived there and the village had shops, a post office and the other usual amenities. These were not for us. A British post office had been set up in the R.A.F. station to cater to our needs. If I wanted to have my shoes repaired, I would go to the village but would find that the cobbler lacked the materials for his trade e.g. waxed thread. Altogether the German economy appeared to be in bad shape. There were hardly any goods in the shops; there were no tractors in the fields and very few horses for ploughing. As the able-bodied men were generally not there, women could be seen working with hoes.

Fassberg was thirty kilometres north of Zelle, the nearest big town and I could sometimes find an excuse for going there. In fact the whole unit had had to pass through there before coming to Fassberg. Outside Zelle was a small Concentration Camp called BELSEN. This was the first Concentration Camp that the British

Army had come across and British journalists saw a concentration camp for the first time. It received adequate publicity in the British press; in fact, it was only after that that most of the British public began to believe that Hitler had confined hundreds of thousands of men and women in these notorious establishments. Details of the treatment meted out to the inmates began to be published. Inmates in their characteristic striped uniforms could be seen wandering about the streets since they were now 'free'. However, they had to return to the camps to eat and sleep because there was no other place for them till something could be worked out. Most of their torturers had got rid of their uniforms and mingled with the local population which seemed to accept them without asking questions. Occasionally a group of prisoners would recognise a torturer and beat him up but this was unusual.

Zelle, of course, was the capital of an ancient Duchy which acquired a connection with the United Kingdom. In the beginning of the eighteenth century it became clear that the Duchy would pass to the daughter of the incumbent. Her name was Sophia Dorothea and she was engaged to Ulrich Anthony of Wolfenbuettel who, by marriage, would become Duke of Zelle. This fact came to the notice of the Electress of Hanover who was heiress presumptive to the United Kingdom. She rushed to Zelle and asked the Dowager Duchess for the hand of her daughter for her own son George. We all know that the marriage was not a happy one and when she expected to become Queen of England, Sophia Dorothea was a prisoner in a small chateau. However, her son became King George II and, to this day, the carriages of the Queen of England are drawn by Zelle Greys.

Educated Germans knew all this history. Some of them thought that the two wars they had gone through in the twentieth century had not done them any good. Much of the British-occupied zone had formed part of the Kingdom of Hanover at the beginning of the nineteenth century when the King of Hanover had also been King of England, Scotland and Ireland – a situation terminated by operation of the Salic law when Queen Victoria acceded to the British throne and her uncle became King of Hanover.

The family name of the house of Hanover was Guelph (Welf in German) so a party calling itself WELFEN came into existence with the intention of linking the old Kingdom of Hanover to the

United Kingdom but there were no takers for this scheme in the United Kingdom.

R.A.F.Fassberg was commanded by Group Captain the Honourable Loel Guinness, M.P. I don't recall any R.A.F. aircraft being stationed there but there were half-a-dozen brand new German planes with their exhaust pipes and other exposed metal parts wrapped up in wax paper. The Luftwaffe had run out of aviation fuel. However the airfield had all the amenities and could not be allowed to lie idle. Very soon three Free French squadrons arrived. Their aircraft were outmoded British ones but they wore French uniforms. The Commanding Officers wore insignia equivalent to the rank of Squadron Leader but they appeared rather arrogant to me; I got the impression that they felt they should be treated like Wing Commanders as Commanding officers of British squadrons were usually of that higher rank. All their Officers ate with us. This did create a problem. The British felt that German water was unsafe to drink and were served tea at all meals. The result was that the evening meal was usually over by 7 P.M. after which they would drink rather more than they were used to – liquor was cheaper than in the United Kingdom. After dinner entertainment was lacking. A film show was an occasional treat. There was no question of gong to a pub in the nearest village or town.

The French were obliged to eat the same food as the rest of us but they could generally get wine of the kind they were used to and they would not eat before 8 P.M. and would linger on at table for quite a while. Most of the French Officers had spent some years in England and spoke quite good English but there was no conviviality between the British and French Officers. I made friends with a couple of French Officers but they made it quite plain that they did not like the British any more than the British liked them.

My unit was a 'lodger' on the station. We were given accommodation for the officers and men but my Squadron Leader reported to an Officer in Zelle. He was given an Office on the ground floor of what had been the Control Tower of the airfield. It was a circular room with huge curved glass windows; we dreaded the coming of the colder weather but it had a tiled stove called in German *Kachelofen* the like of which I have not seen in the United Kingdom. It was about four feet high, as deep from back to front and a little narrower. A chimney came out of the back and left the room at the top of the back wall. In front there was a metal door about 8′ high and 6′ wide through which it was fed. The burning space ran the length of the stove which was beautifully tiled on the outside. It consumed brickets made of coal dust held together by a little mortar. It took effort to light the bricket – a little petrol helped – but once this was done a couple of pounds of brickets would keep the large room warm for the entire working day.

What was the work of disarmament? We would receive intelligence reports of the place where weapons or warlike material was supposed to exist. Teams of an Officer and an interpreter would go out and locate the indicated spot with the help of 1:25,000 *Generalstabkarten* (like British Ordnance Survey maps) which we possessed of the whole *Regierungsgebiet* (smaller than an English county) assigned to our Squadron. I used to be accompanied by another Officer or N.C.O. because I did not want an interpreter. I ended up by interviewing a score of village mayors but we never found anything significant. The Army, as it had gone through the area, had effectively taken away all weapons.

One day everybody became quite excited when the Intelligence report was about 'aircraft factory'. We had visions of a well concealed aircraft factory in the middle of the Lower Saxon Countryside which was not at all an industrial area. The map reference was very specific and as we got nearer I was expecting to see at least a railway line. However, what we found was a village of about a thousand inhabitants only slightly bigger than other villages I had been to. I went immediately to the mayor who denied all knowledge of any factory. After cross-examining him I took him to the map reference where we found the village blacksmith's workshop. It was bigger than others I had seen and the owner was there to answer my questions. He said that he had had a contract with the German Navy to make torpedo nose covers. He showed us a sample. It looked like an unusually broad aluminium bucket. It was designed to be placed on the front end of a torpedo when it was stored in a submarine. Apparently German torpedoes had detonators at the front end designed to make them explode on impact. The cover was to eliminate the possibility of an accidental explosion during transportation or storage.

Of course, the Intelligence reports could be right. The day came when we were told that there was a German Ground Radar scanner of an original design which the Royal Aircraft Establishment at Farnborough wanted to study. As mentioned earlier, the German ground radar was very good and this suggested that they had achieved something more advanced than the boffins of the R.A.F. had invented. We were given the map reference, told to locate the radar, dismount the scanner, load it onto a flat-bed truck and deliver it to a workshop in Hamburg.

I was given a mechanic, and a Coles crane and driver to lift the scanner after it had been dismounted. On going to the map reference I saw the abandoned radar site. It was situated on the south bank of the Elbe some twenty miles upstream from the Hamburg-Harburg bridge. There had been a barracks for the Officers and men maintaining and operating the station. These were now occupied by refugees mainly from Hamburg from where they had been evacuated after the 1942 bombing described earlier.

The operation of dismounting and loading the scanner took a couple of days and we had to spend the night at another R.A.F. post in the vicinity. Non-fraternisation did not extend to children and a charming pre-teen brother and sister turned up from the barracks. The Corporal driving the crane was an Irishman named Murphy who knew no German but had a way with the children and they immediately took to him. It was they who told me of what they called 'Die Terreur'. There was no school in the barracks and, although they were obviously well-brought up middle-class children, they were very badly informed. They asked me if it was true that England was an island. I explained that Great Britain which included Scotland and Wales in addition to England was an island.

'Like those in the Elbe that we can see from here? How on earth do people go to work every day?'

'You cannot compare it to those islands which are not even a hundred metres long. Great Britain is several hundred *kilometres* long and people in London can live and work for months without seeing the sea just as they do in Hamburg.'

I failed to make them understand what was beyond their experience.

Apart from work, there were pleasures to be had at Fassberg. We were told that we could avail of the facilities of a country club. This was some thirty kilometres away in a forest. We could eat in the country club, and ride some excellent Trackaener and halb-Trackaener horses. I enjoyed this very much and, on my next leave in England got Mr. Hume to make me a beautiful riding kit. Thrussell in Bond Street made me very elegant and comfortable riding boots which I still have. This was my introduction to made-to-measure footwear which I have worn ever since. Fortunately, in Delhi, Chinese shoemakers do it very well for a fraction of what it would cost in England.

I have mentioned that I had made friends with some of the French pilots at Fassberg. They managed to arrange air transport for holidays in Paris. I wangled a free week's trip to Paris where I had last been seven years earlier. I availed of the facilities of the Club Interallie which had been installed in a multi-millionaire's townhouse in the Faubourg St. Honore quite close to the British Embassy. I soon discovered that I did not need to buy a ticket for travelling on the metro. On making enquiries, I was told that during the occupation Germans in uniform had refused to buy tickets and insisted on travelling free. After that, the metro had allowed Allied forces to travel free. I wanted to go to Chatellerault to see my friend Jean Lussat with whom I had kept up correspondence. I found there was an R.A.F. office in Paris where I could buy cheap first class tickets for rail travel.

Chatellerault is a town dating back to the sixteenth century and, when I got there Mr. Lussat (Jean's father) told me that an Englishman was Duke of Chatellerault. Later, I researched the situation and learnt that the Duke of Hamilton had escorted Mary Queen of Scots when she travelled to France to marry Francois II. The new town was made a Duchy in honour of the Scottish nobleman who went back to Scotland with his Queen when she became a widow. Many years later I met the present Duke who was serving in the Royal Air Force in Singapore. In 1995, I drove to Chatellerault, had lunch with Jean Lussat and his wife Colette and told him that the Duke of Chatellerault is not an Englishman but a Scotsman.

In 1945, the Lussat family – the parents of my friend Jean – were living in their sawmill. Jean had given me two addresses, one in Chatellerault and the other a flat in the rue Ledru-Rollin in Paris. During the war, correspondence had been difficult but I had resumed it from Fassberg. Mr.Lussat explained to me that he had left Paris when it was occupied by the Germans and shifted to Chatellerault. He had got a flat for himself and his wife on top of the office block of the factory. Jean and his wife had a small flat near the railway station. Mme. Lussat, who appeared less pleased to see me than the rest of the family, arranged a sofa-bed for me in what was the personal office of M.Lussat in the daytime and the family living room in the evenings. M. Lussat explained that they thought I would be better off than in the hotel. It certainly saved me money.

The factory, as I have mentioned, was a sawmill; in fact it sawed only walnut logs which is a luxury wood. M. Lussat said that his men would drive round the countryside loking for odd walnut trees. When they saw one which looked uneconomical as a source of walnuts, they would bargain with the farmer for it.

I had been reading in the English press and it had been confirmed by my French friends in Fassberg that food was short in France and that rations were much smaller than in England. I had therefore obtained some tins of corned beef and spam (mixed pork shoulder and ham) and packed them in my luggage. I now proudly offered them to my hosts only to be greeted by peals of laughter. The French bourgeoisie was not hindered from eating what it liked by rationing. There was not that contempt for the black market which characterised the English gentry. However, I felt that Mme. Lussat appreciated my intention. She had a maid but also worked in the kitchen herself. One of the dishes I ate during my stay was a plate of assorted wild mushrooms (*cepes*) which were delicious and the like of which I have not eaten anywhere before or since.

In addition to this trip, the Air Force arranged winter holidays for us in batches. I got one to Bad Harzberg in the Harz Mountains. I had heard of the Harz Mountains as a source of ghost stories. There were three of us, a Medical Officer of my father's generation, and another Officer of about my own age. I do not remember the names of either of them. We were accomodated in a two star hotel. Bad Harzberg had never been bombed and there had been no fighting in the vicinity. The streets, shops, hotels and restaurants were brightly lit at night and the whole atmosphere was that of a pre-war ski resort. Of course, we had no skis, were not inclined to buy any and I discouraged my companions from hiring any after my Chamonix experience mentioned earlier. We had a good time walking about the streets, sitting in the cafes and watching the few Germans who had found a way to get there. They must have been well-to-do people of independent means or black marketeers who could afford to take a holiday in those days. I do not remember what we ate; probably the R.A.F. had made arrangements to supply rations to the hotel in which we stayed.

The condition of Germans we saw in the streets was not enviable. The shops, restaurants and bars had very little to offer and one seldom saw a well-dressed German. One afternoon in a village I saw a well-dressed, middle-aged squire or well-to-do farmer taking his daughter for a walk. The sight was so unusual that it has remained in my memory for six decades. It seemed to us that one of the most-felt shortages was of cigarettes. I remembered the cigarette factory I had seen in Baden-Baden in 1938; it had used Turkish tobacco. Later in Hamburg I realised that cigarettes were scarce and I was told that the very popular American Virginia tobacco was practically unobtainable. During the war in England cigarettes seemed not to be in short supply. In the Air Force we could get, I think, 200 duty-free cigarettes a week. All this did not concern me because I did not smoke. However, in Germany, I noticed that my colleagues happily threw away their stubs on the footpath and immediately a German would pick it up. It surprised me to see well-dressed Germans (probably of the professional class) doing so. One result I noticed was that some of my colleagues threw their stubs cheerfully into puddles to watch Germans pick them up and dry them. In fact, some of us bought the rationed duty-free cigarettes to which we were all entitled to use them as currency. Of course, the point was that there was hardly anything one could buy with German currency.

An opportunity for me to profit by this situation arose in the Spring of 1946. My friend Clement Bamford had left Cambridge and got himself a job with Courtaulds a firm making 'Celanese' artificial silk. He wrote to me that his laboratory needed a micro-balance and although these were being made in the U.K., the waiting list was very long. He said there was a manufacturer in Hamburg and he gave me the address at which I could go and talk to him.

I found an opportunity for going to Hamburg and drove to the address. The street was clear, there was no one around and rubble was neatly piled five feet high on both sides. How could there be an office or a factory in these ruins? After walking up and down three times, I noticed an improvised cardboard sign with an arrow saying, 'ZZZZZZ WISSENSCHAFTLICHE WAAGEN' which was the name of the firm given to me. I found a gap in the rubble and a footpath which I followed; after several turns I saw a low-lying area which had been cleared of rubble and in the middle of it stood a newly-built austere three-storey brick building with the name-board on it. I found the owner on the second floor. He said, yes, he could make me a micro-balance. It would cost so much. I answered that I understood currency was not much appreciated, would he like cigarettes? He answered in the affirmative and added,

'What I would really like is genuine coffee beans. My wife is not keeping well and the Doctor has prescribed coffee; unfortunately, all I can get is a powder which has no coffee in it at all.'

'I think I may be able to get you coffee beans. Would two kilogrammes suffice?'

I wrote to my friend Ronald Blease in Cambridge. Coffee was not rationed in England and he had no trouble in getting it. He made two neat parcels – there was a weight limit for gift parcels to the forces - and took it to the Post Office. When he filled up the form saying the contents were COFFEE BEANS and gave it to the girl at the counter, she said,

'Oh no! The export of food items is banned. Call it SHAVING SOAP.'

'That won't do, he is a Sikh and has a beard. Shall I call it WASHING POWDER?' So the parcel reeking of coffee was misdeclared and I got what I needed. That was not the end of the story. The manufacturer was delighted with the coffee. I was determined not to do anything against the rules. I wrote to the customs authorities in England to ask how much customs duty

I would have to pay and I got the reply that I would be charged 'key industries tax *ad valorem* at 40%'. I carried the microbalance in its neat plywood box – it weighed less than ten pounds – in my hand and showed it to the customs officer who took the money and gave me a receipt for it. Clement Bamford was delighted. Unfortunately, he was not a good correspondent and I lost touch with him some ten years later when he was Professor of Chemistry at a Northern University.

My knowledge of German produced an unexpected result. The German unconditional surrender had created an army of 'surrendered personnel' whom the Occupation authorities refused to classify as prisoners of war – particularly as the war in Europe had effectively ended. However, there was no intention of releasing them immediately; in the meantime they had to be kept in guarded camps and fed like prisoners of war. All this was expensive in military personnel and resources so it was decided that they should be used as unskilled labour and several hundred were assiged to my squadron. I was detailed to look after them. We really had no work for them but as many of them were skilled we were able to use them – for instance to modify our jeeps for the winter by providing them with sliding windows and heaters. There was no danger of their trying to escape as they would probably have starved. Besides they were disciplined and had their own Officers to look after them. Their Officers would report to me every morning with their problems.

They were not getting enough fuel to keep themseves warm in the winter in their makeshift wooden huts; could I get them more fuel? No, I could not; they should cut down the trees in their camp and use them for heating.

'Oh, then Germany would lose its forests.'

'So much the better; you will have more *lebensraum* which your former rulers were always asking for.'

Mostly they were asking for punishments for their men! It transpired that these Officers were subalterns with limited powers of punishment. Their complaint was that they did not have guardrooms built of cement concrete or brick with barred windows to lock 'offenders' into on a three days 'bread and water diet' which was the maximum punishment they could award and the wooden huts they used as a prison 'makes no impression on them'. I told them that there were no limits on my powers and I would order *five* days detention. Mostly the offences for which they were convicted were such as would not be considered misdemeanours by civilian courts but discipline had to be maintained especially in a defeated army.

One day, in addition to the French Officers in our mess, half-a-dozen Belgians arrived. The Belgian Air Force had ceased to exist in 1940 and any Belgian Air Force personnel who managed to get to England were cheerfully accepted in the Royal Force – distinguished like so many other foreigners by a shoulder-tab reading BELGIUM. There were a number of such shoulder tabs on uniforms because, of course, citizens of allied or friendly nations were welcome to join the British Forces. Before Pearl Harbour a number of enthusiastic U.S. pilots had formed the EAGLE squadron in the Royal Air Force. When the United States declared war on Germany, most of them transferred to the U.S. forces where they got nearly ten times as much pay. One day, in a restaurant in London I noticed a woman in army uniform - the A(uxiliary) T(erritorial) S(ervice) as it was called – with a shoulder tab reading BLAV. She explained that she was a British Latin American Volunteer.

With war over in Europe, the Belgian Govermnent had returned to Brussels and was in the process of reorganising its armed forces. Belgian nationals serving with the British forces constituted the kernel of the revived Belgian Air Force but, till such time as the Belgian Air Ministry could start functioning and aerodromes could be rebuilt, they would continue to serve with the R.A.F.

Taking advantage of my knowledge of French, I introduced myself to some of these newcomers. Foreigners with names which were hard for English-speakers to pronounce were usually given name tabs to stitch on to the left breasts of their jackets/tunics. One of the Belgians wore the tab DE LIGNE. I told him that I had read several books on the history of the Netherlands and was aware of an old princely family of that name. In fact, in 1945 a historical novel FOREVER AMBER figured on the best-seller list. It was set at the time of the Stuart restoration in England and mentioned a Prince de Ligne (Henri II married to Claire-Marie de Nassau) as being the Imperial Ambassador at the Court of St. James. He replied that his name was Antoine de Ligne, he belonged to that family, his father, a diplomat, was the head of the family and had recently returned from Washington where he had been Charge d'Affaires of Belgium. He went on to say that his parents were of an adventurous disposition and had gone to India by car in the twenties when he had been a baby. We soon became friends and this relationship was to affect my life.

In the meantime my parents were getting worried that I had not been called for an interview for the I.C.S. like the serving Officers in India of their acquaintance. I told them conditions were different in Europe but finally Pitaji advised me to write to H.M.Patel who was a Deputy Secretary in the Cabinet Secretariat in Delhi. I did so but instead of getting a letter in reply, I received an obviously official telegram asking me to 'send matriculation certificate in original to Home Department.' I had this document with me in Fassberg so I dispatched it through the Post Office.

It was not long after this that the Air Ministry realised that disarmament was meaningless and my own squadron was disbanded. Early in 1946 I was transferred to R.A.F. Stade – a fair-sized town some thirty miles due west of Hamburg on the

1945 Mussoorie Pitaji & Mataji.

left bank of the Elbe. This had been a Luftwaffe aerodrome but I never saw any R.A.F. planes there and it seemed to serve for holding personnel while the Air Ministry decided what to do with them. There was a 'radar section' of which I was in charge but it was full of disused electronic equipment and my men spent their time trying to make radio sets for themselves. Quite frankly, there was no work and morale was correspondingly low. The only good memory I have is that I made friends with the Church of England Chaplain – whose name escapes my memory - who lent me G.C. Coulton's 'Medieval Panorama' and I learnt about the dispute between the Roman Catholic Chesterton and the Protestant Coulton over English history. Later in the year the Chaplain was demobilised and returned to civil life as Rector at Iwerne Courtney in Dorsetshire where I was his house guest for several days and was able to see English country life at first hand and found it similar to what I had read about in nineteenth century English literature. I was in the neighbourhood again in 1979 and called the Rectory on the 'phone but he had passed away. Today (2005) I tried to look up the village in the index of the TIMES COMPREHENSIVE ATLAS 2000 and it does not figure.

It was therefore with pleasure that I read an incoming official telegram which said, 'Dispatch 161114 Flight Lieutenant G.J.Malik to No.3 Civil Selection Board Purandhar.' The Station Commander asked me where Purandhar might be. I replied that the name was new to me but I guessed that it was in Bombay Presidency. There was no difficulty in releasing me and I travelled by air from the nearest R.A.F. airfield to London where I had to wait several days for the Air Priorities Board to give me a seat on a Transport Command flight to Karachi. The month was July and it was warm enough in London. I expected to arrive at Bombay in the middle of the monsoon but I knew Karachi would be very hot and I needed to get 'tropical kit' for the stay in India.

When I did get the seat it was amazingly good. Most passenger flights in those days were by twin-engined 'Dakota' aircraft. It so happened that a new plane was being delivered to India for V.I.P.s. The designer of one of Britain's four-engined bombers had modified one for twelve passengers and it was not even full. It was my first experience of a long journey by air. The plane was not pressurised and normally flew at an altitude of 6000 feet. I had the pleasure of flying over France on a fine day at an altitude when I could see villages in the Massif Central. The plane did not fly at night and we stopped at Cairo where we were put up in a 'transit camp' at Heliopolis. In fact this was a pre-war hotel in which two-tier bunks had been installed. There was no air conditioning and it was difficult to sleep at night.

The next day we were to fly to Shaibah, an R.A.F. station near Basra in Iraq. This meant flying over the Sinai Mountains and some of the hottest deserts in the world so the pilot went up to 17000 feet and we were given oxygen masks. That night we had to sleep at Shaibah. The only way I could do so was by pulling my cot some fifty feet away from the buildings which were radiating heat. I was woken up by a blazing sun.

It was only a little less hot in Karachi but my parents were at the R.A.F. station to receive me. I was seeing them after nearly eight years since I had waved good-bye to them in Hamburg. They were living in a house rented by my father because his job (Chairman of the Karachi Joint Water Board – it supplied water to the city and the Armed Forces) was new and there was no official residence for the incumbent. The house was a villa standing in its own grounds but the garden was tiny. However, there were enough servants' quarters for the butler, the cook, the sweeper and the driver. On the great occasion of my return home – for however short a period – the butler had found a sixteen year old from his native British Garhwal (now the Pauri division of Uttaranchal state in the Himalayas adjoining U.P.) named Bharat Singh Rawtela. Bharat Singh is my butler now still working at the age of seventy-five.

The Air Priorities Board in Karachi took its own time to give me a seat on a Dakota to Bombay. I needed the time to acclimatise myself to India's heat after all these years and to equip myself for it. The black shoes I had did not go with the khaki I was wearing. Clothing and textiles generally were rationed in India but dressed in uniform and carrying my identity card (Form 101R) I had access to shops for the Armed Forces and my parents took advantage of the situation to replenish their stock of household linen. They were also able to introduce me to their friends who had either never seen me or only remembered me as a child when the family had left Sind in 1930.

Finally a Dakota took me to Bombay. I knew by now that I had to go to Poona and call a telephone number given to me. In Bombay I took a taxi to have lunch at the Taj Mahal Hotel where I saw a couple of Indians dressed as Army Generals. I knew that the highest rank attained by pre-war regular Indian Army Officers (King's Commissioned Indian Army Officers – KCIOs) was Colonel so these were obviously Princes enjoying Honorary Ranks.

At Victoria Terminus (V.T.) railway station the R.T.O.'s desk was manned by a British Army Corporal and I asked him for a pass to travel by the Deccan Queen. I had travelled by this train before the war when it was the fastest train in India and had the advantage of being electrically propelled. Other trains were hauled by coal-burning steam locomotives so after a few miles even the First Class compartments were full of soot and ash. He told me that to get a pass I would have to go to two other offices which was hardly worthwhile because I could get a First Class ticket immediately for seven rupees (about ten shillings). I had already realised that, after wartime England, every thing in India – taxis, the best hotels and meals appeared very cheap.

In Poona, I went to the best hotel and got a room with attached bath and *all meals* - the morning cup of tea with banana and biscuit known as *chhota hazari,* full English breakfast, lunch, afternoon tea with a slice of fruit cake and a four-course non-vegetarian dinner – for ten rupees a day!

The phone call I made as instructed was answered by a gruff voice,

'You are late. The truck left yesterday.'

'I have come as fast as planes and trains could bring me.'

'Be at the railway station with your baggage at 3 P.M. on Wednesday.'

The war had ended both in Europe and in Asia and it was clear to most of us that constitutional changes were impending in India but an Officer's uniform was quite useful. Moreover, I must say that the twenty-first century's ideas of security did not exist. I believe that the preoccupation with security is exaggerated. The citizen no longer has access to the man or woman in authority and I think this is anti-democratic. We have recently seen, in Europe, that the bureaucracy of the European Union has cut itself off from the people and is living in a cloud-cuckoo land of its own so that the voter in France and the Netherlands has decided to teach it a lesson.

As far as India is concerned, there were terrorists before Independence. They called themselves patriotic revolutionaries and appeared to be particularly numerous in Bengal where they were able to assasinate several Collectors. This was never a reason to cut off officials from the public. Today *security* provides employment to many men and women whose main concern is to prevent access to officials.

In July 1946 the seniormost Officers of the Bombay Secretariat – sheltering from the monsoon in the pleasant climate of Poona - were sitting in non-air-conditioned rooms with open doors and windows with a chaprassi each in the verandah to keep out the public. There were boards indicating the name and designation of each Officer visible from outside. I had no difficulty in gaining access to those whose names had been mentioned to me by my father or whom I had met earlier.

Finally, I got on to the truck which filled up with 'other ranks' so I was able to insist on occupying the only seat – besides the driver. This surprised me until I realised that the Federal Public Service Commission was recruiting not only the few hundred Officers for the All India Services but also thousands for the Central Services. Let me explain that the two All India Services were shared by the Federal Government and the Presidencies or Provinces; they occupied the top jobs all over India. The provinces had their own Public Service Commissions for recruiting the Officers they employed. The Central Services included the Central Secretariat Service, the Customs and Excise, the Income Tax, the Posts and Telegrams and many others. In all these, jobs had been kept vacant for war service entrants and many 'other ranks' aspired to these jobs.

Purandhar turned out to be an old Mahratta fort at an altitude of more than five thousand feet and the weather was pleasant. In fact I felt rather cold in the evening but there was enough activity to warm up.The Commanding Officer welcomed us and explained the programme and procedure for the three-day test. As far as I could make out the procedure for selecting Army Officers had been slightly modified. We were to do what I had known as

TEWTS in the Senior Training Corps – Tactical Exercises Without Troops. A hypothetical situation was related to us and each one had to work out a solution. After that we had to go over some sort of obstacle course as a group – there were thirty of us and we had been divided into groups of ten. The very first included climbing a tree - something I had never done in all my life! I objected that my shoes with leather soles were unsuitable.

'You were all given instructions to come with gym kit.'

'I am sorry; that may have been so in India but in the British Zone of Occupied Germany where I am stationed there was only a signal ordering me to report here. It was on my own initiative that I bought tropical kit in London on the way.'

'If you are interested in taking this test, you will climb that tree.'

I climbed the tree.

Among the thirty, there was only one other Officer and he was not in my group. In my group I had no competition at all, particularly as I was the only one who had lived for years in England and was able to express myself in incomparable English. In fact, someone hearing me speak over the telephone in those days would take me for an Englishman.

There was a three-hour written test which consisted mostly of multiple-choice questions and a short essay. Some of the tests involved recognition of symmetry elements in patterns which I found very easy because of my knowledge of crystallography. We had been told that the questions were very numerous and we should tackle as many as we could. I put down my pen half an hour before the appointed hour to find the invigilator coming up to me,

'Don't give up; carry on writing!'

'Sir, I have answered all the questions; can I get up and go?'

Finally, I had a long interview with an elderly civilian. He was not an I.C.S. officer or an engineer but he obviously belonged or had recently belonged to one of the higher services. He was interested in my background and I was able to rattle off the names of several Bombay Presidency Officers. I explained that I had met them at the Reform Club in Ahmedabad.

'You were seventeen years old when you left Ahmedabad. How could you belong to a Club at that age?'

'Sir, my father is an Officer of the Indian Service of Engineers. At that time his services were on loan to Ahmedabad Municipality as Municipal Engineer. He was a member of the Reform Club and children of members of the appropriate age were allowed to play games. In this way I was able to meet members and since I was a college student, they were willing to talk to me.'

The President of the Selection Board called me,

'As you are probably aware, you have done remarkably well in this test. We shall now send your results and our recommendations to the Federal Public Service Commission in Simla. You may return to your unit and will be called to Simla in due course.'

'Sir, my unit is in Germany. Is it worth while to fly me all the way to Germany and back to Simla?'

'Oh! I shall have to call a meeting of the Board.'

An hour or so later, the Secretary of the Board said to me,

'We are doing something totally unprecedented. Here are two sealed packets containing your documents. Carry them to Simla yourself and give them with the seals intact to the Secretary of the Public Service Commission.'

I realised that it was in my interest to get to Simla as soon as possible without waiting for some Air Priorities Board to give me a free flight. In Bombay I found that a flight of Indian National Airways was available to Delhi and was affordable. The plane stopped on the way in Ahmedabad and was declared unserviceable. To my pleasant surprise, I saw a cousin at the airport. He put me up for the night and took me to the airport next morning.

In Delhi, I had to wait to find a seat on the train to Kalka from where a narrow gauge train would take me to Simla. I stayed in New Delhi with H.M.Patel (who had recently been appointed Joint Secretary to the Cabinet) at 1, Safdarjung Road. This house was subsequently occupied by Prime Minister Indira Gandhi who was murdered there. It is now a museum.

'Do you know what happened to your application?' my host asked me.

'No, Uncle, I am waiting to hear the story from you.'

'Well, when I got your letter I rang up my opposite number in the Home Department and he promised to get the file and tell me. The next day he called and said, 'Here it is, Gunwantsingh

Jaswantsingh Malik, excluded because the candidate is not qualified.'

'How do you mean, not qualified?'

'Well, as you know, in peacetime, only graduates were allowed to sit for the I.C.S.competitive examination. Now, with the war on, we have relaxed that rule because boys are joining up straight from school particularly in England, where they finish Public School at the age of eighteen. However, we *are* insisting that they be matriculates and this Officer has not passed his matriculation."

'So', said my host, 'I replied, 'I don't think we can be talking of the same man. The applicant I asked you about is a graduate of both Bombay and Cambridge Universities.'

'Let me see, yes, B.Sc. (Bombay), B.A. (Cantab), also M.A. (Cantab); the certificates are here. There has been a mistake somewhere. I shall have the application processed immediately but, to observe the rules, will you ask him to send the Matriculation Certificate in original?"

This conversation took place in July 1946 and nearly sixty years later, I keep asking myself how this could have happened. Obviously, the Deputy Secretary in the Home department had never seen my application. How could he with so many other responsibilities possibly go through thousands of applications? He must have relied on a note by a Section Officer. Section Officers, even in those days, were graduates and had passed a competitive examination set by a Public Service Commission. No one could be so stupid as not to know that one cannot be a University graduate without passing the 'matric'. The other explanation is usually corruption; a subordinate official makes a wrong note on an application and waits for the applicant to come and give him a bribe for correcting it. I have seen this happen with my son Kiran's college admission application. The Head Clerk changed one of his marks from 65 to 56 which excluded him. I was abroad at the time. A good friend of high social status had to go and see the Principal to get the mistake corrected.

In my case, such an explanation will not hold water. The best I can imagine is an unknown clerical official seeing the application saying to himself, 'This candidate who is not all deserving will get in, just because his father is rich and could afford to send him to the most prestigious Universities in India and Europe. He himself is a mediocre student and never got a First Division in Bombay or a First Class in England. If I can exclude him, perhaps my brother who graduated from Meerut College may stand a chance.' No better hypothesis occurs to me. I am certain that without H.M.Patel's intervention I would not have got into the Indian Foreign Service.

In Simla I was the houseguest of H.S.Malik, my father's cousin, whom I have mentioned several times. At this time he was not in Simla but his wife, whom I always called 'Auntie Prakash' and who was a cousin of my mother's, was living in his official residence with their three children and some other relations – his services were on loan from the Government of India to Maharaja Yadvendra Singh of Patiala as Prime Minister of that Princely State. Traditionally, the Maharajas of Patiala refused to live in Simla because they claimed that a Viceroy in the nineteenth century had illegally seized the land from their ancestors. Patiala had its own summer capital at Chail some twenty miles away where the Maharaja, a brilliant cricketer, had built the highest cricket ground in the world.

The interview with the Federal Public Service Commission (as it was then called) went very well and I was going down the stairs when I was recalled.

'Mr. Malik, we have only just noticed that you have also applied for the Indian Political Service. We cannot understand this; the Indian Political Service looks mostly after the tribal territories in the North West Frontier Province. What would a man of your education knowing several European languages do with semi-literate Pathan chiefs?'

'Sir, I am thinking of the future. India is bound to have a diplomatic service and, in fact right now, one member of the I.P.S. is Ambassador in Chunking and another, Sir Girja Shankar Bajpai, is Minister for Indian Affairs in the British Embassy in Washington.'

'Oh, the future. We are thinking of the present. Thank you. Good bye.'

The attitude is very interesting. Only 10% of I.P.S.Officers were Indians and, as the Chairman had said, they were mostly posted in the N.W.F.P. which had an inhospitable climate and was very backward. Only hunters and polo players would find such postings attractive. What made the I.P.S. so much sought after were postings in princely states where there was plenty of entertainment by the princes and the 'Residents' received a sumptuary allowance so that they could also entertain suitably. Such posts were seldom given to Indian Officers, much less were they posted to the Persian Gulf or Aden where the 'Political Officers' had vast powers and were not subject to criticism in the Indian press or Parliament. Many years later I met an Englishman who had been posted in the Gulf and he told me that his powers had included being 'Manumitter of slaves'.

I went from Simla to Karachi by train in leisurely style stopping on the way in Lahore where I stayed and met several relations. When I got to Karachi, the Air Priorities Board was not in a hurry to fly me back to England so I really had a six weeks holiday in India which did not count against my leave entitlement.

This period in India was not a pleasant emotional experience for me. I had spent six years thinking mainly about the war and the importance of beating the Germans who had had those horrible concentration camps and the Japanese who (according to the Allied press and media) had treated prisoners of war so abominably. In India everybody I met other than government servants was praising the Indian National Army whom I thought of as men who, when the fate of the world was in the balance, had thrown in their weight on the side of the forces of evil. There were even men and women who praised black marketeers and tickteless travellers for 'getting the better of the government.' I could understand the desire for Independence but I was convinced that if Hitler or Tojo had won the war India would have been worse off than under the British. I was worried that if men and women who admired Hitler were to rule India it might not be a country worth living in.

Fortunately, Pandit Nehru and his colleagues had sound political instincts and built up a functioning democracy. Many countries in Asia and Africa which attained independence in the next two decades did not have equally brilliant leaders.

Back in England I reported to the Air Ministry where I found that it was not the intention to send me back to Germany. In fact, no one had any idea what to do with me and I spent four or five weeks on leave while a post was being found for me. I began to feel that England was rather rudderless. The Labour government was dealing with major political issues like independence for India and creating a socialist state. They knew very well that no one would accept Stalin's Soviet Socialism much less Hitler's National Socialism but there were Ministers like Dr.Gaitskell who thought they could and should control every aspect of the economy and they failed miserably. Bread had not been rationed at any time during the war but it was rationed in peacetime. Instead of dismantling controls imposed during the war, new ones were thought of.

Finally I was posted as Radar Officer at Scampton in Lincolnshire. Men and women who had been conscripted or, like me, had joined up during the war were anxious to return to civilian life but the Ministry of Defence had worked out a plan for demobilisation which created groups numbered according to a formula based on age and length of service. My group was 52 and there was no stated date for my 'release'. In the mean time, the permanent, pre-war Officers and N.C.O.s were anxious to recreate a peace-time Air Force which seemed to consist of meaningless inspections, church parades and spit and polish. Few wartime entrants were keen to join such a force even though they did not have jobs to go to.

As I have mentioned earlier, Station Commanders were not fond of technical officers who would never be pilots. The Group Captain at Scampton was particularly disgusted with my marching on parade so when I asked him for early release and repatriation, he was only too happy to recommend my application. The procedure involved going to a 'release depot', being 'issued with' a civilian outfit, and waiting for few days to get a berth in a First Class cabin on the Royal Mail Ship ANDES which was doing duty as a troopship. I was given paid leave for three months and allowed to wear uniform during this period.

The Royal Mail Lines normally operated between the United Kingdom and South America. I would say that the accommodation was better than on P&O ships. I was given a berth in a First Class cabin which would normally have been occupied by a single passenger but it had been adapted to hold six bunks so it was short on 'lebensraum' and 'ablution facilities' although I remember only three of us sharing it. One of these was an Englishman who had served as an Officer in a Gurkha regiment and had been appointed to a 'Ceylon cadetship'. This was similar to the job I would hold if appointed to the I.C.S. I learnt a lot from him about the qualities of the Gurkha soldier. Most of the passengers were British going out to postings in Malaya, Singapore, Hong Kong and other places in the British Far East.

There were a couple of Indian Army Officers returning from courses in U.K.; they were probably envious when I told them that I was expecting to get into the I.C.S. However, they pretended that there would have been no future for me in the Indian Army because I was not a Jat. This was completely incomprehensible to me. In Patohari as I had heard it spoken, a jat was a boorish, uneducated person whom I would not have wanted to be associated with.

It was not only in Patohari that the word jat had this meaning. A few months later, I met a colleague who had served in the Indian Army and been awarded the Military Cross. His name was Avtar Singh and he was the son of the Secretary of the Punjab Legislative Assembly named Abnasha Singh. He had been born and brought up in Lahore and had never been outside India till he joined the Army. He had been brought up as a Keshadhari Sikh and was a few months younger than I. He applied for a commission in the Indian Army after getting his B.A. degree. He was interviewed by a Board of three Officers, two of whom were British. In the course of the interview, one of the latter asked him

'Mr. Singh, are you a Jat?'

'No, Sir! I am a graduate.'

He got the commission, shaved off his beard and had a brilliant career both in the Army and in the Indian Foreign Service – he retired as Ambassador in Japan.

There was a time, before joining the R.A.F., when I had sought the advice of the most famous retired British I.C.S.Officer, Lord Hailey, about learning languages which might be useful in the I.C.S. Hailey was the only ex-I.C.S. Peer I could find. He told me that Dutch might be useful because of the nearby Dutch East Indies.

Years later I learnt that in U.P. of which he had been Governor, Lord Hailey was known as 'the butcher of Ballia'.

Anyway, I bought an English-Dutch dictionary and a Dutch grammar. The third lesson of the grammar began with the words,

'The following twelve diphthongs are pronounced very similarly. To hear the difference, ask a native.'

I threw away the grammar. I still have the dictionary.

Like most people in England, I have heard of the Boer War and the foreign word is pronounced by my English friends as two syllables but I am told that the Dutch pronunciation is nearer to the English word BOOR. During the Boer War, the Dutch in South Africa were proud of being farmers but the public in the United Kingdom was amazed by their military ability.

I am mentioning all this because of the similarity between Jats and Boers. There is a large population of people who call themselves Jats in Northern India, particularly in Western U.P (the area where the BRAJ dialect is spoken – this dialect was considered the most appropriate for composing poetry, like Galician in Spain), Haryana, Northern Rajasthan (Bharatpur district) and Indian Punjab. In the course of centuries, some Jats were converted to Islam and are called MEOS, others to Sikhism. There is a slight difference of pronunciation between the way Hindus and Sikhs pronounce this word. Jats are known to be physically strong, hard-working and talented farmers and soldiers. The British recognised them as a 'martial race' and only Jat Sikhs are enrolled in the ranks of the '11ᵗʰ Sikhs'. Thus, the Indian Army recognises 'Jat Sikhs' and 'Mazbi Sikhs' who are enrolled in the 'Sikh Light Infantry'. There are plenty of Sikhs – like myself – who are neither Jats nor Mazbis who join the army's other units, Engineers, Gunners, Electrical and Mechanical Engineers, Army Supply Corps, etc. Officers are not subject to caste restrictions. Nor are caste differences recognised in the Indian Navy and the Indian Air Force.

As I have explained earlier, the Gurus tried to abolish the caste system but they were not successful as can be seen above. Before Independence, well-educated middle-class young men and women were unaware of our own castes and felt that the British were keeping the caste system alive to divide and rule us. We were quite mistaken. Today everyone is aware of his or her own caste. Our politicians have used caste to create vote banks.

My Jat Sikh friends claim that they are all equal whereas the non-Jat Sikhs can be Khatris, Aroras, Brahmins, Ahluwalias and God knows what else. Of course, this is not so. The Jat Sikhs divide themselves in a number of other ways e.g. by their territorial origins. In Singapore I was officially invited to visit the Singh Sabha, a large and imposing gurudwara in a very prominent location. It was a wooden building. The prayer hall was upstairs. On the ground floor were the kitchen, the living quarters of the priests and servants and a *dharamshala*. This is a free hotel where anybody can find food and lodging irrespective of age or religion. The German Consul General told me that when he had deserters from ships or other impecunious backpackers he was always able to accommodate them in the Singh Sabha dharamshala, until a German ship came along!

I soon found that there were a number of other gurudwaras in Singapore less conspicuously located in small houses. It took me time and effort to be invited to visit them. They were known as Doaba, Manjha, Malwa, etc. gurudwaras depending on the various regions of Indian Punjab from which the congregations originated. The congregations were all Jat Sikhs. When I asked,

'Why can't all Sikhs pray in the Singh Sabha?'

'Oh! the Singh Sabha – we don't know where they come from. Perhaps they are not Punjabis at all and come from the old North West Frontier Province.' They really meant that the worshippers in the Singh Sabha were not Jats.

In fact, the gurudwara is not only a place to pray. The priest is often also a teacher and runs a school. Depending on the size and resources of the congregation, there can be a secondary school as in Bangkok where I found a very talented headmaster. In addition to all that, the gurudwara is a meeting place, something like a medieval English church.

I have gone into this rather lengthy digression about Jat Sikhs because of the social, military and political significance of these divisions. Let me add that nothing in the last hundred years has prevented Sikhs of all 'communities' from becoming doctors, lawyers, engineers or distinguishing themselves in professions of their choice – except politics!

GETTING INTO THE INDIAN FOREIGN SERVICE 1946-47

I disembarked from the R.M.S. Andes at Bombay on 22nd November 1946. My parents had come all the way from Karachi to receive me. They were jubilant. They held in their hands a three-day old newspaper which contained a list of 164 successful war service applicants for the I.C.S. Beneath the list, was a small note.

'Because of impending constitutional changes, the I.C.S. and I.P.S. may be abolished but the successful candidates will be accommodated in the successor services.'

My parents were staying in Bombay with the Governor of the Reserve Bank of India who accompanied them to the dock. The beaming smiles on the faces were due to the fact that the list was arranged in order of merit and my name was fourth on the list of 164. Moreover they had found out that the F.P.S.C. (The Public Services Commission) had considered the first four to be equal and arranged us by age. The three above me were:

Shailendra Eknath Sukhthankar
Percival Theophilus Chalappa Shastri
Mohammed Attaur Rahman.

It may be of interest to know what happened to them. I met Sukhthankar in R.A.F. uniform. He wore the Distinguished Flying Cross, pilot's wings, a Squadron Leader's rings and a small wing worn only by personnel of No.8 Pathfinder Group which was a Bomber Group commanded by Air Vice Marshal D.C.T. Bennett. Bennett had been an Australian civil airline pilot and was the only Air Officer of a combatant R.A.F. unit who was not a pre-war regular Officer. His group used to go ahead of the main force to drop Target Indicators on the night's objectives. I gathered that he was not popular with Regular Officers.

Sukhthankar was not interested in the Foreign Service, opted for the then Bombay cadre of the I.A.S. and, I am told, ended his career as Municipal Commissioner of Bombay.

Shastri's case was tragic. I never saw him. I am told that he wanted to join the I.F.S. but was rejected 'because he had buck teeth'. He was so upset by this decision that he refused to accept an appointment in the I.A.S. and became an Anglican clergyman; however he is said to have committed suicide.

Rahman opted for the I.F.S., ended his career as Ambassador in Bonn and now (2005) lives in Delhi. He was always very interested in sport so our interests are not the same but we remain in touch.

Constitutional changes were indeed taking place at the end of 1946 and I would have been a loser – again, but for H.M.Patel who soon became a Secretary and was appointed Partition Secretary a few months later.

One problem was that I had not been selected for the Indian Political Service of which the Indian Foreign Service was the successor as had been foreseeable to every one except the British Chairman of the F.P.S.C. – The I.P.S. list did not appear in the press. The Home Department had my name in the I.A.S. list and allotted me to Sind because I had been born in Karachi and had given my address:

'c/o J.S.Malik, Esq., O.B.E.,
Chairman,
Karachi Joint Water Board,
Karachi'

There were elected governments in all the Presidencies and Provinces. The Congress governments accepted the advice of the Home Department that the war Service entrants (known in bureaucratic language as E.C.O.s – Emergency Commissioned Officers) were exceptionally good human material because they had been chosen out of thousands of applicants who all had 'field' experience. However, the Muslim League governments of Punjab, Bengal and Sind found that the majority of the names in the lists sent to them were of non-Muslims and rejected the Home department's recommendations saying they would make their own choice if and when Pakistan was created. I and dozens of other 'successful candidates' were jobless.

These developments were not published in the newspapers which we read in Karachi. We were kept informed of them by H.M.Patel's letters. He managed to persuade the Department of Foreign Affairs that I should be considered for the Indian Foreign Service and I was called to Delhi for an interview. When I got there I found there were four candidates who were going to be interviewed. The Board for the interview was headed by the Foreign Secretary an Englishman named Weightman. The other members were Sir Akbar Hydari (an I.C.S.Officer) whose appointment as Governor of Assam had just been announced, K.P.S.Menon (the Ambassador in China mentioned earlier). There was also a younger Indian Officer whose name I have forgotten.

After this hurdle came the final interview with Pandit Nehru who was the Member for External and Commonwealth Affairs in this interim government. He asked me several awkward questions which I answered frankly opposing the underlying concepts in the questions, such as,

'If the Russians want to, they can overrun the whole of Europe tomorrow.'

'Yes, Sir, but not the British Isles; the Soviet Union is not a naval power.'

'Hum. There is no understanding between U.S.A. and the U.K.. Britain has refused to accept American potatoes.'

'Sir, there is a reason for that. The American potatoes are infested with boll weevils and these do not exist in the United Kingdom so they would probably overrun British agriculture.'

Panditji did not seem happy with my interview but I was told a decision would be taken in due course and I went back to Karachi. This was early in March 1947. A letter from H.M.Patel came announcing that I had been selected and should arrive in Delhi on 20th March which I did.

THE I.F.S. – INDIA 1947-48

I reported to Metcalfe House hutments in the Civil Lines area of Old Delhi and found that there were 64 'hutments' and that meant that 64 of the original list of 164 successful candidates had joined the I.A.S. Training School. Some of the others were already working in various provinces or in the Central Secretariat while a large number of Punjabis, Bengalis and Sindhis had not got letters of appointment as I have explained on the previous page. In fact, my name appeared on the list at Metcalfe House but I had no letter of appointment and I had to go to Mr. P.V.R.Rao, the Deputy Secretary in the Home Department to collect it. H.M.Patel had got advance information probably from him and asked me to come.

Of the 64, the I.F.S. officers were less than 10, the others having been selected for the I.A.S. Some officers never came to Metcalfe House as I have mentioned above.

Jagat Singh Mehta (from the Royal Indian Navy) had got admission to St. John's College Cambridge after his F.P.S.C. interview and would only come after the end of the academic year. He was the only one of our batch to become Foreign Secretary – in 1977.

M.A.Rahman ('Ishi' to his friends) mentioned previously was working as Under Secretary in the Ministry. He was the son of a wealthy Muslim landowner, Col. Rahman, a member of the F.P.S.C. who, of course, had not sat on the board for interviewing

217

candidates for the I.C.S. and I.P.S.. Ishi had gone to Public School in England and had been my contemporary at Cambridge but we had never met while we were there. In March 1947, he was said to be engaged to Ingrid Hydari, the eldest daughter of Sir Akbar Hydari and his Swedish wife.

There were three Muslim Officers of the I.F.S. at Metcalfe House who opted for Pakistan a few weeks later in the month of August.

What was Metcalfe House? It was a very imposing building overlooking the Yamuna River which had been built for Sir John Metcalfe when he was the Envoy of the East India Company to the Mughal Emperor. In March 1947, it was kept locked up and I was never able to see the inside. In its extensive but neglected compound, 64 hutments had been built during the World War to accommodate Officers of the Armed Forces. Of course, there was a Mess Hall and some offices alongside. This group of buildings had been allotted to the I.A.S.Training School which was a residential institution. We ate English food in the Mess Hall. It was provided by a contractor and I have no hesitation in saying that it was bad. I lost a lot of weight that summer. Since I have never been fat, this meant that I became emaciated.

The Principal of the I.A.S. Training School was M.J.Desai, an I.C.S. Officer who was later absorbed in the Indian Foreign Service and ended his career as a Secretary in the Ministry of External Affairs. In fact the school had been set up in a hurry without adequate planning. Before the war, all I.C.S. probationers whether selected in India or in England used to be sent to Oxford, Cambridge or London Universities where special courses used to be organised for them before they arrived to serve in India as Assistant Collectors.

This seemed inappropriate in an India soon to be independent and in the case of men who had already served as Officers in the Armed Forces. However, some training was necessary. The I.A.S. Officers were all going to be magistrates so they had to study the Indian Penal Code and the Code of Criminal Procedure. They had to learn driving and motor mechanics; Pandit Nehru wanted them to learn riding because he was convinced that riding instilled courage in a man – there was no woman among us. They were taught Urdu which had been the second official language of India for a century but by this time it was obvious that Urdu would be replaced by Hindi so Hindi classes were started.

I had no interest in Urdu – an attempt in childhood to learn this language had not got beyond the character *aliph* – and little in Hindi but I was glad to learn about Indian law of which I felt I did not know enough. However, it was obvious that the course had not been planned for future diplomats and we were being 'parked' in the Metcalfe house till the Ministry could work out what to do with us. A factor which was slowing this up was the political change in progress.

In all this time, Pitaji had retired. The retirement age for the higher services - except the I.C.S. who had the choice of serving for thirty-five years – was 55 so Pitaji should have retired on 13th April 1945. However, on that date, the World War was still on and he was given a year's extension because it was better 'not to change horses in mid-stream'. A year later, in April 1946, the British were thinking that they did not want to lose a trusted Officer just before they might be leaving India, so he was given another year's extension.

As I have said, I was to report in Delhi on 20th March but Pitaji was already packing to leave Karachi on 13th April. Fortunately, he had been offered and had accepted a new post created for him – Chief Engineer, Ahmedabad Municipality. This gave him a salary higher than he had been receiving in Karachi. At the same time, a new official residence had been built for him in Ahmedabad.

By the middle of March the killings associated with the Partition of India which had started in Calcutta and then in Bihar had spread to Punjab also. I have mentioned Gurbachan Singh, the son of Sardar Mohan Singh, as a schoolboy in England in 1938. By this time he was married and working in the India Supply Mission in Washington where his wife Shyama was expecting their first baby. The Mohan Singhs were anxious to be present for this important event. They arrived in Karachi by train from Rawalpindi and stayed for a few days with Dr. Harnam Singh Chhachhi who was a Medical Officer with the North Western Railway. The Chhachhis were a prominent family from Rawalpindi. The newspapers we read in Karachi were tactfully silent about the happenings in Patohar but the North West Railway had its own telephone network and the Chhachhis learnt that riotous mobs had burnt scores of houses that Mohan Singh and his elder brother owned in Murree and the Civil Lines of Rawalpindi. The Chhachhis discussed this matter with my parents and decided not to inform Mr. and Mrs.Mohan Singh who flew off cheerfully by Trans World Airways to New York without knowing that they would never see their property again.

We were expecting similar trouble in Karachi so Pitaji decided not to sell his furniture or his cars but to take everything by train to Ahmedabad. I decided to go to Delhi by train with a suitcase, an attaché case and a bedding roll. I had brought all my books, clothes and pictures from England in a couple of trunks and tea-chests from England and these were now in Karachi so they all went to Ahmedabad. In July 1946 I had left Stade with a small bag by fighter aircraft on my way to London. The rest of my luggage containing more books, spare uniforms and expensive riding kit had not reached me from R.A.F. Stade when I left England. They got to Karachi after my parents had left and some of them were rescued by H.M.Patel during one of his visits there as Partition Secretary.

Pitaji was able to sell his Studebaker convertible in Ahmedabad for a good price. No cars were being made in India, import licences for cars – especially American cars – were hard to get and he was able to sell even his ancient Ford tourer. At the same time, he ordered a fleet of garbage trucks for the Municipality. There was no difficulty in importing trucks, the production of which had increased during the war, and General Motors (India) were glad of this order so when he asked for a Chevrolet and a Vauxhall Wyvern for himself, he got them quite quickly. In the heat of May, I became the happy possessor of a brand new Vauxhall Wyvern. Of course, the petrol ration was very small and I could only allow myself a couple of trips a week to New Delhi. However, I was the only possessor of a new car in Metcalfe House hutments – it was a present from my father.

As I have mentioned, the Home Department which was in charge of the I.A.S.Training School was not very sure of what it wanted to do with us and gave us a summer vacation like Delhi University gave. Pitaji decided that he wanted to avail of leave also and arrived in Mussoorie where he rented a house named FIRDAUS (*paradise* in Persian) at the top of Gun Hill. I was able

INAUGURATION OF INDIAN DOMINION
FLAG HOISTING CEREMONY

South East of King George's Statue near Memorial Arch.

15th August 1947 — 6 p.m.

Admit......*Mr G. J. Malik*........................

Block   E..............Row....~~XX~~........Seat..388.

Spectators must be in their seats by 5-40 p.m.

1947 Delhi Indian Independence 15 August.

to drive to Mussoorie and park my car in the car park at the end of the Cart Road. Only the Governor of U.P. was allowed to drive in Mussoorie although permission could be obtained in special circumstances e.g. illness. Rickshaws pulled and pushed by *jhampanis* (human rickshaw pullers) were numerous. We felt that we would have liked to be drawn by animals but not by human beings so a rickshaw was only hired for Aunty Bansi.

I got back to Delhi in time for the Independence ceremonies and I still have the invitation to the flag hoisting on 15th August. In 1997, RTV – the French equivalent of the B.B.C. – asked the French Ambassador to find someone in New Delhi who could speak French and remembered India's Independence. I was interviewed first by a radio reporter who carried a tape-recorder and, a few days later, by a television crew which made a video recording.

The radio journalist asked me,

'Do you remember your feelings at the time of Independence?'

'Yes, I felt sad.'

'Sad? Why on earth?'

'I was very much aware that people were being killed at this time in hundreds of thousands.'

The journalist came to see me again a few days later and said that he had listened to the tape over and over again because it had surprised and shaken him.

In fact, the killings which had started in Punjab in March had been going on intermittently on both sides of the new dividing line in Punjab but Delhi was still peaceful on 15th August. The killings started a few days later and the new Home Ministry immediately decided that the probationers in Metcalfe House, with their military experience, were the best people to deal with it. Half were sent off to East Punjab and the other half were assigned work in Delhi. I was sent along with some others to the Town Hall. I drove my colleagues there. I was advised to approach it from the back – Chandni Chowk – instead of the front which faced the Old Delhi Railway Station because 'the train system is overloaded with Muslim refugees fleeing from Delhi and Hindus and Sikhs arriving from West Punjab.'

I entered Chandni Chowk from the southern end facing the Red Fort to find all the streets deserted. I drove along slowly and saw dead bodies lying on the asphalt. There was a solitary policeman who tried to stop us but I explained that we were on official duty. As there was no other traffic, it was not difficult to weave my way between the dead bodies.

At the Town Hall, there were few people but I soon saw Officers I recognised and I was told to sit down at the only telephone in a large and otherwise empty room. I had a table and chair and was told to deal with visitors as best as I could. There was a smaller room accessible only by going past me which was occupied by K.B.Lall, an I.C.S.Officer who had been sent there from his normal job of Joint Chief Controller of Imports and Exports. He was very quick-witted and often solved problems immediately without worrying too much about the veracity of what he was saying. A prominent Muslim scholar, Dr. Zakir Hussain (he was President of India when he died many years later) who was heading an institution of higher education, Jamia Millia Islamia, came with a delegation,

'Mr. Lall, we have come to see you because reports have come to us that you are disposing of Muslim dead bodies by burning.

This is entirely contrary to our religion and we would like you to stop it immediately.'

'Doctor Sahib, there are thousands of dead bodies decomposing and endangering the health of the surviving population. The Officer in charge is a Zoroastrian who cannot tell a Muslim from a Hindu. I estimate that the dead of the two communities are in equal numbers. He is burying half the bodies and burning the other half. This should leave both communities equally satisfied or dis-satisfied.'

Dr. Zakir Hussain and his delegation went away although they must have known that in Delhi very few Hindus and Sikhs had been killed. I knew that my good friend Rustam Feroze Boga was throwing dead bodies into pits and then pouring petrol on them and dropping a match. Earth was thrown on the pits only when the ashes were cold.

In fact Russi Boga's work was beyond all praise. He had been given a car from the Governor-general's garage in which an official had succumbed to stray firing so that the car stank. This car still carried crowns fore and aft instead of number-plates so the police seldom dared to stop it. He personally supervised the work which was done by admirably self-sacrificing boy scouts. A Congress Party leader named Deshbandhu Gupta who had offered to provide workers for the job never showed up. After working uninterruptedly for three nights and two days Russi Boga returned to Metcalfe House and had a hot bath but he still stank after that and we were not happy to see him in the mess hall. He had been at Blundell's school, then at Oxford before serving as a Cavalry Officer, was married and both he and his wife Mehroo had private fortunes.

My own role was small and relatively inactive. One day Fori Nehru, the Hungarian Jewish wife of B.K.Nehru (I.C.S. and a Deputy Secretary in the Finance Ministry) whom I knew from having met her in H.M.Patel's house, came in and said blankets had to be bought for Muslim refugees who were leaving for Pakistan and were, at present accommodated in a refugee camp. The first problem was to get petrol for the car we were using. Only a few petrol pumps were operating and we had to get special coupons from my colleague Avtar Singh. Then, we had to find a shop which was not closed. At the shop, Fori said to me, in French,

'It is a good thing the Hindu shopkeeper does not understand French otherwise he would probably kill us rather than sell us goods to be used by Muslims!'

There were horrible incidents too. A man walked into my office with a dagger stuck in his back. On another day I was driving back to Metcalfe House for lunch when I saw a boy's body lying on the road. His trousers had been taken off.

In the middle of all this, normal life went on. The post brought me a letter from Antoine de Ligne in Belgium – a friend who has probably written three letters to me in all his life. The letter said that his father had been selected to be Ambassador to India and I should expect him to arrive in the middle of September. I went to see Ishi Rahman in the Ministry because he was the Under Secretary dealing with Europe. Not a single West European country had an Ambassador in New Delhi – the United Kingdom had a High Commissioner but France and the Netherlands only had Charge d'Affaires; Germany and even Spain did not exist – the Allies had boycotted General Franco. For Belgium to send an Ambassador straightaway was an important political gesture. For years, Belgium had maintained Consuls General in Bombay and Calcutta and the one from Calcutta arrived to be Charge d'Affaires. I went to see him; he was staying in a suite in Cecil's Hotel – now a Roman Catholic school – had no secretarial assistance and kept his correspondence with his shirts!

One problem was that all accommodation in New Delhi was controlled by the Government – the Ministry of Works. To get a room for long-term stay in a hotel, one had to go to the Estate Officer. The Belgian Ambassador, his family and staff, were to get rooms in Maiden's hotel in Old Delhi, less than a kilometre from Metcalfe House. I and some of my friends were in the habit of going there occasionally for a drink in the evening. There was only one dining room and one had to go through the bar to get there.

I was at Safdarjung airport when the special SABENA flight arrived. I had managed to drive on to the tarmac and greeted the Prince as he came down the step-ladder. Eugene de Ligne was accompanied by his wife, whom he used to describe jokingly as

'Philippine de Noailles, Mouchy, Poix, Princesse de Ligne, Amblise, Epinoy'

They were accompanied by their attractive daughter Yolande aged about twenty, a First Secretary named Charles Pigault de Beaupre and his wife. The Prince's Private Secretary was an unmarried woman of about forty was introduced to me as Meme de Croy.

Also on board was the Chairman of Sabena, Tony Orta. He had brought this four-engined plane on an exploratory flight to see if a service could be started between Belgium and India. This was a fanciful idea because, of course, there was not enough traffic to justify it and in 2006 there is still no direct flight between India and Belgium. I got the impression that Mr.Orta overestimated his ability and his own importance.

The Ligne family was very good to me and I saw a great deal of them. I found that Marie-Helene de Croy – Meme to her friends – lived with the family. She told me her father had been an Austrian Army Officer who was ruined by the Great War and the subsequent inflation in that country. She had emigrated to Belgium where she had got herself naturalised and had got this job because she was a very distant relation.

I had read a lot about the European nobility and was conversant with the Almanach de Gotha which at that time was published every year in German and French. I found that Meme was entitled to be addressed as 'Your Serene Highness' while her employer was only 'His Highness!' Of course, 'Highness' outranks 'Excellency'. It appears that Napoleon put an end to the Holy Roman Empire after Austerlitz and the Ruler of Austria declared himself 'Emperor of Austria and King of Hungary'. His descendants in the tail male were all addressed as 'His/Her Royal and Imperial Highness the Archduke/Archduchess.....' They could marry into the Royal families of Europe or Princely and Ducal families which were declared 'mediatised'. Otherwise they would lose their 'Royal and Imperial' status.

The Ligne and Croy families both originate from North West Europe. Ligne is a village in Belgium near Ath whereas the Head of the Croy family has a large estate in Germany not far from the Belgian frontier at Duelmen. When the Austrian Empire was created, both Ligne and Croy were classified as 'mediatised' but soon after that Field Marshal Prince Eugene de Ligne was obliged to sell the County of Edelstetten to which the mediatisation was attached so he ceased to be 'serene'. In fact, through the centuries, there have been several marriages between the Ligne and Croy families.

The Ambassador had been an Army Officer in the Great War after which he had been appointed to the Belgian Foreign Service. He had received the education of an Army Officer after leaving school. The family was not very rich but had managed to hold on to Beloeil which had been the seat of the Lignes for centuries. It is a few kilometres from the village of Ligne where there is no country house. He had married Philippine who had inherited property in U.S.A. from her American grandmother. This enabled them to maintain Beloeil and a very high standard of living.

Philippine herself was a woman of great ability and personality. She had been the Head of the Belgian Red Cross during the war and this had enabled her to maintain contact legally and officially with the occupation authorities and obtain concessions for individuals who might otherwise have ended up in the notorious German concentration camps.

As I have mentioned, the Lignes were good to me and invited me to several of the many parties they gave. I, in turn, introduced them to my Officer friends in particular the H.M.Patel family and also to some of my relations who were socially prominent in the then very limited society of Delhi. I don't think that in 1947, there were ten thousand motor cars in the Union Territory the population of which was said to be eight hundred thousand. I also served them as a tourist guide.

By this time, law and order had been restored in Delhi and we had all returned to our increasingly meaningless classes at Metcalfe House. By October, I think, the Foreign Service probationers had been transferred to the Ministry and I had obtained accommodation in a 'cubicle' in Kotah House. This was the Delhi residence of the Maharao of Kotah which had been taken over by the Government of India as a hostel for Officers. As a bachelor I was given part of a large first floor room which was separated by a seven foot partition from the rest. There was minimal furniture. There was a common lounge, a shared bathroom and a dining hall where the food was quite good if rather expensive.

At the Ministry, I was assigned 'protocol' work. I soon found that this meant dealing with foreign missions and ticklish questions of precedence. I found there was a library and I was able to borrow several books on international law. Some of these dealt with protocol problems including one written by a British diplomat named Satow who had been Ambassador in Japan – Sato is a surname in Japan.

Since accommodation was controlled, the Ministry had to find a house for the Belgian Ambassador. They identified a house belonging to a wealthy Muslim landowner who had emigrated to Pakistan. Obviously, hundreds of thousands if not millions of Muslims had done so. A law was quickly passed for dealing with such 'Evacuee Property' and a 'Custodian of Evacuee Property' appointed with vast powers. The result was that 24, Harding Avenue was allotted to the Belgian Embassy. I rushed to tell Prince de Ligne about it and soon the family was visiting the place. The French Charge d'Affaires had not been allotted a residence and he wrote an angry letter to the Ministry.

The Prince told me that since his wife, mother and grandmother were all French and he was very friendly with several French diplomats and also because Belgium has the best of relations with France he had visited the Quai d'Orsay before leaving Europe. There he had given the good news to his friends that he was going to be Ambassador in New Delhi. The reaction was quite cold,

'India does not merit an Ambassador. We shall only be sending a Minister Plenipotentiary.'

In fact many years elapsed before the Charge d'Affaires was replaced by an Ambassador. At that time the French attitude to India was not very friendly and the Charge d'Affaires was told that he should be happy that he had been allotted office accommodation in a prime location. Today, in the twenty-first century, the French Embassy in Delhi is one of the largest French Missions in the world.

With the onset of what we call the 'cold weather' in India and what the French call 'la belle saison', the Lignes were anxious to see Agra, Mussoorie and so on. They invited me to accompany them on these two trips. For Agra, they extended the invitation to the two older Patel daughters. I had been prepared to pay for the hotel accommodation in Agra for the three of us but the

Prince had stationed Meme to make sure I did not do any such thing.

Early in December, H.M.Patel – who was Defence Secretary at this time - announced that he would be driving down to Bombay over Christmas/New Year for Usha's marriage and invited me to join him with my car because his car – a new Chrysler – could not hold all the family. This wedding was the event of the season and was to be attended by my parents (from Ahmedabad), the Home Minister and Deputy Prime Minister of India, Vallabhai Patel, and several other friends of H.M.Patel who would travel long distances to be there.

Pitaji had been getting worried about me. He was delighted that I had returned from eight years abroad with my turban and beard intact and he knew that I would soon be going abroad again on a foreign posting. He was keen that I should get married to a suitable girl, particularly from a Sikh family. I had not shown any interest in girls from the baradri some of whom I had met after many years. Of course, the conditions were very difficult. Many members of the baradri who had been comfortably off in Rawalpindi or Lahore were now living in improvised accommodation, even tents, in Delhi. Some had been ruined and it would take years for them to be rehabilitated. A girl brought up in such conditions might not fit in too well in society in Europe.

Pitaji had heard that there was a Sikh Forest Service Officer in the Bombay cadre who had a very high reputation for honesty and ability and had a pretty daughter. Mr.J.A.Singh - that was how he wrote his name, Jiwan Amrik (his father's name) Singh - was not only a highly competent silviculturist but also a very good administrator. In December 1947 he was posted in the Bombay Secretariat as Director of Civil Supplies. Since so many consumer goods were controlled or rationed in some way, this was an important post. Moreover, it had considerable potential for corruption and Mr. J.A. Singh was above all suspicion. Having come to Bombay for Usha Patel's wedding Pitaji went to the Secretariat, walked into the Office of the Director of Civil Supplies and introduced himself. Of course, J.A.Singh had heard of Pitaji who was some ten years older than him. He immediately invited us all to a buffet dinner he was giving for his sister-in-law and her family.

The drive from Delhi to Bombay had been quite an adventure. Neither the roads in India nor the cars were really suitable for long-distance travel. We had stopped on the way in Gwalior, Indore and Nasik. Gwalior and Indore were princely states and had luxurious guesthouses but Nasik turned out to be rather austere. At a time when the future of princely states was very uncertain, several high officials and prominent persons wanted to see the Defence Secretary. In Indore, for the only time in my life, I saw a man wearing a necklace of egg-sized, uncut emeralds! He was a businessman who had made an enormous fortune speculating in some commodity – probably cotton.

The road was full of potholes. The Chrysler took all these in its stride, suffering only a couple of punctures but the Vauxhall's bottom was quite battered by the time we arrived in Bombay. However, after a day in the workshop it was drivable and I could drive my parents around the city. They were staying with friends in Marine Drive not very far from where H.M.Patel had arranged for me to stay. My main problem was that all the Gujratis involved in the wedding were vegetarians and I had studied Egyptian history so I knew that between the first and twentieth dynasties everybody who had eaten vegetables had died!

I was quite looking forward to the dinner in a Sikh family where I was confident of finding a non-vegetarian meal. The Singhs were living in Rocky Hill Flats overlooking the Arabian Sea on Malabar Hill, one of the most prestigious flats in Bombay. Of course, they did not own it; it belonged to the Government and went with the job. I saw the family for the first time. Mr. Singh was a Sikh of average height, certainly not slim, who did not trim his beard but did try to darken it. Later, I was told that he was rather dark for an aristocratic 'Dhai ghara Khanna'. Let me explain that Khanna is a 'jati' of 'Khatris' and are one of two-and-a-half jatis which are highly considered among non-Jat Sikhs. I have mentioned his rather dark complexion as something which had to be brought to my attention. The reason is that North Indians and Punjabis in particular are very colour-conscious and regard a dark skin as the ultimate ugliness. I, having lived for eight years among white people did not regard a white skin as beautiful by itself. It was fat which still disgusts me.

Mrs. Jiwan Singh (Balbir Kaur) was nearly as tall as her husband and not slim either. She had a good personality, spoke English well and was a good hostess. The son, Harinder, was six feet four inches tall, weighed over four hundred pounds and suffered from leucoderma. This disfigurement had obviously made him very self-conscious and was probably the reason for his obesity. Otherwise, he was strong and healthy; he was about five years younger than me and was reading law. He told my parents that he drove a Harley-Davidson – no other motorcycle would carry his weight. My parents had had a Harley-Davidson so that was common ground between them.

The daughter, Gurkirat Kaur – Kirat to everybody, was sixteen but looked quite a young lady in her salwar kameez (traditional dress of long shirt and baggy trousers). She stood five feet six inches tall and was very slim and pretty. There were few women of that height in Bombay at that time. A Sikh of about my age came up to me, introduced himself as Jagjit and said that he was a Lieutenant in the Army. Later I learnt that he had expressed an interest in Kirat only to be laughed at and told her age at which the parents were not thinking of marriage for her.

My parents got to know quite a lot about our hosts during the course of the evening. Mr. Singh was the eldest of several sons – by two marriages - of a Civil Surgeon. He had been a brilliant student as a result of which he won a scholarship to Oxford from where he had been selected for the Indian Forest Service – this had the same salary scales and prestige as the Indian Service of Engineers to which Pitaji had been appointed at the age of thirty. Because of this and his high caste, he had been offered the eldest daughter of Sardar Bakhshish Singh Butalia, an important landowner in Gujranwala District – now in Pakistan. The name was familiar to Pitaji. A Jhanda Singh Butalia had been a General in Maharaja Ranjit Singh's army and a Butalia had been Tehsildar of Pindighep and a drinking companion of Khazan Singh Malik.

Pitaji invited the Singh family to tea at the Taj Mahal hotel. I got a chance to speak to Kirat. She had passed her Senior Cambridge from Queen Mary's School in Lahore while her brother had been at Aitchison Chiefs' College. These were the schools set up by the British for the children of the landowners in Punjab. Mr. J.A.Singh had given his children the best education available in

India. Kirat was quite talkative and had a sense of humour. She was not interested in higher education but was good at dancing and painting and was taking classes at the J.J.School of Art in Bombay.

Also present in the lounge of the Taj Mahal hotel while we were having tea was another group which appeared to be headed by an elderly Sikh. Pitaji recognised him as Sant Singh who had been a member of the Central Legislative Assembly before Independence and went over to speak to him. He came over and was introduced to us. He had been employed by Mataji's father as a tutor for his two sons. He had read law after that and made a fortune as an advocate in the new district town of Lyallpur in west Punjab. He was interested in politics and had got himself elected to the Central Legislative Assembly. Sikh politicians in those days used to belong either to the Chief Khalsa Diwan or the Akali Party. The Chief Khalsa Diwan represented the interests of the landowners and generally supported the British government. The Akali party was quite radical but was mainly interested in Sikh problems. Sant Singh called himself a 'nationalist Sikh' and often supported the Congress Party so Pandit Nehru thought well of him.

My parents went back to Ahmedabad after this tea while I stayed on in Bombay till H.M.Patel could finish paying the bills for the wedding and we could go back together. In this time, the Singhs invited me to go to the cinema with them. There was no chance for me to talk to Kirat but Mr. Singh talked to me about my career and what I expected to be doing. I realised that there was no possibility of my talking to Kirat alone.

When we got back to Delhi, I found that my tactics had worked out and I was being posted to Brussels as Third Secretary. I wanted this not only because of the French language but because I knew that Belgium was the European country which had the least problems of rationing and restrictions – most countries like France and England had had extensive war damage which Belgium had been spared. Besides, the Belgian Government believed in a liberal economy.

I immediately wrote to Mataji saying I was interested in marrying Kirat and that she could start negotiations. A week or ten days later, on a Saturday, I got the answer that my letter had arrived at the same time as a letter from Mrs. Singh proposing the name of her youngest sister. This letter had said, inter alia,

'It has not been the custom among us that girls should be seen by their prospective husbands before marriage. However, we gather that you think differently and we are willing to comply. My sister is living with our parents in Poona and if you and your son will go there, a meeting can be arranged.'

Mataji had immediately replied,

'Thank you for your kind offer but none of us have seen your sister. On the other hand we have all seen your daughter Kirat and are delighted with her. In fact, Gunwant has written to me to ask you for her hand. The matter assumes some urgency because he has been selected for posting to Brussels and will be leaving India at the end of the month and we would like to celebrate the engagement before he leaves, if you are agreeable.'

Mataji's letter went on to say that an affirmative reply had been received and asked for my travel plans.

As I have mentioned, this letter arrived on a Saturday. I realised that in the prevailing conditions, Tayaji would expect to be informed of this event. On Sunday morning, I was going to my car when I saw Tayaji arrive in his car accompanied by his youngest son Daljit and, of course, his driver. I may mention that Daljit (1925-2005) was handicapped because he had osteomyelitis as an adolescent and had an open wound in his right leg so that he could not wear normal shoes. Besides, from time to time, the wound would become infected and he could not walk till it had been treated. I said to Tayaji,

'I was just going to see you to tell you about my engagement.'

'Does your father know about this engagement?'

'Yes, indeed. I can show you the letter from my mother which contains the news.'

'I see; I came with a proposal.'

Naturally, I cut him off before he could give me any details about the proposal he had come with. However, there were to be consequences which none of us could foresee.

I have described how accommodation had been provided for the Belgian Ambassador in Delhi. The groundwork had been done by the Consul General in Calcutta talking to the protocol department in the Ministry with a very little help from me. India had no one in Brussels to help. Finally, I think Prince de Ligne found some one who offered to find a house which would serve both as residence and office for the Charge d'Affaires – we were not thinking of finding an Ambassador for Belgium.

The Charge d'Affaires had been selected. It was B.F.H.B.Tyabji. He belonged to the Tyabji family which I have mentioned – B stood for Badr-ud-Din which was also the name of his great grandfather, hence the second B. Like most of the Tyabji family, his patriotism was unquestionable but Partition and the Delhi riots had been difficult. At one stage, he and his wife Suraya had had to take shelter in the house of a Hindu friend. He was an I.C.S.Officer and had served in Punjab and as Collector of Customs in Karachi while Pitaji was there but, somehow, they had never met and he was unaware of the friendship between his first cousin once removed Salman and Pitaji. His English colleagues were surprised by his opting for India – they thought that it was unnatural for a Muslim not to prefer Pakistan.

Anyway, I had the feeling that he was not particularly happy about having a Sikh as Third Secretary. He has written his autobiography in which I have been mentioned very favourably but he does say that both he and his wife were amused by my appearance until they got to know me better. I think he was about twelve years older than me and they had two sons and a daughter, Laila, who was born just before they left India.

Telegrams were exchanged between the presumptive landlord in Brussels and the Ministry in Delhi. The house in fact belonged to a lady whose nationality of birth I never found out but she was the widow of a British diplomat, Sir Constantine Phipps. He had apparently bought the house before the Great War, telling her she would be quite safe as Belgium was a neutral country by ratified agreement between the Great Powers. Of course, the Germans invaded Belgium soon after he died. At some time she had been married to a Brazilian and her affairs were looked after by her middle-aged son named Gomez Brandao. I got the impression that he was pleasant, polite and spoke several languages but had never worked in his life. The exchange of telegrams was unfruitful because nobody in the Ministry could understand the French words for 'meter rental' and French or Belgian laws about leasing were totally different from the English laws we were used to.

In the meantime, Mahatma Gandhi was assassinated in Delhi on 30th January 1948 and, of course, national mourning was declared. I left shortly afterwards for Bombay where the engagement ceremony was held in the flat of the Singhs in the presence of my parents. It was then that I got to know what had happened when Mataji's letter had arrived.

'We were stunned', said Mrs. Singh, 'because we had never thought of Kirat getting married; she was too young. We put the letter in the wardrobe while we discussed what to do. Kirat was away at her art class. When she came in, we asked her to look at the letter. She did but it was in Gurmukhi in which she is not very proficient and we had to help her to understand it. Her comment was, 'Well, why not?' We asked how she could think of leaving us so soon but she thought she could.'

XIII

BELGIUM 1948-50

I flew off to London all by myself, picked up my new car an MG 1.25 litre saloon and drove to Brussels where I was the house guest of Antoine de Ligne in the family's *pied-a-terre* in the Square de Meeus. Mr. Tyabji had already arrived alone and was staying in the Hotel Cosmopolite. He was to have an official car, a Humber Pullman limousine as supplied to Indian Heads of Mission but this had not yet arrived so I drove him around. He told me he had bought an M.G. 2.5 litre convertible just before the war and had only recently sold it off.

The staff was arriving in instalments. A Second Secretary, V. S. Charry, was expected to arrive with his wife and baby daughter. We went to occupy the house in Boulevard St. Michel. It turned out to be a twenty-five metre wide townhouse which had been divided into two. The bigger portion was fourteen metres wide and was the Legation of the Union of South Africa! Dr. Verwoerd had not yet declared apartheid and we still had a Mission in Pretoria but relations were quite strained. However, good personal relations were established with the South Africans.

The living room on the ground floor was made into the Chancery of the Embassy. The house was deep and there had been a small sitting room in the front which became Mr. Tyabji's office while the rest of us, the two secretaries, the stenographers, the cypher assistant and the office boy occupied the long dining room – it was really quite inconvenient.

There was a good drawing room on the first floor which became the Tyabjis' living room but, again, there was no proper dining room for giving sit-down dinners as are expected in an Embassy. The Tyabjis had their bedrooms on the second floor – the kitchen was in the basement.

I soon found a boarding house in which I was given the second floor. Actually, what I had was a huge bedroom. The bed was in front, and the back of the room overlooking the garden was furnished as a sitting room. I had my own bathroom and had meals with the family and two other boarders on the ground floor. It reminded me of my boarding house in Goethestrasse in Hamburg nine years earlier except that I had much more room and really appreciated having a bathroom to myself. However, once again, it was quite unsuitable for entertaining.

What surprised Mr. Tyabji and me was that, just before the War, France had been much cheaper than England and Belgium had been cheaper still but now we found Brussels nearly twice as expensive as England. The World War had caused much more inflation on the Continent than in England and the post-war exchange rates had been so fixed that Allied troops could not deprive the civilian population by buying scarce goods cheaply.

Tyabji asked me to speak to the Deputy Chief of Protocol to ask him to help us to find appropriate affordable accommodation as we had done for the Belgians in New Delhi. I was told that the Belgian Government neither owned nor controlled property – except for its own use – so there was nothing they could give us. But could we not be helped, I asked.

'Well, no, it would be embarrassing. There are, for instance, Belgian diplomats who are serving abroad and might like to let out their houses or flats. However, if I were to put you in contact with them, I could be accused of corruption for misusing my official position to act as a house agent. It would also be embarrassing for my colleagues, the diplomats abroad.'

The point was that we were still living in a colonial society with a controlled economy and could not understand the situation in a democratic country with a market economy.

I had never lived in Southern India and my Downing friend Raja Raman had never explained the intricacies of Southern society to me. My new colleague, Charry as I started calling him, was an

Oxonian and realised immediately that I did not understand his name. He explained that Charry is the Tamil version of Acharya (teacher in Sanskrit, a word understood by everybody in India) and is used as a suffix by many Brahmins to show off their high caste. For instance, he explained,

The Acting Governor General of India's name is Chakravarty Rajagopalachari. This translates literally into English as 'Emperor King Cowherd Professor'! The Hindu God Krishna was a cowherd by caste and Krishna is a fairly common name in Northern India. If he had been born there he would probably have been called 'Rajkrishan Pandit'. My given name is Siddhartha and the V represents my father's name 'Venkata''.

So, of course, we call each other Siddhartha and Gunwant to this day (2006).

Siddhartha also told me that his father was a barrister and practised law in Malaya where he was the Legal Adviser to the Sultan of Johore. Since there were no appropriate schools in Johore at that time, his father had sent him to a small public school in England from where he had gone to Oxford and ended up as a Master at the Doon School. He had applied for the I.F.S. and was selected. He further explained that his father had become interested in Buddhism – which many Hindus recognise as a form of Hinduism but not subject to domination by the Brahmins. In fact, I knew that the Hindu Law applies to Buddhists, Jains, Sikhs and four Shia Muslim 'castes'. His father had, therefore, given him the name Siddhartha which is one of the names of the Buddha. However, he had received his primary education from a Brahmin priest and was a practising Brahmin; he was proficient in Sanskrit in addition to Latin which he had learnt at school in England. The family spoke Tamil at home but lived in the princely state of Mysore so they were bilingual in Tamil and Kannada – the official language of Mysore state.

I also found that his wife, Andal, who was remarkably light-skinned, was the daughter of a Mysore Civil Servant – Mysore and Baroda were the only states to have a civil service on the lines of the I.C.S. and as good. Andal spoke English as well as any of us and we all felt at home in each other's company except that Andal was a vegetarian and Siddhartha preferred to avoid meat as far as he could without embarrassing his host or hostess.

By now we had all realised that although we might belong to the upper middle class in India or in England where Tyabji, Siddhartha and I had all lived for several years, and were accepted by the Belgian aristocracy, we were in fact quite poor. I had a car because Pitaji had generously given me its predecessor but the Charrys did not – They had a child instead. Siddhartha was able to get a loan from the Government of India to buy a car and he was able to maintain it by doing without a maid. We had to have a maid because Kirat was still learning how to cook! Of course, when the Charrys arrived in late February, I was still unmarried. I used to take them out to the countryside in my car. All that Spring and Summer I met many people in Brussels either through my work or through Antoine who was very generous in inviting me to Beloeil where I met several of his friends and relations. In this way I got to know the Belgian aristocracy; I even became well acquainted with the Almanach de Gotha of which I found several volumes in the library at Beloeil.

Before the Great War, the Gotha had been required reading for all diplomats – most of whom were Europeans – but it is no longer an annual publication and many of today's Ambassadors have probably never heard of it. As I write this, I have before me the 'Gothaischer Genealogischer Hofkalendar nebst diplomatisch-statlichem jahrsbuche 1905.' It is the hundred and forty-second edition published by Justus Perthes in Gotha – hence the name. I bought it in this century in a second-hand bookshop in Bonn.

It is illustrated with pictures of the Grand Duke and Grand Duchess of Saxony – both quite young and good-looking, the Prince of Solms-Baruth and the Foreign Minister of Russia who happened to be a German Count. It contains Protestant, Roman Catholic, Jewish and Mohammedan calendars and the times of sunrise and sunset in various European cities.

The main body of the work contains the genealogies of Europe's ruling families in alphabetical order in the first part. The second part contains details of the German mediatised families. The third part contains genealogies of other princely and ducal families of Europe – if I remember right some families were selected each year and described in detail. This takes up 482 pages. After this come 640 pages containing information and statistics about various countries including colonies of the European powers and North and South American republics – such information is published today in various yearbooks. Finally, there is an appendix containing dates - national days, birth and accession days of various rulers etc..

A hundred years ago it was an essential book because the vast number of U.N. publications available today did not exist. However, by the time I got to Belgium all it had was a snob appeal – 'My aunt's name appears in this year's Gotha.' For the lesser aristocracy, there was a Gotha of Counts. Politically, the Belgian nobility was no longer important. Of course, there was no bar to a nobleman standing for election and as some of them were rich, they had scope for various activities which did not provide a comfortable livelihood - like the Armed Forces or Diplomacy but these were equally available to the much larger number of wealthy bourgeois.

Among the latter and the middle class, there were various jokes about impoverished noblemen working as headwaiters; I met a Hungarian with a famous name who was a cellarer. Or people would say, 'He has a 'de' in his name as in 'pomme de terre''. Still, there was a certain social value to a title. In fact, there was an annual publication called 'Le High Life de Belgique' which many Belgians liked to see their names in because it contained so many aristocratic names also.

Tyabji associated me with much of his work, taking me to accompany him on the calls he had to make on Belgian Ministers and on foreign Heads of Mission. Of course, my rather better knowledge of French was helpful to him on these occasions. In the office, I dealt with administrative problems like hiring of local staff and negotiating leases. As I have explained, the property in Boulevard St.Michel was particularly inconvenient for the Tyabji family and he soon found a house for himself and another for the Chancery in the Avenue Franklin Roosevelt which was a new development with more modern houses. There was a problem about persuading the Indian Ministry of Finance to approve the expenditure which appeared high in New Delhi. However, there were a number of conferences in Brussels which were attended by Secretaries to the Government of India and they were able to see conditions for themselves. That helped to obtain the necessary approvals.

He also assigned subjects to Siddhartha and me to study and write reports about for sending to the Government of India. Because of my experience in British industry, I did a study of Belgian industry which was circulated to several offices in New Delhi. Pitaji happened to go to one such office in connection with his work in Ahmedabad. The person he was meeting asked him if he was related to the secretary in Brussels whose report had been sent by the 'Ambassador there'. I did another on the Catholic Church in Belgium and its missionary activity abroad. This was relevant because a Belgian missionary had just returned on leave from India and written an article about our country in which he said that Hindus performed 'human sacrifices'. Siddhartha was dealing with the press and saw the article which resulted in our refusing a visa for this missionary until he had written a more favourable article and had it published.

For this study I went to the office of the Primate of Belgium, the Archbishop of Malines, and asked the clergyman who received me,

'Monseigneur, how is it that Belgium with its comparatively small population sends so many more missionaries abroad than other Roman Catholic countries?'

'The Grace of God descends upon the earth without regard for manmade frontiers.'

One of the problems we faced in dealing with the press and even with individuals was that everybody referred to us as 'hindou' while we insisted that we were 'indiens'. It was objected that the latter word was used for American Indians who objected to being called 'peaux rouges' (redskins). Some years later (in 1954) I was an observer at the Third Inter-American Indigenous Congress in La Paz, Bolivia where the word 'AMERINDIAN' was adopted.

Our problem arose from the fact that the Academie Francaise in its dictionary had called Indians 'hindous', relegating Hindus to the word 'hindouiste'. The influence of the French language in all countries where languages of Latin origin are spoken was enormous. Throughout Latin America, in the fifties, before I became fluent in Spanish, I was able to get on in Society with French. In all those countries I had to explain that I was not a 'hindou'. As one can imagine, Tyabji with his memories of the massacre of Muslims in Delhi in 1947, was quite unhappy to be referred to as 'hindou'. It has taken a lot of effort by our Embassy in Paris to get this situation corrected. However, I must mention that there was a Shia Muslim judge of the Bombay High Court – M.C.Chagla - who was fluent in French and became Minister of External Affairs who used to say, 'Je suis hindou.'

I took leave in early September to get married and flew to Bombay. Members of the Ligne family were travelling from time to time between Brussels and Delhi. At this time, Yola (as everybody called Yolande) had to travel to India and so she took the same flight and I was asked to look after her. I had been seeing her in Delhi and in Brussels. I had introduced Kirat to the Lignes in Bombay where they happened to be visiting at the time of my engagement. We had to change planes in Geneva where her brother-in-law (her sister Margot's husband) the Marques de Villalobar y Guimarraes was Spanish Military Attaché. I never understood why the Military Attaché of the Spanish Embassy in Berne should reside in Geneva. It was the first time I was meeting him. He gave us lunch in his apartment. We were to see a great deal of each other many years later in Madrid.

In September 1948, Mr. J.A.Singh had become Conservator of Forests in Poona so the marriage was to take place there. Pitaji hired a house in Poona and rented a railway compartment with twenty berths to bring our relations from Delhi to Poona. The wedding took place on the 15th of September. I could not get enough leave for a honeymoon so we were just a couple of days in Bombay before taking the flight to Brussels via Geneva.

With Kirat's arrival in Brussels, my social position improved still further. She was dubbed an 'Indian beauty'; in fact, both Suraya Tyabji and Andal Charry were very good looking but Suraya was only four feet seven inches tall and Andal was no more than five feet two and they both wore chappals without heels whereas Kirat in high heeled shoes stood out at parties. We travelled quite a lot at weekends driving not only in Belgium but even to Holland and France. In the summer of 1949, we took ten days' leave and drove to Switzerland.

The Tyabjis were also fond of travelling. In fact, they went off to Austria and Switzerland on a holiday in the Humber Pullman with their three children.

1948 Poona The studio photograph after the wedding

In 1948, there was a new development in India. Vallabhai Patel was Deputy Prime Minister and also Home Minister. In addition, he was also Minister for States. This was a department peculiar to India. Before Independence one third of the territory of India was ruled by Princes with various titles. In fact, their rule was carefully watched by Residents and Agents from the political department as I have mentioned earlier. Each of these five hundred odd Princes had a *sanad* – a treaty with the Crown Representative (who was no other than the Viceroy). The bulk of these states fell to India's share. The Crown Representative wrote to each of them abrogating the sanad – thus, in fact, setting them free. Obviously India could not tolerate several hundred foreign countries within its geographical area. Vallabhai Patel demonstrated Talleyrand's ability in dealing with them so that they accepted 'privy purses' and something like diplomatic or parliamentary immunity and gave up all their ruling rights.

In the course of these negotiations, it was suggested on behalf of the Princes that some of them might be suitable for the Indian Foreign Service and about a dozen were accepted. They did not all serve till the age of superannuation, finding government service rather restrictive. One of those who did serve till superannuation was Surendra Sinh, Raja of Alirajpur. He was posted in the Office of the Chief Controller of Imports and Exports for some months to learn about the routine of Government service and then he arrived in the Embassy in Brussels with his wife Babli, his 1.5 litre Jaguar car and an Indian servant.

I have mentioned Vallabhai Patel's success with the Princes. One Prince he did not succeed with was the Nizam of Hyderabad who was advised by his Prime Minister Mir Laik Ali not to accept integration with India. The 'police action' led by General Chaudhry put paid to that while I was in India for my wedding. My friend Russi Boga was appointed Collector of Hyderabad.

In Brussels we took over the lease of the Lignes' pied-a-terre in Square de Meeus while they moved to a bigger flat higher up in the same building. Our first home had a bedroom, a dining room to seat six and a living room which was, of course, also my library. We had a part-time maid so we could give lunch parties but most of our entertaining was done at cocktail parties for which we would get a waiter to serve the drinks.

I was being advised by my batch-mates in Delhi that I should be senior to Siddhartha by virtue of my war service and I should not be a Third Secretary while he was a Second Secretary. He was a few months older than I and his appointment had been made on that account. I was promoted to Second Secretary with retrospective effect but I was still junior to him because it would have been embarrassing to reverse our positions. It was some years before a new seniority list was published making me senior to him. All these details did not affect our personal relations or our work in the office.

Tyabji managed to organise an official meeting with the Government of India's representative in Berlin. Berlin was a curious Mission which existed because of the important part that the Indian army had played in the World War. Our representative had to be a General who was accredited not to any German personality but to the quadripartite Allied *Magistrat* which was ruling Berlin. An I.C.S. Officer, Khub Chand, who was a Deputy Secretary in the Defence Ministry had been selected for the I.F.S. and arrived in Berlin in the uniform of a Major General.

Neither his figure nor his bearing were those of an Army Officer. His Secretary dubbed 'official secretary' was my batchmate Ishi Rahman.

Ishi had broken off his engagement to Ingrid Hydari to marry an Indonesian of Eurasian race who had come to New Delhi in President Soekarno's entourage. India had played an important part in the Indonesian freedom struggle and a wealthy Oriya businessman, Biju Patnaik, who flew his own aeroplane had been Soekarno's pilot while he was fighting the Dutch. Pandit Nehru felt very close to 'Bung Karno' so he was delighted when he was told that Ishi was not marrying Ingrid but Tania and he was a guest at the wedding which took place in Delhi according to Indonesian Muslim rites – Tania insisted on washing Ishi's feet during the ceremony which Indian Muslim brides do not do.

In fact Tania was older than Ishi and had been married twice before. Her first husband had been a wealthy Chinese businessman by whom she had a daughter named Mai Ling. This marriage had ended in a divorce. She had then married a Eurasian Protestant police officer who had played a part in fighting the Japanese occupation of Indonesia and been killed in the process so she was regarded in Indonesia as a 'war widow'. She had a daughter by this marriage also.

We arrived in Berlin by air during the siege of Berlin and Kirat and I were houseguests of Ishi and Tania. There were three daughters in the family of whom, of course, only the youngest was Ishi's.

On his next visit, Tyabji took Surendra Alirajpur with him to Berlin. General Khub Chand had just got a Buick as his official car and regarded it as an invaluable asset. In India, the bourgeoisie regarded a Buick as the height of automobilistic ambition while the landed aristocracy preferred English cars. As I have mentioned earlier, Officers like Pitaji who had to tour extensively on country roads used American cars because they were sturdier but could only afford Fords or Chevrolets. Tyabji who had a private fortune and could afford to buy a car to his taste preferred convertibles. When Khub Chand suggested that the Buick should not be taken along a certain minor road, Tyabji said,

'Oh, don't worry. Surendra has a stable full of Buicks and he uses them to shoot tigers.'

In fact, in 1949, Surendra used to get depressed every time he got a letter from Alirajpur saying that a villager had been eaten by a tiger. He felt that he was not doing his duty of protecting his subjects from tigers.

In the twenty-first century, one can land in jail for shooting a tiger.

One family we saw a good deal of in Brussels were called May. They were Jews by race but practising Roman Catholics. I think Madame May was related to the French Rothschilds. Paul May had joined the Belgian Foreign Service. He had risen to be Minister Plenipotentiary in China at a time when it was considered inappropriate for European diplomats to take their wives to that country. He had brought back a large quantity of Chinese silk brocade from China. After China, he was appointed Ambassador in Washington and Eugene de Ligne had been his Counsellor. He had died in Washington and Mme. May had returned with her two daughters to Brussels. She had looked long and hard for a house where there would be closets and bathrooms attached to every bedroom as was the custom in the United States. Such things were unknown in Belgium. She was shown one house where the agent took her to a room, saying,

'This is the study-cum-bathroom of Monsieur le Comte.'

Finally, she had bought a house of appropriate size and had it remodelled with a closet and a bathroom for each bedroom. She had also used the Chinese brocade as wallpaper for the three reception rooms. I was introduced to the daughters by Antoine de Ligne and had dinner at their house several times. The daughters had managed to escape to England after Belgium was occupied by the Germans. To get asylum, they had to be interviewed. The Officer who interviewed the elder daughter had, at her suggestion, rung up the Belgian Embassy, but the 'phone had been picked up by a servant who, of course, denied all knowledge of any one called May. The younger one was interviewed by an Etonian who asked,

'Belgian? May? I knew a Belgian boy named May at Eton, but he died.'

'Yes, he was my only brother.'

So both the sisters got asylum. The younger one trained as a nurse and continued to work in that capacity after returning to

Brussels. While I was there, she married a Doctor – not of Jewish race – in the hospital where she was working. Years later, I heard that the marriage had ended in a divorce. The elder one married a French Comte but I think that marriage did not work out either.

With Surendra's arrival as Commercial Secretary, the Embassy in Brussels was becoming too big for Belgium. I think an Embassy had been opened in Brussels in early 1948 only because Belgium had taken the trouble to send an Ambassador to New Delhi. Once opened, it was regarded as a training ground for young diplomats who would then go on to open new Embassies. The time had come for this.

Pandit Nehru was very conscious of the fact that the old 'balance of power' in Europe had to be changed. Even before Independence, as soon as he became Member of the Governor-general's Council for External and Commonwealth Affairs in 1946, he had organised an 'Asian Relations Conference'. An elaborate and colourful opening ceremony had been held for this in December 1946 in the Old Fort of Delhi. I was there with my parents on our way from Bombay to Karachi. Yes, from Karachi, most people who travelled by train to Bombay would go via Delhi because the line from Mirpur Khas to Ahmedabad was a smaller gauge and passed through the Thar desert which could be very hot or very cold – there were no air-conditioned carriages on that line.

At this conference, I saw people in magnificent costumes representing 'countries' – they were not independent and therefore not subjects of International Law – of whose very existence I was not aware such as Tibet, Annam, Malaya, Indonesia and Cambodia. Now that India was independent and had a handful of experienced diplomats he was anxious to reach out to new emerging countries. One he had chosen was Ethiopia. A decade earlier, the Emperor of Ethiopia had won the admiration of most of the world by his resistance to Mussolini's aggression and the dignity with which he had accepted defeat and lived as a refugee in Geneva before being replaced on his throne by British intervention.

When we had met Sant Singh at the Taj Mahal hotel in Bombay in January 1948, he had been on his way back from Addis Ababa where he had gone with a delegation to express India's solidarity with this African country and to explore the possibility of closer relations. Sant Singh who was a refugee in Delhi without any assets was delighted to find any kind of employment since he was in his late sixties and did not think he could resume his earlier highly successful legal career in a new court. His report on Ethiopia had been favourable. There was a prosperous Indian community of Gujrati merchants in Addis Ababa who had established good relations with the authorities. At another social level, there were Indian carpenters who were quite successful. It was said that the Italians had killed off the men of the official and middle classes and the Emperor, as soon as he got back in the middle of the war had prevented the British from carting off Italian civilians to India as 'enemy personnel'. There were therefore Italian carpenters, plumbers, motor mechanics and other skilled workers who had to be replaced by Ethiopians as soon as they could be trained. Indian school teachers of whom there were a few were much appreciated and the Government of India could help to supply them.

As a result of all this, Pandit Nehru had selected Sant Singh to be Ambassador in Addis Ababa. Only the United Kingdom and the Soviet Union had Ambassadors. U.S.A. and France had Embassies but the last was headed by a Charge d'Affaires whom I recognised because he had held the same charge in New Delhi earlier. I was selected to run the Embassy as Second Secretary especially as Sant Singh had no experience of government service or procedures. When I got the news, I was shocked at the idea of leaving Brussels, the most comfortable post in Europe for the wilds of Africa. Of course, I realised that I had to serve wherever the Government sent me. Tyabji wrote to Delhi saying that it would be a waste to send a talented diplomat's wife to a country where presumably women played little or no part in social or official life.

The result was that the Government decided to transfer my friend Avtar Singh who was a bachelor from Cairo to Addis Ababa and to post me to Cairo. Kirat was horrified at this idea. She had vivid memories of the massacre of Sikhs in Lahore in 1947 – Keshadhari Sikhs were immediately recognisable while Hindus could not always be easily distinguished from Muslims – and did not want me to be seen in a Muslim country! Of course,

I knew that no Sikh had been killed in Egypt but, equally, I could not argue with her when her reasoning was essentially emotional. The result was that I was selected for Addis Ababa. Tyabji also felt that I should be happy with a Sikh Head of Mission. As I have said, all this had come as a shock to me.

Yola's engagement to the Archduke Charles had been announced. Who was the Archduke Charles? Austria had never been a kingdom. In the ninth century when the Holy Roman Empire had been created, there had been set up a Council of Electors who had to choose one among themselves to be the Emperor whenever the incumbent died. The identity of the Electors kept changing but the Prince Bishop of Liege and the Archduke of Austria appear always to have been there. Finally, a time came when the Capital of the Empire could no longer be shifted with each new Emperor and it was fixed in Vienna; this was because the Archduke managed to pack the election. Becoming the permanent Emperor he decreed that all his descendants in the tail male should be styled Archdukes. The Austro-Hungarian Empire ended with the Treaty of Versailles after the Great War. The last Emperor went into exile. His successor in 1949 was Robert who maintained his claim and was, therefore, debarred from entering Austria. He spent some time in France where he styled himself Duc de Bar – a title and territory which his ancestors had held centuries earlier in France.

Robert's younger brother Charles had no territorial claims in Austria and was perfectly willing to earn his living. In fact, he found employment with the biggest Belgian bank. It was he who was to marry Yolande. This was a great event for the Ligne family because by the decision of 1806 they had been excluded from intermarriage with the Imperial family. The wedding was attended by and is described in Badr-ud-Din Tyabji's autobiography. To my surprise, Surendra was invited to the wedding but I was not.

Thirty years later, Yola's brother-in-law Villalobar told me that Charles had turned out to be a financial genius and occupied a high position in the Societe Generale de Belgique. More recently, I have read that the Archduke Robert has abandoned his claim to the Austrian throne and is now a citizen of the Republic of Austria. I have never met any member of the Austrian Imperial family.

Since I was to go to Ethiopia and am very fond of driving, I thought this was an opportunity to see a great deal of Europe and North Africa. I put the proposition to my Head of Mission and he agreed that Delhi's permission should be asked. This was done and obtained.

We were now in the month of January 1950 and the Constituent Assembly (of which Badr-ud-Din Tyabji had been the first Joint Secretary) had decided that India would become a Republic – ceasing to be a Dominion – on 26th January so I was asked to stay on for the party. Kirat and I left Brussels the next morning in the M.G. which had no heater. Nor did it have a spray for the windscreen wiper. The weather was freezing and our breath congealed on the inside of the windscreen. Of course, I was wearing my overcoat and Kirat was wearing a duffel coat. We decided to open the windscreen which was designed for that but that did not help. We closed the windscreen but by now the weather had changed slightly and frost was forming on the outside of the windscreen. We had to stop more than once to scrape the frost off the windscreen and the journey to Paris which normally took four hours took much longer. We reached our hotel before dark.

After a day's rest in Paris during which we sought advice for dealing with the windscreen – a thermos of boiling water – we set off and reached a restaurant just after Fontainebleu. The restaurant was warm and we felt comfortable even before the meal arrived. In addition to pictures on the wall, I noticed what looked like a letter. I went to examine it and was pleasantly surprised to read a certificate by King Louis XV saying he had found a good meal and relaxation after hunting.

I was, of course, interested in tourism as much as getting to Naples from where we were to take a ship to Alexandria so I had made hotel bookings along the *route des alpes d'hiver*. This meant driving on snow; fortunately I had done this the previous winter in Belgium so it was no problem. Still we were glad to get to the Fifi Moulin hotel at Serre which we found well equipped with double glazing. Fifi told us that it was the recognised stop for motorists on the route des alpes d'hiver. The food was also satisfying and plentiful. After Serre the weather became less cold or perhaps we had put on more sweaters. To our surprise, when we got to Rome we saw fresh snow which is not very common there.

We had to wait for our ship in Naples so we went to see Pompeii which was very impressive. This was Kirat's first experience of sea travel and as it was winter the Mediterranean was quite rough and she became rather sick. I was able to enjoy the Italian food.

I had been driving the M.G. for two years and had enjoyed its gear-box and good acceleration but the quality of this post-war car was not up to expectation and the engine had given us so much trouble that I had had to have it rebored. After that things had improved and we had a trouble-free drive from Brussels to Naples but on the excellent road from Alexandria to Cairo it stopped. An Egyptian motorist who spoke very good French was able to get it started.

In Cairo we were welcomed by my friend Avtar Singh. He was a bachelor staying in a hotel. He arranged for us to stay with the First Secretary, Abid Hassan Safrani. Safrani was also a bachelor but his sister was living in their spacious flat, keeping house for him. Safrani's history was remarkable. He was from Hyderabad and had gone to Germany for his studies. Of course, he spoke fluent German; he had also developed a taste for wine and beer and this made him a secular Muslim. He was in Germany when the World War broke out and there he had met Subhash Chandra Bose who had appointed him his secretary.

Bose had joined up with the axis powers and tried to create an Indian National Army. He did not have much success because the number of Indians living on the Continent was small and very few of them belonged to 'martial races' or were interested in the Armed Forces. He had tried to recruit among prisoners of war but there were hardly any Indian prisoners of war in Germany or Italy. When Japan entered the war and, within a matter of days, the British Commander-in-Chief in Singapore surrendered, the situation changed dramatically. Hitler agreed to send Bose to Singapore. So Bose and Safrani travelled by U-boat to Singapore which must have been a harrowing experience for the two civilians. They got an enthusiastic welcome from the large Indian communities in South East Asia. Most of these Indians had been taken there by the British as indentured labourers and were very badly treated. These local Indians said:

'When we used to go to any government office, we were not allowed to sit on a chair or even on a bench. Bose told us that Indians were as good as any other race and that we must be self-assertive. "Unless you show self-respect, why should anybody else respect you?" he had said to us.'

This was what many middle-class Indians told me a decade and a half later when I arrived in Singapore. I found all this very strange because I knew that many Indian shopkeepers and merchants had made their way to South East Asia through the ages. Then, again, the British Empire in Asia was a British-Indian Empire with large numbers of Indian Non-Commissioned Officers in the Armed Forces and also Indian clerks, accountants, foremen and supervisors. Then, after the Great War, there were Indian professionals like my friend Siddhartha's father who were educated in England and must have been treated like equals by their British colleagues. I could only infer that these upper class Indians took no interest in their working class fellow-countrymen.

Such people were not likely to make good soldiers but many Indian prisoners-of-war were glad to join the Indian National Army. This was known as the First Indian National Army. The trouble was that Bose had no military experience or tradition – he did not belong to a 'martial race' – and did not know how to treat soldiers so that many Officers and men were unhappy. The First I.N.A. was not a success and there were several deserters – among them my cousin Tony Bhagat.

Then the Japanese decided to use Indian labourers on their civil works – any one who has seen the film BRIDGE ON THE RIVER KWAI will understand what this meant – and Bose was able tell the Indians that, as soldiers, they would get proper food and be looked after by their own Officers. General Harbaksh Singh (the hero of Khemkaran) told me half-a-century later that he had been a Captain and prisoner-of-war in Malaya at that time and had been interviewed by Bose. He had said to Bose,

'We are mercenaries of the British. If we now become unfaithful to them, who will ever want to use us as mercenaries and what will our own morale be like?'

General Harbaksh Singh said that Bose had appreciated this argument and not tried to recruit him. The Second I.N.A. was never a great military force but it became a successful political organisation after the War and in Independent India. The Army was not keen to re-employ its members after Independence but H.M.Patel managed to get Tony Bhagat re-integrated and he retired as a Brigadier.

This digression was to explain Safrani's background. He was not a soldier but he was a very sincere person and had remarkable political instincts. Somehow, he never got married and had a different life style from the rest of us.

The first thing was to get the car fixed. They were able to solve the problem at the Nuffield garage in Cairo –it was the carburettor – but I was not happy at the prospect of the car breaking down on some rough track far from workshops. However, we set out going up the Nile Valley. We had an introduction to an Egyptian gentleman at El Miniah and he and his wife gave us an excellent lunch. They both spoke very good English.

The reason for having lunch with an acquaintance was that there seemed to be no restaurants of the international type. In fact, after El Miniah the road ceased to be paved and became a well-maintained dirt track – the thought of all that dust getting into the carburettor made me even more worried. We had a reservation for a hotel in Assyut but when we got there we were very disappointed. The staff did not speak English and the food was entirely Arabic. I am not adventurous about food and generally eat European or Punjabi food. Everybody at this hotel wore fez caps and this terrified Kirat. She thought that so many visible Muslims were sure to murder me – the fear mentioned earlier. She absolutely refused to go any further so we returned the next day to Cairo and moved into a comfortable European-style hotel where the waiters and the chambermaids spoke fluent French and I ate the best *piccata aux champignons* I have ever eaten.

ADDIS ABABA 1950

We flew from Cairo to Aden and from there to Addis Ababa where we moved into the newly built Ras hotel. Sant Singh and his wife were already there. He had presented his credentials to the Emperor the day before we arrived. It was obvious that Mrs. Sant Singh knew no English at all. She spoke Punjabi - her mother tongue - and Urdu. She was also uncomfortable wearing a sari as she was used to wearing a salwar kameez. In those days, all Indian 'ladies' wore saris when they went abroad. She had solved the problem to the best of her ability by wearing the sari on top of her salwar kameez. She also confessed to Kirat that she was unhappy seeing so many dark-skinned people. 'Why aren't there people here with complexions like Punjabis?', she asked. There were European women staying at the hotel but she made no attempt to try and communicate with them which she could have done using Kirat as an interpreter.

They had taken a Sikh servant with them. Officially, he was a messenger but in fact he was their domestic servant. This was not an usual practice in those days. The Tyabjis had taken two of their servants with them, showing them as office boys. The real problem was about food. Sant Singh ate European food but she would only eat 'Indian food' served by her servant. There were no cooking facilities for the residents in the hotel. They solved the problem by having their food brought to them twice a day by a local Gujrati merchant.

There was, of course, the problem of language. In the hotel, English was enough and so also in the Ministry of External Affairs. Most of the Ministers and high officials spoke very good English although I did come across some of the older ones who were more comfortable in French – one of these was the 'Minister of the Pen' who was said to be the strong man of the Government.

Communication with people in the street, taxi-drivers, shopkeepers and so on was easiest in Italian. Mussolini had not conquered Ethiopia as an economic venture such as India was for the British. He was looking for space for his rapidly increasing population. He wanted territory under his own control rather than have his unemployed emigrating to the United States, Argentina or Venezuela. Correspondingly, Italians had been thick on the ground and their were still thousands of them in Ethiopia. They also had close personal relations with Ethiopians cheerfully sharing their food and drink. A number had taken Ethiopian wives – perhaps common law wives. On the other hand, it was not 'politically correct' to speak Italian. When one asked an official if he spoke Italian as well as he did English, the answer was usually in the negative.

Sant Singh had never been to Europe. I don't think he had any European friends. In fact, I think his visit to Ethiopia in 1948 had been his first trip outside India. He thought that if he saw a European speaking a language which was not English than he must be speaking French. He was not interested in the political significance of Italian which I necessarily used in my conversation with non-official Ethiopians. Obviously, he could only speak with Ethiopians who spoke English.

At the hotel, since I did not have a sitting room, Kirat and I spent a good deal of time in the dining room where we had all our meals. The Government of India was paying for our accommodation but not for our meals which were rather expensive. Sant Singh seldom ate in the dining room and he never entertained. He was fond of whisky and appreciated Scotch. I don't think it ever occurred to him that he should entertain Ethiopians and diplomats while he was still in the hotel and serve them food and drink of their choice.

Of course, we had to rent an Embassy, a Chancery and houses or flats for me, and the non-diplomatic staff. This took time because there were not many suitable houses and flats were not to be found. The British, the French and the Americans had large compounds in which they had built all the accommodation they needed. We could not do that immediately. A house was found for the Embassy which stood in its own grounds and had outhouses which could temporarily accommodate the Chancery. Furniture was a problem. The Government of India was providing rent-free furnished accommodation to its staff abroad. In Europe and in other rich countries such accommodation existed and could be rented but in Addis Ababa landlords had to be persuaded to do so. Sant Singh wanted to do everything as cheaply as possible. Fortunately, he was in constant touch with the Indian merchants – the only people that Mrs Sant Singh could communicate with – and they told him quite firmly that the Indian Embassy staff must maintain the same standard of living as Europeans. It was thanks to them that I was able to buy – for the Embassy – the furniture of a British businessman who was leaving the country – and rent a two bedroom house for us to live in.

We could import goods from shops in Aden which supplied duty free goods to Embassies or Consulates in neighbouring countries and there was an airline flying goods from Aden to Addis Ababa. The surface route meant trans-shipment at Djibouti – where very few ships called – and the expensive French-operated railroad from there. Crockery and cutlery were obtained and I was able to get various supplies for myself in this way. Sant Singh, of course, only imported whisky.

Having found a house, I engaged an Ethiopian cook, a butler and a watchman. The watchman had worked for a Gujrati family so I would speak to him in my very imperfect Gujrati and he would translate to the cook whom Kirat taught the dishes she knew. He had worked with Europeans so that part went very well. The butler spoke enough English for our needs. We were now able to give a cocktail party to which, of course, the Head of Mission and his wife were invited.

While we were still at the hotel, the Emperor had invited the entire Diplomatic Corps to the inauguration of a bridge over the Blue Nile several hundred miles from the Capital. I was very impressed by the arrangements for our transportation. It involved flying several hundred persons in Dakotas to an improvised airstrip and then taking us in a variety of jeeps and cars to the site of the bridge. This was some thousands of feet lower than Addis Ababa (itself about seven thousand feet above sea level) and therefore quite hot. Suddenly I noticed Kirat looking rather agitated and then she collapsed at my feet. She soon recovered when water was splashed on her face. I guessed the reason for this and the next day I took her to the Embassy doctor who confirmed in due course that she was pregnant but we did not tell anybody. Of course, Mrs. Sant Singh who had already expressed her displeasure at Kirat's fondness for ballroom dancing, said this kind of 'publicity' was very improper.

An amusing incident took place shortly after this. One afternoon Kirat told me that she had an irresistible longing for Dundee cake. The Head Waiter at the Ras hotel was an Austrian and had never heard of such a thing. The M.G. was out of action with a broken half-shaft, taxis were hard to find so we took a 'calesa' – something like an Indian Tonga but much more lightly built and without any kind of roof – to go to the area where there were shops catering to the European population. We were very lucky and found a tin of Dundee cake.

It is not that Kirat was unadventurous about food like me. One evening we were invited to dinner by an Ethiopian official. When we got there we found the arrangements were similar to what we were accustomed to in Delhi. There was a buffet laid out with European food and another with Ethiopian food. I made a beeline for the first and helped myself to ham and chicken. Then I saw that Kirat had gone to the other table so I went to see what was going on. She looked at a dish and said,

'Ethiopian curry, I must try that.'

I replied,

'That is not curry; that is raw meat in blood.'

In the meantime, I had come to the conclusion that the Ministry of External Affairs had fixed our allowances on the basis of the prices reported by Sant Singh when he had led the delegation to Ethiopia in 1947. After that, Sterling had been devalued which meant that the Indian Rupee which was linked to the Pound had lost its value in relation to Ethiopian currency (the Maria Theresa Dollar) which preferred to follow the U.S. Dollar. I suggested to the Ambassador that we should write to Delhi to ask for Exchange

Compensation Allowance. Of course, he had never heard of this and his first-class legal mind was slow in understanding financial reasoning. However, he agreed, I made the request and after the normal bureaucratic delay we were given an exchange compensation of 43% on our emoluments.

Everybody in the Embassy was delighted, no one more so than Sant Singh who had wanted this post mainly because he hoped and expected to recoup his losses from Partition. Unfortunately, his appreciation of my initiative did not last long which is the normal course in human affairs. As for me, I found myself saving money for the third time in my life – the previous occasion was when I was serving with the R.A.F. in Germany where there was nothing to buy. About the same time, the Ministry took a decision that all personnel in Missions could take leave after thirty months abroad and I immediately applied for leave.

Leave was granted quite quickly but the funds to pay for air tickets took time to arrive. Kirat was keen to go to her mother as is normal at such a time. Fortunately, I had made friends with one of the Gujrati merchants, Dulu Varia, and he lent the money for the ticket. Dulu Varia was exceptional among the merchants in Addis Ababa because he was the only one to have a college degree – and that too from England. His family which was from Kutch had been trading in Ethiopia for three generations. Of course, they were very well off and he and his elder brother had ideas beyond commerce. The elder brother became a medical practitioner while Dulu took a degree from the London School of Economics. I never met the brother – he was practising somewhere else – but later I learnt that he had a stroke and became completely paralysed so that only the muscles of the eyes were functioning. I was told that he was given a board with the letters of the alphabet on it and his wife could understand what he wanted to say by watching his eye movements. Dulu continued to be my friend as long as he lived.

I mentioned that I met Alan Rowley in Addis Ababa and that he had served in the Indian Army. He was Second Secretary in the British Embassy. When the British Ambassador, a bachelor, gave a dinner for the Indian Ambassador it was Alan who made the arrangements. Having been informed of Mrs. Sant Singh's dietary problems, he arranged for the Sikh servant to serve her usual Indian meal in a thali while the rest of us had a traditional Embassy dinner.

As I have mentioned, we were able to get crockery and cutlery from Aden and once the Embassy had been rented, Sant Singh knew that he had to entertain at least the diplomats whose hospitality he had been enjoying. I expected that since my Ambassador, who was an intelligent man, had seen how dinners were served in other Embassies and how much trouble the British Ambassador had gone to for his guests, he would entertain appropriately. It was the monsoon season and Europeans had fires in their drawing rooms – as much to dispel the humidity as for warmth. The host had lighted a fire but he had not taken the precaution of trying this out beforehand. When the guests arrived, the drawing room was filled with smoke from a height of about four feet upwards so everybody was coughing and conversation was impossible.

There was no fire in the dining room but other pleasures were in store for the guests. The only servant in sight was the Sikh. He was not carrying serving dishes but a tiffin carrier (large multilayered metal lunch box commonly used in India) – where the (Indian) food had come from I do not know – and the guests had to help themselves from its containers. One tiffin carrier proved to be enough for twelve persons because the food was so spicy that neither the Ethiopians nor the Europeans could eat it. For drink there was a choice of whisky or water from the tap. Economy was more important than the needs and tastes of the guests.

Shortly after this, I was able to proceed on leave. Pitaji's contract as Chief Engineer, Ahmedabad Municipality had ended in April and he had gone into partnership with a retired colleague, Newandram Mathrani who had secured a contract for building the 'followers' lines' at Khadakvasla where cadets for the Indian Armed Forces were to receive their preliminary training before going off to the various 'academies' for the Army, the Navy and the Air Force. It is located in a very attractive valley near Poona. A younger colleague of my father, Francis Xavier Mascarenhas had led a delegation to England and U.S.A in late 1945 to look at the military training facilities in those countries. In London he was put up by the Indian High Commissioner at the National Liberal Club and we had recognised each other. Subsequently, he had been given the job of constructing the buildings for the Khadakvasla institution. Of course, the actual construction was done by a number of contractors but Mascarenhas had the overall responsibility.

Newandram Mathrani was one of the seven sons of a Sindhi Amil (a clan of Hindus from Sindh) Schoolmaster. I think three of the sons got into the Indian Service of Engineers while the youngest, Kewalram, made it to the I.C.S. Newandram was in the provincial service and had retired as an Executive Engineer. He had invited Pitaji to be his partner because of his seniority and his friendship with Mascarenhas. The 'followers' lines' were to be the living quarters for the cooks, waiters and other civilian workers of the Khadakvasla institution. Newandram had created a company for this contract and this company had hired a house for Pitaji and was paying him a salary equal to what he had been receiving in Ahmedabad. Kirat and I stayed in this house during most of my two months' leave. Pitaji realised that he was not cut out to be a contractor. To make a profit, a minor contractor has either to live a life of Gandhian austerity or resort to imaginative accounting - practices which were unacceptable to Pitaji.

Pitaji had planned all his life to live in Rawalpindi after retirement. He had bought a plot near where his father lived and, since childhood, I had seen plans for the house lying around whichever house we were living in.

Now, in 1950, all these plans had evaporated; Rawalpindi had ceased to exist as far as we were concerned. The Ministry of Rehabilitation had announced plans for compensating refugees out of the sales proceeds of 'evacuee property' – the property of Muslims who had emigrated to Pakistan. An important Officer in this Ministry was Tarlok Singh whom I have mentioned previously. The quantum of compensation was to be worked out on Nehruvian socialist principles in which Tarlok Singh also sincerely believed. This meant that the richest refugees from West Punjab got about 1% of the value of their loss while those who had only a small hut got full compensation. Of course, this was the theory. In practice, things could be very different. I heard of a middle-aged man who had had a house in Rawalpindi. By the time compensation was physically awarded, he had passed away but his four sons got a house each in New Delhi. Imaginative form-filling and helpful officials can work miracles!

Pitaji was confident that he would get his provident fund, amounting to over seventy thousand rupees, to which he had contributed all his life, from the Government and this would suffice to build a house if he could get land. For this he had even gone to the U.P.Terai. This was an area of dense jungle adjoining Nepal which the Government had thrown open to cultivation. It is now called the Udhamsinghpura district in Uttaranchal after the man who, in 1939, shot dead Sir Michael O'Dwyer in London. Sir Michael was the Lieutenant Governor of the Punjab when Acting Brigadier Dyer had carried out the notorious Jallianwala Bagh massacre and had justified it. To live in the Terai it was necessary to cut down the forest, kill off the wild beasts whose habitat it was and then cultivate the land. Pitaji realised that this work was not for him.

While Kirat and I were in Poona, Pitaji took us all to Bhopal. Bhopal was an important princely state before independence; in fact the Nawab of Bhopal was the second richest Muslim prince – after the Nizam of Hyderabad. He had emigrated to Pakistan taking his family, his jewellery and other valuables in seven Dakotas. As was to be expected, several important Muslim families in Bhopal had followed his example. Therefore there was a good deal of 'evacuee property' for which registered refugees could apply.

However, Mataji was able to persuade Pitaji that as they had only one child and that child, being in the foreign service, could only be posted in New Delhi on the rare occasions when he was not abroad, they could not consider living anywhere but in Delhi.

I am sure at that moment Pitaji must have remembered the letter he had received in 1934 from his cousin Teja Singh Malik. Teja Singh Malik was the son of his elder uncle Mohan Singh Malik and was not much older than my father. They had both been born and had grown up in the same house in Rawalpindi. Later they had both studied engineering in England. Teja Singh had been selected for the Indian Service of Engineers and, in 1934, was serving in the Central P.W.D. in New Delhi. He had been the senior Indian engineer working on the construction of the Viceroy's House since 1911. He wrote, I quote from memory as is the case with most of this book,

'I have decided not to go back to Rawalpindi when I retire in a few years' time but to settle down here in New Delhi where I have been living for over twenty years. I have bought a four-acre plot on which I propose to build my house. The adjoining plot is available and I would be more than happy if you would buy it; it only costs four thousand rupees. If you don't have that amount handy, I can advance it to you.'

Pitaji's reaction was adverse. He discussed the matter with Mataji, saying,

'I can not possibly think of agreeing with our cousin (Teja Singh's wife Raj was a cousin of Mataji's). The very idea of leaving our beautiful Rawalpindi and living among these southerners depresses me.' Mataji agreed so Pitaji sent a polite refusal.

After going to and fro between various government offices, Pitaji managed to get a plot of land in a new development adjoining Nizamuddin village. When the plots had been demarcated and allotted the address was A-21 Nizamuddin West. It faced Mathura Road – the main highway of India connecting Delhi to Calcutta – across a small park. When Pitaji mentioned this to his cousin Iqbal Singh , his reaction was, 'Oh, yes, I used to go there to shoot partridge.' This conversation took place in 1951. Today, in the twenty-first century, 'hunting' is forbidden all over India and it is many years since I saw a partridge in the open.

I left Poona towards the end of November (1950). Of course, this journey was performed by train via Bombay where I left Kirat in the care of her mother who had made a booking for the delivery of the baby in the best maternity clinic. In New Delhi I stayed with H.M.Patel for several days before the 'Estate Officer' could find me accommodation. H.M.Patel had moved across the road from 1, Safdarjung Road to a bigger house (as he was entitled to, having become Defence Secretary) at 11 Roberts Road. This house had a guest room separated from the main house by a porch where cars deposited and picked up passengers. I was in this room when I got the telegram early one morning that a baby boy had been safely delivered. Kiran (Kiran Bir Singh Malik) was born on 11th December, 1950.

Before the end of my leave, I had made a short trip to Delhi. I had realised in Addis Ababa that I was not getting on with my Head of Mission although I was convinced, modest as I am (!), that there could not be a better Secretary of Embassy than I. As a precaution, I had written a letter to H.M.Patel. During this visit I learnt that the precaution had been very timely. I also met my successor, Rajkumar Raghunath Sinha of Sitamau. Raghunath was a few years older than I. He was a Cambridge graduate and the younger brother of the Raja of Sitamau - a princely state in Rajasthan. He had been serving as his brother's Chief Minister when he was selected for the foreign service. He had a private income. We agreed to keep in touch.

I wrote and told Raghunath of the birth of a baby boy. A few weeks later, I got a letter from him,

'I mentioned to the Ambassador and his wife that you had become the father of a son. I was very surprised when Mrs. Sant Singh exclaimed in Punjabi,

'Our Kanwal only had a daughter.''   It was after receiving this letter that I made enquiries and found that the offer of a bride for me (the proposal mentioned earlier) concerned Sant Singh's daughter and this was the reason for his giving me a bad 'confidential report'. Later, when the question of granting an extension to Sant Singh came up, Tyabji who had to deal with this case told me he had written on the file that this Head of Mission seemed difficult to get on with because he had complained about two secretaries who were of different ages and backgrounds and who had been reported on favourably by other Officers under whom they had served. Sant Singh did not get an extension or another Embassy much as he wanted and tried to.

DELHI – UNDER SECRETARY IN THE MINISTRY OF EXTERNAL AFFAIRS 1950-52

In Delhi, I was appointed Under Secretary for South East Asia, a region of which I had no experience. My charge did not include Burma (now Myanmar) which because of its importance to us at that time – it had been a province of India till 1934 and still had a substantial Indian population – had an Under Secretary all by itself. He occupied the room next to mine and was named K.R.Narayanan. He was a few months older than I and was a bachelor; I think he was staying with an uncle and aunt who were both Members of Parliament.

In view of Narayanan's exceptionally brilliant subsequent career, I think I should say something about him. He was from Kerala and belonged to a 'scheduled caste'. This is the constitutional name for those who had previously been known as untouchables and for whom the Constitution of India has created reservations in legislative bodies and in government posts. Much has been written in the press about the poverty and deprivation of Narayanan's childhood. I find this rather hard to believe. I read recently that he has donated 'his ancestral house with several acres of land to charity'. Besides, if one is the nephew of two Members of Parliament, that surely entitles a person to belong to the 'creamy layer'.

As far as I am concerned, I always found him to be a loyal, friendly and very polite colleague. His wife is a Burmese – he was posted to Rangoon (now Yangaon) shortly after I met him – and changed her name to 'Usha'. As I said, his career was unprecedented. He became, in due course, Ambassador to Washington, Vice President of India and retired as President and earned everybody's respect in all these high charges. He honoured me by coming to a party I gave while he was Vice President.

In my charge of South East Asia, I had two 'sections', one was called Malaya and the other included Australia, New Zealand and whatever is known in the geography books as South East Asia. The Malaya section also dealt with Emigration. This is a long and painful chapter in Indian history and in Indian bureaucratic jargon an emigrant is *not* 'a person who leaves his own country in order to settle permanently in another' as in the 'The New Oxford Dictionary of English'.

In the nineteenth century, British planters in several colonies found that the natives were not able or willing to do agricultural labour on a regular daily basis – in several countries the tradition was that agriculture, if any, was done by women while the men hunted or fished. British tea, rubber, opium and indigo planters in India were finding Indian agricultural labour very satisfactory. The result was that 'indentured labourers' were leaving India in tens if not hundreds of thousands for Malaya, Fiji, Ceylon, the West Indies and several other countries. They were, in fact, replacing the slaves whom Pitt and Wilberforce had emancipated. The conditions of their travel and work in the countries they went to horrified not only the Indian public but also the British Parliament. In 1922, the Indian Emigration Act was passed. Effectively, it prohibited the 'departure by sea' of any unskilled worker and all agricultural work was classified as unskilled. 'Skilled workers' – there was a list of specified skills - had to have contracts drawn up according to rules laid down for the purpose. There were 'protectors of emigrants' in the ports to check these contracts and make sure the worker understood it. Finally Representatives and Agents were posted in the receiving countries to whom aggrieved workers could complain. The Joint Secretary under whom I worked was the Controller General of Emigration and all these officials in the ports and abroad reported to him.

I found from the files that some decades earlier my predecessor had decided that 'any work which is not classified as skilled and, in point of fact is not unskilled is not work at all for the purposes of the Act'. This freed the professional and managerial classes from the Act. This genius had signed his note as 'G.S.Bajpai, Under Secretary'. In 1950-51, Sir Girja Shunker Bajpai was Secretary General of the Ministry of External Affairs and Commonwealth Relations.

I thought I would do something similar for Indians in Singapore who were having difficulties because they were being treated as foreigners. I consulted the Law Ministry and wrote to the Representative of the Government of India (R.G.I.) in Singapore that under the British Nationality Act 1948, Indians were Commonwealth citizens and, as such, indistinguishable from British subjects. The relief of the R.G.I., Singapore was short lived. Pandit Nehru found out what had happened was furious at being classified as a British subject, and had a letter written to the High Commissioner of the United Kingdom. Of course, this also adversely affected the emigration of Indian skilled workers to the United Kingdom.

After a year at the South East Asia desk, I was transferred to the post of Under Secretary (Administration) where I succeeded my friend Jagat Mehta. The work gave me administrative control of all the staff in the Ministry below the level of Under Secretary. Of course, this only related to leave, transfer, promotion and so on; their work was not my concern.

At that time all this staff belonged to the Central Secretariat Service and it was felt that a separate cadre should be created of staff who could be rotated between the Ministry and the Missions and Posts abroad. This meant weeding out those who did not want to go abroad and those whom the Ministry wanted to exclude – generally because they had more than two children since neither the accommodation nor the allowances would suffice for them. Necessarily, it would mean recruiting large numbers of new staff since the Ministry was expanding and new missions were being opened. Many of those we recruited had worked in the tribal areas of Baluchistan and the North West Frontier Province – that is to stay they had been subordinates of the Indian Political Service Officers and therefore had a claim on the successor service.

All this was done by setting up a committee of which I was the secretary. Finally, I was given the authority to recruit 'clerks'. In the meantime, the way of working in the secretariat was changing.

Before Independence, most of the Under Secretaries were British and, therefore expensive. A file could only be opened by a Section Officer who would authorise an Assistant to write the first note on the incoming letter which usually started any file. The file would then travel upwards. I heard a story about an Assistant's note which was so good that none of the officers could add anything until the Viceroy drew an arrow to the note and wrote,

'I agree with him also!'

With Independence, more Under Secretaries were appointed, more stenographers' posts were created and there was an increasing need for copy-typists because approved drafts were being held up in the 'typists' pool'. The committee approved the creation of four posts of typist-clerks and I sent off a requisition to the Employment Exchange.

The following Saturday morning, a Sikh walked into my office, He was probably five years younger than I, a couple of inches shorter and wearing a tweed coat and contrasting trousers just like me; the only difference was that his clothes were tailor-made by the neighbourhood durzi whereas mine were the mass-produced 'demob kit' issued by the British Air Ministry. He announced that he had come from the Employment Exchange in response to my requisition.

'Oh, that is very good. What is your typing speed?'

'Sir, I don't type.'

'Oh, I am sorry. We urgently need typists but no non-typing clerks.'

'Sir, you have got to take me, I am a graduate.'

'Congratulations, but I still only have jobs for typists.'

'Sir, you have to take me, I am a scheduled caste.'

'Don't give me that! You are a Sikh like me and we don't have castes.'

'Sir, please make enquiries. There are four scheduled castes among the Sikhs.'

I was shocked. In those days we used to work half day on Saturdays. After lunch I drove several miles to Rajpur Road in Old Delhi where Tayaji had a bungalow – he had exchanged it with a Muslim lawyer who had emigrated to Pakistan. Pitaji was staying with him. I told them my story. Pitaji had not lived in Punjab for many decades but Tayaji was a lawyer with political ambitions. He said that, in the twenties, Sikh missionaries had converted a number of untouchables. Then a brilliant untouchable Mahrashtrian lawyer, Dr. Ambedkar, had started agitating for his fellows and had persuaded the British government to create reservations for them in government service. The new Sikhs had converted back to Hinduism to avail of these reservations! This was how Sikh politicians had agreed to, indeed insisted on, the creation of Sikh scheduled castes. Later, I discovered that the Indian Army which only accepted Jat Sikhs in the 11ᵗʰ Sikh Regiment had a regiment of Mahzbi Sikh Light Infantry. Apparently earlier Ranjit Singh's army had had Jat cavalry and Mahzbi infantry; at least my great grandfather had been a cavalryman!

I remember that, at that time, I was very upset. I knew very well that there were rich Sikhs and poor Sikhs, highly educated Sikhs and those who could just about read but I was not at all aware that – as it turned out – there were high caste and low caste Sikhs. Suddenly, I felt that Sikhism had failed and that we were subject to Hindu rituals. Now I know that Indian society is very complicated.

I have mentioned that Pitaji had obtained a plot of land in 1951. By being very active and energetic he managed to obtain all the permits he required to start building without paying any bribes. The plan was signed by an architect, as required. He purchased all the materials himself and got several contractors for the various works to be done – masonry, plastering, reinforcement, plumbing, electrical, woodwork and so on. At that time components like doors, windows, flooring tiles were not available ready made and were built in situ. Some of these procedures Pitaji were not familiar with from his experience in Gujrat and Maharashtra and he learnt about the economic advantages of the techniques in use in Delhi. To complicate life, Nehruvian socialism had put an end to imports so that copper pipes and wires were not available and aluminium ducts and wires had to be put in. Pipes had to be galvanised iron.

All these problems put a considerable strain on an engineer who had, all his life, given orders for work to be done and then monitored the execution. Now he often had to carry materials from the shop to the building site in his own car. Moreover, inflation was in full swing so that his budget provisions were clearly going to be exceeded. In the middle of all this, he got a severe toothache. The dentist said the tooth could be saved but the adjoining teeth were also infected and the process would be long and expensive. The cheaper, quicker solution would be to have half a dozen teeth extracted. Worried at the cost and time involved, Pitaji decided he would like *all* his teeth removed which the dentist obligingly did and gave him a complete denture.

Then he started having lumbago which he used to have in Ahmedabad twice a year when the season changed. But this attack was much worse and appeared to be interminable. He was lucky to have a cousin who was a general practitioner – Dr. Gurdit Singh Malik (1899-1966) whose father Dogar Singh (1878-1946) had had a villa opposite Tayaji's Ajanti residence in Rawalpindi. G.S. had not had a successful career as an Army surgeon. He had been found sleeping on his watch and had had to look for a civil job but even there he had not been a success so he had taken up private practice in New Delhi. Anyway, he gave Pitaji some analgesics which brought relief within a few weeks.

Immediately, he resumed work on the house under construction which had slowed down in his absence. He also found that the money he had for the job was not going to be adequate and he would have to borrow on his life insurance policy.

Of course, the time (two years) during which I could expect to stay in Delhi was coming to an end. Because I was at headquarters and had made friends at higher levels, I had a limited choice of countries I could go to. I chose Buenos Aires where a younger colleague Ajai Mitra who had been attached to me for training had just gone as Third Secretary; he was sending me good reports about the living conditions there which were similar to Europe. I was confident of learning Spanish on my own as Mitra had done earlier in Madrid where he had been attached to the British Embassy specifically for that purpose. Mitra's wife, Shanta was the daughter of the most successful radiologist in Delhi Dr.Satish Sen and her mother was a Jewess, Hannah who was the Principal of Lady Irwin College. Both of them were socially prominent. The Mitras had a son Kamal who was nearly the same age as our Kiran.

Preparations for departure started. Accommodation in Delhi had been a perpetual problem. In January 1951, we had been allotted a 'hutment' in Kota house. The location was excellent, within three miles of my office, but messing was expensive for the whole family – we had a manservant and a nanny – and the single storey 'temporary structure' would get very hot in summer so one could not manage without an air conditioner which had to be rented and the electricity paid for at a very high rate. We were living beyond our means because we were maintaining the life style which our parents had had at our stage in life. Salaries had been fixed in 1890 and revised downwards in 1948! We had, therefore been moving about between different makeshift flats. October 1952 saw us living in a flat built for Members of Parliament and lying vacant in the parliamentary vacations.

Kirat had a friend from her schooldays who had had a very unhappy arranged marriage. Her husband had conveniently died but her parents were averse to her remarriage. Kirat had found her a Bengali who appeared compatible – in fact the second marriage appeared to be working out well ten years later when I last happened to meet the husband – but the parents who had been supporting her in every way refused to have anything to do with the ceremony and she desperately needed a friend to be a witness. The upshot was that Mataji and Pitaji moved in with us in the M.P.'s flat to look after Kiran while Kirat went off to Simla to help her friend.

Kiran (several weeks short of two years) of course, understood nothing of all this and although he was used to Mataji he objected strongly to his mother's absence. Pitaji was in bed with his lumbago so Mataji went off by herself in the car to buy a pair of sandals for Kiran in an attempt to pacify him. The sandals had buckles and we all tried in turn to help Kiran to put them on. His reaction was strong and violent, the first indication I had of his independence of spirit. Somehow he knew the Punjabi word for 'I will do it myself.' Curiously enough this whole sentence can be expressed by the word AAPE and Kiran used it to such effect that all of us, including the servants, were doubled up with laughter. Pitaji who could hardly get up from bed because of pain laughed more than I had ever seen him do in all my life. Unfortunately, it was the last time I was to see him laugh wholeheartedly.

The rule was that all transfers had to be by surface route. A move to Buenos Aires would take about two months. Kirat and Kiran left by train for Bombay where Mr. Jiwan Singh had managed to get a three bedroom flat – he was posted in Poona. I went to Rajpur Road with my parents for the few days till I could be relieved of my post. Pitaji's lumbago was very much better but he was having fever and shivering so much that his whole bed shook noisily. Apart from G.S.Malik, other doctors were called and various ailments were diagnosed including malaria and dengue, but the tests were negative. However, he recovered sufficiently to see me off at New Delhi railway station which involved climbing a high footbridge twice. I left for my journey rather concerned about him but not seriously worried.

The journey to London was one I had made more than once by P&O liner. The only new thing was that instead of paying for accommodation in London, Mr. J.A.Singh had arranged for all of us – we had taken Pitaji's butler Jeevan as the Indian servant allowed under the latest rules – to be the house guests of Dr. & Mrs. Hingorani in Harley Street. Dr. Hingorani was a very famous eye surgeon and we were very well looked after. We left London by the boat train for Southampton on, I think, 5th November just as the last pea-soup fog was rolling into the city.

The ship we took was the ALCANTARA of the Royal Mail Lines. It was smaller and older than the ANDES – converted into a troopship – on which I had travelled to India six years earlier. In spite of its age, it was more luxurious than the P&O ships I was used to. The journey was a very long one with eight intermediate stops. The first one was at Cherbourg which I did not notice because it was in the middle of the night and I love my sleep. We had acquired fellow passengers named Shahane; he was to be Press Attaché in Buenos Aires. He was considerably older than I and had two grown sons whom I never met because they were already working in India. Apart from Mrs. Shahane – whose first name was not used by any of us – he was accompanied by a teen-aged daughter. I found Mohan Dattatreya Shahane very knowledgeable about English history and literature. He was being transferred from Nairobi where he had been Press Attaché. He was of course a journalist by profession and had been the editor of the well-known Marathi paper HITAVDA. He had also written some books in Marathi.

I had bought Hugo's Spanish Self-taught in London and started reading it. The grammar was not unlike Italian but the words although structurally the same were sufficiently different (particularly the terminations) as to be confusing. On the ship we met a French-speaking Swiss couple who gave me a book on Spanish verbs – one hundred of them – called 'TRATADO DE VERBOS ESPANOLES por CARMEN COMPANY de KEMPIN' which I found most useful. After I had mastered the hundred verbs I only needed opportunity and experience to speak Spanish. I began to understand Spanish and even Portuguese names. For instance, the author of the book was a married woman named Carmen whose maiden name was Company and she had become Kempin by marriage.

On the ship we became friendly with a man named John Blydenstein. He was about the same age as Kirat and told us he was the son of a banker of Dutch descent in London. He was going to Argentina at the invitation of an aunt (his deceased mother's sister) who wanted him to look after the *estancia* she had inherited from her father – John's maternal grandfather – and which she felt needed a man to look after it. I found him a very friendly and sincere young man with whom I had very little in common.

Our first stop after Cherbourg was Vigo. I had never heard of the port which was at the end of a huge sheltered bay. The Shahanes and we rented a taxi to go around and I tried my Spanish on the taxi driver. Shahane told me that the British navy had anchored in this bay several times in the previous two centuries.

The next port was Lisbon. India's relations with Portugal were getting strained because the Portuguese were refusing to discuss the possibility of a hand-over of Goa. In fact they had amended their constitution to make Goa a Portuguese province which they called the STATE OF INDIA. In spite of this provocation, we had a Charge d'Affaires in Lisbon named Kewal Singh. He was an I.C.S. Officer, a Punjabi and a Sikh but had cut his hair. I called him on the phone from the ship. He sent us his car, invited us for tea and then showed us around Lisbon and its surroundings. The place seemed pleasant enough but the country was obviously poorer than England and I was struck by the fact that the Army uniforms were almost indistinguishable from German uniforms and there were a great many of them around. Of course, the country was under a military dictatorship which had been well-inclined to the Axis powers during the World War.

We did not get off the ship to see Madeira but we did in Las Palmas in the Canary Islands. This is a duty free port but we had done our shopping in London. The Canary Islands (they belong to Spain) were home at that time to the second largest Sindhi population outside the subcontinent – the largest being in Hong Kong. Again we took a taxi to see the sights but there was no very impressive scenery and we ended up eating squid, for the first time in our lives, for lunch.

About shopping, there was a duty-free shop on board the ship which was opened when we were outside territorial waters. We began to understand the raison d'etre for this as we approached the first of four Brazilian ports we were to call at.

It is difficult for those living in market economies in the twenty-first century to understand what life was like under the command economies prevailing in many countries in the middle of the twentieth century. I have referred rather disparagingly in these pages to 'Nehruvian socialism'. I must be fair to Jawaharlal Nehru and say that he did not invent it. He was merely following the example of his British friends and trying to create a Fabian socialist society in the country which it fell to him to govern. Probably, he did not make sufficient provision for the difference between wealthy England and poor India. Then again, there was a tradition of individual liberty in England which did not exist in India. In any case, a system of controls on consumption was created; one got the impression that only Ministers and High Civil Servants could have cars. Even they were limited to the choice between two cars, the Hindustan Ambassador (a Morris Cowley) and the Premier President (a Fiat *millecento*). There came a day when the waiting time for an unprivileged person to get a Premier was twenty-five years! Vallabhai Patel had promised the Princes that they would not be taxed like ordinary mortals. Nehru invited Nicholas Kaldor, a British economist and politician of Hungarian Jewish birth, to invent new taxes which he intended would be payable by the Princes because they had not existed at the time that the Sardar had given them the assurance. Later Kaldor said that he had intended that these taxes (death duties, a wealth tax and an expenditure tax) should replace some of the existing taxes. Instead the new taxes were added on to the old taxes so that some persons were asked to pay taxes greater than their income. The result was that the exchequer received less than before.

In Brazil the Military Government had imposed a number of fiscal and non-fiscal restrictions on imports so that many consumer goods disappeared from the shops and others became unreasonably expensive. To do their shopping, some Brazilians were boarding the Alcantara at Recife to get off at Bahia. The Brazilian customs argued that the ship was sailing in territorial waters. Customs inspectors came on board to see the situation for themselves.

When we got to Rio de Janeiro, Ashok Bhadkamkar (First Secretary and my batchmate in the I.F.S.) and Hitinder Singh Vahali (Press Attaché) came to meet us on board the ship. Let me explain the relationship between Hitinder and me. Our mothers-in-law were half sisters. Hitinder is the same age as I am and his wife Jitinder was about five years older than Kirat. Jitinder was a direct descendant of Guru Nanak and her father was a prominent landowner in the area around Nangal. He owned the small town of Oona. I had got to know them in New Delhi because of the relationship and subsequently he became one of my closest friends. When I met him he was a news reader on All India Radio and he applied for a job with the External Publicity division of the Ministry of External Affairs because, 'I got fed up with the odd hours I had to work'. The Vahali family had been among the biggest landowners in West Punjab but his grandfather had ruined himself through litigation. His father was, in 1952, a senior Officer in the Punjab Civil Service. He himself had been educated at Aitchison Chiefs College, Lahore where he had become friendly with my colleague Gurbachan Singh and my brother-in-law Harinder Singh.

Ashok and Hitinder the invited us to lunch and Ashok insisted that I ride in his car. It was then that he broke the news of my father's death on 16th December.

The Register of the Notified Area Committee of Delhi gives the cause of Pitaji's death as 'heart failure'. Apparently, the infection in his tooth had dripped into his blood stream and caused a septic endocarditis. Apart from Dr. G.S. Malik, several other doctors including the best-known cardiologist of the day had been consulted. One Doctor had prescribed a new drug 'penicillin' and this had brought the fever down but other Doctors were afraid of it and discontinued it.

At this stage let me say something about my father which I have not mentioned so far. Several people said to me both during his lifetime and later that they were amazed that a man who was so handsome and so successful in life was never even rumoured to have been unfaithful to my mother who had never been pretty. Another merit of his was his charity. He not only gave money to charities like the construction of gurudwaras but he paid for the professional education of a couple of young men of the baradri. Most important of all was that he sheltered and fed Mataji's sister, Aunty Bansi. Traditionally, in our baradri and among other Punjabis that I know, the wife's relations are not supposed to accept a husband's hospitality.

BUENOS AIRES 1952-56

I do not remember the exact date but the ALCANTARA docked in Buenos Aires after Christmas 1952 and before the New Year. Apart from the Embassy staff, my friend Thomas Traube whom I had not seen since he and his wife Tania had briefly visited Brussels in 1949 was there to welcome me.

Of course, this was because we had maintained a regular correspondence. While I was still in Zurich in 1939, he had received an official intimation that the German government had declared him stateless. He was of Jewish race on both sides – like me he was an only child - but did not practise the Jewish religion. His father's family had been very rich and his father had become an Officer in the Imperial Guard by bribing the Officer who was measuring his height because he was not tall enough to qualify. I never met his father who had emigrated to South Africa where he had the Eastman Kodak agency in Johannesburg. The parents were divorced and his mother to whom he was close was living comfortably in a 'pension' in Geneva. In fact at Whitsun 1939, he had invited me to go with him to Geneva and spend the weekend there as his mother's guest. Later, during the war which he spent in Switzerland, he had finished his studies but could not get a work permit, he had met a Jewish girl born of a mother of French nationality and a father who was a Jewish refugee from one of the Baltic states. By some quirk of French law which was then granting citizenship to Europeans fairly easily, Tania was described as 'French by birth from the age of twenty-one years'.

He was able to communicate with me because the post, though slow, existed between Switzerland, a neutral country, and the United Kingdom. In fact, I became the channel of communication between him and his father in South Africa.

Later, I learnt that during the World War the Swiss Government was quite anti-Semitic and Jews who arrived in Switzerland from Germany often disappeared. Anyway, Thomas and Tania lived in Switzerland throughout the war. In 1949, some months after their visit to Brussels, Kirat and I went for a holiday to Zermatt and had dinner with Tania on our way back to Brussels. She was living comfortably in a flat and had a maidservant. She told us Thomas was in South America trying to find work because he could not get naturalised as all the Swiss cantons wanted immigrants to have money to be naturalised and he did not have enough. I did not enquire further because Thomas had told me that Tania's father was a multi-millionaire financier who owned three cars and a huge villa in Rome.

At the end of 1952, the Traube family was comfortably installed in a house which had earlier been occupied by the Thyssen family which had recovered its steel mills in Germany after Hitler and gone back there. The Traubes had a Buick car and three living-in servants. He told me he had three Czech partners in a factory making artificial pearls. We were to see a lot of the Traubes and their three sons, the youngest of whom was a couple of years older than our Kiran.

When we arrived in Buenos Aires, the Ambassador Nawab Ali Yavar Jung was away in New York where he was a member of the Indian delegation to the U.N.General Assembly session led by Vijayalakshmi Pandit. The Charge d'affaires was the Commercial Secretary V.C.Vijaya Raghavan. He was due to go back to India by the Alcantara so I saw very little of him. His wife was Australian of Polish Jewish birth.

I immediately became Charge d'Affaires for a couple of weeks and had Ajai Mitra to assist me and interpret for me. I found that there was not much occasion for me to speak Spanish except on the rare occasions when I dealt with Argentine officials who were instructed to speak Spanish although most of them were quite fluent in other European languages. There was a large, wealthy and influential Anglo-Argentine community and those members of Argentine society who did not speak English were fluent in French. For quite some time, I spoke Spanish mainly to the Embassy drivers.

One new factor I came across in Argentina and which was to persist in most other South American countries was exchange control. Of course, we had exchange control in India and even a black market but this was something else. The Argentine Central Bank had a rate of exchange of the Argentine peso for imports, a different rate for exports, yet another rate for 'financial transactions' and, of course, a flourishing black market through which Tania Traube received her allowance from her father with which the Traubes maintained the life style which I have described. In the Embassy, we Officers and staff received about half our emoluments at the 'financial' rate while the rest was paid into accounts in Sterling in London which we had to open for that purpose, There were no clear guidelines about what we could do with the money in London and, from time to time, this led to disciplinary departmental proceedings.

Nawab Ali Yawar Jung soon came back from New York. He was perhaps twenty years older than I and educated at Oxford. He spoke fluent French – his first wife had been French and was reported to be running an antique shop in Hyderabad. He belonged to a wealthy family in Hyderabad State and had served as Deputy Finance Secretary before becoming Vice Chancellor of Osmania University. He told me quite frankly that in Hyderabad it was gossiped that he had been rewarded with the Embassy in Buenos Aires in exchange for giving up his prestigious university to the Government of India's nominee.

In fact, the Embassy of India in Buenos Aires had a curious history. A Trade Office had been opened in Buenos Aires before Independence during the World War in connection with an Indo-Argentine Wheat-Hessians Barter Agreement. This agreement was still running in 1952. When the office was opened a Parsi businessman in Calcutta whose office building had been requisitioned by the Government of India had been appointed Trade Commissioner. At that time, Argentina had a very influential landowning polo-playing class and it was felt that a 'mere businessman' would not be able to have access to the levers of power so a prince of the Kapurthala family had been included as Social Attaché. After Independence, hardly anybody in the Ministry of External Affairs knew the difference between Argentina and Brazil and Panditji had appointed a wealthy Parsi engineer with an American wife as Ambassador to Buenos Aires. For some reason he fell out of favour and Nawab Ali Yavar Jung was appointed. He proved to be an excellent choice.

I was now a First Secretary and what the Americans call a Deputy Head of Mission. I did not have a car. I had sold my four-year-old M.G. for a pittance before leaving Delhi because small English cars were not appreciated in India. The money I got just about paid my debts. I asked the Ministry for an advance. This took time.

In India, Mataji sold Pitaji's Chevrolet for double what he had paid for it five years earlier because American cars could no longer be imported into India and there were plenty of nouveaux riches who wanted a big car. She used half the money to buy an Austin and sent me the rest with which I bought a Vauxhall Velox and returned the loan I had asked for. Of course, four months elapsed before the Vauxhall arrived in Buenos Aires.

One of the first problems which came to our attention was the question of 'address commission' – something of which I had never heard. In fact, I had no knowledge of business problems at all. We were concerned with the export of Argentine wheat to India. It was delivered to us F(ree) O(n) B(oard). The first thing was to find ships on which to load it. This was being done by the Indian High Commission in London. This meant that ships were chartered in London, paid for by the High Commission there and we were sent a copy of the 'charter party' so that we knew when the ship would arrive, how much it could carry and so on. In fact, all this meant very little to the Ambassador or to me. The work was handled by one or other of the shipping agents in Buenos Aires whose business it was. It had been decided much earlier that we would use four large international firms and the division of the work between the firms was determined by a formula which left nothing to our discretion. Nearly half the ships were loaded by a firm called Bunge & Born – it used a different version of the name in other countries. Other firms were 'Louis Dreyfus', 'La Plata Cereal' and 'La Continental de Granos'. Bunge was the only one to have its headquarters in Buenos Aires, so it was the one we saw the most of.

There were two or three Bunge managers who kept in touch with us. One of them came to see the Ambassador and asked him what was to be done with the 'address commission'. Since we did not know what this was, he explained to us that according to well established shipping practice, when a ship is chartered, an address commission (4%?) is paid to the 'client' which in this case meant the Embassy. Scrutiny of the Embassy accounts showed that no such amount had ever been credited there.

'Oh, no, it would not appear in any official accounts. It would be paid in a currency of the recipient's choice in whichever country he wants it.'

The Ambassador had associated me with these conversations, so we asked why the freight could not simply be reduced by the amount of the commission to ease the burden on the Indian taxpayer.

'Oh, no, that would be contrary to business practice and tradition. In fact, we as shippers expect half the amount to meet our office and other expenses.'

So, of course, the shippers must have kept the commission but with their experience, contacts and organisation they were invaluable to the Embassy. Whenever we imported anything whether it was a car for the Embassy or duty-free liquor for serving to our guests, we did not have to go to grasping 'handling agents' but had the work done for us by 'our' shipping agents.

Nawab Ali Yavar Jung lived in a rented furnished house which his beautiful young (she was about my age) second wife Begum Zehra – I may have the spelling wrong since I never addressed her by her name - maintained in appropriate style. They entertained very well within the resources provided by the Government of India and we could all, Mohan Shahane, Ajai Mitra and I learn from them. They were both very formal and addressed us all as Mr. and Mrs. which we found amusing because the other officers under whom we had served would address us by our first names.

Among the foreign diplomats with whom we became friendly were the Second Secretary of the British Embassy, Mervyn Brown and his wife Beth. I am still in correspondence with them. Sir Mervyn Brown retired as High Commissioner to Nigeria. There was a lot of entertainment in Buenos Aires among the diplomatic community. Argentine officials had to be careful in dealing with us because the ruling class (the President General Peron who was generally addressed as 'Mi General' and his associates) did not trust them, since they belonged to the landowning class which they had ousted from political power. However, there were non-political well-to-do Argentines who were accustomed to living well and appreciated invitations from diplomats.

One of the first parties we went to was given by the Browns where we met the recently arrived Second Secretary of the Canadian Embassy, C.F.W. (Bill to his friends) Hooper and his wife Patricia. Patricia asked Kirat if she liked dogs.

'Oh yes, I love dogs but not, of course, those horrible dachshunds which look more like rats than dogs.' Patricia gulped but said nothing. Soon after we went to their house and saw her dachshund! As it turned out, Patricia suffered a lot from asthma in Buenos Aires and blamed it on the damp climate, because whenever she went away for a weekend she did not have it. She tried all kinds of tests and medicines for her asthma which pursued her to Ottawa but it only disappeared several years later when the dog died. We could understand her attachment to her dog because she had no children.

Kiran was beginning to talk mainly in Hindi because he spent more time with Jeevan than with us. Besides, Kirat had been accustomed to talking Hindi with her parents. We spent our Sundays with him because the Traubes would arrange outings to restaurants in the surrounding countryside where children were welcome. Their favourite restaurant was called, in Spanish, 'El Chencho Rengo' (the lame pig – why? Apparently the expression is used in Argentina for a man who pretends to hear only what he wants to hear) which was run by a Hungarian couple. There we got to know several Hungarian aristocrats who had run away from the Communist regime in their own country.

Then Jeevan fell ill. He was diagnosed with a duodenal ulcer and operated upon at the British Hospital but he did not survive. After that, we only had Argentine maidservants and Kiran became fluent in Spanish.

Nawab Sahib took me along on a visit to Cordoba about five hundred kilometres north-west of Buenos Aires. We arrived there just after lunch and quite soon the receptionist said that a journalist wanted to interview the Ambassador. We asked for him to be sent up and offered him tea. To our surprise and disappointment he knew no English and hardly any French. Nawab Sahib had been in Buenos Aires for about nine months and could speak enough Spanish for ordinary conversation but was by no means fluent and far from being elegant as in English and French. Normally, diplomats who converse fluently in a foreign language prefer to have an interpreter for official talks and press conferences – then they can blame him when things go wrong! But my Ambassador was full of confidence and I, knowing even less, learnt a good deal. The journalist asked,

'Your great writer Rudyard Kipling ....' To be interrupted by the Ambassador,

'I think there is a mistake somewhere. Kipling was an Englishman.'

'No, no, I have reread his biography today. He was born in India.'

So far, there had been no language problem. We knew that much Spanish. But now we had to be careful and the Ambassador said in English,

'You are quite right but he was not attuned to our national aspirations.' Of course, the journalist was at a complete loss. Nawab sahib said the same in French translating 'attuned to' as 'd'accord avec' but again this was insufficient. Fortunately, I had a Spanish-English dictionary and found that the Spanish expression is very similar to the French which solved the problem and we went on to talk of Tagore.

After he had gone, we discussed the contretemps and the Ambassador said that in Argentine thought *jus soli* (the principle that a person's nationality at birth is determined by the place of birth) seemed to prevail whereas in India and England we went by *jus sanguis* (child's nationality determined by father's nationality). Kipling would have been just as horrified as we were if he had been called an Indian. In his ESPRIT DES LOIS, Montesquieu had explained how, in his time, France was divided legally between the North and the South. In Northern France, where five hundred years earlier, *langue d'oil* had been spoken there was customary law (as in England) but where *langue d'oc* was spoken, Roman Law prevailed.

Nawab sahib took advantage of the visit to Cordoba to introduce me to the Honorary Consul of Lebanon. He was a wealthy businessman named (Abd-el) Malik. He was quite old but his young and rather brash son was Vice Consul and he took us around in his car which had a CC (Consular Corps) number plate which he used to put traffic policemen in their place. His sister Alicia was an attractive young blonde. Nawab sahib said 'It certainly helps in life if one is good looking.' Up to that time, the only Arabs I had known were Egyptians who are as dark-skinned as Indians. It was a new experience to see a blonde Arab.

I was under orders from Kirat to get a particular kind of poncho which she said was available in Cordoba. Enquiries at the hotel gave me the name of a shop in Arab Street. I reflected that there must be a lot more Arabs than Consul Malik in Cordoba. The shop had the poncho but I was surprised when the name of the shopkeeper sounded very German. I asked the shopkeeper and he replied,

'Of course, we are Jews.'

'But...... but, how can there be Jews in Arab Street?'

'You know we all come from the Middle East so we are neighbours here as well.'

'What then is all this about Israel and Palestine?'

'Oh, that is politics. We businessmen are not concerned with that.'

After this visit, I got to know a lot about the Syrio-Lebanese community, as it was called in Argentina. They appeared to be Roman Catholics and, at that time, numbered about four hundred thousand. They had started coming to Argentina at the end of the nineteenth century when they were known as TURCOS because the documents they carried were issued by the Turkish Empire. They had started by opening country shops, usually at crossroads in the countryside miles from any other human habitation. They had done well under Peron who had been friendly with the Axis powers and was anxious to break the economic power of the Americans, the British and the Jews. In 1953, it was said that the richest businessman was a man named Jorge Antonio who was referred to as a Turco. I never met him.

I was already well acquainted with the Israeli Embassy because the Mitras had made a point of cultivating them and also because of my own sympathy with the Jews dating back to pre-war Germany. The Jewish community was also about four hundred thousand strong. The most important Jewish firm was 'Bunge & Born' which I have already referred to. At the Israeli Embassy I became friendly with the Counsellor Jeonathan Prato whose father had been the Chief Rabbi of Rome. His wife Klaere was German and they had both been able to save some silver and china from their families. Jeonathan was very well up on Italian history particularly of the old aristocratic families. There was a large Italian community in Buenos Aires. Every other shopkeeper, taxi-driver and artisan I met said he was the son of an Italian immigrant.

At the other end of the Italian community was Silvio Tricerri to whose house I was taken by Nawab Ali Yavar Jung. He was not well educated but was quite a genius at business administration. He said he had read five books in his life. His father who had been a trader had now become his subordinate in his office. He was said to be second only to Jorge Antonio in his wealth. He kept open house and Kirat and I used to go there almost once a week. We became very friendly with the second-in-command of his business empire an Italian named Renzo Ghiotto and his wife Olga. I am still in correspondence with Renzo.

Silvio Tricerri's wife was named Susanna; they had seven children in 1953 and the process was continuing. I am told that with the fall of Peron, his firm also fell but Renzo escaped in time and became an industrialist in Vicenza which is reputed to be the richest city (by per capita income) in Italy.

I have mentioned that the Mitras had a son Kamal, of the same age as our Kiran. They had a daughter born in 1953 who did not survive. Cremation was not allowed in Argentina. There were two Roman Catholic cemeteries. The Anglicans had managed to get a British cemetery. Others, i.e. non-Christians could be buried in a plot adjoining the larger Catholic cemetery and that was what we had had to do with Jeevan. When his daughter died, Ajai Mitra was told she could be buried there but that pets were buried there as well. Shanta was horrified; she discovered that her daughter could be classified as a Jewess because by Jewish law the religion is inherited from the mother ad infinitum. There was a Jewish cemetery but, of course, the grave would have to be the minimum because graves are expensive and the Reserve Bank of India would not release foreign exchange – Shanta's father was very well off – for a burial, at any rate not in time.

Nawab Ali Yavar Jung and I went for the burial where there was a Rabbi and an Israeli diplomat present. The Mitras were very hospitable and we both knew it because we had enjoyed their hospitality. Nawab sahib expressed his disappointment to me that none of the Mitras' friends had come to 'throw earth on the grave' as is, he told me, the custom among Muslims. It was my first experience that serving whisky to guests does not ensure their friendship.

The Ambassador and his wife also had a child, a boy. This created a legal problem because, under Argentine law, a child born in the country automatically became a citizen and, in the case of a boy, would in due course be obliged to do military service. I was told by my British colleagues that there was a very distinguished British Ambassador who could never be posted to Argentina because he would be arrested on arrival for non-performance of military service! He would not be recognised as a foreign diplomat. This British diplomat had been born in Buenos Aires when his father was a Consul there.

Fortunately, there was an exemption for the children of diplomats – as distinguished from consuls – and their births could be de-registered. This proved to be a long and complicated process and, before it was completed, the Nawab was Ambassador in Cairo.

I see I have been referring to my Ambassador as NAWAB without explaining what this means. Before Independence, the Viceroy would give titles, some hereditary but mostly 'personal', twice a year. This was in accordance with British practice but it was an old Indian tradition for rulers to award titles to their subjects and several of them continued the practice after they had signed a *sanad* (agreement) with the Crown Representative. In earlier centuries, a Nawab was a Muslim who was given charge of a district rather like a Collector in British India. In practice, the Viceroy regularly awarded the title of Nawab Bahadur and the lesser Nawab Sahib as a 'personal distinction'. The Nizam of Hyderabad had given the title of Nawab to Ali Yar Khan for his distinguished services and, at the same time, changed his name to Ali Yavar Jung. Muslim women whether their husbands have titles or not are addressed formally and politely as Begum.

The Ambassador was very fair. He took us all on tours by turn. As far as helpfulness was concerned, Ajai Mitra was an easy winner because he was the only one who spoke Spanish fluently; I spoke it less well than the Ambassador and Shahane hardly spoke any. As it turned out, Ajai was on tour with the Ambassador when Shanta delivered her baby and it was I who had to take her to hospital.

The Ambassador was accredited concurrently to Chile but in that country he was only an Envoy Extraordinary and Minister Plenipotentiary; it was not till some years later that the designations of E.E. & M.P. and Minister Resident were abolished so that a country only had the choice of appointing an Ambassador or a Charge d'Affaires in another country.

He took me on a trip to Santiago, Chile. I enjoyed this very much. For one thing I did not like the humid climate of Buenos Aires which was cold and clammy in winter and hot and sticky in summer. Santiago was about a hundred kilometres from the sea and there was a range of hills between Santiago and the coast which kept the humidity away. Then again, being a couple of thousand feet above sea-level, it never became oppressively hot. At the same time, it received very little rain and the sun shown brightly on most days. The fertile central valley of Chile depends for its water supply on the run off from the melting snows of the Andes.

In more material terms, Chile did not have exchange control or many non-tariff barriers to trade; it was more like a market economy. One could see American and English films which Peron would not let into Chile to save foreign exchange and to promote the Argentine film industry. Diplomats are supposed to be immune to customs duties and non-tariff trade barriers but it is one thing to order something from a catalogue and wait months for it to arrive and something else to see an item in a shop and buy it if one can afford it. I studied the list of the Indian Foreign Service, made an actuarial calculation and decided that I would never be an Ambassador but would be happy to end my career as E.E. & M.P. in Santiago.

Towards the end of the year (1953) the Ambassador told us he was being transferred to Cairo and that he had no news about any successor. I was sorry to see him go because I had been very happy to serve under him but, of course, the prospect of being a Head of Mission (Charge d'Affaires ad interim) for a few months was quite delightful. I had had experience of this already because the Ambassador had been away as a member of the delegation to the U.N.General Assembly in New York for over two months and he made the announcement on his return. This was the third year in which he had been a member of the Indian delegation. The reasons he was chosen were his diplomatic ability, the fact that he was a Muslim and his ability to speak Spanish. At that time, there were no African members of the U.N. except South Africa, Liberia, Ethiopia and Egypt. The countries of Latin America were a large voting block; though they generally voted with the United States on issues of importance to that superpower they appreciated it if an Indian Ambassador spoke to them in their own language.

Nawab sahib told me that one morning in New York when the Indian delegation had its working meeting, a new member asked the leader, 'Why is the Mexican Ambassador attending our meeting?' The new member had not been introduced to Ali Yavar Jung, had seen him greet someone in Spanish and decided that he must be the Mexican Ambassador because Mexicans have about the same skin colour as Indians! In fact this facial similarity of Indians to Mexicans has an unfortunate consequence. The Mexican government has an overpowering fear of its country being inundated by millions of Indian immigrants and very few Mexican Ambassadors – to say nothing of Consuls – are empowered to give visas to Indians.

The Ambassador duly departed and I was left in charge of the Mission. The rented and furnished house which he had occupied was returned to its owner. The Embassy's cutlery and crockery were stored in the Press Attaché's office and I got the use of the Ambassadorial Buick and its driver. The problem was where to keep it. I was staying in a beautifully furnished first floor flat where I had place for one car on the ground floor. This space was occupied by my Vauxhall. We had to find a secure place for the Government owned Buick. The Government agreed to its being parked in a public garage within walking distance of my flat.

Normally a comparatively junior Officer like myself would not be able to afford the petrol which a Buick consumes but in

Argentina petrol was produced locally and was very cheap. I decided to go off to the North, to the provinces of Salta and Jujuy, where there were Indians working in the sugar mills. This meant being accompanied by Kirat, Kiran, the Ambassador's Private Secretary (named Kawatra who had previously been Private Secretary to our High Commissioner in Ottawa, H.S.Malik) and the chauffeur Luis Baladron.

Kawatra was an admirer of H.S.Malik. No one he had worked for before or since was the equal of that 'boss'. I only knew H.S.Malik as an 'Uncle', had never seen him in his office and listening to Kawatra gave me an idea of how I should behave to win the respect and affection of my staff although I was quite satisfied with what I had learnt from Ali Yavar Jung.

More valuable for me was the conversation of Luis Baladron, the chauffeur. He only spoke Spanish and spoke it non-stop discussing everything and every one including the Ambassador's friends. I often had to stop him. This was really my first opportunity to speak Spanish because as I have mentioned earlier in the office and at home I spoke English; French was appreciated at parties and so I found I was speaking Spanish only to servants. Of course, I realised the risks of this situation. In all societies, the speech of servants is different from that of their employers. Fortunately on this trip I got the opportunity to speak to provincial Governors and other officials many of whom only spoke Spanish and I returned from the trip talking Spanish quite easily. Back in Buenos Aires I started speaking Spanish to Argentine acquaintances (who knew English and French) which they appreciated.

The official object of my tour was to see the Indian communities in the North. I should explain the origins and nature of the Indian presence in Argentina. Of course, there were odd middle class persons who had got to Argentina somehow and settled there following their professions or doing business with varying degrees of success. Most of them would have married local women. Such people were generally not interested in meeting other Indians and would only come to the Embassy if they needed a new passport. In practice they would have non-Indian passports so there would be no need for them to come at all. They could hardly be considered a community.

I consider a community to be a group of people who meet regularly and usually pray together. There was such a community but not in Buenos Aires. I found two gurudwaras in the course of my tour to the north. I did not come across a Hindu temple or a mosque. I have read that units of the Indian Army had been brought to England for Queen Victoria's Diamond Jubilee and had returned to India via Canada. In Canada, there was a great demand for immigrants and the Sikhs made a good impression. A few were allowed to settle there. The remainder when they returned to India gave glowing accounts of this vast underpopulated country with plenty of farmland. Very soon Sikhs started emigrating to Canada by whatever ships were available.

As was to be expected, a movement started in Canada opposing 'Asiatic immigration'. Canadian and British shipping lines were instructed not to bring passengers from India. Not to be outdone, some enterprising men chartered a Japanese ship the 'Komagata Maru' and it sailed to Vancouver with a full load of Sikh and some Muslim emigrants. When it arrived in Vancouver, the ship was fired upon. I am not clear how but it seems that the majority of the Kamaghata Maru's passengers managed to land in different parts of the Americas mainly in California, Argentina and Uruguay.

The problem was what were they to do and how were they to get work permits. The railways in Argentina were built by British companies. Most of the engineers employed by them had worked in India and were familiar with the abilities of Indian workmen and they were glad to employ them. They were able to convince the Argentine authorities that since Indians regarded cows as sacred, they would be able to help with Argentina's vast cattle wealth!

These illiterate unskilled workers constituted the Indian community. Of course, many of them learned to read and write Spanish and most of them became skilled workers. A few were successful in trade and became quite rich. I met dozens of them but only one was a keshadhari Sikh. Unfortunately no Indian women migrated to Argentina. The result was that most of them had Argentine common-law wives. Those who did not generally took to drink and came to a sad end.

One day the receptionist told me that an Indian tourist named Ismail wanted to see me. When he came in I immediately recognised him from photographs I had seen in the ILLUSTRATED WEEKLY OF INDIA. I said, 'Ah, Mr. Ismail you are the Honorary Consul General of the Dominican Republic in Bombay. I have just received an invitation from the Syrio-Lebanese Club to an Id party. I hope you will accompany me?' He was delighted but he said he wanted to pray on Id day rather than go to a party and wanted to know if there was a mosque in Buenos Aires. I called up the Syrian Minister whom I knew rather well but his answer was so equivocal that I told Mr. Ismail that I had been unsuccessful so he said he would pray in his hotel room.

Anyway, I took him to the party which was held in the hall of the Bakers' Guild. The President welcomed us and offered Mr. Ismail a ham sandwich! I asked him if there was a mosque in Buenos Aires to which he replied,

'There must be.'

Before this, in 1953, I had felt a pain in my abdomen after lunch. When this recurred on three consecutive days, I decided to consult the Embassy Doctor. He asked for a number of tests, urine, blood, sputum, stool etc. I got all these done and went back to him with the results. He said there was a septic focus somewhere but he could not say where. He suggested I go to see a specialist and he recommended a Dr.Caul. This was not a Kashmiri Brahmin (spelt KAUL) but a Welshman, i.e. an Argentine of Welsh descent.

I was worried because Pitaji had been diagnosed as having a septic focus during his rather long undiagnosed terminal illness. Anyway I went to see Dr. Caul who, to my surprise, ordered a spinal X-ray. I got this and it looked perfectly normal to me. When I was a child I had swallowed a torch bulb and a relation who was a medical student had taken me for an X-ray which had revealed the brass part of the bulb travelling harmlessly through the digestive system. Except that I was now correspondingly bigger the X-ray looked much the same to me. I took it to Dr. Caul, who looked at it and said,

'Ah, as I suspected, you have spondylitis.'

'Doctor, what is spondylitis?'

'Spondylitis, Mr. Malik, is rheumatic arthritis of the spine. You can see it here as small incrustations on the lumbar and dorsal vertebrae.'

'Doctor. I don't understand. The pain is in front, the spine is behind. Besides, how can I have spinal arthritis? At the age of thirty-two I can touch my toes.'

'Mr. Malik, have you never heard of deferred pain? This is caused by the pressure of the incrustations on the sensory nerves leading to the abdomen. Within five years you will be immobilised.'

'What does that mean?'

'You will either be in a wheel chair or flat on your back in bed.'

'What should I do now?'

'You can go on drinking but drink only wine, not whisky.'

'Doctor, I only drink water.'

'Well, cut down on smoking.'

'How should I do that, since I don't smoke?'

'You can continue to swim but don't sit around in a wet swimming costume.'

'Doctor, I don't know how to swim.'

'I am prescribing B-complex; that should ease the pain for the time being.'

It did but I could not believe what this 'specialist' was saying.

I have not mentioned so far that one of the first Argentine friends I had made was a tall, well-built sharp-featured man named Julio Pardo. He seemed to be about fifty years old and his wife Isolina was perhaps ten years younger and not good-looking. They had no children and lived in a small apartment but entertained lavishly in their 'quinta' (literally a fifth – of a hectare - meaning 2000 square metres) where they had a beautiful garden and a swimming pool around which social life was lived on Sundays. Lunch was usually a barbecue but, if it rained, there was a dining room, an ample verandah, a couple of bedrooms and changing rooms. Service was provided by the caretaker and his wife who lived there permanently. Of course, this was only possible during the warmer months. The Ghiottos, the Hoopers, the Mitras, some relations of the Pardos and a few other diplomats were the habitués of the Pardo quinta.

Julio Pardo was obviously making a very good living as a stock and exchange broker. He drove a Cadillac and was of a very generous disposition. During this period he acquired control of a small textile mill and presented me with a suit-length of brown woollen material. Politeness required that I should have it made into a suit and wear it at a party to which I would invite the Pardos so I took it to the English tailor Wagstaffe. The piece was so large that he was able to make a double-breasted suit with a waistcoat. When he had done so, he asked me,

'Now that I have made that suit, Mr. Malik, may I let out the suit you are wearing by three inches?'

My vanity had lost the battle against good and plentiful Argentine beef and he had to let out all my suits. That was the only reason for the abdominal pain. More than half-a-century later, I am still walking about.

I enjoy driving, so on Sundays I would drive the Buick myself and on trips I shared the driving with Luis. Actually, I preferred driving the little Vauxhall to the big Buick because the latter had 'fluid drive' which meant that when driving downhill I could not use the engine as a brake and the brake kept giving trouble. I had gone in the Vauxhall with Kirat and Kiran right across Argentina to Mendoza where the climate was beautifully dry and good wine was grown by irrigation – the run-off from the melting snow in the Andes – rather than by depending on the rain. The only fault I found in the Vauxhall was that it had a tendency to overheat so it became very thirsty like me except that it cheerfully consumed any water available while we preferred still mineral water.

Having the Buick and the driver, I decided to make the trip to Santiago by car. The road goes through a pass in the Andes just below the Aconcagua peak which is 6959 metres high. The pass, I was told at the time, was about fourteen thousand feet high and only accessible in summer. Even then the odd summer storm could block it with snow. Fortunately there is a trans-Andean railway which goes through a tunnel which is kept open throughout the year. Passengers and freight have to be trans-shipped before and after the tunnel because the European-gauge line gives way to a narrow-gauge one through the tunnel. Cars are loaded on flat-bed open trucks and the whole system is well-managed.

We were lucky with the weather and managed to drive over the pass into the beautiful hilly country of Chile which was so different from the flat pampa in Argentina. On the other hand, in Chile, only Santiago and its suburbs had paved roads, the rest being gravel whereas in Argentina we had only found gravel in the Northern provinces of Salta and Jujuy. On previous visits to Chile, I had only seen the city and this was the first time I saw the surroundings. To Kirat and Luis it was all very new.

Nawab Ali Yavar Jung had told me that he had met the wife of a Chilean surgeon named Urzua who claimed to be of Indian descent. She said that, early in the twentieth century, a Jam Sahib (a prince) of the State of Jamnagar-Nawanagar in what is now Gujarat (who was a Hindu) had fallen in love with a Muslim girl and wanted to marry her. This had shocked the family because while it would have been normal to have a Muslim concubine the idea of a Muslim Maharanee or even a Rani – some Maharajas (a ruler of a state who are usually Hindus or Sikhs) had 'secondary wives' of lower birth and designated them as Ranis – was unacceptable. The British resident had been approached. This was about the time when Ranjitsinghji (the famous M.C.C. test cricketer Ranji) who was a prince of Jamnagar returned from England so he was installed as Jam Sahib and his predecessor pensioned off to live like a Maharaja in France. The infatuation with the Muslim girl had not lasted and he had 'married' one or more European girls. The last was an Englishwoman named Winifred who had presented her husband with a daughter whom she named Dolores so she was, in 1953, Dolores Jadeja de Urzua known to her friends as 'Lola'. She was a little younger than I.

On this visit in the Ambassadorial Buick, we got in touch with them. Lola was much younger than her husband Rafael. They had three children, a boy and two girls, the last of them born deaf. Rafael had been married before and had grown sons by his first wife who was alive but I never met her or her offspring. He told me that his family had been moderately well off and he had studied medicine. In Chile there was no specialisation and all surgeons and physicians got the same degree. He had not been particularly good at studies but happened to have a talent for surgery. He did all kinds of surgery but was the only one in Santiago doing cosmetic surgery. He spoke some English and read French and English perfectly. He gave me a book he had written on Surgery in Spanish which I have just looked at to make sure of the spelling of his name. He was obviously very well off and drove a Cadillac.

Our principal contact in Chile was Juan Marin who had been Charge d'Affaires in India and, now retired, was President of the Amigos de la India – Friends of India. His wife Milena was of Yugoslav descent. They were both very tall. He related how when he was in Delhi there had been another Chilean, also named Marin, who was the Representative of one of the United Nations agencies. One afternoon Pandit Nehru had told his Private Secretary, 'Get me Marin, the Chilean.' They found Juan playing tennis and he had arrived in the Prime Minister's Office in his tennis kit, sweating, only to find that he was not the man the P.M. wanted to see.

By the end of 1954, it became obvious to me that Ajai Mitra was a womaniser. This would not have been my concern but for the fact that his activities were extending to the office, the staff, the premises and so on. Apart from that, the 'commerce of women' as Montaigne calls it is an expensive sport and he was not rich. Shanta, his wife, was the only child of well-to-do parents, but that source of funds was not available for this pastime. Diplomacy is not generally a source of wealth. In fact, in certain countries only men with personal fortunes were allowed, in the early twentieth century, to become diplomats. Correspondingly, there are not many ways of making money illegally. A complaint was made to me that he had sold his car, in advance of the end of his tenure in Argentina, to two persons and obtained advances from both of them. No documentary proof of such a sale could be produced so the charge failed but I was glad to see him go in spite of my friendship for him and the good company he and his wife were.

In India, we were well aware that Pandit Nehru did not approve of the foreign policy of the Latin American republics. It was rumoured that he had referred to them collectively as 'American lackeys.' In 1954, he was doing his best to promote the Peoples Republic of China. With this objective, he sent Krishna Menon to South America. When he arrived in Buenos Aires, the Argentine Government put him up in the best hotel and placed a car and driver at his disposal but he was unable to see either President Peron or Foreign Minister Remorino.

I arranged a small public meeting, within my budgetary resources, for him to address. Of course he spoke no Spanish so the Embassy's Argentine interpreter was there. This man was able to interpret our speeches, sentence by sentence, quite well but this would not serve Krishna Menon who did not like the flood of his eloquence to be interrupted and told the interpreter so. He was accustomed to the 'simultaneous interpreters' of the United Nations. In those days there was one school in Geneva where such interpreters were trained. The diploma of simultaneous interpreter required five years of study and the drop-out rate was quite high. My second cousin Divya Veena Malik only got as far as 'consecutive interpreter'. Anyway, our 'interpreter' had to wait till Menon finished his oration when he said, in Spanish, 'Ladies and Gentlemen if you did not follow all that, I can only tell you that you missed a very good speech.'

Krishna Menon was getting more and more frustrated. He told me, 'If this problem of China's representation is not solved, the Third World War could break out in the Taiwan Strait in a few weeks.' We all know now that it was Pakistan, not India, which succeeded in establishing diplomatic relations decades later between U.S.A. and China and that did not do India any good. I could see very well that no third world war was in the offing but it was not for a First Secretary to tell a Cabinet Minister that he was talking 'nonsense on stilts'.

Finally, Krishna Menon was able to see the very distinguished retired diplomat who had led the Argentine delegation to the United Nations General Assembly for several years. This gentleman listened politely to Menon and treated him with due respect but, of course, he was not able to reverse his country's foreign policy.

I was more successful in Chile where President Ibanez agreed to receive him. I had had an interview with him some weeks earlier to present him with Tendulkar's LIFE OF MAHATMA GANDHI when I had spoken to him in Spanish. This event had provoked a newspaper cartoon in which I am saying to the President,

'Mr. President, I have the honour to present to your Excellency the life of Mahatma Gandhi – the greatest 'faster' in the world.'

The ghost of a typical Chilean 'roto' (tramp) is standing behind us and he says,

'*I* am the greatest faster in the world.'
Of course, I had never said anything of the kind but the cartoonist had to voice his own opposition to the ruling establishment.

The meeting did me no good because, after listening to Krishna Menon's praise of the Communist regime in China, Ibanez ended the meeting rather abruptly saying,
'We have plenty of non-conformists in this country.'
Krishna Menon's comment to me, as we left the Presidential Palace, was,
'This would not have happened if we had had an Ambassador here.'
My own impression is that Krishna Menon was a great orator but his greatest talent was his ability to make enemies for India every time he made a public speech.
Of course, such failures can not be concealed. Shortly afterwards, the Vice President Dr.S.Radhakrishnan was sent to South America. Apart from the protocol value of a Vice President, the personal stature of Dr. Radhakrishnan as a scholar was unequalled. However, the realities of politics were inescapable. The question everybody asked me was, 'If something happens to Pandit Nehru, would this gentleman take over?' No one except perhaps the most enlightened members of the Anglo-Argentine community could understand the working of Parliamentary Democracy. They only knew the Presidential form of government – because it is more easily replaced by a military dictatorship? President Peron had been duly elected – there were no allegations of rigging against him – but he was addressed as often as 'Mi General' as 'Senor Presidente.' We cannot blame Latin America for this. Charles de Gaulle in his many years as President was often addressed as 'Mon General'. When a President of a French-speaking African country addressed him as 'Papa', he advised him to use the expression 'Mon General'. When he finally retired, he only accepted a Colonel's pension – he had served as Acting Brigadier for a few days – to use British or Indian terminology.
Vice President Radhakrishnan, of course, talked more culture than politics except when he referred to India as a 'bridge to be trodden on' between the Eastern and Western blocks. He was received at a formal dinner in the Argentine Congress by the Vice

President. There was no language problem there. The problem was that he was a vegetarian – an idea incomprehensible to Argentines, 'If you don't eat meat, you will eat chicken, won't you?'

Other problems arose. He had been given a Counsellor (an educationist) by the Embassy in Washington because it would have been inappropriate for him to have only a Private Secretary to travel with him. This gentleman had violent cramps in Buenos Aires – a duodenal ulcer – and the Doctor ordered him to be flown back to Washington when his pains subsided. The Vice President asked me to accompany him to La Paz, Bolivia in addition to Santiago, Chile as I had planned. He appeared disappointed that the Argentine government did not give him a decoration and said, 'Kirat will be my decoration!' So Kirat got a chance to see La Paz where I had spent two weeks earlier that year as an Observer at the Third Inter-American Indigenous Congress.

I had not received any briefing for this Congress and did not even know what it was all about. In fact, it was only during the session that they were able to arrive at a consensus on the English name – 'Amerindian' – for the subjects of their discussions. I was conversing quite easily in Spanish by this time. In Spanish, the word in use was 'Indio' and my presence caused some hilarity as some one circulated a slip of paper in Spanish which said,

'The only real Indio among us can not speak to us because he says he is only an Observer.'

In my travels in Argentina, no one had pointed out an Indio to me and I had not seen one in Chile either. At the Congress in La Paz, I learnt that the difference between Indios and Blancos (whites) is more economic and cultural than racial. I have explained this earlier. Bolivia and Ecuador were the only countries half a century ago where there was an Indio majority.

The problem with the Vice President's going to Bolivia, as I saw it, was going to be something else. I explained to him that the airport of La Paz was on the *altiplano* (the Andean plateau) at an altitude of 14000 feet and the main city was down in a valley at 11000 feet. The Presidential Palace, the hotel we would be staying at and the main official buildings were at about 12,000 feet. Breathing at such altitudes takes getting used to. When I had gone to La Paz, a bus had deposited me at the hotel. I had to pick up my own suitcase and climb three steps to get to the reception desk; to my great surprise, I found myself panting! Twelve days later I was able to run up and down stairs. It suddenly dawned on me that I was not holding Dr. Radhakrishnan's attention when I explained all this to him – he had no intention of running up and down stairs and had no experience of life at high altitudes. I ended up by saying that I would ask the airline to provide an oxygen cylinder. What I was concerned about was that the Vice President was exactly twice my age.

In Chile, apart from the protocol visits, Juan Marin had arranged for the Vice President to address a university audience and Dr. Radhakrishnan spoke on the 'Cultural Unity of India'. As soon as he started, the interpreter who could only interpret consecutively asked him to make his sentences shorter so he could translate them one at a time! This was virtually impossible and Juan Marin produced another interpreter. When the speaker mentioned the Buddha, he backed down saying it was not an English word. I felt I could do a little better than that so I took over but, of course, I am not at all a trained interpreter so the audience

1954 La Paz, Bolivia At airport with then Vice President Dr. Radhakrishnan, an unidentified Bolivian, Vice President Hernan Silez Suazo of Bolivia and the British Charge d'Affaires.

lost the brilliance of the great man's eloquence. However, there was none of the unpleasantness which had characterised Krishna Menon's visit. On the contrary seeing and meeting some one of Dr. Radhakrishnan's eminence enhanced India's status among the intellectual class. We had one of his shorter books translated into Spanish for the occasion.

In Bolivia, things worked out as I had foreseen. At the airport, the Station Manager of PANAGRA - the airline which carried us from Santiago to La Paz – brought us a portable oxygen cylinder and showed Dr.Radhakrishnan how to use it. He appreciated it because his first experience of an altitude of 14000 feet gave him the personal explanation of what I had told him a few days earlier; he was, as usual, very considerate and asked, 'Why only one cylinder? What will the three of you (Kirat, I and his Private Secretary) do?' I explained that he was the one whose health mattered to all of us. In fact, he was in good health, his heart was strong and he only needed the cylinder when he had to climb steps in the older buildings.

Shortly after these two visits, I was told that Mohan Shahane's term had expired and he was to be replaced by Hitindar Vahali. This was a very pleasant surprise for Kirat and me. For our Argentine friends and acquaintances, it was a great surprise. They saw two keshadhari Sikhs as the only Officers of diplomatic rank in the Embassy. I was asked, 'Are the Sikhs some kind of aristocracy that you two senior diplomats are both Sikhs? I had to point out to them that there was another Sikh in the Embassy who did not enjoy diplomatic status. For Kiran it was company because there was now another little Sikh boy (Dilbir) in Buenos Aires. Unfortunately, a house of affordable rent could not be found for the Vahalis near us and they had to live in a suburb; of course, a house was an advantage for them because they had two children – the daughter Jaiji was older than the two boys who were of about the same age.

Living near us were the Hoopers. As I have mentioned, we had a luxuriously furnished first floor flat on the fashionable Avenida Figueroa Alcorta. Three streets behind us lived the Hoopers in a 'petit hotel' which backed on to the Railway Line. From the point of view of noise, our homes were equal. We had the noise of the avenue which was, in fact, the beginning of an arterial highway so that we could not use our balcony but had to keep the plate glass windows perpetually closed. The Hoopers had no children so they really had very little use of their back garden. They tried to have Sunday barbecue lunches but conversation was rendered impossible by the noise of the railway line on which ran not only the trains to the North but also the suburban trains to the fashionable northern suburbs. However, they had a proper lock-up garage. Patricia and Kirat used to rent bicycles and go around the neighbourhood for shopping and so on. As Patricia's hair was brown and Kirat's was black, they became known as 'La rubia y la morocha' – the blonde and the dark one.

As I have mentioned, Juan Domingo Peron was a constitutionally elected President. For the election he had been opposed by an older candidate belonging to the traditional Radical party which was supported by the Governments of the United States and the United Kingdom who were afraid of American and British-owned firms being nationalised. One of the American firms was a mining company called BRADEN COPPER. Its virtual owner Spruille Braden had been appointed U.S. Ambassador in Argentina. This was indiscreet enough but a bank clerk named Margueirat – I do not remember his first name and no one ever used it – managed to see a cheque signed by Braden in favour of the candidate opposing Peron. The photograph of this cheque became Peron's election poster. When he won the election Peron appointed Margueirat Chief of Protocol. I never met his wife and he himself was brash, vulgar and very aggressive. Of course, he did not have the traditional education of a diplomat – candidates for the Argentine foreign service in those days had to have law degrees. He was very intelligent, popular with Peron and could overrule the Foreign Minister on matters which he was interested in. He managed to get a diplomatic number plate (CD 111) for his car – the only Argentine to have one. The diplomats who won his 'friendship' could import anything they liked; others would be harassed for a minor traffic violation.

Generally, in South America, there is the tradition of the CAUDILLO (the leader) and this suited Peron very well. However, South American dictators are usually removed by a *golpe* (coup d'etat) and with increasing corruption and abuse of power by the President's friends, the time seemed to be drawing near. With the death of his charismatic wife Eva in July 1952, he had acquired a reputation as a womaniser. This would normally be an asset but the women became younger and younger until he founded an association of secondary students who got various privileges like the use of one of the Presidential residences. He thought he would reach out to India as a non-aligned country because he wanted to get away from the U.S. apron which usually covers Latin America under the name of the Monroe Doctrine. I was approached and asked if I would like to arrange an Indian cultural performance at the suburban Presidential residence being used by the secondary school students. Nawab Ali Yavar Jung had been very favourably impressed by Peronist foreign policy but I was prejudiced against the Axis Powers which Peron had supported as long as they existed and was not an admirer of the 'populist' policies being followed. Of course, we (Kirat was a good dancer and choreographed part of the performance) went all out to arrange the cultural show but we knew that it would produce no lasting benefit for India.

In June 1955, we heard strange sounds in our Chancery (Office) on the fourth floor of an office block in Calle Lavalle in the centre of the city which faced the police station where, according to common report, prisoners were routinely tortured. I recognised the sounds as aerial canon-shells. I went down to drive towards the Presidential Palace but found cars coming from the opposite direction – i.e. the wrong way in a one way street. It became obvious that a coup d'etat was in progress. Later in the day I learnt that the coup had failed. The Navy had refused to participate – the Vice President was a Naval Officer. Only some units of the Army had revolted. The Air Force was leading the coup and its pilots had been bought off while they were in the air with the promise of import licences for cars. The popular joke was, 'The Air Force are pancakes – they turn over in the air.'

The National Day of Chile falls on 18th September. Some of our friends were keen to see Chile and the National Day parade which included at that time a charge by horsed cavalry and a gallop by horse artillery – probably one of the last in the world. So the Pardos and the Hoopers accompanied us on the flight to Santiago. We left Kiran with Renzo and Olga Ghiotto to whom he was accustomed. As it turned out, they could not handle him as they had no children of their own and no experience; finally, in our absence they turned to the Vahalis who were able to look after him.

While we were in Santiago, we learnt that a coup had taken place in Buenos Aires, that a General Leonardi had seized power and an Admiral Rojas had become Vice President. Peron was a prisoner on a ship anchored in the Rio de la Plata (River Plate in English). Because of the coup, all flights had been cancelled. We were obliged to stay longer in Chile than we had planned. I had managed to import a car into Chile and the six of us used it to explore the surroundings of Santiago and to go down to Valparaiso, the biggest port in Chile. Chile is known as the 'stringbean country' because it is so long and so narrow. It has a number of ports at which Yankee Clippers used to take water on the long voyage from Calcutta to Boston and back in the tea trade. For this reason Chileans drink tea while other Latin Americans are addicted to coffee.

1955 Buenos Aires, Argentina Kirat, an unidentified Argentine, President Juan Domingo Peron, and the President of Secondary Students Union, at a display of Indian fashions organized in co-operation with the Union.

We returned to Buenos Aires to find that Margueirat had disappeared, that some of our friends in the Palacio San Martin (the Argentine Foreign Office) were now able to talk much more freely and the old land-owning class was working hard to return to power. The Army was not very visible and there was not the atmosphere of a military dictatorship. General Leonardi soon fell ill, went to U.S.A. for an operation and returned to die. He was succeeded by a General Aramburu. None of these Generals had a charismatic personality. Peron had been granted asylum in Paraguay.

All the time that we had been in Argentina we had been going to parties given by a remarkable childless couple, the Salverdas. The dominant partner was the wife, Edith Mitchell de Salverda who appeared to be about twenty years older than her husband who looked about the same age as I. The husband (I can not remember his first name) was a tall and handsome young man while Edith appeared to me to be an old woman who had had more than one face-lift. Edith was a woman of extraordinary vivacity and energy, a real 'party animal' who could dance all night, interrupting that exercise with food, drink and cards (canasta and bridge) generally at very high stakes. Her parties would some times go on for twenty-four hours.

She told us that she was the daughter of a wealthy Chilean couple named Mitchell who had gone on their usual trip to Europe after the Great War. She had been of an inconvenient age for extensive travelling and had been left in Buenos Aires. In the absence of her parents, she had fallen ill with typhoid – at that time a very dangerous disease. She had been treated by a Dr. Roth who was of German descent and a widower. When the parents returned from Europe, they were told the whole story and Dr. Roth asked for 'her hand in marriage'. The parents were shocked,

'She is so young and, besides, can you maintain her in the style to which she is accustomed?'

'I think I can keep her in better style than you can and, besides, she wants to marry me.'

Their honeymoon was a world tour by ship during which they had visited India and been entertained by some Indian Princes including the Raja of Mandi.

We had first been taken to a Salverda party by Nawab Ali Yavar Jung. We were not at all used to such parties where there were guests of all ages all addressing each other as 'tu', liquor flowed so freely and the guests helped themselves from a buffet or were served at their card tables. I was accustomed to bridge which my parents used to play but not for money. Kirat had been going to women's parties in Buenos Aires and learnt to play canasta and I learnt from her. We could not afford to play for money. At these parties, there were usually one or two Ambassadors and a lot of people whom I could only think of as the 'idle rich'. The Salverdas appeared to belong to this class and entertained a great deal and very lavishly.

Raja Joginder Sen of Mandi had been appointed Ambassador in Rio de Janeiro in 1952. Hitindar Vahali had served under him and found him a great gentleman. Both of them had been unhappy with the First Secretary – Joginder Singh, a keshadhari Sikh. Anyway, the Raja was keen to see Argentina before he went back to India. Edith was equally keen to reciprocate the hospitality she had received decades earlier. Of course, since then she had lost her first, rich husband and remarried Salverda who appeared to be dependent on her ample fortune for their lavish life-style. The Mandis came, were entertained by everybody, and were a great social success.

It was at the Salverdas' that we met Francisco Elizalde. He was, at that time, a handsome twenty-eight year old, belonging to a well-known land-owning family and had returned from U.S.A. with an M.D., specialised as an eye surgeon. He was quite outspoken in his views and had been overheard saying something against the Peronista regime. He had been arrested and tortured but released. The Salverdas were apolitical and so were the Pardos to whose quinta we took Pancho Elizalde. 'Pancho' is the abbreviated, familiar form of FRANCISCO.

When the Peron regime was toppled, Pancho was appointed Subsecretario in the Health Ministry. Subsecretario translates into English as Under Secretary and that is probably a good translation in the American sense. A civil servant as understood in India or England would not aspire to such a post. Pancho was the only subsecretario whom I ever addressed as 'tu'.

By this time the lease of my flat had expired and Kiran was big enough to need a house with a garden to play in. We moved to a terrace house in Acassuso, one of the northern suburbs. We were no longer in the city of Buenos Aires where nearly half the population of Argentina (a country with an area only 20% less than that of India) lived but in the Province of Buenos Aires, the capital of which is the port of La Plata.

We gave a cocktail party to which we invited a hundred persons, expecting to have seventy. Our dining table could only accommodate eight but we decided that we would invite ten persons to stay on for supper after the party. We felt that our single living-in maid would not be able to cope so an older woman who was a good cook spent the day preparing snacks. Everything went according to plan. The guests had been invited for 6-8 P.M. and by 8.30 twelve of us could sit down to an informal supper at small tables, one in the dining room and the other in the drawing room.. The cook had left by then and the maid served the meal. By 11 P.M. everybody had gone, the maid had gone to her room and Kirat had also retired after having worked hard all day.

I started to rearrange the furniture which was of the light Scandinavian type. Several items had been stacked in the garage which was accessible from the dining room. It must have been 11.30 P.M. when I went out into the road to bring the car into the garage. As I was getting into the car, I noticed a pair of headlights approaching. I immediately guessed the worst and rushed upstairs where I found Kirat in bed so I told her a guest had just arrived. It was Pancho Elizalde who had been working all day and had come straight from his Office. Of course, he needed dinner! Kirat rose to the occasion – in red corduroy slacks instead of the sari she had been wearing all evening – and prepared a hot dish to supplement the left-over snacks from the cocktail.

I have mentioned John Blydenstein who had travelled with us on the R.M.S.Andes from England to look after his aunt's *estancia* (ranch). He would come and see us on his visits to Buenos Aires. His father came from England to see him and they both came for dinner. I was very impressed by Mr. Blydenstein's manners, dress and politeness. He told us he owned a small bank which bore his name but that the days of small private banks were over and that he was planning to sell his bank (to the Bank of England?) and to retire. Some time later John announced that he had got engaged and brought his fiancée, Nelly, for dinner. Nelly was Argentine, spoke some English but created no impression on us. She was only a little younger than John. He had decided to go to the United States to take a degree in agriculture.

By the end of 1955, the Ministry in New Delhi remembered Argentina and found an Ambassador for the post. He was Mr. Nedyam Raghavan. I had heard quite a lot about him. He belonged to a very prominent Nayar (a land-owning warrior caste) family from Kerala but it was in Penang that he had made a name for himself as a barrister. Penang was at that time a British colony, part of the Straits Settlements, off the Malay Peninsula. In fact, the land facing the island was one of the British protected states and the Sultan had handed over a little bit of territory to the British so they had a port there in what they called Province Wellesley. Mr.Raghavan had joined Subhash Bose as soon as he arrived from Germany and Bose had made him a Minister in his 'Azad Hind government'. I was told that of all Bose's 'ministers' Raghavan was the only one who had a car of his own; the others were proudly showing off the cars which they had expropriated from their British or Chinese owners. Pandit Nehru had taken a liking to him and appointed him Ambassador in Prague where my batchmate Amreek Mehta had accompanied him as First Secretary. Amreek had passed through Brussels on his way to Prague and had been full of praises for his Head of Mission and of his 'closeness' to Pandit Nehru but it transpired that they did not get on. I had faithfully related all this to Badr-ud-Din Tyabji whose comment was, 'The idol turned out to have feet of clay'.

I think the Raghavans arrived in Buenos Aires in March 1956. I was overdue for leave but Raghavan asked me to stay to provide continuity particularly as he knew no Spanish or French. Kirat's parents were clamouring to see her and she left (by air) soon after the Raghavans arrived.

In view of my experience with Sant Singh and Amreek Mehta's not having got on with Raghavan in Prague, I was determined not to give any cause for complaint. He was capable and easy to get on with but obviously did not have the character of Tyabji or Ali Yavar Jung. He had come from Berne where he had gone from

Prague and Brussels – Tyabji had stayed on in Brussels as Charge d'Affaires so that Raghavan was the first Indian Ambassador to Belgium and Luxembourg.

Raghavan told me the story of his posting to Berne,

'In Brussels I developed a pain in my upper back which would not go away. The Embassy's doctor was unable to do anything about it. Shortly afterwards, Panditji came to Europe and called a conference of Indian Heads of Mission to Europe in London. I took the opportunity to consult a specialist in Harley street who was unable to solve the problem so I told Panditji about it and he very helpfully transferred me to Berne because, as he said, 'The best doctors in the world are in Vienna and from Brussels you will be concurrently accredited in Vienna and Vatican City.'

'But I found that the specialists in Vienna were equally mystified by my pain. By this time I was due for leave and returned to Kerala where I was told of a specialist in Madras city who might be helpful. I went to Madras where I had been a student many years earlier. The address I had been given was in a street I did not know and, when I got there it did not look a prosperous area. The Doctor's consulting room was upstairs and I had to climb a long and narrow flight of uncarpeted wooden steps. I thought then of the consulting rooms of European specialists with their lifts or magnificent carpeted staircases and felt that I had come down in the world. This impression was accentuated when I knocked on the door and a voice said, 'come in'. When I went in, there was a man sitting facing me at a plain deal table who was writing something. He did not even bother to look at me and said, 'Yes, what is the problem?' I told him my story. It was only then that he lifted his head, looked at me and said, 'If you will do *sirshasan* without a cushion after the age of forty-five, what do you expect?'' Sirshasan is the yoga exercise in which you have to stand on your head.

Mrs. Raghavan was a well-educated good looking woman; Kerala has the highest literacy of any state in India and Malayalis - as people of Kerala are called - have done very well abroad, generally as professionals. When the Ambassador took Hitindar on a trip, I made a point of taking Mrs. Raghavan and separately Jitindar and her children out for tea.

I was spending most of my free time with the Hoopers who gave a dinner for me on my birthday; it was, in fact, my thirty-fifth birthday, the day on which according to Dante a man enters middle age.

There did not seem to be much point in my staying all on my own in Buenos Aires. Normally, I should have gone by the Royal Mail Lines ship on which my successor was to arrive but I persuaded the Ambassador to let me go by the previous ship.

XVII

BETWEEN POSTS 1956

In fact, I had been looking forward to a restful time between posts and asked a friend in the Indian High Commission in London to arrange things so that I would get a certificate saying that I was held up by lack of shipping space. The Ministry had not told me what my next post was so I had my heavy luggage put in a liftvan and left with what the shipping company would allow as accompanied luggage.

In London I stayed in a hotel near Marble Arch; the room was big enough to enable me to repack my luggage. I had left Buenos Aires in the middle of the southern winter early in June. I had arrived in London three weeks later in the middle of the summer. The ship would go through the Red Sea at the hottest time of year and I would arrive in Bombay in the early monsoon. In London rationing had ended and everything seemed to be much more expensive. Thomas Traube was passing through London and we spent a day together. He confirmed what I already suspected – that his marriage was breaking up. In Argentina he had been living rather luxuriously off Tania's money and now he had to get a job. He had found a friend who had invented a new process called 'spark erosion' which enabled metal castings to be accurately shaped without resort to lathes and grinding machines and he had been put in charge of sales. He was leading a bachelor existence. On the other hand the work was challenging and he was glad to be able to use his considerable technical intellect and ability which had got rather rusty through years of disuse.

I also took the opportunity to go to Paris for a week and stay with H.S.Malik and his family in the Embassy which I had never seen before. The house dated back to the beginning of the century when it had been built near the Eiffel Tower by a wealthy Frenchman whom an American Duchess of Marlborough had remarried after her divorce. Naturally, he did not want her to feel that she had come down in the world.

The house must have been bought in 1948 by Sir Raghavan Pillai, but no Ambassador was selected for Paris till late 1949. In the meantime there was great competition for the post and one or more Charge d'Affaires had occupied it without bothering to see if it was in good condition. When H.S.Malik arrived he found it needed a lot of work to make it suitable for an Embassy residence. Fortunately, the firm which had built it could be identified. Not only was it still in existence but the original plans could be found. It took some months to restore it during which the family had to live in a hotel. When we had passed through Paris at the end of January 1950, they had gone away for a few days.

Apart from the lack of a family residence, H.S.Malik's arrival in Paris was a great success. When he presented his credentials to President Vincent Auriol, the latter had wiped a tear from his eye and said, 'You shed your blood for France' referring to an injury he had received while flying a fighter plane over French territory during the Great War. Probably, the French President was also aware that the new Ambassador had served briefly in the French Army as an ambulance driver.

Between 1949 and my visit in 1956, he had made a lot of friends and acquired considerable renown in Paris. When Queen Elizabeth II paid an official visit to Paris, he was the senior Commonwealth Ambassador in France and the magazine PARIS MATCH had, in its centre spread, given him greater prominence than the British Ambassador!

I remembered that in 1948, Sir Raghavan Pillai mentioned by me on the previous page, who was a friend and contemporary of H.S.Malik's (they were both colleagues in the Indian Civil Service) had visited Brussels in his capacity of Commissioner General for Economic and Commercial Affairs in Europe. He had also visited the other Indian Missions in Europe and written a report on the Heads of Mission. This report had leaked out and, when Badruddin Tyabji went to London for a meeting of Heads of Indian Missions with Prime Minister Nehru, Sir Girja Shankar Bajpai had told him about this report,

'Sir Raghavan's remark on R.K.Nehru, our Minister in Stockholm was interesting. He said, 'I don't think R.K.Nehru would be satisfied if he were to be made Prime Minister of India.''

To which Tyabji responded, 'Ah, like Alexander the Great he is looking for new worlds to conquer.'

'Yes, Tyabji, but Alexander the Great had the sense to die young!'

R.K.Nehru was an I.C.S. Officer distantly related to Prime Minister Nehru. By the early nineteen fifties he had become Foreign Secretary – a very important position, as Head of the Indian Foreign Service and which carries the right of direct access to the Prime Minister i.e. by-passing the Foreign Minister. He decided that he could solve the problem of the French possessions in India by going to Paris and discussing the matter with the French government. He arrived in Paris and was received at the airport by the Counsellor of the Embassy, Yog Puri who told me this story several years later. Puri told him that he would be at his (Foreign Secretary's) disposal for the whole of his stay but after the appointments were made, he went to see the French officials alone. On the second day, he told Puri that the talks were not going well and he wanted to know what the French were up to. Puri suggested that he meet the Ambassador. A meeting was arranged and Puri accompanied R.K.Nehru to the Ambassador's residence. He explained that his talks were not going well. H.S.Malik replied,

'Yes, there was a meeting of the Foreign Affairs sub-committee of the Cabinet on the day you arrived and it was decided there that the talks would be *brusqué* on Thursday which is tomorrow.'

'What! You knew this all the time and you never told me?'

'Did you consult me? Do you ever consult anybody? No, you don't. Well go ahead and do your best all by yourself since you know everything.'

Of course, the Foreign Secretary had to return to India without achieving anything.

During my visit, K.P.S.Menon, our then Ambassador in Moscow, passed through Paris – his son K.P.S.Menon, Jr. (Shankar to his friends) was First Secretary and was treated like a member of the Malik family – and a lunch was given in his honour. The elder Menon had acquired a legendary reputation. I have mentioned that he was Ambassador in Chungking in 1946. This had involved going there overland in the middle of the World War. He was a very good writer and had written several books about his experiences. Besides, he took very good care of his staff and was always highly praised by his subordinates. He built up very good relations with the Russian government at a time when Krishna Menon was going all out to wreck India's relations with the West.

At this lunch, he told us how his predecessor, Dr. S. Radhakrishnan – later President of India – had patted Stalin on the back! Stalin was not interested in meeting Ambassadors and was not a friend of India. Besides, he had the curious habit , from his revolutionary days, of working at night and sleeping during the day. It was reported to him that the Indian Ambassador could not stand the Russian winter and spent the whole day in bed – even to the extent of receiving official visitors there. This had intrigued him and he had invited Dr. Radhakrishnan for a meeting at midnight. The conversation on the world political situation had gone very well. Finally, Stalin asked,

'Tell me, what do you think I can do to reduce the tension in the world?'

'I think, Mr. Prime Minister, that you can dismantle the Cominform because it is regarded by all non-communists as a threat to their very existence and it does not appear to be achieving the object for which it was created. The other step I would venture to recommend is withdrawing Soviet Armed Forces from Eastern Europe.'

'No, that I cannot even contemplate; the Americans would immediately move in their Army to replace ours. About the Cominform, I shall think about it.' The conversation had ended on that note and the Ambassador had taken his leave, patting his host on his back and advising him to take care of himself.

I arrived in Bombay after an uneventful voyage. Kirat, her parents and her aunt Simrat were at the quay to receive me in Bombay and they took me to a flat which had been 'de-requisitioned in favour of Mr. J.A. Singh, Chief Conservator of

Forests, Maharashtra'. This piece of jargon meant that a fifty year old three bedroom flat in a prime location a few hundred yards from the Taj Mahal hotel had been requisitioned during the World War for the Government's needs. In 1956, when it was no longer required, instead of being returned to its owner, it was being handed over to a favoured government servant who would have the use of it for a nominal rent. All this was, of course, completely legal. The family was able to keep the flat for many years. In the nineteen eighties, after the demise of Mr. and Mrs. Singh, the original owner – I suppose his successor – got it back from their son Harinder, I do not really know how, shortly before the latter died.

The Singhs did not have enough furniture for this flat and we slept on the floor. Of course, there was no air conditioning, but in Bombay during the monsoon very few people used air conditioning.

I had acquired a cine camera and projector just before leaving Buenos Aires and had taken shots during the long trip. A friend of the Singhs had just returned from a trip to Europe during which he had bought a Zeiss cine camera but no projector. Of course, he was very keen to see his film so we put it in. He had not learnt how to hold the cine camera. There were hilarious shots of people walking in a recumbent position up vertical roads!

We took the train to go to New Delhi where Mataji and some relations received us on the platform from which Pitaji had seen us off in 1952. Mataji burst into tears at the recollection – one of the few occasions on which I have seen her cry.

She had managed the situation very well in my absence. I have related how Pitaji's money ran out before the house was completed. She completed the house with his insurance money and a bank loan. She then rented out both floors to the U.S. Embassy. At that time there was a very serious housing shortage in Delhi and the Government waived income tax on rent from new houses for two years. She had paid off all the loans. With the proceeds of the sale of the Chevrolet car, she had paid for my Vauxhall and an Austin for herself. As she had never learned to drive she kept on the driver, Ranjit Singh. She also kept on Bharat Singh who had been engaged for me in 1946 on the occasion of my brief visit to India.

H.M.Patel had been invaluable at the difficult time of Pitaji's illness. After he died, he had managed to get a hutment for Mataji of a type given to families of Army Officers posted to non-family stations. Perhaps this was misuse of his position as Defence Secretary but we were very grateful for it. When I arrived with my little family, we were invited by Tayaji to stay in the house at 43 Rajpur Road to which he had held on by means of a series of lawsuits – the 'Custodian of Evacuee Property' had claimed it. I found the hot weather unbearable and decided to go to Kashmir. We all flew to Srinagar and Bharat Singh was told to follow by train and bus with the heavy luggage.

I remembered our previous visit to Srinagar in 1936. On that occasion, Dadaji had offered Pitaji a car which he had seized from the English tenant of a shop which the Englishman had rented, when he could not pay the rent because his business had failed. Of course, this car was old and rather decrepit but it did take us to Srinagar. On our two previous visits we had gone by taxi to Srinagar. This time we had the facility of a car at our disposal in Srinagar. Our houseboat was tied up on the left bank of the Jehlum; half-a-mile further upstream were the houseboats of the sons of the Nizam of Hyderabad, one of whom was married to Niloufer the beautiful daughter of the last Sultan of Turkey – she was a head taller than her husband. Two huge new American convertibles were constantly being driven past our houseboat. At the ripe old age of fifteen, I felt humiliated because our car was so old. Pitaji had sold his Ford V8 before leaving Ahmedabad with the intention of buying a new one on his return from leave. I wanted him to buy a new car there and then which, of course he refused to do.

Many things had changed in the intervening twenty years. We took a taxi from the airport to the Tourist Reception Centre. We had lunch there during which we were besieged by houseboat owners. We chose one tied up on the right bank of the river. I was no longer a child but the head of a family. We went up and down the river in shikaras. Mataji showed us a large brick-built riverside mansion which her father had rented from a nobleman in 1900 and which now carried a signboard proclaiming it to be a school. She showed us another more modern two-storeyed house built of wood where they had lived most of the summers that my Nanaji was the Law Member of the Maharaja of Kashmir's council. In 1956 it had become Lambert's Pharmacy. I think I have mentioned that in many Indian cities pharmacies were the only shops stocking imported goods so they tended to be quite large and we were able to go up and down, pretending to be shoppers, and seeing the house. From Pitaji, I had heard the story that when he was a teenager he had accompanied his father on a formal visit to my Nanaji in Srinagar. As they got into the entrance hall, they were shocked to see a tomboy sliding down the banister. Of course, as soon as this pre-teen girl reached the bottom she ran up the stairs and disappeared. It was his first sight of his fiancée.

Mataji knew all the sights of Kashmir quite well and I remembered them from the earlier visits in 1924, 1928 and 1936. Kirat had never been to Kashmir. Her grandfather had been spending his summers in Mussoorie. I was keen to show her and Kiran all the sights. We had to go to places outside Srinagar by taxi which was not very agreeable. Anyway, we had to climb Shankaracharya hill after getting to its foot by shikara. By this time Bharat Singh had arrived and he had to carry Kiran part of the way. I could vaguely remember having been carried up myself in 1924.

Communication while living in a houseboat was a problem. I had left my address in Delhi as 'Poste Restante, Srinagar Post Office' and this necessitated a daily visit to the Post Office on the Bund. One day I found a telegram, 'Call xxx xxxx, NEW DELHI'. This phone call could only be made from the Post Office. Kirat was very excited and insisted on being there when I made the call.

When passing through Delhi I had inquired about my next posting. I gathered from friends that it had been intended to post me to Kathmandu but the Ambassador had decided that he did not want an Officer so senior that he had been a Head of Mission for two years - we had never met but perhaps the word had got around to him that I did not speak Hindi fluently. Officially I had been told that the Kathmandu posting was off and I could go and enjoy my leave.

As we had all anticipated, the call was about my next posting. I was told that the First Secretary in Tokyo had taken ill and would probably require long treatment and convalescence; I was required to go to Tokyo and this would count as a compulsory recall from leave. This last bit of jargon had financial implications favourable to me.

Kirat was of course next to me trying her best to listen in on a call by a rather poor landline. 'Where? Where?' she kept on saying so I said 'Tokyo' to which she immediately replied, 'Say yes!' which left me with no choice.

The background to Kirat's enthusiasm was that her mother's younger sister, Raje was married to an Army Officer, Lt.Col. Joginder Singh. This gentleman was a Cambridge (Peterhouse) graduate and had obtained a wartime commission in the Army. At the end of the war, he had been posted to Japan with the Indian Military Mission. Raje had never been abroad and had lived in cantonments all her married life. She found Japan delightful especially as accommodation, food and all furnishings came out of 'occupation costs' – virtually they were living free and saving all Joginder's pay and allowances.

We returned to Delhi staying this time with Uncle I.S. and Aunt Jeet while arrangements were made for my journey. The final decision was that I should fly and Kirat and Kiran, accompanied by Mataji, would travel by ship from Calcutta. It would take time to find a ship during which time Kirat would find a servant – the government would pay his passage. In the meantime, an Army Officer offered to sublet his house for us – contrary to military regulations but profitably for him and conveniently for us.

I think I should say something about Bharat Singh at this stage. He had been my servant in 1947-48 when I was in Delhi. When I was posted to Brussels in January 1948, my parents took him over. In 1952, when I left for Buenos Aires they gave me Jeevan, their butler as being a more experienced man who would do all our work. Bharat Singh took over the duties of butler. A few days later my father died and his pension ended with him. Mataji knew very well that she could not live in the same style as before. She, therefore, dismissed the cook and told Bharat Singh he would have to do all the work as long as they lived in the Army quarters which H.M.Patel had obtained for her and he did.

When she had arranged her new way of life, she said to him,

'As long as Sahib was there, we were increasing your pay by ten rupees per month every year. Now that he is gone, I cannot do that. You are twenty-two years old and have your whole life before you. You should go to school and then try to get a job as a chaprasi. You will stay in my servant's quarter and work in the morning and evening. I shall find another youngster to work part time while you are not there. I shall go on paying you what I have been paying you so far.'

Bharat Singh gratefully accepted this arrangement. Bharat Singh passed his matriculation and got a job as a chaprasi in an insurance company. He took leave to accompany us to Kashmir in 1956. He did not accompany us to Tokyo because of the job he had.

XVIII

TOKYO 1956-59

I arrived in Tokyo in September 1956 and found my predecessor, Avtar Dar still there but not attending office. He was my batchmate and friend from the time we had been living in Metcalfe House hutments. Since then, he had married Rita Pandit, the youngest daughter of Vijayalakshmi Pandit who, in turn, was the sister of Pandit Nehru. Mrs. Pandit was a politician in her own right; she had been a Minister in the Government in U.P. After Independence she was appointed Ambassador in Moscow. She had also been the first woman President of the U.N. General Assembly.

I found Rita to be a very pleasant and delightful person who behaved exactly as a friend and colleague's wife without putting on any airs as the niece of the Prime Minister. She invited me to lunch in their house which I would be occupying after their departure. Avtar appeared to me to be quite well but he told me he had frequent fits of giddiness which had been diagnosed as Meniere's syndrome. Fortunately this diagnosis proved to be wrong because Meniere's syndrome was incurable at that time and results in deafness. When he got to India, the giddiness responded to treatment and he never had it again.

The Embassy in Tokyo was larger than the three Embassies I had served in. The Ambassador was an I.C.S. Officer, Mr.B.R.Sen, who had been Food Secretary at the time of Independence and a Commissioner in Bengal before Independence. When I arrived he was not there because he was leading the Indian delegation to the annual assembly of the Food and Agriculture Organisation in Rome so I straightaway became Charge d'Affaires for a few days. I met his second wife and youngest daughter, Urmila who was not married. They were a good looking family.

The next Officer to me was the Military Attaché, Colonel Nishi Chatterjee. He and his wife Carol were very popular; they were good looking and very hospitable. Chatterjee is a Bengali Brahmin name but, to my great surprise, neither of them knew any Bengali and they were Anglican Christians. The family had been living in North India for a couple of generations and Carol was actually from U.P. Nishi spoke as good Punjabi as I.

There was a First Secretary (Commercial) Dinker Hejmadi. He did not belong to the Indian Foreign Service but had been sent to Tokyo by the Ministry of Commerce. He and his wife, Sarguna, were vegetarians and served only vegetarian meals to their guests whether Japanese or other diplomats. This did not make them popular. Otherwise they were socially active and he was well informed about commercial matters.

There was a Press Attaché, Emmanuel Pouchepadass and his French wife Christianne. Emmanuel did not belong to the Indian Foreign Service but his reputation as a French scholar went back many years. I recalled vaguely that Eugene de Ligne, the Belgian Ambassador in Delhi nine years earlier, had heard of him and had recommended him to Sir Girja Shankar Bajpai. He was a Pondicherrian by birth so he enjoyed the choice of French and Indian nationalities. Pouchepadass is a Bengali rather than a Tamil name so I asked him about it; it appeared that one of his ancestors had migrated from Chandernagore (also a French possession) to Pondicherry. He spoke no Bengali; his mother tongue was Tamil. He had studied at the Ecole Normale Superieure de la Rue d'Ulm which was the foremost French Grande Ecole before the post-war creation of the Ecole Nationale d'Administration. Graduates were known as 'archicubes'. Most of them got major administrative appointments in government departments or in Industry. In theory, they were qualified to teach in Lycees – Secondary schools. In addition he had got an 'agregation' which entitled him to get a higher salary if he taught in a government school. I found out subsequently that he had won the 'croix militaire' for his war service. Like most

Tamils he was rather dark-skinned; in addition he was fairly bald at the age of 37.

I asked Christianne, whose spoken English was not very good, where she had met this Indian. She said that in 1940, his company had been quartered on her father's estate – he had a wine chateau in South West France not far from Bordeaux - and she had fallen in love with 'his beautiful black hair' which, unfortunately had not lasted very long. They had four children, two girls and two boys, and were living in a rented house – the only Officer in the Embassy of First Secretary rank to do so.

There was a Second Secretary (Commercial) Pran Neville whose job was to collect statistics – I never knew why. His brother died rather suddenly in India and he asked for a transfer home. Later, he got a series of U.N.jobs. In the twenty-first century he has, of course, retired and built up a reputation as a historian writing books about nineteenth century Punjab.

Finally there was Ashok Chib and his beautiful young wife, Padma. He was a Third Secretary and, at that stage in his career, supposed to be learning Arabic! Due to some bureaucratic blunder he had been sent to Tokyo but was recalled soon afterwards. He had a normal career but during a posting in an East European country, an injury to an arm while playing tennis became septic which ruined his health. He died soon after retirement.

Ambassador Sen came back from Rome for a few weeks. He had been elected Director General of F.A.O. to India's great satisfaction. As it turned out he acquired a very good reputation in F.A.O. and whenever I met U.N. Officials they were full of praise for him. Apparently, there had been only one other Indian Director General of a major U.N. Agency who was technically brilliant but not popular, especially with his subordinates.

Before Mr. Sen left, there was an official visit by our Vice President, Dr. Radhakrishnan. He wanted to call on the British Ambassador, Cavendish Bentinck whom I had met in Addis Ababa where he had been Ambassador. I accompanied him on this call. The Ambassador said, 'I always manage to get one or two Japanese Members of Parliament for my parties. I am surprised to find that though they are formally dressed in morning coats, they are usually literally out-at-elbows and down-at-heel. Cabinet changes are quite frequent here and I have noticed that once a man has been a Minister, even for a day, he is never again seen in old clothes.'

I was impressed by the way in which the Head of Mission ran the office. He had a staff meeting every morning so we all knew what was going on in the Embassy. However, he told me that he had always refused to have a Sikh Personal Assistant or Private Secretary because people – particularly foreigners – thought that the Sikh must be the boss! He was a tall, well built, handsome man but he was right. My very next Head of Mission was short, tubby and prematurely white headed and he was unhappy that some Japanese thought that I was the Ambassador which, of course, did not help our relations.

In the meantime I was Charge d'Affaires for six months. During this period, the ship arrived carrying Mataji, Kirat and Kiran. For Kiran the change was very great. The only language he could speak was Spanish which was of no use in Tokyo. Apart from that Kirat was pregnant – she had realised it soon after I had left India! One of the friends I had made on arrival in Tokyo was the Canadian First Secretary John Halstead. I had met him and his American wife Jean at the Dars' and she was obviously going to have a baby within a few weeks. The baby was born at the Seventh Day Adventist Hospital. This information would be useful to us. In fact, Kirat liked the Seventh Day doctors and the administration so much that, in subsequent posts, we always looked for Seventh Day hospitals.

I have mentioned that I was to take over the house of the Dars and I welcomed my family there when they arrived. But it was essentially a Japanese house and it proved very inconvenient in the cold November weather. Shortly after that the Chatterjees left on the completion of their tenure and I quickly moved into their house which had been built for a German doctor at the beginning of the century. It had a garage, central heating and seventeen rooms and one proper European bathroom.

Kirat had been very keen on going to Japan but the inconveniences of life in Tokyo soon became apparent. The house did have a small garden but it was not enough for the activities of a very large six-year-old boy. Kiran was nearly twice the size of Japanese boys of his age. Fortunately, we found a Canadian Catholic Mission school where most of the students were

1956 Tokyo, Japan With Mataji, Kirat and Kiran.

Europeans and North and South Americans who were nearer in size to Kiran. Traffic in Tokyo was slow and chaotic and few diplomats used public transport. In fact, I never saw the Tokyo underground system. Diplomats arranged car pools for their children to go to school. We soon established good relations with the Spanish speaking diplomats. One day, Kiran was to travel to school in the car of the Argentine Charge d'Affaires. When he got in, he greeted the Argentines with 'Buenos dias.' The little boy turned to his mother and asked, in English, 'Mama, what is he saying?' The Argentine boy had been born and brought up abroad and only spoke English – it was the counterpart of our situation! The mother, of course, was covered with shame as she told us when we met her next.

I have mentioned that the Embassy was a large one. The Ambassador's residence was big and beautiful. It had belonged to a very wealthy Japanese nobleman. Apart from several large bedrooms and three drawing rooms, the dining room could easily seat twenty-four. Unusually for Tokyo it had a large lawn in the back garden where several hundred guests could be accommodated for a cocktail party. In Brussels and Buenos Aires, the Embassy had had a car for the Ambassador and a staff car. Here we had two staff cars. When I arrived, I found that one of the staff cars had been placed at the disposal of the Chief Minister of West Bengal whose visit to Tokyo lasted several months - I never found out why. The driver of this staff car had a small flat over the garage of the house where I lived.

Our second son, Arun (Arunpal Singh) was born early on the morning of 6th April 1957. He arrived some six weeks prematurely but he grew up quite fast to make up for it. He was born with bow-legs and had to wear braces to straighten them while he slept. This worked out very well. We got a Japanese nanny for him but communication with her proved difficult and we soon got rid of her. Of its many rooms, the house had two big bedrooms on the first floor directly above the dining room and the drawing room. One of these was ours and the other was Mataji's. A playpen was put in it and Arun used to spend most of the day in the playpen when it was too cold to go outside.

Kiran made friends with a neighbourhood boy - I think he was the son of a Korean physician. They did not have a common language but that did not prevent them playing together. The street in which our house was located was very narrow so that if a car was parked in it, it was difficult for a truck to pass. It had no footpath and gutters nearly two feet deep for the rain water. One day the boys were riding their bicycles and came around a blind corner. A light van - essentially a ten horsepower car - belonging to a multinational company knocked Kiran down and ran over him or rather his left forearm and left leg. The Japanese driver behaved very well and Kiran was taken to the Seventh-Day Adventist hospital quite quickly. I was in my office when I got Kirat's agonized phone call. The doctors were very good and put the broken limbs in plaster using new technologies that I was not familiar with. The epiphesis of the left radius had become detached. This was serious for a growing child because, it was explained to me, the epiphesis contains the growth centre and if it is not properly repaired the arm can become very seriously deformed. This calamity was prevented; in fact, Kiran's left wrist is no more deformed than mine after a similar fracture thirty-seven years later and unnoticeable except to an orthopaedist.

The leg fracture was worse. The tibia had broken and was protruding through the skin. There was also a 'green stick fracture' of the fibula. Seventh Day Adventist hospitals have no specialised orthopaedists but the doctors were very helpful and they arranged for Kiran to be seen by an American specialist with the result that both limbs were properly repaired and he has not had any problem with them in consequence. What we did not know was that the body had supplied so much calcium to repair the fractures that he subsequently had two bone ailments known as Schnurmann's disease and Osgood-Schlatter's syndrome. Apparently there was a genetic predisposition to these on my side of the family.

In the meantime the New Ambassador, Chandra Shekhar Jha, accompanied by his wife Lakshmi and son Prem had arrived. I have described the Ambassador's appearance previously. His wife was good looking. They were both Maithil Brahmins which means that they came from a part of North Bihar where the Maithli dialect of Hindi is spoken. When they spoke to each other, I could not make out a word. Mr. Jha's father was a lawyer and he had passed the I.C.S. competitive examination in India and gone to England for his training as was the practice. Many years later, one of his batch-mates told me that the young I.C.S. probationers were much sought after by the resident Indian gentry in London who had daughters of marriageable age. However, he said, 'Jha refused to take advantage of the available opportunities because he said he was already betrothed to a beautiful girl who, unfortunately, was uneducated and had the mentality of a villager.'

This must have happened nearly twenty years earlier. What we found was that Mrs.Jha's spoken English left something to be desired. She was well dressed and smart and it soon became obvious that she had a very high idea of her own importance. It was rumoured that, in a previous post, she had said to her husband, in the hearing of the staff,

'You do not know how to speak to an Ambassadress.'

Prem was ready to go to Cambridge. His elder brother, known as Shuntoo, whom I did not meet till several years later, got into the Indian Foreign Service. Prem became a successful journalist and, in the twenty-first century writes an economic column in the Hindustan Times. Earlier, he was a foreign correspondent covering the Eastern Mediterranean. His wife was killed in an air raid on an Arab city by the Israeli Air Force.

During C.S.Jha's tenure there was a major attempt to build up Indo-Japanese relations. The Japanese Prime Minister visited India in a tour of Asian countries. Pandit Nehru came on an official visit to Japan, the first by any Indian Prime Minister. There is a background to this. All the Allied countries demanded war reparations from Japan because 'Japan had committed unprovoked aggression' against them'. India proclaimed that it did not want reparations from a country which had suffered so much from the war, particularly from atom bombs. We expected the Japanese to be grateful for this but Dinker Hejmadi told us that the businessmen he talked to had a contrary view. According to him, they were saying,

'Why did you not insist on reparations? That would have opened trading channels between our countries which would have benefited both Japan and India. Look how well trade has developed between us and the countries of South East Asia starting with what were, in effect, free gifts by us to them. We are having so much trouble trying to export our products to you because of your non-tariff barriers.'

Of course, officially, the Gaimusho (Japanese Ministry of Foreign Affairs) did not contradict our view that we had been generous. Pandit Nehru was very well received and his visit was followed by a State Visit by President Rajendra Prashad. This was a very formal affair. For the first time, the President travelled by a chartered Air India plane; Pandit Nehru had come as a passenger on a scheduled flight.

I had gone to the airport more than once as Charge d'Affaires for state visits by Heads of State and had been impressed by the presence of the Emperor and the Empress. When I accompanied the Ambassador to see the Chief of Protocol to discuss the ceremonial of our President's visit, we were surprised to find no mention of the Emperor. I said that the Emperor had received the Shah of Iran some months earlier. The answer was,

'There are family relationships between Japan and Iran.'

'Surely the Japanese Imperial Family is not related to the Iranian Royal Family?'

'I mean Prince Takamatsu visited Tehran last year.'

We could not make head or tail of this so it was finally explained to us that a Crowned Head is different from a President. We returned to our Chancery rather dejected.

I was an avid reader of the London TIMES which we were receiving daily by air, especially of the Court Circular. Chateaubriand wrote, 'The memory is perhaps the quality which goes with foolishness.' He himself had a good memory and so have I. I soon found the item about the visit to the United Kingdom of President and Mrs. Einaudi of Italy. I rushed with it to the Ambassador and next day we were back in the Gaimusho with the paper in my hand. The Ambassador showed the Chief of Protocol the photograph of Queen Elizabeth II and the Duke of Edinburgh greeting the Italian couple. The Emperor went to Haneda airport.

The Ministry allowed the Ambassador and the First Secretary to take one Indian servant each to Tokyo. In addition the Ambassador was paid to employ four Japanese maids while I was expected to have three. I had inherited my three maids from the Dars and, since then, we had got them uniforms of new kimonos. Kirat had managed to establish peace between Barua our Indian cook and the maids. Mrs. Jha was not as successful and her Indian cook had had to be repatriated. They had found a competent cook but Dr. Rajendra Prasad liked Indian food and there was going to be the problem of providing it in the special train which was taking him – accompanied by the Ambassador - to Osaka and Kobe. Jha asked for my cook and, of course, I made no difficulty about that, but Kirat said there would be problems between him and the Japanese catering staff on the train. She said it would be better if she was on the train also to control him. I conveyed this to the Ambassador. That evening we were all at a party for our President and Mrs. Jha accosted Kirat and scolded her. Kirat was naturally quite upset. Relations with Mrs. Jha were never the same again. C.S.Jha was a successful Ambassador in Japan and other countries and a very good Permanent Representative to United Nations.

As I have mentioned, Tokyo was an important post. According to the Japanese, the country was experiencing the 'greatest boom since Jimmo' (the mythical founder of the Japanese Empire) and many Indian V.I.P.s were interested in knowing how it was being done. There were also international conferences and meetings for which Indian delegates came. One day I got a letter from Fori Nehru that her mother-in-law Rameshwari Nehru was going to Tokyo for a conference. I called her on the telephone the day after she arrived and she said the conference arrangements were excellent and she had had no problems; she agreed to come for lunch.

I picked her up in my car and drove her home. During lunch she was full of praise for what the Japanese had done to rebuild their country after the war and the excellent social services – health, education, welfare etc. – they had set up. Generally, how advanced they were when compared with India. I pointed out that many basic facilities were lacking. The roads were poor. There was no such thing as municipal street lighting. In a shopping district like Ginza, there was a profusion of light at night paid for by the shopkeepers but in a fashionable residential street like mine there was one street light provided by a resident. There was no such thing as a sewage system. People had toilets in their homes which municipal employees would empty manually and put into wooden buckets which they would line up neatly on the roadside where they would stand stinking to high heaven until a truck came to pick them up. The contents of the buckets were sold to farmers who would use them to manure their fields. I could see from her expression that the old lady did not believe what I was saying; either her daughter-in-law's young friend was an idiot or pulling her leg.

By this time, she was ready to go back to her conference. As I accompanied her to my car I was still talking,

'Of course, I have the good fortune to be a privileged person. This house was built for a German and it has flush toilets but they drain into a septic tank which has to be emptied from time to time.'

As I said these words, we emerged from the house and the elderly lady started sniffing. With good reason because there was a large truck with a pump which was working away. A four inch flexible pipe was going from the truck to a hole in the courtyard of my house. She did not say much on the way back to the conference. However, she treated me kindly when I met her next a few years later.

I mentioned previously that we had gone to Bombay from Ahmedabad and stayed with the H.M.Patel family in their flat in the Bombay Secretariat. In fact, there were two Resident Under Secretaries at that time occupying adjoining flats; the other was H.V.R.Iengar, a Tamil Brahmin. Obviously, the two I.C.S.Officers were of about the same age and good friends. That must have been in 1936. In 1957, H.V.R.Iengar was Governor of the Reserve Bank. Returning to India from the Fund/Bank meeting in Washington, he came through Tokyo where he was the house guest of the Ambassador. One morning, his host told him that he had to go to a sit-down dinner where he could not take him so he hoped he would not mind having dinner all by himself.

'Dinner alone? Isn't Gunwant Malik the First Secretary here? I will ask him to give me dinner.'

'You know Malik?'

'Yes, of course, he is the son of J.S.Malik, the engineer. I have known him since he was a boy and came to Bombay for an examination.'

Of course, we were delighted to give a dinner for the Governor of the Reserve Bank who was besides very good company. However, such a guest would like to meet others of similar status at a dinner. I could not think of inviting V.I.P.s at eight hours notice for a formal dinner – one can only do that with good friends to whom one can explain the situation. I think we managed to have a sit-down dinner for ten. One of the guests was the Honorary Consul for Lebanon who was, as it happened, a Lebanese importer of non-ferrous metals.

Iengar was very pleased with the dinner and stayed on after the others had gone. He said he had been talking to the Lebanese who had told him that he would like his two sons to go to Oxford – Iengar was an Oxonian – and had asked how it could be done. Iengar explained the requirements and procedure and added that it was fairly expensive.

'What does it cost?'

'In my days it was four hundred pounds a year; today it must be five times that.'

'Four thousand pounds a year for the two boys; no problem.'

Iengar had missed the word 'Honorary' and thought that the man he was talking to was a consul paid by his government and Lebanon was hardly likely to pay more to its consuls than India. He said to me, 'I had no idea that I was talking to a millionaire businessman to whom such trifles do not matter!'

In the meantime my past was catching up with me. The Ministry of External Affairs had found out – I had made no secret of it - that I had sold three cars during my three and a half years in South America and made a profit of three thousand pounds sterling. Each car had been sold with the permission of the 'host' government and according to the regulations for import of cars by junior diplomats. There were precedents. I was charged, as far as I could make out, with conduct unbecoming an Officer and a gentleman in that I had become a 'merchant'. This could mean the termination of my career.

I have asked myself if I had some powerful enemy who wanted me removed and I am convinced that I had no such enemy at that time. Of course, many colleagues would feel envious of me because they had not had the opportunity to be simultaneously accredited in two countries with severe import restrictions and exchange controls which made the import of cars and their subsequent sale by diplomats so profitable. On the other hand, conversations I have had with diplomats from other countries have convinced me that such actions are fairly common but are not appreciated by governments and the individual's reputation and career usually suffer in consequence.

Immediately, the 'political incorrectness' of my behaviour was that there had been a number of such cases and the individual had been let off with a reprimand and the surrender of his profit. There had been questions in Parliament and criticism had been voiced over the 'compounding' of an offence. Others had sold one car; my offence was particularly heinous in that I had sold *three* cars. Informally, the Union Public Service Commission had declared that I could not possibly be saved. My career was considered to be at an end and the question was which of two or three forms of dismissal was to be the punishment to be awarded. Of course, all this was corridor gossip because the administrative procedure is long and complicated and it had not even been initiated. My friends advised me to take leave, return to Delhi, and see what I could do. I did so.

Some years earlier, H.M.Patel had been transferred from the Ministry of Defence to the Ministry of Finance. There has always been more than one Secretary in the Ministry of Finance and the senior one is known as Finance Secretary. In recognition of H.M.Patel's seniority and experience he had been designated 'Principal Finance Secretary' – something which had not been done since pre-Independence times. He still had the same salary as any other Secretary but, in terms of the warrant of precedence, he was practically equal to the Secretary General in the Ministry of External Affairs.

A scandal had occurred in the newly created Life Insurance Corporation of India (L.I.C.). It was said that the Corporation had purchased fake securities from a Calcutta businessman named Mundra. The L.I.C. was under the tutelage of the Finance Minister, a Madras businessman named T.T.Krishnamachari who was a favourite of the Prime Minister. There had been a Cabinet meeting at which Pandit Nehru had defended T.T.K. and the Minister of Education, Maulana Abul Kalam Azad had got up and left, saying, 'I cannot sit at table with this man.' He died shortly afterwards.

A scapegoat had to be found. Who decided that that should be Hiralal Mooljibhai Patel? Politicians are a different class from civil servants in India. On files, ministers give their orders verbally to civil servants who sign the files. The Prime Minister decided that his friend the Finance Minister must be saved at all costs. The Principal Finance Secretary had risen very high in his profession and must necessarily have made enemies who would welcome the chance of hitting him and enhancing the position of the politicians at the expense of the civil service.

The procedure is meant to provide justice. There has to be a preliminary enquiry. This produced an equivocal result but the Government decided to proceed with the charge. There had not been such a charge against a Secretary for several years. The disagreement and subsequent death of the Education Minister who had been President of the Indian National Congress at the time of the Cabinet Mission in 1946 had attracted widespread national interest. The newspapers contained little other news.

I arrived at this stage. My benefactor and principal friend who had treated me almost like the son he never had was in deep trouble when I went to see him and ask for his assistance. He refused to admit that he had problems of his own and listened wholeheartedly to my tale of woe. Other senior friends I spoke to assured me that I had done well to speak to H.M.Patel because, they said, he was widely respected by the bureaucracy and his word would carry a lot of weight.

Fortunately, Sir Raghavan Pillai was Secretary General of the Ministry of External Affairs. I had first met Sir Raghavan Pillai in the beginning of 1948. I have mentioned that I had been posted to the Protocol section of the Ministry of External Affairs. I was working there under the orders of the Chief of Protocol (Joint Secretary) Ramji Ram Saxena. He was a member of the old Imperial Customs Service who had recently returned from the post of Trade Commissioner in Sydney. I think they had been there a long time – probably held up during the World War. He had five daughters and the two youngest spoke only English and that too with an Australian accent. He was quickly selected for the post of Consul General, New York. He gave up his government accommodation and the family went to stay with his friend the Commerce Secretary who was Sir Raghavan Pillai. Lady Pillai was English and, as far as I could judge, of lower middle class origin. Sir Raghavan himself belonged to one of the foremost Nair (khshatrya) families in Kerala. When I went to pay my farewell call on the Saxenas with whom I had built up excellent relations, I met Sir Raghavan and Lady Pillai. I got the impression that they were keen to get a foreign posting.

This posting was forthcoming and he was appointed Commissioner General for Economic and Commercial Affairs in Europe. In this capacity he came to Brussels in a delegation for some meetings in Belgium and Luxembourg and Tyabji and I had to accompany him. The delegation appeared to be headed by the new Commerce Secretary named Venkataraman. One evening the delegation split up, Sir Raghavan appeared to be at a loose end and I took him to my flat where Kirat and I did our best to cheer him up. His problem was that although the British had made him Knight Commander of the Star of India and he was several years senior in service to Venkataraman, the latter was telling everybody – especially European officials and businessmen - that Sir Raghavan was under his orders. He found this particularly annoying and I got the impression that he wanted to do something about it. He returned to India soon afterwards and I learnt from the Indian newspapers that Venkataraman had been charged with corruption – taking a bribe of a case of whisky – and sentenced to a year in jail which meant dismissal from government service.

To return to my own problem and the threat of dismissal hanging over my head, I had spent most of a month, sitting in the office of Manjit Singh, Private Secretary to the Secretary General. This office was not air conditioned and had two doors opening onto verandahs which were kept open. One of these doors faced one of the doors of the Secretary General's office which was air conditioned and one could see who went in and out of the great man's office or even see him on the rare occasions when he went out of his office. Thus everyone in the Ministry knew I was there although I was officially on leave. I also had opportunities of meeting most of my colleagues in the Ministry.

Manjit Singh was an I.F.S. officer a few years junior to me. He was a keshadhari Jat Sikh whom I had never met before. From his conversation I gathered that he had been suspected of being a Communist which would have been disastrous for his career. He had fought off this accusation by pointing out to the policeman on his tracks that he was a very rich landowner! This was hardly a valid defence because some years earlier it had been fashionable for young men of the upper classes to be Communists. In fact Mohan Kumaramangalam, heir to the large estate of that name in Tamilnad, and his wife had had to go underground because the police had non-bailable warrants to arrest them. However, the policeman had accepted that he was not a Communist. Manjit Singh was later posted to San Francisco where he died of undiagnosed diabetes.

After a month of this waiting one of the Secretaries told me that it had been decided not to go ahead with the proceedings against me. I would have to pay the sum of three thousand pounds into the Embassy's accounts and I should not expect to get my next promotion in the near future.

All this time I had been staying with my mother – she had returned to India after a year in Japan to take possession of one of the flats and to let the other one out now that the American Embassy had found other accommodation – whom I had not told of my official problem so she was quite surprised to learn that it was over. Of course, I had suffered a financial loss because, apart from the three thousand pounds, I had to pay for the air passage. After the six months in Addis Ababa, I had not been able to make any significant saving during my service.

Returning to Tokyo, I found Kirat had had a tough time managing the family all by herself. She was expecting that I would bring back a valuable present for her while her friends – the wives of European and Latin American diplomats – had been telling her that I should have given her a fur coat or something like that for having Arun. The only person she had confided in had been Emmanuel Pouchepadass who had gone one day to pick up Christianne from a British Embassy women's function and she had been in the car and had burst into tears under the strain she was suffering.

In nearly two years in Tokyo, we had made no Japanese friends. Of course, Japanese officials and some other socially prominent couples had been coming to our parties but we had not seen the inside of any house occupied by Japanese living in Japanese style. We, generally I alone, had been invited to Japanese meals in Japanese restaurants which I did not enjoy because they seemed to consist mainly of different kinds of soup and rice neither of which I like. Once we had been invited to a particularly expensive restaurant – one of the few permitted to serve blowfish. This sea fish lives at great depths and requires special tackle to catch. It has a special bladder which it can inflate quickly with air and thus rise to the surface. It has a part which is highly poisonous so that a human being eating blowfish inexpertly gutted can die within a few minutes. At this restaurant the main course was blowfish soup which I found totally insipid. Then we were served the fish itself very finely sliced and arranged in beautiful patterns – Japanese food is certainly a feast for the eyes – but feeling like India rubber to chew. When we returned home we found Mataji sitting up waiting for us. She breathed a great sigh of relief on seeing us safe and sound!

I have mentioned a few pages earlier that a great economic boom had started at about the time of my arrival. By the middle of 1958, when I returned from Delhi, there were little Japanese cars to be seen in the streets in addition to the huge American cars of foreigners and the major Japanese industrialists. The revived Japanese managerial and professional classes were only able to afford the little Japanese cars which our European and American friends laughed at. Ten years later, Prakash Tandon then Chairman of the State Trading Corporation of India said to me in New Delhi when we were sitting in his official car.

'These Japanese cars – it was a Toyota Crown – are probably the best cars available in the world today.'

I think he was right and the position is unchanged in 2006.

I think I am a 'foodie' although, as I have mentioned earlier, I am not adventurous about food. After my return from Delhi we were invited to a meal at which a small portable charcoal stove was placed before each of us and we were served slices of meat, which had obviously been marinated, and invited to cook it to our own taste. This was the first Japanese meal where I was offered food I could get my teeth into. Before that, the best had been raw fish – a delicacy in Japan – which I had no wish to eat.

By this time the Ministry of External Affairs had worked out a scheme for building up a small cadre of Japanese-speaking I.F.S. officers. They realised that while one could learn to read and speak most European languages in a few months this would not work for Chinese, Japanese and even Arabic – important languages which should be known by officers working in those areas. It was decided that officers learning Japanese should be posted to Japan for two years when they would mainly be occupied in learning the language with the government paying the cost of tuition. Jagdish Hiremath was the first officer assigned the Japanese language under this scheme.

The bag which contained the intimation of Jagdish's arrival also contained the latest issue of the 'HISTORY OF SERVICES'. This book included Jagdish's entry but with a printer's devil. I wrote to the Ministry,

'We have noticed that J.R.Hiremath the new Third Secretary assigned to Tokyo was born on 11th August 1951. Will he be accompanied by his mother? Will he be entitled to Children's Education Allowance in respect of himself?'

The officer who received my letter stuck it up on the wall of his office.

In fact, Jagdish was joined shortly afterwards by his beautiful eighteen-year-old sister Rajeshwari. Some years later she married an I.F.S. officer named Ravi Tandon who was a keen amateur glider pilot. Unfortunately, he crashed his glider at Safdarjung airport, New Delhi and was killed. In 2006 their son is First Secretary in Paris.

In December 1958, we learnt that our Ambassador had been selected for the post of Permanent Representative to the United Nations in New York which, of course, made him and Mrs. Jha very happy. At about this time we gave a Sunday brunch for the other secretaries and their wives. Our little boys were, of course, present at table. Arun, a year-and-a-half old, was a great favourite with all the women. Rajeshwari took him in her lap. On the infrequent occasions when I meet her I tease her that I know her first boy friend. As it turned out, the 'affair' did not work out well. Sitting in Raje's lap, Arun put his left hand in her hot cup of coffee and screamed. The hand looked quite shrivelled when he pulled it out but fortunately it healed quite quickly and there were no after effects.

A few days later, I was informed one afternoon out of the blue by Dinker Hejmadi that he had been told by the Ambassador that I was being recalled to Delhi and that he would be the Charge d'Affaires until the next Ambassador arrived. Of course, he conveyed his regret at this turn of events. I immediately went to see Jha and found him in a towering rage. He said that he had been told the previous day that I had given a 'champagne party' to celebrate his departure and had been speaking ill of him and his wife to foreign diplomats; when he had sent for me to question me I had not been there and he had wired the Ministry to recall me and punish me for this treachery and calumny which they had agreed to do and I should prepare to leave by the next ship.

Whosoever had made the charge against me had done so at a time when he knew that I would have gone to the airport to receive the new incoming Commercial Secretary and his wife, Indira Jerath, and that this would occupy at least three hours of my time i.e. until the office was closed. It was my practice to receive and see off diplomatic officers. As it happened, Ravi Jerath who was to succeed Dinker Hejmadi was not an I.F.S. Officer. His appointment was in pursuance of a policy to appoint commercial secretaries who had worked in commercial firms and would have experience of the culture of the commercial world. My parents had been friendly with Ravi's parents when they were all posted in Karachi during the World War. Mr. Jerath had been the first Indian to be appointed Director General of Posts and Telegraphs. His reputation in the P.T.T. department lasted many years after his retirement and indeed his demise.

Of course, I denied the allegations against me and asked him who had made them to which I got no answer. I went back to my own room and called up two or three South American Ambassadors who were friends of mine and told them to get in touch immediately with Jha and assure him that I and my wife had never spoken against him or his wife. One of them expressed his doubts about the benefit to me of such a procedure but I assured him it would help me. When I saw Jha half an hour later he was upset that I had mentioned events in the Embassy to foreigners. I assured him that my leaving in this precipitate fashion would be the talk of the diplomatic corps for weeks to come and I am convinced that he began to realise the mistake he had made by acting in such a manner on so little evidence in a fit of temper. I had several long conversations with him before he left and he expressed himself 'mollified'.

He must have communicated this to the Ministry because I received instructions to go on the ship only as far as Singapore where I should succeed Avtar Dar as Assistant Commissioner and First Secretary (Commercial). Avtar Dar was being transferred on promotion to the rank of Counsellor. Jha seemed to be sorry for what he had done but he did not apologise to me till fifteen years later long after his wife had passed away. I have asked myself how such a contretemps could have occurred. Of course, Kirat and I had been very popular in the Diplomatic Corps during the period when I had been Charge d'Affaires and had been treated by most of the Ambassadors as equals. Knowing that I was going away in disgrace, the Australian Ambassador Sir Alan Watt gave a formal farewell lunch for me. Jha was quite popular but his wife was not. The peculiarity of her English pronunciation was the subject of amusement, she had no sense of humour and she made no attempt to make friends with any of the women whether in the Embassy, the Indian community or in the Diplomatic Corps.

Apart from that I must have made an enemy in the Embassy who felt that he should be equally prominent in Tokyo's diplomatic society.

The Jhas left by an American ship towards the end of the year and we left by the P&O Liner on 27th January 1959. The journey was quite pleasant. We sailed through the Inland Sea an area of great scenic beauty which we had not been able to visit. There was good shopping to be done in Hong Kong.

It is difficult in the twenty-first century to understand the passion for shopping which possessed most middle-class Indians in the middle of the twentieth century. During the World War many Americans had come to India with the fast moving consumer goods to which they were accustomed. These were quite unknown to the vast majority of Indians and somehow they got the impression that they would get them as the fruits of victory. This was, of course, absurd. In 1950 there were very few Indians who could be considered middle class by American or even European standards. All Indians had been very upset when they had seen the Americans destroying unconsumed tinned food before leaving India – tins that thousands of Indians would have liked to pay the market price for. The Americans explained that they could not sell U.S. Army property but that they were hoping to export such items to India very soon. Of course, Nehruvian socialism put an end to that dream. After that the cinema and the proliferating illustrated magazines which came into existence to cater to neo-literates gave the increasing middle-classes an idea of what was available in the outside world – not only in U.S.A. and Europe but also in many parts of Asia and even North Africa. For all these reasons Indians would go berserk in a department store in Hong Kong.

XIX

SINGAPORE 1959

Arriving in Singapore in a depressed frame of mind, because of the Jha episode, we were delighted to meet our friends Avtar and Rita Dar. We cheered up even more when we saw the house we would be occupying and the delights of Singapore.

Bharat Bhavan, the residence of the Assistant Commissioner must have been built fifty years earlier for a wealthy British businessman on three-and-a-half acres of land. He must have had a dozen servants to look after it. The government gave us a gardener, a driver for the Ford Consul with which I was, for the first time, provided and a chowkidar (night watchman/guard) whose purpose I could not understand because he was only supposed to be on duty at night and had no weapon. What was really needed was a large motorised lawnmower to take care of the elephant grass which grew fiercely on account of the 200" of rain that Singapore receives annually but I could never persuade the Ministry to sanction it.

For the house itself we had Barua, our cook, a locally recruited Malay maidservant and an ethnic Chinese *amah* to look after the children, in reality only Arun. The house was in the shape of a square letter **U**. There was a porch obviously large enough to accommodate a coach and horses. Two pillars supported the roof of the entrance hall behind the porch. The space between the pillars and the wall was barred while that between the pillars could be closed by a movable grill which could be closed at night. The hall was spacious. On the left it gave access by a door to the dining room which could have seated twenty-four persons but the blackwood table and the accompanying chairs were for sixteen. Through the dining room one could go to the spacious pantry which in turn was connected to the kitchen and servants' quarters by a covered cement footpath.

Behind the hall, accessible through another sliding grill, was a paved courtyard where one could have six tables for four if the weather was good. The other leg of the U was a guest room with its attached bathroom. The right of the hall which had a tiled floor was occupied by a wooden staircase which led to the drawing room on the upper floor. I use the word 'room' but, in fact, it was open on all sides. The whole floor was teakwood and there was a balcony on the entire front of the house and another overlooking the courtyard mentioned above. The balcony provided protection from the rain when it was accompanied by wind. The space over the porch was an extension of the drawing room but, as it had no balcony, it could not be used when the rain was accompanied by wind.

In fact the space over the balcony was the most pleasant part of the house since it could receive breeze from three sides and we spent most of our time there. I even remember giving a small lunch party there.

Over the dining room were two bedrooms with their bathrooms over the pantry. On the other side of the house there were two more bedrooms over the guest-room. They also had attached baths.

The main problem was mosquitoes. Of the three and a half acres, nearly three acres can only be described as wilderness overgrown with elephant grass – a paradise for mosquitoes. The house being as I have described, it could not be screened. Mosquito coils were the only solution we could find for the evenings. Finally, I managed to persuade the Ministry to have two bedrooms – the ones over the dining room – screened and adapted for air conditioning but I had to buy the two air conditioners myself.

I was now living in the style of Pitaji's house at Nawabshah thirty-five years earlier with the added advantage of contemporary amenities like electricity, running water, a telephone and Indian shopkeepers who could deliver everything on credit at a few minutes notice. The problem was to pay for them on a First Secretary's pay and allowances.

The house had been bought immediately after the war for the Representative of the Government of India created under the Indian Emigration Act 1922. At that time Kuala Lumpur only had an agent of the Government of India. Things had changed since then. Malaya was enjoying some degree of independence and we had a High Commissioner there. Singapore was still a British Colony. The Government of India did not expect the island city to have a separate identity. The High Commissioner in Kuala Lumpur was concurrently Commissioner in Singapore which was why I was designated Assistant Commissioner but, in practice, my boss was five hundred miles away!

Within days of my arrival, S.K.Banerji, the High Commissioner, rang up to say he was coming. I hardly knew him but he addressed me as Gunwant and behaved like a colleague – quite unlike my experience in Tokyo. I decided to do something for him. I persuaded the numerous staff to hold a tea party in the garden of India House – our large office building which had originally been the residence of an Arab merchant and his four wives – for the Banerjis. Mrs.Banerji was not well and did not come to Singapore but S.K. was most impressed – he said such a thing had never happened before.

One wet afternoon I happened to be at home when Kiran, running towards the servants' quarters, slipped on the steep steps leading from the bathroom at the back of the house, and hit the step with his back. He screamed in pain and had a convulsion; however, the doctor at the Seventh-Day Adventist hospital found no damage and Kiran appeared to be quite all right.

INDIA 1959-60

Since I was due to go on leave in July, Kirat left three months earlier with the boys and flew to her parents' place in Poona. I left in due course by a Dutch freighter – there was no passenger liner to Calcutta – with my car and all my belongings. Kirat came by train from Poona to meet me.

We stayed with Lajpat Rai Bhagat, a distant relation of Mataji's at Sodepur Potteries which he owned. He had been employed by Madan Gopal Bhagat in his Gwalior Potteries at Delhi and had later got an appointment as Manager of Than Potteries in what was then called Kathiawar, now Western Gujrat. Than was one of hundreds of princely states in Kathiawar and the Ruler decided to introduce a new industry. Of course, Lajpat Rai could not go to Than except through Ahmedabad so he and his newly wedded wife came to stay with us. When, in due course, she became pregnant they came to Ahmedabad and stayed with us while she was booked into the Civil Hospital – Pitaji knew the Civil Surgeon. The delivery proved difficult, there was an infection and the upshot was that Lajpat Rai Bhagat stayed with us for nearly a month often using our car and driver to go to hospital, etc.

Given this background, I had no compunction about using one of his three cars and a driver - owning a small pottery was much more lucrative than being a civil servant - to go every day into Calcutta to clear my luggage through the Customs. The sticking point was the Ford Fairlane car. The Collector of Customs wanted me to get an import licence and pay import duty on it. I did not have that sort of money. Finally, months later, I was able to negotiate a loan from the Ministry and an import licence from the Chief Controller of Imports and Exports – my old friend Kersi Satarawala.

Lajpat Rai Bhagat told me a story which illustrates social values in India, particularly in Bengal. One day his night watchman came into his office accompanied by his son. He announced proudly that his son had passed his matriculation examination and had come to seek the Sahib's blessing. This, of course was immediately forthcoming whereupon the father said,

'Sahib, that is not all. I want you to give him a job as a clerk.'

'My dear chap, I know your son well. He is a talented artist and has designed several small pieces for me for which I have paid him. I intend to send him to an industrial design school so that he will have a professional qualification and get a highly paid job. Making him a clerk would be downright stupid. Young as he is he earned a hundred rupees from me last month. If I were to advertise a post of clerk at seventy rupees a month, the road outside would be blocked by applicants with M.A. and B.A. degrees to say nothing of matriculates.'

'But, Sahib I want him to be a *babu* (a Hindu clerk who is literate in English).'

Lajpat Rai told me that he had got a Minister of the West Bengal State Government to visit his factory. This dignitary had asked him,

'Mr.Bhagat you employ Bengali and non-Bengali labour in your factory. Is there any difference between the two?'

'Sir, any one you see sitting down is a Bengali. The others are all non-Bengalis.'

When I got to Poona with Kirat, I was horrified to see Kiran in bed on his back, lying in a plaster half cast. I could remember my Aunt Bansi thirty years earlier when she had had tuberculosis of the spine and spent three years (around 1930) flat on her back on a hard bed in a plaster cast which immobilised her spine completely. Kiran's problem seemed to be similar when I discussed it with Dr. Coyaji a widely respected Parsi doctor in Poona who had his own hospital. He said that diagnosing tuberculosis of the spine (Pott's disease) stigmatised a child for the whole of his life so he was calling it Schnurmann's disease. As far as I could make out, his parathyroid gland was not supplying enough calcium to the bones for their very rapid growth. The fracture of the tibia and the radius in Tokyo had aggravated the demand for calcium and the spine could not take the shock of the fall in Singapore so there was decalcification and consequent damage to one of the disks in the lumbar region. It took some months for the spine to recover but, I am afraid, Kiran's back has never stopped hurting him for the last forty-odd years.

A couple of years later he had Osgood-Schlatter's disease (it affects the knees) and subsequently Arun had this also. Shortly before she passed away Mataji told me that her knees had been very painful when she was an adolescent which had made her limp both ways. It looks as if calcium deficiency during adolescence runs in the family on the Bhagat side. I am glad that Arjun – my eldest grandson – born in 1974 has escaped these ailments.

I moved to Delhi after a short stay in Poona and reported to the Ministry where I found that the Jha episode in Tokyo was now forgotten but the Ministry had no idea what to do with me. They decided that I should do a twelve week course at the Administrative Staff College in Hyderabad – the first I.F.S. Officer to do so. I was sorry to leave Delhi because our Canadian friends the Hoopers had arrived there. Bill was the First Secretary at the Canadian High Commission. While posted in Ottawa they had adopted a daughter Alison whose hair was the same colour as Patricia's had been when she was a child.

Hyderabad was quite unknown to me. The staff College was accommodated in what had been the residence of the second son of the Nizam. It was well situated on the bank of the lake and the compound must have been about five acres. Of course, it had tennis courts and a swimming pool. For classes, all the meetings and the meals, we used the main building. For sleeping, a kind of barracks had been constructed where each of us had a room and the toilet-shower-room was shared between two bedrooms. The bedrooms had desert coolers but they were of no use because this was the monsoon. The food was good but the main interest for me was literally to live with men from what were then known as commercial firms and referred to as box-wallahs. In the nineteenth century, the British community in Calcutta was divided into 'competition-wallahs' (the I.C.S.) and 'box-wallahs' (salesmen).

My slightly older I.C.S. colleagues told me that failing the I.C.S. competition often meant getting a job with a British multinational at many times the salary.

In 1959, we were sixty 'members' of the course. I think four were British – they expected to spend their working lives in India, generally Calcutta. We were divided into 'syndicates' of ten members each. There was a member of the 'directing staff' attached to each syndicate. The directing staff of our syndicate was a wealthy Bengali called Potla Sen. His wife Nandita was living on the premises and we saw a good deal of her. The *doyen d'age* was a Parsi named Beham Engineer who was a mining engineer working for the coal-mining company of the Tata Group. There was an Englishman whose name I have forgotten who worked for Brooke Bond Tea. He was manager of a tea drying and packing factory at Kamptee near Nagpur. It is strange that I should not remember his name considering how much I saw of him.

An interesting character was a Maharashtrian named Khanolkar. He was a Trade Union official and a graduate but it was obvious that he did not speak English like the rest of us. Obviously, his primary education had not been in an English medium school. However he did not hesitate to put across his point of view, which was generally at variance with everybody else's, and he did it fluently and forcefully.

Such was not the case with another member named Dua, a Punjabi. It transpired that his family owned a diversified business, and as it was family managed, he was an executive in it. His educational background was similar to Vasant Khanolkar's but he was completely lacking in the gift of self-expression. On one occasion I had to read his mind and answer a question put to him – he agreed with my explanation!

There was a Colonel Ahluwalia from the Army Service Corps. He had a Sikh name but no turban or beard.

Apart from the discussions and projects in the 'classroom', we went on a week's tour of industrial establishments in Andhra Pradesh. I had visited some Indian factories before but, on this occasion, I was able to study the structure and management and see how the managerial staff lived. One of the visits was to a coal mine. We did not go into the 'pit' but from the arrangements, the faces of the miners as they went down and others came back up, it seemed to me that I was seeing an English coal mine such as I had read about or seen in films of the beginning of the century. The countryside in which the colliery was located looked as I felt it must have done for centuries except for the occasional railway line or high-tension power line.

It was a change to visit a newly installed Caltex refinery with an American manager. After we had visited the plant, the manager rattled off the statistics in his office. I asked him,

'You have told us that this installation has cost hundreds of crores of rupees and employs less than two hundred men. How is such a capital-intensive industry helping to solve the unemployment problem in this country?'

'In U.S.A, I could run this refinery with half the staff because I would be able to outsource many services, like transportation, which I have to do myself here!'

All these companies we visited had a guest house for visitors because, obviously, in the countryside there were no hotels of the international type. This illustrates the point made by the Caltex manager because the upkeep and operation of such small hotels makes them more expensive per guest than the most expensive hotels in Bombay or Delhi. The curious part is that companies of any importance maintain such guest houses in Bombay and Delhi also where there are any number of hotels in different star categories. I enquired from a chartered accountant how such wastefulness could be justified and he said that it was because of income tax. The tax rates were so high that the salary of a general manager in a company was less than that of an office boy in another country. The only way that a qualified and trained person could be induced to accept the responsibilities of management was by giving him fringe benefits – subsidised furnished air-conditioned housing, a car and driver, domestic servants, free electricity and water, holidays in resorts belonging to the company, you name it – which were not taxable.

Forty-five years later (2005) tax rates have been reduced to international levels but fringe benefits continue; the latest is that there is a 'fringe benefits tax' and company staffs are complaining bitterly! It is true that Indian salaries whether of workers or top management are lower than in Western Europe.

I was still in Hyderabad when I received an intimation from the Ministry that I had been approved for promotion to the rank of Counsellor from the date when I took charge of my new post which was to be Commercial Counsellor and Assistant Commissioner in Singapore! I was, of course, overjoyed at the idea of going back to that magnificent house with increased pay and allowances which would enable me to live in appropriate style. At the Administrative Staff College, I was told that it was proof of the merit of the College that an alumnus was being promoted! Actually, of the sixty members of the course there were only two – the other was a railway officer – of us who had studied at a prestigious university – Cambridge. We were the two who were always selected for making speeches, welcoming V.I.P. visitors and so on.

I was also told that I could avail of the leave I had applied for and then spend some weeks in the Ministry of Commerce being 'trained for commercial work'. Of course, as soon as the course was over, I returned to Delhi to solve the problem of the car – the Ministry gave me a loan for paying the customs duty and the Chief Controller of Imports and Exports (my old friend Kersi Satarawala) gave me an import licence. I was also informed that I would be allowed to sell off the car which would enable me to pay off the customs duty and leave me enough money to buy another car.

The next step was to arrange a holiday tour of Central India with the Hoopers. They had the right car, a Chevrolet station wagon, and I offered to arrange cheap official accommodation in dak bungalows, rest houses, circuit houses and so on. I could also, as a fairly senior officer of the Ministry of External Affairs count on support, if needed, from district collectors and other officials all over India. The Hoopers arranged to leave Alison in the care of friends and her ayah, Ruby. Kiran and Arun were with their maternal grandparents in Poona.

We set out after Christmas and went to Ajmer. We had all seen Jaipur several times. It was Bill Hooper who told me that Ajmer was old Hindu holy ground on which the Muslim conquerors had built several mosques. The nearby lake of Pushkar was a place of pilgrimage for Hindus where they came to take holy baths. None of us had seen Chitor which is very important in Rajput history.

The residential arrangements there were poor but we managed to stay in Udaipur which is much visited by tourists and where both the Lake and City Palaces had a rather dilapidated appearance. However, the setting was beautiful and we drove round the lake. Conditions were much less comfortable than they are in the twenty-first century but correspondingly there were fewer tourists and *security* was not the problem it has since become. For instance, part of the City Palace was occupied by the princely family but the rest was abandoned; when we went into it there were frescoes on the walls of great historical interest but there was no charge for entering and we found cows wandering on the stairs!

Similarly, we could see small forts on the hills round the lake. There was a motorable gravel road to one of them. We drove there, saw a caretaker who was delighted to show us around. It would have made a nice week-end resort if it had been in good condition.

Chitor, which figures so largely in Todd's ANNALS AND ANTIQUITIES OF RAJASTHAN must have been a huge walled city. The rubble walls were still more or less intact but there were very few people inside. We saw an encampment of nomads but we had to drive quite a long way to find the *Jaisthamba* (Tower of Victory) which is quite unique because it is asymmetrical. From an architectural point of view, the *Kirtisthamba(Tower of Fame)* is more interesting because it incorporates Buddhist elements from the famous stupa at Sanchi.

The most remarkable thing was the lack of knowledge or interest of the local people in these monuments. More information and better maps were available in guide books printed in Europe than in anything available locally.

After Rajasthan, our next important objective was the caves of Ajanta and Ellora. Kirat was particularly keen to see these because she was upset that I had seen them in a week-end trip from Hyderabad a few months earlier and she had missed out on that. I had arranged for us to stay at a dak bungalow from which we could visit both sets of caves. The Ajanta caves were dug around the seventh century A.D. in the sides or cliffs of a gorge through which a small river flows after a waterfall. They were discovered by an Englishman in the middle of the nineteenth century in the course of a shooting expedition. The peasants cultivating the fields around the top of the cliffs had no knowledge of them. Now a footpath connects the entrances to all the nearly score of caves but even in 1960, looking from outside the gorge, it was very difficult to spot them. One cannot see them without a guide. All that we know about them is from archaeological studies which have revealed that they were constructed by Buddhist monks for their residences and meditations. After having been dug, they were plastered inside and some of the fresco paintings on the plaster have survived. I have in my library where I am writing this, a copy made by a local artist of the most famous figure, THE DARK PRINCESS, which I purchased *in situ* in 1960.

Conservation of the caves presents a problem. The footfalls of visitors bring dust into the caves which, for centuries, were not visited by human beings. There is no electric lighting in the caves which are of a stygian darkness. The guide carried an electric torch to show us around. To see the paintings and attempt to photograph them – unsuccessfully as it turned out – he lit an open magnesium flash the smoke from which cannot possibly have done any good. Decades later I attended a lecture by a photographer who took pictures by what he called the 'available light technology'. He explained that any artificial light cannot possibly show the true natural colour of the paintings. He found that there was *some* light in the caves during daytime and by using a special photometer he was able to measure it. Putting his camera on a good tripod he was able to take superb photographs by giving exposures of several minutes. Not only do the photographs reveal details not visible in the published books but the colours are fantastic.

The Ellora caves, many miles away, are of much later date and easily visible and accessible. They are wider and shallower and everything inside is visible in daytime. The decorations are sculptures rather than fresco paintings. They are Brahminical rather than Buddhist. The entrances are beautifully carved and have been copied in some twentieth century buildings. The most interesting is not a cave but the Kailas temple carved out of the mountain – the 'living rock' as one guide book describes it. The rock is granite which is why, exposed to the elements such detailed and fine sculpture has survived so well.

After Ellora we visited Aurangabad where the Emperor Aurangzeb is buried in a simple grave open to the sky. He said that his predecessors had transgressed the Muslim faith by being buried in elaborate tombs. His wife is buried nearby in a tomb which is a poor imitation of the Taj Mahal.

Another ancient ruined city in the region is Daulatabad, the city built by Mohammed bin Tughlaq when he decided that Delhi where he had built the walled city of Tughlaqabad was not the centre of India. Later he decided to come back to Delhi but he was murdered a few miles before completing the journey. The two journeys from Tughlaqabad to Daulatabad and back totalling abut two thousand miles were particularly arduous and few of Tughlaq's courtiers survived. I call this bad logistical planning and worse execution. At Aurangabad we stayed at a hotel of international class – the only one on the whole tour.

Our next major objective was the Marble Rocks near Jabalpur. Normally, we would have stayed at Nagpur on our way to Jabalpur but I had written to my English friend in Kamptee whose name I have shamefully forgotten. We were very well received, lodged and fed. The result was that we started rather late on our next journey. We passed through Seoni and entered the Central Indian forest which for decades used to provide the best teak in India. By this time Indian road conditions had had their effect on Bill's slipped disk and he was having considerable pain while driving so I was driving the Chevrolet Station Wagon. The forest road was paved but not wide. I saw a narrow high bridge ahead and, to my horror, a bus coming straight at us. I realised that while the bridge could not possibly accommodate the two vehicles, even the approach road along which I was driving was only just wide enough but the bus driver seemed quite oblivious to the presence of our vehicle. I stopped and engaged reverse gear and that was when we were hit head on.

The next thing I remember is that I was not seeing very well with my left eye and my left hand was covered in blood. What had happened was that since there were no seat belts in those days my head had moved forward and hit my left hand on the steering wheel. This had caused the left lens of my spectacles to shatter against my wristwatch. Bits of the lens had penetrated the skin around my left eye – hence the blood. I was seeing less well with my left eye because there was only a right lens in my eyeglasses. Nobody else in our car was bleeding. Later we found that the impact had worsened Bill's slipped disk but this was not immediately apparent. Nobody was injured in the bus.

In fact, the bus had suffered very little damage. Its solid bumper had protected it. The station wagon was undriveable. Its battery had been shattered and its engine had moved six inches in the chassis. It is only because Indian workers are paid very little and are highly skilled that the car was repairable and did not have to be written off. It had to be towed by a tow-truck with its front wheels up in the air.

The police arrived a couple of hours later, understood the importance of a diplomat and his car, and arranged a bus to take us back to Seoni which is a district town with a general hospital. There the doctors stitched up my seven wounds and we all moved to the circuit house. We stayed there for two nights while I was kept under observation.

Then we got in touch with my English friend in Kamptee. He sent a car to pick us up, another vehicle for our luggage, gave us his hospitality and also arranged railway bookings for us and the station wagon to Delhi. Getting berths on long distance trains in India was quite a problem in those days. I heard of an industrialist in Kanpur keeping an air-conditioned compartment reserved for him on every train to Delhi just in case he happened to need it! My friend knew the Roman Catholic bishop of Nagpur. There were a number of Roman Catholics in the railway administration and we travelled very comfortably back to Delhi.

Mataji was horrified to see me with half my face covered in bandages but not altogether surprised. She said she had received a mysterious trunk call from Bombay – trunk calls were few and far between in those days – asking for Pitaji. This surprised her because Pitaji had passed away nine years earlier. When she asked who wanted to speak to him, the 'phone went dead. She felt that this was some sort of message for her from the Other World so she was worried and could only pray for our well-being.

As soon as my bandages could be removed, I reported to the Ministry of Commerce for my 'training'. The Commerce Secretary was K.B.Lall whom I knew from the time of the Delhi riots. He told me that as Commercial Counsellor I should devote less time to office work and more to people, particularly the business community in Singapore. Of course, I knew quite a lot about the commercial work in Singapore but I was glad to meet the officials I would be corresponding with and to find out what they wanted from me.

Going to Singapore from Delhi, I was expected to go by train to Madras and by ship - an Indian shipping company kept up a regular service from Madras to Singapore touching Nagapatam and Penang on the way – to Singapore. It was now the month of April which is the hottest season in the peninsula; I was only entitled to travel by first class but I had sold my car and decided to pay the difference and booked a spacious air-conditioned compartment for the four of us. The thirty-six hour journey was a delight because the four of us seldom had the opportunity to be so close together.

The journey by ship was something else. The ship had been built many decades earlier for carrying Indian labourers between India, the Malay Peninsula and Singapore. It had 'de luxe' cabins on the upper deck with windows instead of portholes but no air conditioning anywhere and the food was mediocre. However, sea travel was not as hot as land travel because of the breeze.

SINGAPORE 1960-63

Much had happened in Singapore during the nine months I had been away. The British Governor had been replaced by a Malay politician. This is as good a place as any to explain the meaning of the word MALAY. Forms which had to be completed by individuals having dealings with the bureaucracy in British South East Asia always contained an item NATIONALITY. This really meant *race* and the recognised words for this item in Singapore were European, Eurasian, Malay, Indian and Chinese.

I think EUROPEAN I have explained much earlier. EURASIAN had the same meaning as 'Anglo-Indian' in India. It meant a person of mixed race claiming patrilineal descent from a European. MALAY was legally described as a person 'professing the Muslim religion, who speaks the Malay language and observes the Malay *aadat* (customs) in his home'. Indian included everybody coming from pre-partition India. In practice I found that the only negro I saw in Singapore was classified as an 'Indian'. He was the Sergeant-at-Arms of the Legislative Assembly. I never raised any objection to this designation on the principle 'the more the merrier.' *Chinese* meant a person of Chinese race. This again is stretchable because not everybody claims to be able to distinguish a Chinese from a Japanese and marriages between Chinese and other Asians do take place.

In addition to the Governor, the Commissioner-General for South East Asia had also changed. In 1959, it had been an English civil servant whose previous post had been Permanent Under

Secretary in the Ministry of Defence. I do not remember his name but both he and his wife were very accessible. I remember speaking to him. He had been a colonial civil servant in Singapore in 1941 and had been held in a prison camp by the Japanese along with several Indians. Once at a party given by the Governor I was surprised to see the chowkidar of the Indian Commission staff quarters and even more when he was embraced by the Commissioner General!

The new Commissioner General was a politician whose previous appointment had been First Lord of the Admiralty. This was the post held in 1939 by Winston Churchill! He was the Earl of Selkirk. This is a Scottish peerage and he explained to me later that it has a curious history. In the seventeenth century, the title of Duke of Hamilton – the premier peerage of Scotland – had been inherited by a woman. Unlike English peerages which are only inheritable 'in the tail male' – a 'special remainder' is only for one occasion – a Scottish peerage is infinitely transmissible irrespective of sex. The Earl of Selkirk (family name Douglas) who married this heiress did not want his title to disappear. He therefore obtained a special remainder to enable the earldom to be transmitted to a younger brother. 'Geordie' as he was known to his friends, was the younger brother of the Duke of Hamilton. They were four brothers who had all become pilots in the Royal Air Force. The Duke in 1960 had been Marquis of Douglas and Clydesdale before the death of their father and had become famous as the first man to fly over Mount Everest. Later, during the World War, he had become known as the man whom Hess 'had flown to England to meet'.

The Prime Minister of Singapore, still a British Colony, had changed. Lim Yew Hock had been replaced by a younger man, Lee Kuan Yew. He was a Chinese like his predecessor but Cambridge educated and known to be brilliant. He was expected by my British friends and acquaintances to perform miracles. In the twenty-first century, he holds no constitutional responsibility but carries the designation of 'Senior Minister'. I would say that such of my contemporaries as are still alive find their expectations fulfilled.

In Kuala Lumpur, Malaya had attained its independence. All the Malay kingdoms (previously known as Federated and unfederated Malay States) had formed into a Federation and the rulers – with various traditional titles – became Heads of the Federation by rotation. Later on the Federation of Malaya absorbed the British colonies of Malacca and Penang (which included the mainland territory of Province Wellesley). These were republics and their presidents could not officiate as the Head of State of the Federation. The British Governor General of Malaya had ceased to be.

More important for me, there was a new High Commissioner of India, Yog(endra Kumar) Puri. He was from Peshawar and married to Savitri one of the several daughters of Bakshi Tek Chand a famous lawyer of Lahore. I had met Yog Puri once during the Delhi riots in 1947 and I had gone to see him in 1958 to elicit support when I was being threatened with dismissal. On that occasion he had suggested that it might be advantageous for me to hold on to three thousand pounds and accept dismissal – advice which I did not relish.

In 1960, I found his attitude completely changed. To my delighted surprise, he asked us to address him and his wife by their first names. No Head of Mission had ever done that. He told me something of his background. He belonged to a wealthy Hindu family of Peshawar. He said that, as a child, he had spoken five languages effortlessly. Like other Hindus in Peshawar, the family spoke Punjabi as their mother tongue. In the street he spoke Pushto, the language of the Pathans who constituted the majority of the population of the North West Frontier Province. At school, he spoke English and Urdu, the official languages of Northern India. At the *akhada* (Hindu gymnasium) he had to speak Hindi. His family had managed to get compensation for their substantial urban and rural property and, after the death of his father, he was fairly well off. So was Savitri who had no brothers.

One day he told me a heart-rending story. In the I.C.S. he had been allotted to the province of Assam where he had become a Collector during the World War. Shortly after the war ended, he was taken into the 'Finance and Commerce Pool'. This was a much coveted appointment because most I.C.S. Officers preferred to serve in Delhi rather than the provincial cities to say nothing of the districts. Besides, there was the possibility of becoming a

Trade Commissioner in Milan or New York at a time when India had no foreign service.

With Independence, he was suddenly appointed to the new Ministry of Relief and Rehabilitation where he had to work ten hours a day including Saturdays and Sunday afternoons. On a Sunday morning he was relaxing in an easy chair in the verandah of his house with his eyes shut when he heard someone calling,' Yogji!' Who would dare to address an I.C.S. Officer by his first name? He opened his eyes and saw two rather ragged-looking Sikhs at the wicket gate. On reflection, he recognised them as peasants from one of the villages which his family had owned in Punjab. It was a village where they used to go shooting. He invited the men in and asked them what he could do for them. He told them that he was working in the Ministry of R.&R. and he could get them housing, relief allowances and so on. They replied,

'We know all that but please first listen to our story. When Partition took place, we knew that we were in for trouble because our village was surrounded as you know by Muslim villages. We were well off and had enough guns so we got hold of all the ammunition we could and alerted the nearest army unit of our apprehensions telling them that if trouble broke out, we would expect them to come to our rescue. The British Officers assured us that we could count on them.

'It all turned out as we feared. The Muslims came in hundreds and surrounded our village from where all our Muslims co-villagers had disappeared. The invaders asked us to surrender our weapons and assured us we would get safe conduct out of the village. We did not trust them and refused and the shooting started. We defended ourselves and waited for the army to come but no one came and it dawned on us that the army had left us to our fate. When we saw the ammunition getting exhausted, we shot our own women, children and old people and fought till we had nothing to defend ourselves with. The two of us managed to escape and are the only survivors from the village. We know that there are millions of Muslims living in Central and Southern India undisturbed by the holocaust which has taken place here in the North.

'We have nothing left to live for and our only aim in what is left for us in life is to kill as many Muslims as possible before we die. The Muslims in and around Delhi are now well protected and we know that there is an 'inner line' which refugees are not allowed to cross to go to Ajmer or Lucknow. We also know that you are authorised to issue 'inner line permits'. We have come to beg you to give us these.'

Yog told me that it was the most difficult decision he had ever had to take, but he had to refuse their request.

One day a delegation of Indian merchants came to see me. They said that the head of an important Indian industrial group (Singhania?) was passing through Singapore with his entourage on his way back to India from the United States. Would I like to give a lunch for the party. I said that my table could only accommodate sixteen. They accepted that and said the party were all vegetarians. I decided I would have the lawn mowed.

Barua, our cook, was a Bengali – actually from what is now Bangladesh. Of course, he was used to preparing vegetarian meals. The industrialist's wife was sitting on my right and her very pretty daughter-in-law on my left. Suddenly I noticed that the lady was raking the lentil dhal with her fork. It was only then that I realised that she was pushing away the fried onions which Barua had used to decorate the dhal so she must have been a Jain because Jains do not eat root vegetables – no one had warned me of this.

Some months later, I visited Sarawak. This was a British territory in North Borneo. Until a few years earlier, it had been ruled by a 'white raja'. At some time early in the nineteenth century, an English adventurer named Brooke had persuaded the local tribes that he could establish law and order in the territory and put an end to the tribal wars which were killing them off. He had been outstandingly successful which was all the more remarkable because some of the tribes were head-hunters and their customs only allowed a boy to be recognised as a man if he could produce the head of a man from another tribe. The Brooke family had been succeeded after the World War by a Colonial Governor who gave a dinner in my honour. I have mentioned the five 'nationalities' which were recognised. In Sarawak and the two other British territories there was yet another nationality – native. In India this word has a pejorative connotation. In British times, it was used to describe us; in the words of a Dundee jute merchant, 'India is a grand country; a pity the native is there.'

At the dinner I noticed that there were two or three other Indians and some Chinese. The dinner was a typical Embassy dinner of those days with five glasses and seven sets of cutlery at each place. I asked my hostess if 'natives' were invited to her table. She replied,

'Of course, even in the times of the White Rajahs, every chief and his wife had to eat here at least once a year.'

'Like this, with seven sets of cutlery? Didn't they feel embarrassed?'

'No, I have never noticed anything.'

The grandsons of head-hunters could learn European customs but not the repositories of our ancient civilisation!

The most prominent Indian socially in Singapore was a Muslim from Western Gujrat called R(ajaballi) Jumbhoy. He had made his fortune many decades earlier and the Indian Army officers who had been in Singapore or adjoining Malaya when the World War broke out all remembered him. He had never had a college education but was a member of the Royal Island Club and accustomed to British company. He spoke good English. When I had arrived in Singapore the previous year, Avtar Dar had told me that he would take me to see the Indian member of the Cabinet, Mr. Jumabhoy. I said,

'Ah! The old man that everybody has been talking to me about?'

'No! No! They don't talk to each other although they are uncle and nephew.'

I got to know them both quite well. They had entirely different personalities. The younger man, J.M.Jumabhoy, said that his father had established their family in Singapore. He had been much older than Rajaballi – no one used that name – and his (J.M.'s) grandfather had died fairly young. He possessed a letter written by Rajaballi to his father in Gujrati in which he addressed him as 'Brother like a Father.' J.M. was a very serious man with no sense of humour.

Rajaballi was a jovial and very hospitable man. He had a tennis court in his house and was a member of the Turf Club. He would frequently invite the Puris and us to spend the Sunday afternoon at the races. His main source of income appeared to be the Agency of the Indian steamship company which plied between Singapore and Madras. No other company was allowed to run ships on this route. The poorest Indians in Singapore were unskilled Tamil labourers and the only way they could go home on leave or retirement was by buying third class tickets from Jumabhoy. I have referred to the austere travelling conditions for first class passengers on the STATE OF MADRAS. Third class passengers were not fed but could cook their own meals in a space indicated for the purpose. The third class fares were ridiculously low by international standards so there was a long waiting list for tickets.

Two or three Indian businessmen had told me that there was a black market in third class tickets from which Jumabhoy was making a fortune. I had mentioned the matter to Mr. Banerji who said he had discussed it with Jumabhoy who had responded,

'Let them say it publicly and I shall sue them.'

I quoted this to my acquaintances and it always ended the conversation. After I left Singapore Jumabhoy sent me a book MULTI-RACIAL SINGAPORE bearing his name as the author. He used to complain that there were now Indians in Singapore who twenty years earlier 'had been nobody.' Like many other successful older people in the world, he did not accept change.

It was clear to me that if I was to have a social position in Singapore I would have to learn to play golf. There were two golf clubs in Singapore to which top people belonged. The older one was the Royal Island Club. At one time it had been reserved for Europeans but this was no longer the case; in fact the President of the Club was a very wealthy Cambridge educated Chinese businessman named Loke Wan Tho. R.Jumabhoy was also a member and most consular officials belonged to it. There were European members also but many boxwallahs had started a new club called the Bukit Timah Club. The name Bukit Timah was that of a nearby hill (it means TIN HILL) which was the highest point of the island. It only had European members; yes, they would accept me as they did all diplomats but I chose the Royal Island; I am not enamoured of boxwallahs.

One day Lee Kuan Yew (who was a member of the Royal Island) mentioned to me that the Club was getting overcrowded.

I said there was adjoining forest land which could be cleared. The Prime Minister replied that it had been found in Malaya that the cutting of forests brought about an immediate decrease in rainfall; the Bukit Timah was short of golfers and he would 'persuade' the two clubs to grant reciprocal facilities. When he did so, I immediately availed of the facility to go and practise on the driving range which was lit up at night unlike the one at the Royal Island.

Yes, I did take golf lessons from the pro but it was of no use because I am no good at games. Kirat was much more successful and became an active and popular golfer. In fact, there were occasions when I thought that she was breathing and eating golf. How to get myself recognised as a golfer? I invited Ashok Malik and his rival in Delhi Billoo Sethi to visit Singapore. They played a foursome with the Prime Minister and the Finance Minister, Goh Keng Swee. The reputation of Maliks as golfers was established.

However, more could be done. There was some tournament in America for 'senior golfers' and the Indian team going back home included H.S.Malik (as non-playing Captain) and I.S.Malik. Once again the Royal Island Club arranged a match and H.S.Malik decided to participate. He was paired off with the Finance Minister's brother who was a regular player and a good golfer; I knew him better than I knew the Finance Minister who, like the Prime Minister, was seldom seen at the Club; I think they played at dawn. I decided to follow this pair and watch its performance. Mr. Goh – I can't remember his given name – said to me after watching H.S.'s putting, 'Mr. Malik, I think I am being taught golf.'

'Well', I replied, 'You have to admit that I have found you someone of an age at which you should not mind accepting him as a teacher.' H.S.Malik was approaching seventy years at the time.

I have mentioned Loke Wan Tho as President of the Royal Island Club. He owned a chain of cinemas including THE CATHAY. This cinema was the ground floor of a skyscraper built against a cliff. The rest of the building was a hotel in which Wan Tho had reserved a floor for himself as his residence; it was accessible from the top of the hill. Below this floor was the Cathay restaurant which was large and popular. His sister was married to a rich Malaysian Chinese who owned tin mines and rubber plantations in Malaya.

It took me some time to understand the structure of Chinese society in Singapore. The first thing was its division into provincial groups, distinguishable by the languages they spoke. The Chinese government had decreed that Mandarin was the language of China; the Singapore government, politically quite anti-communist, accepted this and Mandarin was the only recognised Chinese language. However, the majority language in Singapore was Hokkien. The Hokkiens considered themselves superior to the other groups. The most despised were the Hakkas. If one saw a Chinese sweeping the road, one was told he must be a Hakka. In addition there were Cantonese – the language spoken in Hong Kong - and Shanghainese. Then, they were divided by clan. The clan was indicated by the first name as used in Chinese. Thus Lee Kuan Yew belonged to the Lee clan and Goh Keng Swee to the Goh clan. One Lee might have no traceable biological connection with another Lee but they were both supposed to be registered at a Lee temple somewhere in China. Personally, I am sure that poor and even rich illiterate Chinese – and practically all the Chinese I met were illiterate in Chinese having been educated in English medium schools – had no knowledge of where their clan originated from and had never been there so they could not register their children there.

Education in Chinese was a problem. The government had no Chinese medium schools. The Chinese community, very attached to its language and culture, paid for and managed its own schools for all ages up to eighteen. They were referred to as C(hinese) M(iddle) S(chools). 'Graduates' of these middle schools (who were particularly strong in mathematics) could not get admission to the University of Singapore because their English was not good enough. To avoid political difficulties with the 'two Chinas', Singapore passports were not made valid for China or Taiwan. Products of the C.M.S. could not get a University education. An illiterate Chinese named Tan Lark Sye who did not know any English made a fortune and became President of the Chinese Chamber of Commerce. He donated three million dollars to found a Chinese University called Nan Yang (South Seas) University. I visited this institution. In the library there were no books but scrolls. I noticed a shelf with a score of large scrolls of uniform size and appearance and asked what they were. I was told they were the official annals of the Chinese Emperors. In India we have nothing comparable. The first history of any part of India is the Chhachhnama in Persian written after the conquest of Sind by Mohammed bin Kassim.

My experience in a classroom was quite different. I was taken to it as the students were trooping out and the blackboard was being wiped. I said,

'Stop. I can read that blackboard. It has the chemical equations for Fischer's Pyridene synthesis and is written in English. I thought this was a Chinese medium university?'

'Yes, I am afraid we are not allowed to import books from China or Taiwan so we have to teach the natural sciences in English.'

To return to Loke Wan Tho, whom I got to know quite well, he was a keen bird-watcher and bird photographer. He had spent most of the World War in India, mostly Bombay, as a refugee having escaped from the Japanese Army in a small boat. In India he had made friends with Salim Ali the ornithologist who was related to the Tyabji family. His interest in birds was shared by the then British High Commissioner in Delhi, Sir Malcolm Macdonald who had earlier served in Singapore as Commissioner General.

Loke Wan Tho's wife Christina (they were not Christians) was the most beautiful Chinese woman in Singapore. Not only did she have a lovely face, but her figure was the envy of much younger women. I remember having a dinner in the Cathay restaurant in 1959 at which Kirat and I were seated at the same table with Christina Loke and the British Commissioner General's wife. This lady who must have been nearing sixty was intrigued by Christina's figure. When Christina left the table to attend to another guest, she turned to Kirat and said,

'I could not believe that Christina was not wearing a corset, so I pinched her bottom just now and, you know, no corset!'

Wan Tho had, of course, the most up-to-date equipment for his bird photography. In late 1960, Macdonald decided to write his book THE BIRDS IN MY GARDEN which became a great success. It seems hard to believe in the twenty-first century that he was able to identify a hundred different species in the garden of the High Commission in Rajaji Marg. Macdonald wanted his book to be illustrated and Wan Tho offered the services of Christina who had become quite proficient in this art. When she came back, she mentioned to me,

'I wish I had had Wan Tho's new equipment. I was using his old one which is not nearly as good.'

Rather tactlessly, I happened to mention this to Wan Tho who said,

'Christina should not complain about the equipment; I took very good photographs with it.'

To which I replied, 'Wives can always complain' and he responded, 'and generally they do.'

The next thing I knew was that Wan Tho had engaged a Q.C. from London to fight his divorce proceedings in Singapore. Macdonald had to come from New Delhi to appear in court as co-respondent. Of course, Wan Tho won his case. It was said that he paid a million Singapore dollars to Christina. I was also told that he had originally 'bought' her for a hundred thousand pounds from an Englishman.

There was a rival cinema firm to Loke Wan Tho in Singapore. It was called Shaw Brothers. The brothers were named Run Run and Run Me; they had reversed the Chinese way of writing names to correspond to English practice. The elder was emaciated and unhappy about it; when asked why he should be unhappy to be thin when it was universally believed to be healthier, he replied,

'Because my friends look well-fed and I feel the odd man out.' He was said to have suffered from tuberculosis. His wife did not speak English too well. They had several grown-up children who had attended English-language schools.

Run Me Shaw spoke English quite well and his wife had been a beauty queen some years earlier. They entertained magnificently in their large and well-furnished villa. The family used Rolls-Royce cars. The fact is that they were showmen. Apart from owning several cinemas in Singapore and Hong Kong they also produced films in both places. Finally, they owned one of three amusement parks in Singapore copied from the Tivoli Gardens in Copenhagen, Denmark.

I had found a golfer at the Royal Island Club who was almost as bad as I. He was Ahmed Ali Khan the Pakistani Trade

Commissioner. He had been born in Meerut. He explained to me that he was not from the Pakistani Foreign Service but reported to the Department of Foreign Trade. He was a sincerely friendly person and had a weight problem and so did his wife Qamar who was also his cousin. We used to play golf regularly twice a week. Pakistan did not have any other representative in Singapore.

There was however a Pakistani High Commissioner in Kuala Lumpur who was also accredited to Singapore. He was also Indian-born, being the younger brother of the Nawab of Pataudi who had played test cricket for England. This diplomat visited Singapore and Run Me Shaw gave a dinner in his honour. I had attended Run Me's dinners before. Most dinners I was invited to in Singapore were Chinese meals and the food was always good but its presentation generally left a good deal to be desired. At the end of the meal the table cloth would be covered with stains. Dinners at the Shaw residence were served on beautiful damask table cloths in their garden at tables for six. The waiters were well trained and there was silver cutlery for those who were not accustomed to eating with chopsticks. There were beautiful

1961 Singapore Greeting the Pakistani Trade Commissioner and Mrs. Ahmed Ali Khan.

bonbonnieres full of European chocolates. The Pakistani High Commissioner's wife and Ahmed Ali Khan were at my table. Kirat recognised this lady with whom she had been at school.

On 6th March 2006, at a dinner of the Oxford and Cambridge Society, I happened to meet Mansoor Ali Khan Pataudi, the famous cricketer and asked him if an uncle of his had been Pakistani High Commissioner in Kuala Lumpur in 1961. He replied, 'Yes, General Sher Ali. I have just been to Pakistan where I met his family.'

As I have mentioned earlier, my friend Ahmed had a weight problem and his lunch usually consisted of fruit so by dinnertime he usually had a ravenous appetite so he attacked the soup with gusto.

'You are not going to eat that soup, are you?' asked the guest of honour.

'Yes, indeed, how can I refuse my host's soup?'

'Can't you see the bits of lard floating in it?'

The next course was fish and Ahmed thought it could not be objectionable but the orthodox lady told him that it had been fried in pork fat. Then came roast suckling pig..........

The last course at all the Chinese meals I had been to was always rice which was not usually consumed as it was polite to say to the host – if only by implication – that one had eaten so much good food that there was no room left for a plebeian course such as rice. However, by now Ahmed was really hungry and prepared to tackle this humble dish but he was told it contained specks of ham. Ahmed survived by eating all the chocolates on the table.

We were told that the President of Pakistan was passing through Singapore so, of course, all the Commonwealth Commissioners and Trade Commissioners had to be at Changi airport to receive him. Ahmed and Qamar were very much in evidence. When the General came down the steps he was followed by his suite and I had to shake hands with all of them. One tall man embraced me. Normally, I do not embrace men, even my relations – I have no problem with embracing good-looking young women - but of course I had to be courteous; besides he was an old friend.

Qamar ran up to me and asked, 'Who is that man who greeted you like a long-lost brother?'

'He is called Khan.'

'Oh, come off it!'

'He is Sahibzada Sultan Mohammed Khan, Foreign Secretary of Pakistan.'

Sultan and I were batchmates. We had been together at the Administrative Service Training School at Metcalfe House from 20th March 1947 till Partition when he had opted for Pakistan like all the Muslims except Ishi Rahman.

In 1962, the Ministry of External Affairs decided to have a conference in New Delhi of Heads of Mission and Posts in South East Asia so, of course, I had to go. This was very convenient for me because it was time for Kiran to join the Doon School where he had been registered soon after he was born. I took him along with me and left him with Mataji in New Delhi. She would take him to Dehra Dun for the beginning of the winter term by car. In Dehra Dun my cousin (Mataji's brother's son) Prem Bhagat was the Commandant of the Rashtria Indian Military Academy and would be his 'local guardian'.

While I was in India, we annexed Goa. This was done at that time to enable Krishna Menon who was not a particularly popular man to win a bye-election in Bombay and get into the Lok Sabha – the Lower House of the Indian Parliament. The move was successful but widely criticised in the West, particularly in the United States where it was characterised as 'naked aggression'. Many years later, B.K.Nehru who was Ambassador in the United States at the time, told me he had had a bad time till he gave a television interview in which the question came up. He asked the interviewer,

'Supposing in your War of Independence, there had been a small territory, say Rhode Island, held by a country other than Britain, say Turkey, would you have allowed them to hold on to it?'

'No, of course not, we would have thrown the rascals out.'

After that, he said, he had never faced any more criticism on that account.

I returned to Singapore. Kirat had worked hard to make friends with the Countess of Selkirk. There was a fad at that time for physical fitness, the two rival systems being Yoga and Chinese 'Shadow Boxing'. Kirat had no problem with physical fitness because she was very figure conscious and got enough exercise playing golf. However, she found out that Wendy Selkirk had taken up shadow boxing so she would wake up at the crack of dawn – she was normally as fond of her sleep as I am – and join the shadow boxing class. This tactic paid off and we became firm friends on first name terms in spite of the difference in age (fifteen years) and status (Commissioner General and Assistant Commissioner). This friendship continued as long as the Selkirks lived and was particularly beneficial for Kiran.

The Commissioner General's office was located in 'Phoenix Park' – it was said that the British Empire had been resuscitated after the World War like a phoenix arising from the ashes. His residence was a huge house called 'Eden Hall'. I have seen thirty four persons at his dining table where I met various British noblemen and Ted Heath who became Prime Minister shortly afterwards.

The staff at Phoenix Park included my old friend, Mervyn Brown. Both he and Beth had plenty of opportunity to play tennis at which they were so good. As I have mentioned, the Commissioner General had a co-ordinating role and his annual 'Eden Hall Conference' was attended by the High Commissioner in India along with the representatives in other countries.

Mervyn had occasion to go to Laos where he was taken prisoner by the 'Pathet Lao'. Apparently he was well treated but the country was very short of food and when he returned to Singapore he had visibly lost weight. Fortunately his strong constitution and the good food available in Singapore soon put him right and they were both in good health forty years later when they had lunch with me in London.

In the meantime we were getting miserable letters from Kiran who was most unhappy at the Doon school. With hindsight it appears that he could not adjust to being away from parents or grandparents. We thought that he had frequently been away from us in New Delhi and Poona and with his independence and strength of character he would be able to adjust to a boarding school. However, we were wrong. We pointed out to him that he had more than one second cousin at school of whom the one he knew best was Dilbir – Hitindar Singh Vahali's son. Moreover, he was bigger than other boys of his age so he should be able to stand up to bullies. A letter to a teacher elicited the response that he was no good at sports on which there was considerable emphasis at the Doon. He was also unused to the school's ideas of discipline whereas many other boys had been at Colonel Welham's preparatory school in Dehra Dun. We decided to withdraw him from the Doon early in 1963.

The next problem was to find a school for him in Delhi. There were several reputable 'public schools' in Delhi but the most famous secular one was the Modern School which was co-educational and had been attended by the children of Sir Teja Singh Malik. Unfortunately this head of the family had passed away ten years earlier. Admission to a prestigious school is always difficult and requires contacts. I could not manage this from Singapore.

When we had been living in Kotah House Kirat had made friends with the wife of the caterer, Manohar Singh. He had been a prosperous baker in Lahore and after Partition had managed to get a bakery in New Delhi where he was baking MANOHAR bread. Many bakers in India are Muslims. He had also got the catering contract for Kotah House which was a residential job so he lived in a hutment like ours. He was a workaholic but his wife, Roop, had a talent for making friends and she made full use of living in a 'hutment' in Kotah House to get to know some of the top civil servants in New Delhi. Because of her and his own business contacts, Manohar Singh knew several bourgeois in New Delhi and his three children – the youngest 'Bibloo' not much older than Kiran – had been educated at the Modern School. So Manohar Singh got Kiran into the Modern School. He was much happier there because he was a day scholar and was living at home with Mataji.

In late 1962, the Chinese army invaded India. Krishna Menon was the Defence Minister and was not popular with Army Officers; to make matters worse, he had appointed an Officer of his own choice as General Officer Commanding Eastern Command. This General was a good administrator; he had been able to arrange a hot lunch in the field for over a thousand men when the Prime Minister had visited his troops.

The background to this military encounter between India and China is interesting. We have no knowledge of any war between any kingdom in India and the Chinese Empire. In the nineteenth century, Britain had gone to war with China to oblige the Manchu Emperor to allow import of Indian opium into China – the notorious Opium Wars. After the Great War, the relations between Britain and China had been good. The Indian people had a great deal of sympathy for China for various reasons – cultural similarities, Buddhism, the common struggle against the white man's economic and military domination of Asia , etc. After Pearl Harbour, American and British support for China became more than lip-sympathy and this became one field in which the British Government of India was not at variance with India's national aspirations. The dispatch of an Indian medical team to Chunking – as it was then called – received full support and its leader Dr.Kotnis became a national hero.

There were also good personal relations between General Chiang Kai Shek and Pandit Nehru. When Mahatma Gandhi launched the 'Quit India' campaign and Vijaylakshmi Pandit could see the prison gates about to close on her and feared for the fate of her three unmarried daughters, she wrote to Chiang Mei Ling for help. A Chinese diplomat quickly arrived in India and took the girls away to Universities in Europe and America. These good relations continued till the Communists entered Peking. Then, facing up to reality, Pandit Nehru quickly recognised the new government. Chiang Mei Ling wrote a very 'nasty' letter to Vijaylakshmi as she later told me. Of course, the Nehruvian decision was strongly criticised by the U.S. government.

Nothing daunted, Pandit Nehru sent a special plane to fetch Chou En Lai to the Bandoeng Conference. This plane was sabotaged by some one in Hong Kong so it made a forced landing on an Indonesian beach. At the conference, Panditji took Chou by the hand and introduced him to various Asian leaders among whom his own prestige was then at its peak.

I have never met Chou en Lai or any other Chinese leader and I have never been to China. Postings in Singapore and Manila gave me some idea of what the Chinese are like. In Singapore I became acquainted with the Agence France Presse representative mainly because he could talk to me in French. He told me an interesting story,

'I was quite poor when I was a student at the Sorbonne but I became friendly with a Chinese student whose name was Chou En Lai and who was obviously rich. One day he said to me,

'I don't like your tie.'

'I am sorry but it is the only tie I have. Would you like to give me one of your choice?'

'The next day he gave me one. Many years later, here in South East Asia, I was going to a function in his honour and I found and put on that old tie and when I was formally introduced to him by my host I pointed to my tie and said, in French,

'Mr. Prime Minister this is the tie which you so kindly gave me in Paris.' He looked at me with complete incomprehension and his interpreter said to me, in English,

'The Prime Minister does not speak French.''

In India the Government did everything in its power to help the new Chinese government.

In the eighth century A.D., the Chinese Emperor had conquered Tibet and maintained an Officer in Lhasa ever after but he was not very effective and was unsupported by troops. There were cultural and religious links between India and Tibet. I have seen Tibetan monks in the Golden Temple in Amritsar in the thirties and Indian Buddhists travelled freely to Lhasa. The British were keen to protect India's frontiers from other powers. They tried to find out more about Tibet where they were not allowed to enter. They sent Indian Hindu spies dressed as Buddhist pilgrims to Lhasa. Two of them carried long staffs with which they measured the distance from the frontier to Lhasa! This led to clashes with the Tibetan authorities and in 1904-05 Colonel Francis Younghusband of the Indian Political Service led an 'expedition' to Lhasa which the Tibetan troops opposed in vain. Younghusband was an indologist and a diplomat more than a soldier. He succeeded in setting up a British Resident in Lhasa much as if it were an Indian princely state. He also established two Agents, one of them in Gyatse (Western Tibet's frontier with India) to 'facilitate' frontier trade which had been going on for a long time. A telegraph line was built from Calcutta to Lhasa. When thieves started stealing the copper wire, Indian troops were assigned to protect it. Thus in 1949, when the Chinese Army occupied Peking, there was an Indian military presence in Tibet and a functioning fair-weather road from India to Lhasa.

For over a century, Governments in Peking had been unable to have any say in Tibetan affairs. They had protested against

Younghusband's invasion but could do nothing about it. Protests had also been made about the British-Tibetan agreements about stationing of troops in Tibet but they were equally ineffective. The new Communist government was determined to put an end to the autonomous or semi-independent territories surrounding Chinese territory proper. They could do nothing about Outer Mongolia which was under Soviet Russian protection or Taiwan which is still (2006) protected by the United States but they quickly re-occupied Inner Mongolia which had religious relations with Tibet and Sinkiang (then known as Chinese Turkestan) where the British were influential.

Tibet was a little more difficult because of its location and because its large monastic society was unwilling to have a secular, even atheistic, government. However, the Tibetan army proved as ineffective against the Red Army as nearly half-a-century earlier against Younghusband. The Chinese Army arrived in Lhasa but the route through the mountains made it impossible to provide supplies. Chou En Lai approached Panditji for help in transporting supplies through Calcutta to Lhasa by the overland route. This was granted without even obtaining ratification of the forty-year-old Indo-Tibetan agreements. When the Chinese Army had established itself in Lhasa, there was a request for the withdrawal of Indian troops. Pandit Nehru agreed, justifying it to the Indian Parliament, as a 'colonial heritage' which the Republic of India did not wish to continue.

On the ground in Tibet, the Dalai Lama found his authority completely eroded. He visualised Lamaistic Buddhism being wiped off the face of the earth and decided to move to India and save his religion even if he could do nothing about his country. The Chinese Army was unable to stop this monastic procession from crossing the mountains into India and the Indian public welcomed this holy man as it had through the centuries welcomed so many others.

After this, relations with China deteriorated quite quickly. The inaccessible frontier between India and China in the high Himalayas had been demarcated on maps drawn by British cartographers without – in several places – being marked on the ground. Younghusband had obtained Tibetan signatures on these maps and the Chinese had protested vigorously but ineffectively.

The first indication that the Chinese were occupying Indian territory was given to Pandit Nehru by the Agent in Gyatse who was immediately transferred. A patrol was sent into Aksai Chin, an uninhabited part of Jammu and Kashmir in its North East. The patrol never returned. It was then found that a road had been built through Aksai Chin connecting Lhasa with Kashgarh in Sinkiang. This was the Western Portion of the India-China frontier where there was a high uninhabited plateau. In the Eastern Portion, near the then Indian princely state of Sikkim, the Chinese army had learnt mountaineering and reached the 'inaccessible' heights. A new map was published in Peking showing the frontier considerably south of where it appeared on the old British Indian maps. It included in China cultivated territory and some middle-sized towns among them a district headquarters. Pandit Nehru was getting more and more upset that his Hindi Chini Bhai Bhai (Indians and Chinese are brothers) policy had collapsed. The Indian public was getting increasingly angry with Chou En Lai. Even the Communist party was finding it difficult to justify the actions and statements of the Government of the 'workers' paradise' and split on the issue into the C.P.I. (Communist Party of India) and the Marxist C.P.I. (M), the latter becoming pro-Chinese. A last attempt was made to settle matters by inviting Chou En Lai to India but there was no welcome for him nor any acceptable offer from him.

Finally Pandit Nehru gave the order to evict the Chinese from the positions they had occupied. Neither Nehru nor Krishna Menon had any military experience although Menon belonged to a 'martial race' – the Nairs of Kerala. They did not realise that it is difficult to fight uphill. Our troops had never been trained, acclimatised or equipped for mountain warfare. The Chinese whom they were up against had been on the Tibetan plateau for many months and were accustomed to the cold and the lack of oxygen. We had our own advantages. We had tanks and aircraft which the Chinese did not have - in Tibet. If we had waited for them in the plains we could have destroyed the Chinese infantry on ground of *our* choosing. The Army Officers knew all this. Did they fail to advise the Minister? Did he ignore military advice? What we do know is that the Minister and the Army Commander lost their jobs.

For me in Singapore a difficult situation arose. About 70% of the population of Singapore were Chinese. I asked Wee Kim Wee, the English educated and, I would say, very anglicised Vice President of the Chinese Chamber of Commerce whether he felt more Singaporean or more Chinese and he replied,

'Of course I feel more Chinese, although I was born and brought up here and have never visited China and speak English better than Hokkien.'

The Indians were equally nationalistic. A constant stream of men I did not know poured into my office and offered to join the Indian Army. It was obvious from their appearance, physique and body language that were unlikely to make good soldiers. I told them that the war might be over before they could get to India and certainly before they could be trained. Of course, they were very disappointed and even unwilling to accept my answer. I told them that it would be much more useful if they could give money which I could send immediately to India. Apart from its rupee value the fact that it was convertible currency would be particularly useful because India was short of foreign exchange which was needed for buying advanced weapons we did not produce ourselves. This argument worked well and substantial contributions were received.

Whenever I had to speak about the war I would blame it on Communism since that doctrine was anathema to the Singapore government. Of course, I was reporting all this to New Delhi. To my great surprise, I received a long letter from Yezdi Gundevia, the Foreign Secretary. I was surprised because Secretaries to the Government of India do not usually condescend to write to comparatively junior Officers unless they have something unpleasant to communicate. This letter was very friendly and explained to me at some length that we were not really fighting Communism because the Soviet Union was our friend. It just happened that a mis-guided and ill-advised Chinese Government had invaded Indian territory. It did create a difficult situation for me especially when Lee Kuan Yew told me officially that the majority Chinese community was siding with China in this war and might want to send money to China if I did not stop sending money to India! Fortunately, the Chinese decided to stop fighting and restored the status quo.

I could appreciate the validity of Lee Kuan Yew's remarks because I found that Loke Wan Tho who knew India well and had many friends in our country told me he was very upset that India had turned anti-Chinese and 'Hindi Chini Bhai Bhai' had changed to 'Hindi Chini Bye Bye'. He seemed to think that it was India's fault – an idea which had never occurred to me!

Run Me Shaw never mentioned the war to me.

To everybody's surprise, the wife of a Chinese businessman whom we all knew suddenly divorced him and married Loke Wan Tho. The surprise was because we were not at all conscious of that marriage with three children being in trouble. Loke's previous marriage had been childless. The new couple went to Taiwan for their honeymoon where they perished in a plane crash.

The colonial as distinguished from the political hierarchy was headed by the Governor. The next lower rung was the Chief Secretary, a European, with whom Yog established cordial relations. I decided to give a dinner for the Under Secretary, a Eurasian named Stewart who was reputed to have half a dozen children. I had met him and his wife at parties and she had a good face and figure in spite of her age and fecundity. She told me,

'When I got married, my husband was District Officer in Penang. We lived in a nice bungalow outside Georgetown. When the Japanese occupied Malaya they did not interfere with the administration and the only difference it made to me was that I had to go and register. An English-speaking Japanese sergeant was the registrar and he was questioning me and entering the answers in his book. When he came to the column 'nationality', I answered

'Eurasian'

'Where is Eurasia?'

'Oh! It means a kind of mixture.'

'Ah! Mekishko.'

'So I became Mexican. Life was quite normal after that till one afternoon twenty Japanese soldiers marched into my sitting room. We could not communicate because they did not speak English or Malay and I knew no Japanese. I realised that I should offer them something, perhaps tea, so I rang for the maid. She was not there; normally at that hour she should have been having her siesta but obviously she had found something better to do.

Fortunately I knew where the kitchen was so I went there and soon found a tray in which I arranged twenty cups and saucers. I also saw a tin labelled TEA which contained tea-leaves. I realised that the teapot in which our tea was served to us would not do for twenty people.

'We did not have running water in the bungalow. Ewers full of water and basins were kept in the toilets. I got an ewer and put a teaspoonful of tea-leaves in it. To my surprise, the tea-leaves sank to the bottom leaving clear water which did not look at all like the tea we were served. It dawned on me that one teaspoonful would not do for twenty people so I emptied the tin into the ewer but, except for a little dust on top, the water was clear. I found a long wooden spoon in the kitchen, stirred the water, poured it quickly into the cups, took the tray to the sitting room, put it on the centre table and ran out of the house. When I came back a couple of hours later the Japanese were no longer there. It was only next day that I learnt about boiling water.'

Was she pulling my leg? No, I don't think so. At about the same time I got to know the Professor of International Law at the University of Singapore. He was an English Jew. During the World War he had served in the British Army in the Judge Advocate General's Branch and was posted in India. There he had met a young Jewess surnamed Levi and married her. I must explain that in the nineteenth century there was a large and wealthy Jewish community in Basra in the then Turkish Empire. When they learnt about new wealthy cities under British rule further to the East, they emigrated to Bombay, Madras, Calcutta and Hong Kong. The most successful ended up in England – Siegfried Sassoon the writer and Victor Sassoon who was a friend of Lloyd George's at the time of the Great War. In India, because they were light-skinned and rich they were accepted in the DOMICILED EUROPEAN AND ANGLO-INDIAN COMMUNITY. This young woman joined the W.A.C.(I.) - the equivalent of the A.T.S. in the United Kingdom, of course as an Officer. One day there was a meeting of half-a-dozen W.A.C.(I.) Officers and the Junior Commander who chaired the meeting said,

'We need some tea. Levi, you are the junior most, please make tea.'

'But, Madam, I do not know how to make tea!'

I myself have a second cousin who has told me that when she got married she did not know how to cook.

There were incidents less amusing than these. I managed to persuade the Ministry of External Affairs to let me air condition my office room because I had to receive the Flag Officers of the British Forces there. This meant fitting spring doors. One day I heard someone struggling to open the door. I got up to open the door. I saw an old and emaciated Sikh on crutches covered with bandages rather than clothes apart from his kachha. I invited him to sit down and arranged for a cup of tea for him. His story was that he had been a policeman.

Until the war the police and prisons in British South East Asia had been staffed with Sikhs recruited from Ludhiana district in Punjab. For this, British police and prison Officers used to be stationed in Ludhiana where they learnt Punjabi and saw to the recruiting and the domestic problems of the recruits. In Singapore, the government servants got no pension but a 'provident fund' to which the Government and the employee contributed so they got a substantial amount when they superannuated (reached pensionable retirement age). Only very senior ones brought their families to Singapore but the others got generous leave to go home.

My visitor had returned home to his family after retirement. One afternoon when he was having his siesta he woke up to overhear a conversation between his wife and his son.

'This old man is not earning anything; he only eats. Do you know where he keeps his money?

'Yes, Mother, not only that, I also know how to get hold of his money.'

'Then let us kill him now with his lathi; here it is.'

Because he had happened to wake up he survived the beating with only a few broken bones. He decided that he had no friends in Punjab and had made his way to Singapore where his friends would look after him and keep him alive.

I was greatly impressed by the way the Singapore Government dealt with the housing problem. The problem differed with race. Indians did not have a major problem. The rich and the middle class could live in the kind of accommodation they would have had in India. The poorest were the workers for the Harbour

Board and other unskilled workers in the public sector who had come from India with contracts and they were usually housed by their employer in tenements which they found acceptable. The problem only arose with those who met with a misfortune – death of a breadwinner, sickness etc. and they were few.

The majority community, the Chinese, were quite different. The poorest were drivers of 'trishaws' (cycle rickshaws) who generally did not have families. I was amazed to learn that hundreds of them lived in a large building in the centre of the city which appeared to be well maintained – of course, I never went inside. Apparently they were very well disciplined and there was no problem over toilets or kitchens as generally happens with Indians.

In that respect, the Malays resembled Indians. They did not like living in flats. With a few exceptions they wanted to live in individual houses. For the poor this meant building shanties in areas (kampongs) where they could find land. Such areas were unlikely to have electricity, water or sewage facilities. When a fire broke out in a kampong, the Housing Board moved in quickly before the ashes were cold and bulldozed the whole area flat. Then they quickly built multi-storey blocks of flats and let them out at affordable rents. Before this initiative was taken, the original slum-dwellers used to come back as soon as the fires had gone out to retrieve any unburnt belongings and rebuild their shanties. As multi-storeyed blocks could accommodate far more persons than shanties in an given area, it only needed a few fires to put an end to the slums.

We were sorry to leave Singapore when my term expired.

INDIA 1963-65

I had been told that my posting in Delhi would be in the Ministry of Commerce. There was a policy of having some I.F.S. Officers in the Ministry of Commerce so that that Ministry would get advice about conditions abroad. These postings were not popular with my colleagues because we were not made to feel very welcome in the Commerce Ministry where we were regarded as 'birds of passage'. Besides, there were very few posts corresponding to Counsellor in the Ministry of Commerce. I was too junior to be a Joint Secretary and a post of Deputy Secretary would have been be a demotion. It became necessary to create a post of 'Director'. The Ministry's full name was 'Ministry of Commerce and Industry' and the Minister had Cabinet rank. Under him was a Minister of State for Commerce and another Minister (both of them without Cabinet rank) for Industry. At the officer level, there was a Secretary for Commerce and Industry who was one of the four members of the Foreign Service Board which had the effective power over the Foreign Service. The Ministry of Commerce had a Special Secretary; he got the same salary as the Secretary but was of inferior status.

I knew this Officer, D.S.Joshi, a Maharashtrian in the I.C.S., because I had met him the previous year when he had been Textile Commissioner in Bombay and I had gone to see him about some consignments of textiles exported to Singapore which had been found by the Singapore Customs to contain only rubbish. He had explained to me that 'corruption has not been eliminated.' I had been horrified. The scam was that A would export rubbish declaring it as high value textiles (for which he got a cash 'incentive' from the Ministry of Commerce) passing it through the Indian customs by bribing the inspector. Since Singapore was a free port, there was a good chance that the customs would not open the consignment. The importer B was a friend or relation of the exporter and they would amicably settle the financial part of the transaction which might also be profitable because of exchange control.

Fortunately, the wife of the Secretary (Ranganathan, a Tamil) had gone to Malaya a few months previously on a private visit to meet relations there. She had rung me up before arriving in Singapore to ask me to find a suitable hotel. I had invited her to stay at Bharat Bhavan and she had appreciated my hospitality for her and her cousin who was accompanying her. I think that helped in expediting the creation of a post of Director to accommodate me.

In the Ministry of External Affairs, the Officers were designated by their duties e.g. J.S.(Ad.) was the Joint Secretary (Administration). No one had carried out such an exercise in the Ministry of Commerce and sections were allotted ad hoc to senior Officers depending on the experience of the Officer or the whim of the Secretary. I was therefore known by my initials as Dir(GJM). Another Officer, a Muslim from Kashmir was Dir(MMM). I asked him to amplify his initials and he said his name was Mufti Muhammad Maqbool. I said I thought 'Mufti' was a religious rank. He replied that he was a qualified Mufti and this had become hereditary in his family so it had been adopted as a surname like Malik. Before the arrival of the English language it was not unusual to write the family name before the given name.

I was allotted some sections of which the only one which interested me was 'Americas'. I was supposed to formulate policy for dealing with my area and to correspond with Commercial Secretaries and Trade Commissioners. Trade Commissioners were an older, pre-independence, institution and used to report directly to the Department of Trade. With Independence and the opening of diplomatic missions, they were slowly absorbed into Embassies and High Commissions. This situation is not peculiar to India. Many years later, after I retired, a South American Ambassador asked me to compile information for him in Spanish on the Commercial and Economic situation in India. I said that his Commercial Secretary probably had it all. He replied that his Ministry of Foreign Affairs had instructed him not to mention the matter to the Commercial Secretary who reported to that country's Ministry of External Trade!

The Minister of Commerce was a Gujrati named Manubhai Shah. He was industrious, had a good grasp of his subject and an excellent memory. He would spout voluminous statistics in his conversations with us. D.S. Joshi, whom he treated rather shabbily, told me that more than 90% of the statistics were correct. However, although his vision of India's economic future was good, he was over optimistic about the timing of our economic progress. His manners and his inability to appreciate what was practical and what could not be immediately achieved led to the early termination of his political career.

Since I was dealing with the Americas and the principal object was to export and thus earn foreign exchange, I decided to study the export statistics and see what we were exporting to the United States which was the only significant market we had in those two continents. I was surprised to find that the biggest exports were hessians (cloth made of jute and used in U.S.A. for carpet backing) and cashew nuts. The Jute industry was concentrated in Calcutta where British businessmen had started it a hundred years earlier and was based on jute grown in the Ganges delta. Jute is a very thirsty crop and its cultivation was very labour intensive so it was suitable for local conditions. Exports to America were also well established since pre-Independence days.

Cashew nuts were a more recent development. Americans, particularly in the Southern States had developed a taste for roasted, salted cashew nuts with their 'sundowners' but they were very expensive. They then discovered that they were grown as a marginal crop on the rubber plantations of Kerala. This made the fruit very cheap. The problem was that, to get at the nut, the fruit had to be broken and it exuded a very acid juice which burnt the fingers of the worker. In Kerala these workers were young women. They were able and willing to do the work. I was told that their nimble and skilled fingers distinguished them from other workers. It may have been that they accepted the damage to their fingers and even developed immunity to the acid.

The next problem was to transport the nuts to the United States. It was found that when packed in tins they quickly became stale and unappetising. Here again the Americans developed a technique for packing them in nitrogen which enabled them to arrive in U.S.A. with their taste unchanged. Our Consul General in New York, my friend and batchmate Sunil Roy, reported that the price we were getting free on board New York was a quarter of the wholesale price in U.S.A. When he protested to the American importers, they replied that India had done nothing for this trade and they had discovered the benefits of nitrogen packing without which there would have been no cashew exports. My own feeling was that there was an innate hostility on the part of our bureaucracy to business and the profits that businessmen made as the reward for their enterprise. This bureaucratic attitude matched perfectly with Nehruvian socialism which had set up an Office of Chief Controller of Imports and Exports – the nomenclature indicating that trade was not desirable and must be controlled.

Sunil Roy had suggested certain steps to change the situation in our favour but the Financial Adviser – a Joint Secretary detached from the Ministry of Finance – would not allow expenditure to be incurred on a project the return from which (if any) would accrue not to the Government of India but to businessmen. I understand things are better now in the twenty-first century because businessmen are able and willing to do things themselves instead of asking the Government for handouts or even just help.

I must give credit to the Minister for wanting to help exports instead of succumbing to the inertia of the bureaucracy – especially the Ministry of Finance. He asked me to take a commercial Mission to South America to establish contacts with the businessmen and officials and study the possibilities on the spot. Of course, this would be a new experience for me.

The first problem was to find businessmen who would agree to absent themselves for a month or more from their profitable businesses to explore a continent so far away, to which there were no shipping services and where they would have to deal with languages of which they had no knowledge. On this point I encouraged them by saying that I spoke Spanish and would interpret for them and that Spanish was understood even in Brazil. The next problem was finance. They wanted the government to pay half their fares. This the Minister was able to arrange. The Secretary as a Maharashtrian, was not happy at businessmen from Calcutta monopolising this jaunt. Finally, we were able to find a Gujrati, a Konkani (the area around Goa) and a Marwari from Calcutta. An export executive from the Birla group who knew one of these businessmen attached himself to us saying he would pay his own expenses but would like to profit by the introductions and contacts which Indian Embassies would provide to an official delegation but not to a private businessman. We would benefit because his group could provide exports not covered by the other three businessmen. We accepted his proposition but we were not too happy because at that time Birlas were known mainly for their AMBASSADOR car which was quite unpopular.

We were due to start at the end of May (1964) when suddenly the Prime Minister passed away. I was afraid that it might put paid to our trip but the Ministry of External Affairs advised that there would only be a week's mourning during which Embassies would not be able to entertain. This did not affect our programme.

Our first port of call was Rio de Janeiro where Vincent Coelho was our Ambassador. He was a Goan and spoke Portuguese. This facilitated our work. There was, however, a problem with our diets. I ate everything but did not drink. The Gujrati who was the oldest, the most experienced and the wealthiest among the businessmen was a vegetarian but liked to drink; however, his capacity for alcohol was small and he did not know when to stop. The Marwari was a vegetarian and teetotaller; moreover, this was his first overseas trip and he had to learn everything about international customs and manners; he really had very little to say for himself.

The Konkani was the one person I could identify with. He came from a well-known family of academicians. He would normally have gone to England or America for his higher education after graduating from the University of Bombay but the war prevented this. When the war ended, there was a rush for such families to send their sons and daughters abroad, of course to U.K. and U.S.A. In both these countries, ex-servicemen were getting preference and financial aid for higher education. It was very difficult for foreigners (especially those who had not served in the Allied Forces) to get admission. My new friend could only manage to get into the University of Denver in Colorado! He ate everything and drank in moderation.

We could not do much in Rio because it is not the industrial or commercial capital of the country. However, we did meet a Minister in the company of the Ambassador. I suggested to him that preferential treatment might be accorded to our handicrafts and handlooms which are produced by the poorest and most deprived sections of the population; he replied that the situation in Brazil was very similar. It took me time to understand that there is greater social and economic inequality in Brazil than in India. In fact, in those days, undeveloped land for industry or for 'industrial' (large scale mechanised) farming was advertised as 'dirty' or 'clean'. The latter was land from which the Amerindians had been removed (how?). There was no question of an Amerindian (corresponding to our tribals) becoming a diplomat, much less the President of the country. This has only happened in Peru and Venezuela forty years later.

In Sao Paulo where India had no consular presence, we were greeted at the airport by an active young-looking Indian and his daughter. We asked him how he happened to get to this very distant country. He said that he had been a contractor in Nagpur when his marriage had broken down and he had decided to go abroad. The only foreign country where he had friends was Switzerland so he bought the seven hundred and fifty pounds foreign exchange which the Reserve Bank of India used to allow every three years to tourists and went to Switzerland. There his friends told him that Switzerland does not accept immigrants and he should go to Brazil.

'But I do not even know what language is spoken in Brazil. What on earth shall I do there and whom should I turn to for help?'

'You are a resourceful businessman and you will surely succeed. People less educated and talented than you have made their fortunes in Sao Paolo. Go there.'

When he arrived in Sao Paolo he decided that he could teach yoga without knowing any Portuguese so he hired a classroom and set to work. At the end of a year, he could speak Portuguese, he knew forty people and he had some knowledge of the local economy. He noticed that buildings were being sold and knocked down to enable larger, higher buildings to be constructed on the terrain. Quite often due to the endless inflation, the man who bought the terrain found he did not immediately have enough money to build and the land would lie empty for a year. He rented such a plot by the month, hired a Brazilian and turned the plot into a parking lot – traffic congestion in the largest and fastest-growing city in Brazil was everlasting. This established his reputation as a businessman and in a couple of years he was better off than he had been in Nagpur. It was then that he decided to invite his daughter over.

Our fame preceded us and we found photo-journalists waiting for us at every airport. In Sao Paulo we had found everybody speaking English in the Chamber of Commerce. When we mentioned Hindustan Machine Tools, a member said that the factory had been set up with Czech collaboration, that he had used the same Czech partner for his factory, that ours was bigger but his was more up-to-date. He knew more about it than we did! It was arranged that I should speak on one of the local television stations in Spanish. This was done and we got enough publicity.

Our next port of call was Buenos Aires, Argentina. The Ambassador there was a retired Cavalry General. I did not know him but I had sent him a list of people I knew and requested him to invite them for the party he would give for our delegation. He did so and, this time, I was able to give a radio interview.

In Santiago, Chile, our Ambassador had recently arrived from Laos and furnished his drawing room with Laotian artefacts. We spoke to some businessmen and our jute expert made contact with his clients. The history of our trade relations is interesting. Before the construction of the Panama Canal, even as early as the eighteenth century, sailing ships trading between Calcutta and Boston used to come via the Pacific Ocean and touch at the first Chilean port they found to get fresh water and food supplies. One of the items they carried was Indian tea – the Boston Tea Party – and they would sell some in the Chilean and, on the East Coast, Argentine ports. The result was that these two countries acquired a taste for Indian tea and that market was still there in the twentieth century. Today, in the twenty-first century I believe Argentine tea competes with us!

Our next port of call was Lima, Peru. We had no Ambassador there. In Japan, I had known the First Secretary of the Peruvian Embassy and Kirat and I had had a meal with him and his wife when they were transferred to New Delhi. Unfortunately, very soon after getting to India they had met with a traffic accident on a trip to Agra. The First Secretary died in the accident and his wife who was expecting a baby had been very severely injured. She had survived and delivered a little boy; due to his mother's (Mercedes, abbreviated to Mecha) injuries he had been born paraplegic. I found out from the Peruvian Ministry of Foreign Affairs where she was. She was living with her parents in their large house. The father was a famous Doctor and had been Health Minister. When I called, the whole delegation was invited to dinner. The ex-Minister was very kind to us. We told him that our next visit would be to La Paz, Bolivia. He said there were dangers involved in flying to La Paz for a short visit because there would be no time to acclimatise our bodies to the altitude and in the three days we would be in La Paz we would be rushing around and not be able to rest. He examined us and advised our oldest member not to go to La Paz but to stay in Lima and re-join us in Bogota, Colombia.

In La Paz, the business class was so small that we found hardly any prospects for trade but India was known because my friend Vikram Sarabhai was doing research in PHOTONS. These are sub-atomic particles which are found in sunlight. However, not many reach the earth because they are stopped by the earth's atmosphere. They are best studied at high altitudes where the atmosphere is much thinner. With the collaboration of the Bolivian Government, he had set up an observatory at an altitude of 17,500 feet – La Paz is spread out between the airport at 14,000 feet and the lower city at 11,000. There was an Indian scientist working for Vikram, who was living in La Paz. He came to see us, had a meal with us and offered to take us to his observatory. The others were not interested but I went (in a truck) and was very uncomfortable with mountain sickness.

Colombia was the only country where we had a big deal under discussion and that too without an Embassy to help.

Geographically, the country has several advantages. It has coastlines and ports on both the Pacific and the Caribbean. It has a choice of climates varying from the altitude of Bogota (like Ooty in South India) to the coastal plains (like Bombay). It also has plenty of rainfall. Indeed, we were told that a frontier region adjoining the Isthmus of Panama has more rain than Cherrapunji. However, the forest is so thick and so unhealthy that it was, at that time, the missing link in the Pan American Highway and it was not possible to go there.

It was the plentiful rainfall which gave Indian exporters an opportunity. There were several hydro-electric projects in the country, of course located in mountainous and forested areas. The problem was to get the electricity to urban centres where there was a demand. At that time, India had practically a monopoly in the manufacture and supply of transmission line towers. If we could install them and link them up, a public sector company called 'Interconexiones S.A.' would give us a contract.

With its natural resources, why is Colombia one of the poorer countries in South America? The 'politically incorrect' answer is that it has a majority aboriginal or Amerindian population which has not benefited by education. The other answers are the lack of infrastructure and law and order. While we were there, an amusing anecdote was related to us. Bogota had a problem of burglary, armed robbery and pick-pocketing. The Government asked Scotland Yard for assistance. The team from London duly arrived but had its luggage stolen between the airport and the hotel!

There were positive aspects. The country produces high quality coffee. It is also the major source of emeralds in the world. There is a pre-Columbian legend of 'El Dorado' – the golden man. It was said that there was so much gold in the country that every year one man was dressed in gold and then ceremonially drowned to appease the local divinity. There were gold mines at one time but no significant gold has been produced for a hundred years. We visited the 'gold museum' housed in the building of the Central Bank; it contains very beautiful gold artefacts which have been dug up. The urban population is highly literate and even literary. The standing joke is that every man has a manuscript ready for publication in his pocket. When two friends meet in the street, both pat their pockets and say,

'I will read yours if you will read mine.'

An old friend in Buenos Aires, a hotelier named Ottocar Rosarios, had given me an introduction to a playwright named Osorio in Bogota. I went and called on him and he and his wife, who both had a working knowledge of English, invited me and my Konkani friend (the others being vegetarians had no interest in Colombian food) to see his play in the theatre and dine with them. Osorio claimed that he was the only dramatist in the world who had been able to build a theatre with his literary earnings. His wife explained that they made much more money by showing films in this theatre than from his comedies. We both enjoyed the dinner and I was able to translate some of the jokes for my friend. Our presence at a Spanish play got us favourable publicity in the newspapers.

Our final destination was Caracas, the capital of Venezuela. By 1964, Venezuela had attained the same per capita income as Argentina by its substantial export of petroleum to the United States. But the economic and cultural situation in the two countries was not comparable. Argentina was an exporter of cereals and meat – products which are fairly labour intensive. While the countryside is poor, a large middle class had been built up particularly in the capital where, at that time, over a third of the country's population lived. The oil industry employs very few people and once pipelines have been laid from the oilfields to the harbours there is no need for much infrastructure. In Venezuela, the oil fields are mostly situated in and around Lake Maracaibo which is more lagoon than lake because it communicates through a short navigable channel with the Caribbean. Much of the oil can be loaded directly from the rigs onto tankers, diminishing the need for an extensive network of pipelines. There was a refinery to supply domestic needs but only crude was exported. The government had built up a system of superhighways connecting half-a-dozen important cities but otherwise the countryside lacked modern amenities. I got the impression that the wealth was concentrated in Caracas which looked like a prosperous city but it still lacked the vibrant cultural life of Buenos Aires.

There was no Indian Embassy in Caracas. There did not appear to be any prominent Indian resident either. One well-to-do woman called on us. She was the daughter of an Indian intellectual who had been India's representative to U.N.E.S.C.O.

in Paris. There she had met a Venezuelan whom she had married. We invited her for lunch but she came without her husband.

The Venezuelan government was very good to us. They placed a couple of cars at our disposal as also an English-speaking Officer who accompanied us on our calls. Of course we invited him to dinner and he came accompanied by two sisters. When I addressed them as 'Senorita', he explained that they were both married and had both been abandoned by their husbands who had left them with babies and nothing else. While I was used to seeing divorces in the West and even in India, this situation seemed strange to me and gave me a bad impression of Venezuelan society.

While we saw possibilities for Indian exports to Venezuela, nothing could be done immediately.

After Caracas our delegation broke up and we went our separate ways. I have asked myself what we achieved. We made India and its industrial and commercial capabilities better known in official, commercial and industrial circles in South America but any businessman in international trade new quite a lot about India anyway. The deals resulting from the activities of the members of the delegation may have paid for it but my impression was that India was not producing enough manufactured goods of international quality. Our exports were mainly of agricultural or mineral produce very slightly worked on – jute woven into textiles, grey cotton fabrics still requiring processing before they could be commercialised, iron and manganese ore, bauxite processed into alumina etc. In the twenty-first century things have changed; we are exporting motor vehicles in substantial quantities. Machinery, fashion fabrics and even garments are significant in India's foreign trade. Unfortunately, India's share of world trade is less than it was two hundred years ago.

I returned to Delhi and the problems of the house. I have mentioned that Pitaji had started construction of the house in Nizamuddin West in 1952 and Mataji had completed it in 1953. It was designed to occupy the maximum permissible built-up area on the plot and consisted of two flats, one for him and Mataji and one for me and my family on the upper floor. His idea was that he would be able to live comfortably on his pension. His pension expired with him. Mataji had been living in one flat and letting out the other to give her an income and pay house tax. If I were to occupy the other flat she would have no income.

1964 Delhi The house at 21 A Nizammuddin West, as remodelled by K.M. von Heinz.

Fortunately, the municipal bye-laws had been changed and it was now permissible to enlarge the house. We could build another bedroom with attached bath on each floor so that each flat would have a drawing room, a dining room, a kitchen, three bedrooms and a prayer room. This would provide room for all of us and a flat to let to provide an income. A loan for building could be obtained from the Life Insurance Corporation of India. We would have to find a place to live for the better part of a year. Before I left for my trip we had shifted to a house which my cousin Bhupinder had built in Defence Colony. When I came back, Tayaji told us he had to sell that house and we rented part of the house adjoining ours which had the advantage that we could see the work going on in our own house and this may have expedited its completion. The architect was a German, Karl Malte von Heinz whose houses were very popular. Of course, there was a cost over-run and I had to pledge my own life insurance policy but that probably happens to most people. Anyway, we did manage to live very comfortably on the upper floor and let out the lower one before I was posted abroad again.

I produced a hundred page report on my trip and it was read – I got comments from men who had been to South America - but I have no idea whether it brought about any noticeable increase in exports to South America.

The time was approaching for my promotion to Joint Secretary. This would also mean my transfer from the Ministry of Commerce where there had never been a Joint Secretary from the Indian Foreign Service. Changes were taking place in the Ministry of External Affairs. With the demise of Pandit Nehru, a new Prime Minister had been installed. This had been not very easy. At first the senior most Minister was elected. This was Gulzarilal Nanda. Nanda was a Punjabi who had joined Mahatma Gandhi in his Sabarmati Ashram. From there he had become a labour leader in Ahmedabad's flourishing textile industry. Naturally, Pitaji knew him and had invited him to my wedding in Poona in 1948. However, he did not last long and, within a week, Lal Bahadur Shastri became Prime Minister of India.

Pandit Nehru was the son of a famous and wealthy lawyer and had been educated in England at Harrow and Trinity, Cambridge. He was also a successful writer and had been known in the West before India's independence. I doubt if anyone outside India had heard of Lal Bahadur Shastri before 1962. In fact, even his name was inexplicable. When, during the course of what H.M.Patel called the Hindu Renaissance, B(enares) H(indu) U(niversity) was founded in the nineteenth century, its medium of instruction was Hindi not English. Hindi was a new language with, at that time, only one literary work, the Ram Charitra Manas which was a translation of the Sanskrit Ramayana. Of course, there was a corresponding Muslim Renaissance which created the Aligarh Muslim University where the medium of instruction was Urdu – a well established language with many literary treasures and the official language of Northern India along with English.

Since the medium of instruction of B.H.U. was Hindi, it wanted to confer degrees with Hindi names and the word Shastri was chosen to replace 'Bachelor of Arts'. By caste, Lal Bahadur was a *kayastha* (writer). Traditionally, a kayastha could be a humble letter writer sitting cross-legged on the pavement outside the post office writing petitions for illiterate villagers or he could be a powerful and wealthy Minister. Lal Bahadur was left an orphan when he was still a child. It is said that there was no school in his village and he had to swim across a river to get to school. To make matters worse, he was small and insignificant in appearance. To make up for these deficiencies, he was a man of great administrative and political ability and an iron will. He graduated from B.H.U. and people started addressing him respectfully as Mr.Shastri which really meant calling him 'Mr. Bachelor of Arts'. His wife was his childhood sweetheart from the same socio-economic background as himself but without a college education.

Lal Bahadur got his first job as a teacher but he soon entered politics at the village level and rose quite rapidly to get elected to the Lok Sabha – the lower house of the central legislature whose members are directly elected. By 1960 he was Minister for Railways. When a major railway accident took place, he accepted personal responsibility and resigned. There have been scores of railway accidents on the world's second biggest rail network but I do not know of any other Minister of Railways who has resigned. This act of self-denial gave him a national reputation and Pandit Nehru re-appointed him to the Cabinet. Apparently he thought of him as a possible successor but this is conjecture. When he was asked, on the floor of the Lok Sabha to name a successor in case 'anything happened to him', Panditji replied that he expected to be around for quite some time. Three days later he was dead. Apparently a consensus emerged to appoint Lal Bahadur as Prime Minister.

By the time I became Joint Secretary (Economic Division) Lal Bahadur was Prime Minister and he decided to hold his first press conference. I was able to attend this conference. His small stature, undistinguished appearance and modesty did not create a good impression but his answers were cogent and clear. He never held another press conference.

The Foreign Minister was Sardar Swaran Singh who had made his reputation and fortune as a lawyer in Punjab. He was a keshadhari Sikh, older and taller than I. He was approached by a Punjabi industrialist who wanted to re-activate his cement factory in East Pakistan. The situation was peculiar. This industrialist had built a factory in Bengal before Independence. It was situated among rice fields on the left bank of the Brahmaputra river. The principal raw material for cement is limestone which he quarried from a cliff across the river. At this point, the river was the border between the then provinces of Assam and Bengal. At the top of the cliff was the small town of Cherrapunji reputed to be the rainiest spot in the world with an average annual precipitation of five hundred inches. The quarry was not easily accessible from Cherrapunji but was connected by a ropeway with the factory across the river by which both limestone and passengers could be carried. The industrialist had sent a General Manager to negotiate the details of what he wanted. This man was a retired I.C.S. Officer with a Muslim name but he was a Christian. He had opted for India at Partition but his name had made him unpopular.

Independence had closed down the factory because the Pakistani government would not allow its Indian Sikh owner to import limestone from India. 1965 seemed to the Sikh industrialist to be a good time for the two governments to come to an understanding and allow the factory to resume work. India would earn foreign exchange and Pakistan would have cement on the spot in its eastern half instead of having to import it by sea from West Pakistan – a journey of several thousand miles. I was to go to Shillong, the capital of the then state of Assam to persuade the government of Assam which had not been willing to listen to a Punjabi industrialist. I got a chance to see Shillong and Cherrapunji at government expense but the scheme was doomed by politics.

One incident happened on this trip which has remained in my memory all my life – or at least for the next forty years. I had to travel from Calcutta to Gauhati (now Guwahati) on a Dakota. I was in no hurry to get off the plane while others were pushing and jostling to get to the door. When I did get up I noticed a diminutive young woman encumbered by her baby. She had got up but her seat was full of little bags and bundles which she must have needed to feed and pacify the baby. I noticed another Sikh coming from the front. I picked up two of the woman's packages and gestured to him to pick up the remainder which he did unhesitatingly. When we got down the stairs the woman was being received by a young man. She looked at us and spoke to him so he came towards us. We gave him the packages and he shook our hands and thanked us profusely. When this was over, I spoke to the other Sikh,

'Nobody else came to help the poor girl.'

'I do not know what power the Guru has endowed us with to serve others.'

Relations with Pakistan were not good. There was a Military Government there and it must have seemed to General Ayub Khan that it was a good time to finish off India when there was a new and un-charismatic Prime Minister who had no world reputation and was obviously not martial. The first incursion was in Kutch (Western Gujrat). A settlement was reached after our Army successfully stopped it. At this time, for a short period, C.S.Jha was Foreign Secretary. A meeting between the two Prime Ministers was arranged. Ayub Khan was a foot taller than Lal Bahadur so he was naturally asked how he would hold talks with a man who would be looking down on him,

'Well, he may be looking down but I shall be looking up and I always like to look up.'

The next incursion took place in Kashmir but the war was soon extended to Punjab. The Pakistani Army attacked with their new American tanks at a place called Khemkaran. The Indian Corps Commander was Lieutenant General Harbaksh Singh whom I have mentioned earlier. He had been a class fellow at Dehra Dun of the Pakistani General opposing him. The Indian tanks were also new and of Soviet manufacture; in fact I was told that their guns had not been 'zeroed' – tried out in practice to check their sights. There was a new railway embankment a few kilometres inside Indian territory. Harbaksh decided to hide his tanks in the ripening wheat to the east of the embankment. He expected the Pakistani tanks to come over the embankment with their guns blazing, which they obligingly did. As they climbed the embankment they exposed their 'soft underbellies' and were hit by Indian shellfire completely disabling and stopping them but leaving the armour apparently intact. We captured 105 tanks of American manufacture. For over a week, an American tank with Pakistani markings was standing outside the U.S. Embassy in New Delhi. Khemkaran was the largest tank battle in the world after the last World War. A cease fire was soon arranged but the war did not officially end till the following year during which time there were no diplomatic relations between India and Pakistan.

At this time, we had an Ambassador named Mohammed Suleiman Saith in Manila, Philippines. He was an Oxonian and the reports he sent were excellent but he had a reputation for being quick tempered. He belonged to a wealthy (Shia?) family of Bangalore and had been a friend at Oxford of several I.C.S. Officers. In fact, he made friends easily over a glass of whisky. He was a secular Muslim in all respects and even had a Hindu wife; she had been a government servant, a private secretary. One of his close friends in Manila was the Pakistani Ambassador. Saith apparently did not make friends with the Indian community in Manila most of whom were Punjabi businessmen with some Sindhis thrown in. As our relations with Pakistan deteriorated, the Indian community became more and more irritated with his very overt friendship with the Pakistani Ambassador. The Republic of the Philippines has a very vigorous free press and a photo-journalist managed to publish a photograph of the two Ambassadors embracing each other at a party. This was the last straw for the Indian community. Several wealthy Indians came to Delhi to see Ministers and Secretaries and demand that Saith be replaced. I think the photograph was mentioned in Parliament.

I knew nothing of this situation so I was quite surprised when C.S.Jha called me one day, related the story to me, and told me that I had been selected for posting as Ambassador in Manila. Obviously a Sikh who was a teetotaller would be the complete contrast to the existing Ambassador and assuage the feelings of the furious Indian community.

I had not had much success as Joint Secretary, Economic Division. There was a Minister without cabinet rank in the Ministry of External Affairs. Raja Dinesh Singh was my effective boss. He had been a student of Siddharthacharry's at the Doon School after which he had been appointed Private Secretary to H.S.Malik when he was Ambassador in Paris, I think on a salary of one rupee a month which meant that he was, in fact, an unpaid volunteer in the Embassy. He had then entered politics. He was a wealthy landowner in U.P. He was keen to take away international economic affairs from the Ministry of Finance which was handling the subject and transfer it to the Ministry of External Affairs. This was, of course, impossible and Swaran Singh knew it but Dinesh Singh, I think, felt that I had not tried hard enough.

I was glad to have an Embassy because I was convinced that I could do much better 'in the field' where I could build up relations with foreign leaders by my own personality and actions rather than trying to frame policies in the abstract in New Delhi. I had hoped that by being in Delhi I should be able to wangle a post in the West but there was no point in trying to avoid Manila where I was being offered a challenge which I welcomed.

It is the practice for an Ambassador going to a new post to do a tour of India. This is mainly for meeting businessmen and others dealing with that country so that they can tell the new Ambassador what they would like him to do for them. It is also meant to enable the Ambassador to see, at first hand, what is happening in India because sitting at a desk in Delhi reading newspapers one is liable to get a warped idea of our large and varied country. I went inter alia to Kerala where the climate and topography are rather like the Philippines and the products compete with our own. I was to learn that we use much more labour intensive processes than the Philippines where much industry was in U.S. hands and management was using more economical and efficient technologies. By 1965, there were a number of firms in Cochin with old English names but I never saw a European manager.

An acquaintance in Delhi, Dhan Singh Bawa a wealthy builder, introduced me to the local representative of SAN MIGUEL. This is a brand of beer and a large diversified industrial group which is controlled by what we would call a 'domiciled European (Spanish)' family which is probably the wealthiest family in the country. In this respect, Philippino society is very different from Indian society. There is reason to believe that, at some time in the remote past, there was an indigenous religion containing Hindu elements but these effectively disappeared when neighbouring Indonesia was converted to Islam. The Spanish conquerors in the sixteenth century did a very thorough job of converting the population to Roman Catholicism which is now the prevailing religion. There is still a Muslim minority in the South and those that I met told me that they are proportionately as numerous as Muslims in India.

This Muslim minority was not visible in Manila while I was there. All the rest being Roman Catholics, they appeared to be graded by wealth and race. Anthropologists classify the Philippinos as 'Malays' and they are a fairly dark-skinned race. There has been a fair amount of intermarriage between Spaniards and Malays and no one tries to hide his or her ancestry. The nineteenth-century national hero, Rizal described himself in Europe as 'metis filipinois' (half-breed Philippino). It would not be much of an exaggeration to say that a person's social position depends as much on the shade of his skin as on his wealth. The wealthiest families are often described as 'white Philippinos'.

When we arrived in Manila, we were greeted at the airport by the Chief of Protocol named Katigbak. Later I found that the Katigbak family had been prominent in society from Spanish times. We met him again that evening when we went to a supermarket with our cook to buy provisions and to show him what a supermarket is like – he had, of course, never seen one.

Next morning, when I got to the Chancery, the Second Secretary Charge d'affaires told me that the most urgent job was to go to the bank and get my signature registered; of course, I also had to open an account for myself otherwise I could never get any pay.

The Bank was, I think, the Hong Kong and Shanghai Bank and I met the English Manager. He explained to me how the Philippine polity works,

'There has just been an election in which a new President and eight Senators have been elected. Senators here do not have constituencies and are elected nationally i.e. every voter ticks the names of eight candidates on the long list before him so each candidate has to campaign all over the country which is very expensive. In this election, it cost eight million Dollars to be a Presidential candidate and two million to stand for the Senate.'

To cut a long story short, I relate what he said to me on my next visit a couple of months later,

'There is a Tariff Committee of the Senate. Early this month, its Secretary called up the President of the Textile Industry and told him that the Committee would be considering import tariffs on textiles the following week and he could bring his delegation to present their case on Tuesday. Then he rang up the President of the Association of Textile Importers – there is a flourishing trade in import of second hand garments from U.S.A. - and invited him to come on Thursday. Of course, the final result was that after collecting 'contributions' from both businessmen, textile tariffs remained unchanged.'

In the foregoing pages I have not tried to conceal the existence of corruption in India but I am convinced that in 1965, it was greater in the Philippines than in India. It was certainly more open. I have read a book by a Philippino diplomat in which he refers to 'Our Kleptocracy.' Perhaps in India we are more secretive and prefer to call a spade 'an agricultural implement'

The election had taken place just before I arrived. I think I have mentioned earlier that in the American style of Presidential democracy, the installation of a new President is an important ceremony. A Ministerial delegation was to arrive from India; I could only be present if I had assumed my duties. This was quickly arranged and I presented my credentials to President Diosdado Macapagal. I was prejudiced against him because he had invented the policy of 'konfrontasi' against Malaya when that country had absorbed the colony of British North Borneo. In fact, both Malaysia and the Philippines were market-oriented democracies at a time when President Soekarno in his dotage had handed over his country (Indonesia) to the communists. It behoved them to act in unison against that philosophy. Anyway, his term had ended. Today (2006) his good-looking daughter is ruling the Philippines.

Philippinos are very hospitable and sociable. They also love spectacles and the installation of the new President in Luneta Park provided a great spectacle. I was impressed by Marcos. It was said that he had been elected on the strength of his young wife's good looks and singing ability. In fact, I did not find her beautiful. She was nearly as tall as her husband and therefore avoided high heels. She looked broader than him on account of the *terno* (formal dress with 'leg-of-mutton' sleeves) which she wore on formal occasions. She did however provide the spectacle which Philippinos love.

I was more interested in his speech. He said, inter alia, 'Our founding fathers built this republic on a very narrow social and economic base.' He was perfectly right. The first Presidents had all come from a small group of predominantly Spanish families. The first President not to have a Spanish name and not to belong to this group was Ramon Magsaysay who carried out a number of admirable reforms. One of his meritorious acts in this respect was to promote an Army Officer, on the spot, when he found that he had refused a bribe. But, in the words of Lord Acton, 'All power corrupts and absolute power corrupts absolutely.' I never knew Magsaysay but the deterioration of Marcos happened before my eyes.

I attribute it largely to Imelda and her love of spectacle and display. When a revolution toppled the Marcos family, the world was appalled by the collection of her shoes found in Malacanang Palace. I had come across such a collection before when Juan Peron was overthrown in 1955, his various residences yielded a huge collection of the shoes of his deceased wife Eva Maria Duarte de Peron's footwear mostly designed to make her look taller – the reverse of the case of Imelda Marcos.

President Marcos's speeches and conversation in the early days were good. In a small gathering, he related that, for his honeymoon (he was already a Senator when he got married) he had taken his wife on a round-the-world trip. They had visited Thailand and he had remarked to the official from the Ministry of Agriculture who was taking him around,

'Your landscape and climate are very much like what I see at home. Even the people are only distinguishable by their dress. How is it that you export rice to us who can never succeed in growing enough of it?'

'Well, Senator we send our agronomists to Los Banos for training.'

The International Rice Research Institute in Los Banos is in the Philippines. I met a couple of Indian scientists there.

Marcos could never broaden the base of Philippine society or persuade his peasants to practise what they were taught at Los Banos.

The climate in the Philippines is very much like that of the coastal regions of India. Being an island country it has more storms – typhoons – than we have. Manila is situated on the Pasig river which is fed by a huge fresh water lake, the Laguna de Bay. When I was there, it was said that the water of the lake was fit to drink a hundred meters from the shore but by the time I left it was no longer so.

There are several volcanoes in the Philippines, and one or other of them becomes active every year. One of the tourist spots within a couple of hours of Manila is a lake in the middle of which is an island the top of which is the crater of a volcano. It had a minor eruption while I was there. Since then there has been a major eruption of Mount Pinatubo which blocked out the sun from Manila for many weeks and destroyed the cultivation of tens of thousands of acres of land by burying it under toxic ash. I had never heard of Pinatubo while I was in the Philippines.

If one accepts the theory that different races have different aptitudes, it would seem that Philippinos are not great seafarers or possessed of trading and entrepreneurial skills. Yet the Malays must have been great sailors to occupy lands as far apart as Madagascar and Luzon. Chinese seem to have settled in the Philippines many centuries ago. When I was there they were the major trading community. I could not easily tell a Chinese from a Philippino by their faces. After a generation or two many Chinese families Latinised their names to sound like the Spanish names that many Philippino families use and adopted Roman Catholicism. Intermarriage is very common.

Philippinos have not rejected their Hispanic heritage. For two centuries, a galleon used to sail every year from Acapulco in Mexico to Manila and back. On the Westward journey it carried silver coins and European luxuries and on the return it was laden with Chinese silk, porcelain and the valuables that Asia had to offer. Even from Spain, most goods came by this galleon. The largest of several copper mines in the Philippines is called LEPANTO from the great sea battle of that name won by Don Juan of Austria over the Turkish fleet in September 1571. The news reached the Philippines a year later when the mine was discovered. I visited the mine and was told that they had recently uncovered a Chinese mint with coins dated over a century before this date. The Chinese must have used and exhausted a shallow mine.

Not long before I arrived, for the first time a President of Mexico had visited the Philippines. When he was being driven around, he noticed a large compound and asked his guide,

'What is behind that wall?'

'Your Excellency that is the Chinese cemetery. Many Chinese have not become Christians and still practice their traditional rituals so we have to have a separate cemetery for them.'

'You mean Chinese die in your country?'

'Of course, your Excellency.'

'We have Chinese in Mexico but no Chinese ever dies. It seems that the deceased's name and identity are immediately taken over by an illegal immigrant.'

It seemed to me that many Philippinos were unable to distinguish a Chinese from an Indian like the Swiss woman I mentioned earlier.

As I have stated above, the richest Indians in Manila were Punjabi merchants. I found they were Jat Sikhs who had shaved off their beards. They probably started off as money lenders but when this was banned, they took to 'instalment trading' which was the same under another name. Some had made fortunes in real estate and construction. Of course, there were professionals who were assimilated in the Philippine population like Ramon D. Bagatsing of Indian descent who had been Mayor of Manila and knew nothing of India.

For our first dinner party, we invited the Chairman of the Science Development Board, an elderly scientist (dietician) of Cabinet rank and his wife. We had also invited a relatively young society couple named Gonzalez. Kirat had met the wife Vicky who was the same age (about 35). To my surprise, the elderly cabinet member refused to go in before Vicky. He explained that she had a special place in the warrant of precedence.

When we got to know the Gonzalez better, she told us her story. In 1942, her father surnamed Quirino was a lawyer in a city a hundred or more miles north of Manila. Suddenly, the Japanese army arrived; her father was not at home and her mother decided to take the children and run from the house. They saw a section of Japanese soldiers running towards them with fixed bayonets and thought of taking shelter behind the wall of a park. Vicky managed to get over the wall and looked round for her mother who was carrying her baby sister. To her horror, a Japanese sergeant shot her mother dead. As the baby fell from her hands, the sergeant bayoneted it.

Quirino did not remarry and entered politics after the war. He was elected President in due course and Vicky became his official hostess – hence her special rank. Gonzalez, a very wealthy young Armed Forces Officer, was one of his aides-de-camp. She married him. He had his own aeroplane in which in 1965 he flew Marcos around the country during his election campaign. Vicky joined Imelda Marcos in the campaign. They decided that there should be a group of (relatively young) women accompanying the candidate all dressed in uniform dresses. Gonzales presented them with dresses in his racing colours so they were know as 'the ladies in blue'. This 'chorus' and Imelda's singing ability contributed to the success of the campaign. Of course, Marcos was duly grateful and appointed Vicky as Ambassador in Brussels. Just before they were due to leave, she was diagnosed as having cancer of a kidney so her life was despaired of. However, she survived the operation and I understand she outlived her husband.

This kind of ostentatious wealth among politicians was new to me and I was surprised that the relatively poor people of the country appeared to accept it. It is a good indication of the national character. I was particularly struck by the fact that neither Vicky nor the other Philippinos we met showed any hatred for the Japanese who soon became the second trading partner of the country – after the United States. It is only in the twenty-first century that I have read of hatred felt by the Chinese and people of some East Asian countries towards Japan's World War activities.

All this fits in with the love of spectacle of the people. Philippine society, as I have mentioned, is very fond of parties which, at that time, were mainly held out of doors. An American specialised in providing lighting for dinners. In 1967, he was charging three thousand U.S. dollars for an evening's illuminations. Poor people would gather outside the gates to watch the spectacle. They were grateful for a bun each handed out to them by the servants.

One afternoon in 1966, the Philippino maidservant told Kirat that an Indian lady had come to see her. She went down to see a smartly-dressed, good-looking young woman who said to her,

'I am Kamal Sehgal. I came to call on your mother.'

Kirat laughed and replied,

'I am Mrs. Malik. We have no daughters, only two sons.'

Kamal's husband known as Pasha was a Punjabi about ten years younger than I. He had been trained as an Engineer in Canada but had made his reputation and fortune as a salesman for ENCYCLOPAEDIA BRITANNICA in Canada. He had received an award for being the best door-to-door salesman having sold a million dollars worth of merchandise in less than a year. He had arrived to open and manage an Encyclopaedia Britannica office in Manila. The two families - they had two daughters and adopted an Indian orphan boy - soon became good friends on first-name terms. There were a few Indian professionals in Manila holding U.N. jobs or employed by multi-nationals as also an Indian Methodist Bishop but Pasha Sehgal was the first wealthy Indian businessman with a professional education. The Sehgals were accepted in international society and entertained in Embassies.

The Philippines had a curious constitution. It is a unitary republic but provinces enjoy a degree of autonomy. Even more autonomy is enjoyed by the 'cities' which do not come under

1966 Manila, Philippines The family in the garden of the Embassy Residence.

the provincial administration unlike 'towns' which are often only villages. The police is either municipal or the Philippine Constabulary. Law and order was not a strong point while I was there. Our residence and chancery were both located in the city of Manila. The Capital was in Quezon City but this only meant certain offices which I never had to visit. Several Embassies had moved their residences to 'gated' (I would say fortified) suburbs bearing names like 'Forbes Park' and 'New Forbes Park.' Forbes had been an American Governor General. There was another conurbation which contained new office buildings, shops, blocks of flats and hotels.

We were living in a spacious two-storeyed rented house with outhouses and a garden behind high walls. These walls were intended for security but served the additional purpose of protecting the ground floor from the awful noise of the traffic. The upper floor where the bedrooms were situated did not have this protection but the master bedroom had a glazed balcony which helped. Finally, all the rooms except the principal drawing room (which was an atrium) had separate air conditioning which made the house very comfortable. The dining room could seat eighteen.

Arun was with us and enrolled at an English-medium Roman Catholic school, Letran College. Kiran was in India but the government paid for him to come to Manila for the vacations. One morning, Kirat was in the balcony where she kept some of her wardrobe when she saw Kiran opening the front gate of the compound. She opened the window and shouted,

'Kiran, where are you going?'

'Mama, I am going round the corner to buy a comic.'

'You can't do that.'

'Mama, I can't go out to buy a comic?'

'No, you can only go out of the house in the car.'

Kiran was seventeen years old and with his plentiful beard looked like a man in his twenties.

The story was told that a newly arrived German Ambassador had set out with his wife for a walk. A large car passing by had stopped and the occupant in the rear seat had told this well-dressed distinguished-looking white middle-aged gentleman,

'Sir, you must be new here. It is not safe to walk. Please get into my car and I will be happy to take you to your destination.'

The British Ambassador who was a tall well-built bachelor told us his story,

'I was going for a walk on the sea-front boulevard, when two young men, one of them holding a knife, accosted me and asked for my purse. They were quite small and did not look like hardened criminals. I knocked their heads together making one man drop his knife and run. I held on to the other one and, seeing a uniformed policeman shouted to him to arrest the man but he replied that he was from Pasay City and this was Manila.'

In our stay in Delhi we had become very friendly with Jai and Veena Raghavan. Veena is my second cousin being the daughter of H.S.Malik. She had married the son of Nedyam Raghavan whom I have mentioned as my Ambassador for a few weeks in Buenos Aires. He had subsequently succeeded H.S.Malik as Ambassador in Paris but his health had given way and he had retired. Jai had married Veena without the prior concurrence of his parents. In Delhi he was working for the Association of Indian Chambers of Commerce and Industry. He was able to arrange for A.I.C.C.I. to pay for most of his and his family's holiday passage because it did not cost much more to fly from Delhi to Manila than to his 'home' in Kerala. They had stayed with us and the children (their daughters Sarita and Surekha) had also got on well with ours. We decided that next year we would go on a motoring holiday to Sikkim where his cousin Appuni Menon was the Government of India's Representative and my cousin Preet Malik was First Secretary.

In fact, I knew the Chogyal (Monarch) of Sikkim. He was a widower and had come to Tokyo for a brief visit at a time when the Ambassador was gong to be away on tour and C.S.Jha had asked me to look after him. He had arrived on a week end and we (Kirat, Kiran and I – Mataji had stayed behind with Arun) had taken him to Karuizawa, the local mountain resort. To his great surprise, he had found the Japanese looking very much like the Lepchas and Bhutias of Sikkim – he himself was a Lepcha. Of course, correspondingly the Japanese seeing him thought that he was one of them and spoke to him in Japanese of which he could not make out a word. They would ask him who were these queer people with him – and only we had any idea of what they were saying. After our entertainment of him, we had a standing invitation to go to Gangtok and be his guests.

I was due for leave and was very keen to see the ruins of Angkor in Cambodia. I worked out that the air fare to Delhi would cover the detour to Saigon, Phnom Penh and Bangkok where I asked K.R.Narayanan to arrange our stay in an economical but clean hotel.

To our stupefaction, as the plane was taking off from Manila, the pilot announced that the Viet Cong were attacking Saigon – the Tet Offensive – and the plane would land in Bangkok! I never got to see Saigon and Angkor.

We got to Delhi, made our last minute arrangements and set out in the two least suitable cars for our long trip – a Triumph Herald belonging to A.I.C.C.I. and Mataji's Fiat 1100. The trip was uncomfortable being hot in the plains and cold in the mountains – neither air conditioners nor heaters in the cars; besides the Herald kept breaking down - but we managed to see Gangtok, Darjeeling and Kanchenjunga which the Chogyal proudly announced was his personal property inherited from his mother. In Gangtok the Representative gave a lunch for us and produced a telegram for me which told me I was posted to Dakar and that this was a compulsory recall from leave, thus paying for the Gangtok trip!

As it turned out, this trip had taken place in March and we did not get to Dakar till late July what with the journey to Manila, the farewell formalities there, the journey back partly by ship from Manila to Hong Kong and the long wait for *agrements* which had to be obtained from five governments (Senegal, The Gambia, Mauretania, the Ivory Coast and Upper Volta) to which I would be accredited. This period included the month of May (1968) during which it seemed that President de Gaulle would be toppled and that a revolution was taking place not only in France but in some other countries also. In fact it was a period during which a substantial socio-political change took place. In the words of Louis Heren, the English journalist, the English ceased to be a deferential people.

The approved route for the transfer to Dakar was by Air India to Paris, by train from Paris to Marseilles and by ship from Marseilles to Dakar. There was a problem with the servants,

Joseph and Ruby who were not allowed to travel by air. They left Manila with us but had to continue by ship to Madras city. Their home was in the Tirunelveli district of Tamilnadu. They got to Bombay after their leave and then they had to travel by ship all the way to Dakar. This was quite complicated for a couple not accustomed to travelling by themselves. They had previously worked with the Hoopers. Working for an Indian employer who received an Indian salary was a come down for them but there were not too many Europeans or Americans looking for servants.

For us, Kirat, Arun and myself the journey was fun. We were travelling first class. We had to stop in Paris and the Embassy put us up in a three star hotel in the Rue de Berri opposite to the office of Le Monde. Of course, the daily allowance was minimal and we could not eat in the hotel or in any restaurant in the neighbourhood. Kirat had the brilliant idea of buying bread and various delicious French spreads from the shops nearby. 14th July, the French National Day, occurred during our stay but having read about the troubles which the government had faced a few weeks earlier we decided not to go and watch the parade. We had tea in a café on the Champs Elysees by which time the avenue looked deserted. In many ways, France seemed a backward country. I wanted to speak to my friend Jean Lussat in Chatelleraut but I was told I would have to go down to the basement of the hotel where the telephone operator would try to connect me. When I finally got the connection it was not very good. This was very much like India at that time. Malaya, eight years earlier, had had much better telephones.

The journey by train to Marseilles included lunch and since we did not have to pay for it that was the only really satisfying meal we ate in France.

Marseilles, which I remembered vividly from 1939, had not changed very much in nearly thirty years except that everything was very much more expensive. We were to travel on a ship of the Messageries Maritimes on its way to East Asia. The difference between travelling on a French ship and a British one was noticeable. On P&O ships there was a very senior Officer known as the Staff Captain to look after the entertainment of the passengers and the food was guaranteed to make one put on weight but not particularly tasty. On this French ship, although facilities for games, swimming and so on existed one had to find them or ask for them. On the other hand, the food was very varied and delicious. It made no difference to us that good wine was free with the meals since none of us drank.

The ship stopped at Casablanca and we got off and visited the city. The weather was hot and sticky and the place did not feel like the film I had seen many decades earlier.

XXIV

DAKAR 1968 -70

When we got there the port of Dakar was enjoying a boom. The Egyptians had closed the Suez Canal to British and French ships so they all had to take water and supplies at Dakar. The port authorities and ship chandlers were doing a roaring business. I soon discovered that there was a very real French presence in Dakar. A Brigade Group of French forces was stationed outside the city. Apart from that many shops were owned by Frenchmen. Those that were not, belonged to Arabs – almost all Christian Lebanese. There were even a couple belonging to Indians – Sindhis. There were also French artisans working there. When I asked for a plumber, a Frenchman turned up. His bill appeared exorbitant to me and he explained that he was from Marseilles and he was only working in Dakar's insalubrious climate because he could earn twice as much as in Marseilles. I decided that I would insist on a Senegalese electrician next time. He came accompanied by three friends in a B.M.W. car – obviously he could not charge less than a Frenchman!

The difference between French and British colonialism became apparent when I went to present credentials in Bathurst, capital of the Gambia. The Gambia is a very small country 300 kilometres long on both sides of a river called Gambia. It is surrounded by Senegal on all sides except for the mouth of the river. The city of Bathurst (a name since changed to Banjul) was named after Earl Bathurst who had been a British Minister when it was occupied by the British. In fact one could hardly see an Englishman in the street. There were shops with English names but they appeared to be run by Africans or Lebanese. Occasionally an English manager would emerge from his back office to deal with an important client.

We patronised the three Indian shops which were very well stocked. We could buy everything from groceries to a car at a much lower price than in Dakar and of brands we were familiar with. We would go back to Dakar (five hours by road) with the boot of the car full of our shopping.

The car.......the car. When I arrived in Dakar, the Embassy car was old and overdue for replacement – I think my predecessor was not a motorist. I wrote to Avtar Singh who was the Joint Secretary (Administration) asking for a Mercedes to replace it. He told me later that he had tried to get me a six-cylinder one but the Finance Ministry would only sanction a 230 – and that was not air conditioned!

I had not had a car of my own since the Ford Fairlane I had bought in Japan and sold in India and I decided to buy an air-conditioned Mercedes Diesel with right-hand drive (for driving on the left of the road) because I thought I would be posted back to India after Dakar. Since we bought hardly anything in Dakar except perishables, I was able to save money for a change and with a loan from the Government I managed to order it in Bathurst. I drove it myself in Dakar, on trips to Bathurst and Nouakchott (Capital of Mauretania), and only used the Office Mercedes on formal occasions.

I have mentioned the insalubrious climate of Dakar above. We had arrived in July, early in the season called *hivernage*. It is what we call the monsoon and lasts roughly from June to September. It is the season when Senegal receives its rain. The difference is in the effect. In India people rejoice when the monsoon starts because 'the sun killeth but the rain giveth life' if I may modify St. Paul's second letter to the Corinthians (iii,6). Indeed, the monsoon ends the intolerable heat of the 'hot weather' and makes everything grow. Poets have sung its praises for centuries and, when it starts, children go out in the rain to dance.

As in India, agriculture in Senegal depends on the rainy season but the attitude is different. Traditionally, the local population does not esteem agricultural activities and they are carried out by women. The men prefer to fish or hunt. When I was there, serious farming was done either by *marabouts* or by foreigners using local labour who were dependent on wages because they could not catch enough fish or find enough game by hunting. A Lebanese businessman named Fifili had a farm from which he was able to supply fruit, poultry and meat.

I must explain the word 'marabout'. These are charismatic religious leaders who can make their followers do anything they want. Many of them believe that they have supernatural powers – or succeed in persuading their followers that they do. Of course, there are marabouts of all shapes and sizes. I only met one or two. The most prestigious in the area I dealt with was the 'Marabout of Kaolack' – the second city of Senegal. He was so important politically that the President of one of the republics presented him with a six-door Mercedes such as he (the President) did not have himself. The conversation of such men is unbelievable. When the American Ambassador got the film of the Moon Landing he arranged a showing at the theatre. The acolyte of a Marabout whom he had invited told him,

'My marabout was on the moon last week.'

Minor marabouts made a living by farming. They were able to persuade their followers to grow peanuts – the only export crop of Senegal.

The evil consequence of the hivernage was on health. The French head of the children's hospital (Hospital Le Dantec) told me that he had once taken his annual leave to go home to France during the hivernage like most Frenchmen; it coincides with the holiday season in Europe. When he came back he found that mortality at the hospital had gone up by 10% in relation to the previous year when he had not taken leave. The following year he took his leave at a different season.

This problem affected me personally when Ruby fell ill. When her ailment was not cured by paludrine (a medication for malaria), we took her to hospital where she was diagnosed as having an 'icthere'. The dictionary described this as hepatitis or jaundice. Of course, her skin was too dark for yellowness to be visible. It proved incurable and she succumbed to it. Joseph was shattered. He had got to know some Pondicherryians (people from the previously French province of Pondicherry in India) who were serving in the French army and they told him that in such cases dead bodies were flown back to Pondicherry at the expense of the French government. At that time, the Government of India would not even pay for the medical treatment of my domestic servants and there was no chance of getting first class fare for a corpse – shipping and air lines charge first class fare for transporting dead bodies. Ruby was a Roman Catholic so funeral rites could be performed but I could not pay for a tombstone. Poor Joseph insisted on returning home.

We were able to find a Gambian and a Guinean to serve us. We lived thereafter on French food.

In a few days, Kirat started showing the same symptoms as Ruby had had. She was terrified when the Doctor confirmed that she had hepatitis. She said,

'I do not want to go to the same hospital and die the same way Ruby did. I want to go home.'

Of course, she was flown back by Air France and Air India. In Poona her parents looked after her and she was back in Dakar a few months later. The illness did have some minor long term effects like not tolerating a bumpy ride in a car or being able to eat certain kinds of food.

The worst sufferer was Arun. He had been admitted as a day scholar in the Dakar Academy - an American boarding school meant for the children of American missionaries in various West African countries. At home he used to play with the children in the neighbourhood – mostly Europeans but also including Africans of the professional and official classes. All this was not affected by his mother's absence but he used to spend much of his time in the company of his mother and the Indian servants and all three had suddenly disappeared. I decided to spend as much time with him as possible. We would read books together, make Meccano models or go out to the headland across the road from our house where there was a large area of wasteland ending in a cliff. Our principal activity there was target practice. I had bought a Mauser .22 rifle with a telescopic sight in Paris and we had a good time becoming marksmen. One day we read in an English newspaper that a supertanker coming to Europe from the Persian Gulf had disappeared in the South Atlantic and I told Arun that a shot he had fired which had missed the target had sunk a supertanker five hundred nautical miles away.

Social relations between Africans and Europeans were interesting. No African ever invited me to his home. Official functions were held in hotels or in office buildings. Of course, many Africans came to my parties. The reason why I was not invited to African homes was explained to me by an American (white) who had a Senegalese wife. He said,

'I never know how many people I shall find at table when I go home for lunch.'

Soon after we got to Dakar we started playing a lot of bridge. I had played bridge since childhood but I am only moderately good and prefer reading a book. Kirat took to it as she had taken to golf. One good result was that she became very fluent in French which I had tried to teach her without much success in Brussels. The only person I have taught anything successfully to is Arun.

She was soon playing bridge with women in society. In this way she got to know the wives of some Ministers and Secretaries of Ministries. She was used to meeting such women in other countries and finding that some of them worked. They would be Doctors or lawyers or follow other professions. In Dakar she found that almost all wives worked and as primary school teachers or typists. Finally, she picked up courage to ask one of them why she had taken up what must be a low paid job. The answer was,

'According to our custom, a man's income has to be shared with his village. Any man from my husband's village can come to Dakar and to our house and demand board and lodging. They are not unreasonable and they understand that we have both to dress according to our station and to keep up appearances but all the rest has to be shared. Thus, we cannot send our children to private schools or take holidays abroad. A woman's income is not subject to this sharing rule and we can do what we like with it. As I earn the same salary as a Frenchwoman would do, this provides money for the activities I mentioned.'

The treatment of professional, managerial or official Africans by Frenchmen was on the basis of equality. However, the French had a curious hang-up about language. The principal local language in Dakar was Woloff but the French insisted that it could only be called a dialect 'because it cannot be written'.

I found by personal experience that this was not so. My chauffeur Ba who spoke excellent French said to me one day,

'Sir, I have received a postcard and I have to go next door to have it read; your neighbour the Rector of the University has a servant who is a Mullah and can read.'

'May I see the card?'

I recognised the Arabic script of the card. West African languages have been written in Arabic script for centuries.

Arabic like Latin does not have a polite plural and Ba told me that this is also the case with the languages spoken in West Africa. This gave some Frenchman the idea that, speaking French, they could get away with addressing Africans as 'tu'. Sometimes a French shopkeeper would address a customer as 'tu' only to find that he was a Minister from whom he would get an earful.

Some years earlier the German Consul General in Singapore had told me that Germany was keen to give a large part of its 'third world grants and loans' to India but when 'Associated countries' were created and India refused to be one, France had insisted that half of all aid should go to Africa. The result was that, according to the statistics, Senegal was receiving a great deal of aid from the E.E.C. as it was then called.

I was now able to see the truth of Gladstone's dictum 'There are three kinds of lies; lies, damned lies and statistics'. The most glaring example was of Dakar airport. France granted 'independence' to its African colonies in 1960. With the aircraft in use at that time, Dakar was a necessary stop on flights between Europe and South America. The French had built and equipped the airport to handle these flights; this included a large number of wireless circuits to handle traffic from and to a number of European countries, Brazil and Argentina. All the professional and technical staff for operating these facilities were French. As soon as Senegal became independent, these men stopped working. There were no Africans in Dakar trained to do this work. The new Senegalese government did not know what to do. The Frenchmen then announced that they had resigned from their government jobs and formed a private company and they would be glad to operate and maintain the facilities but, of course, it would cost twice as much. The cost of this service was met out of E.E.C. (European Economic Community) 'aid'.

During the colonial period, there had been few facilities for professional education in French Africa. The Africans who managed to get to France and obtain professional qualifications often preferred to stay and practice there. French Engineers, Doctors etc. were provided to the ex-colonies and paid generously out of the aid budget. Even the water they drank or cooked in came from France and was shown to the world as 'aid'.

I felt that India could help. I arranged for an Indian meteorologist to come to Dakar and a telephone engineer to go to Upper Volta (now Bourkina Fasso = 'the Country of Honest Men'). The latter, a Bengali, arrived with his wife who turned out to be a qualified electrical engineer. Thus Upper Volta got two professionals whose services they could use and who did not prescribe expensive French equipment but were able to improvise cheaper local alternatives. The Ministers for whom they worked were very appreciative of their services and expressed their appreciation to me. The Indian professionals were receiving international salaries and as they did not consume imported food and drink they returned home with a substantial packet of savings.

One day a smart, well-dressed young Indian turned up in my office. He introduced himself as Syed Mohammed Nawab and said he was a sportsman, a cyclist. He said his specialty was endurance cycling – he could ride a bicycle non-stop for two or three days. In Ethiopia, the Emperor had stopped him on the fourth day because he had noticed a change in his complexion. I was, of course, delighted to see such a prodigy, who was a charming young man and a Muslim. Senegal is a secular state but the vast majority of the inhabitants are Muslim and, in private conversation, they let on that they did not approve of cremation or other 'heathen practices'. This was occasionally exploited by ill-intentioned persons.

I took Nawab to see the Minister of Education, Youth and Sports who subsequently became Head of UNESCO. He was also very happy to meet this young sportsman and offered every help including the free use of a basketball stadium. The Indian shopkeepers helped by providing a person to be there night and day to see to his needs. Nawab went to the Peugeot agent who not only gave him bicycles - one of which he later presented to Arun – but also substantial financial assistance. Mohammed (In India 'Syed' is a title reserved for 'descendants of the Prophet') did all that he had said he would and got a lot of very favourable publicity. I then took him to see President Senghor. Naturally, I talked a great deal about him. The Belgian Ambassador, Trouveroy, must have got fed up with all this and said to me, in English,

'But tell me, this cyclist of yours, isn't he a little bit of a Muslim?'

'Do you think he is more Muslim than the President of India?'

'Oh, I forgot. You are very tolerant in your country.'

'It is not a question of tolerance. India is a secular state. The Government chooses people whom it considers appropriate for the job without bothering about their sex, religion, mother tongue or other consideration. I myself belong to a minority community.'

More than thirty years later, I met this Ambassador's son who was Ambassador in New Delhi. I did not tell him of this conversation.

1969 was the year of the Mahatma Gandhi Centenary. I discussed the matter with the Professor of English at Dakar University – a Frenchman with an English wife. In Paris, on my way to assume my new post in Dakar, I had called on the Officer in the French Ministry of Foreign Affairs dealing with Senegal and invited him to lunch. His name was Lebel and he said his family had made its fortune as arms manufacturers before the Great War; apparently Lebel rifles had been sold to many armies in Eastern Europe. He had told me that the University in Dakar was, in all respects a French University. When I visited it and talked to the Rector – who was my neighbour as I have mentioned – I found out what Lebel had meant. The building was in the recent French style and most of the students were French, the sons and daughters of the large French expatriate community in French-speaking West Africa. Africans were only admitted if the National Plan in their country provided for a job corresponding to the subject that the student wanted to study. There were therefore no unemployed African university graduates.

This shows how the French visualised the development of West Africa. The public sector was to be Africanised and these African students only foresaw their future as government servants. When an independent writer had called on an African headmaster and talked to him about the future of his students, he realised this and expostulated,

'But everybody cannot be a civil servant!'

the latter had replied,

'That is very unfortunate.'

Apparently the intention of the French Establishment was that they would retain control of the French-speaking African economy.

To return to the Professor of English, he suggested that on 2nd October (Mahatma Gandhi's birthday) I should deliver a lecture to the University, on Mahatma Gandhi. The Rector agreed to arrange a Convocation. In the Philippines, whenever I visited a University the President would arrange a convocation for me to address and I would answer the questions of the students about India but I realised that this was different. The University was honouring the Mahatma, India and (indirectly) me and that this was unprecedented.

I am well aware that I am not an orator; I can give a good lecture in English, French or Spanish on a subject I know e.g. aero engines. My speech is clear and I have a strong voice so I seldom need a microphone. Here I was to speak about a man whom I admired as the greatest man of the twentieth century but whose economic and social policies I disagreed with. I could not possibly be insincere or hypocritical and say things I did not believe. I decided to make a factual speech about his life and quote his famous phrase, 'My life is my message.'

I managed to get a French translation of a one-volume 'Life' and set to work. One problem was that we did not have any local staff in the Embassy other than peons and the driver. I had to write my speech by hand, get a French typewriter, and then a talented Malayali Assistant typed out what I had written. Finally, I took the typescript to the Professor of English who corrected the mistakes saying, 'You write better French than you speak.' I knew that already because Arun had told me that my pronunciation was execrable.

The great day, or rather evening, arrived and I put on my achkan and proceeded to read out my speech. The audience was in evening dress and, for the first and last time in my life I saw a man wearing the full dress uniform of a member of the Academie Francaise which resembles that of a British Ambassador, covered with gold braid. There were only a few African faces in the audience but the diplomatic corps and Dakar's French society did not let me down. Next day, the local French language paper carried the full text of my speech.

Of course, I reported all this to the Ministry in New Delhi. There was no reaction. Does any one read the despatches of Ambassadors in South Block?

Apparently in Islamabad someone did take notice. A month or so later the newspaper which had published my speech put out a two-page supplement to celebrate the birthday of a Pakistani poet. I went to see the Editor and ask him how this had come about. He appeared rather sheepish but his comment was illuminating,

'What could we do? The Ambassador brought us the text along with blocks of the pictures and the advertisements and pleaded with us saying that if we did not publish it he would lose his job.'

In our Ministry of External Affairs there exists an Inspectorate of Missions. It was the turn of Dakar to be inspected. The team consisted of my batchmate Ashok Bhadkamkar and a Joint Secretary from the Ministry of Finance who, I found, had also studied Physics and Chemistry so we had that in common. They were interested in our accounts but, knowing Ashok I knew I had to lay on a party. The population of Dakar was about three hundred thousand of whom a tenth were French. The people who could be invited to an Ambassadorial party were only about two hundred. I invited them all and engaged a caterer; of course, I provided duty free liquor and cigarettes. The accounts of this party would be scrutinised by the inspecting team so they would know what sort of parties I gave and what they cost. I had learnt all this from a British diplomat in Tokyo who had had to go through this sort of ordeal because we had copied the British system. It was my one and only experience of an inspection. The point was that Ashok was the son of an I.C.S. officer and I knew he enjoyed good food and drink – unfortunately he did not know when to stop and he died a few years later of the consequences of his life-style.

Shortly after this, the Ministry in Delhi announced that one of the Secretaries, Kewal Singh was going to visit several African countries including Senegal and giving his programme. I had to do at least as much for him as I had done for the Inspectors so I rang up the caterer, sent out invitations to the people I had invited for the Inspectors – there was nobody else to invite – and made appointments with the Minister of Foreign Affairs and so on. The Secretary's tour was starting in Kenya and then going through a number of countries before getting to Dakar from where he would return to India via London. I must explain that at that time there were not many flights between African countries and hardly any between English-speaking and French-speaking countries. Even to go from Dakar to Antananarivo (Madagascar) one had to fly via Paris – a remnant of colonial times. This complicated Kewal Singh's itinerary and then he kept on changing it. I got the impression that he was probably not coming at all. I cancelled the party and the appointments.

Finally, on a Thursday I got a telegram that he would be arriving next day in the evening and leaving late on Sunday night. There was no time now to send out invitations for a party and it proved impossible to make appointments with officials at a week-end. I decided to put him up in the Embassy residence. Most official visitors appreciate this because they can save the daily allowance and foreign exchange was hard to get in those days.

It was however very inconvenient for me. The house had a master bedroom and another bedroom which had been divided by a partition. I had asked the Ministry for Air Conditioners and they had agreed to the public rooms being air conditioned but insisted on sending three machines from India. These were badly packed and proved to be unserviceable when they arrived. Senegalese mechanics were unable to repair them. I had obtained an air conditioner at my own expense and installed it in my bedroom when I found that the humid climate was giving me lumbago. I gave this room to Kewal Singh and moved into the partitioned bedroom the other half of which was occupied by Arun. Kirat was in India at this time.

Kewal Singh expressed his appreciation of the hospitality and appeared to understand that his programme had had to be cancelled. Apart from the meals he had at home, I took him one of the best French restaurants in Dakar. I could not charge this to my entertainment grant as I could bigger, formal parties.

All this about one infructuous visit may appear excessive but it had subsequent consequences.

One thing we did appreciate about Senegal was the good law and order situation. I have mentioned that in Manila where the population is almost entirely literate, Kirat would not allow seventeen-year-old Kiran to go out of the compound at 11.A.M. In Senegal where the literacy was less than 50% one could see young women in their very showy clothes waiting all alone for the bus in the countryside. As regards twelve-year-old Arun, he would get on to his bicycle after dinner to see a friend in the neighbourhood without our feeling worried in any way.

I notice that I have not mentioned the Ivory Coast. Before Independence, Dakar had been the capital of West Africa with the Residence and offices of the Governor General. Most of these buildings dated from before the war. Only the University was post Independence. Few important commercial buildings had been built because Senegal had only phosphates and peanuts to export. The economy of the Ivory Coast was much more diversified. It received much more rain than Senegal and was naturally an area of tropical rain forest. This circumstance had been used to grow rubber, coffee and cocoa. Some of these plantations had been broken up and had passed into Ivoirian hands. With this diversification the country had become much richer. The port of Abidjan also served land-locked Upper Volta. With all this, Abidjan looked more prosperous and modern than Dakar.

In French-speaking West Africa the per capita income of the coastal countries was generally double that of the land-locked ones. Upper Volta's main export was labour. I came across an interesting development. Abidjan had plenty of unionised workers in the offices and factories which processed, packed and handled its export crops. The politicians had organised these unions and the workers were very well off. It occurred to some one to investigate the situation in the ever-growing harbour. He was surprised to find that the harbour employed over a thousand

Voltaics at less than the minimum wage. The union leaders were in habit of saying to the Voltaics (I translate literally the very expressive but ungrammatical 'pidgin French' commonly used),

'Train comes you comes; plane comes you comes, truck comes you comes; even foot you comes.'

The unions insisted that the foreigners be replaced by unionised Ivoirians getting the minimum wage. So far so good, but then the Ivorians realised that the work in the port was much harder than work as clerks or machine-minders. Finally the Voltaics got their work back at the old rates but the Ivoirians pocketed an equal amount for signing the attendance registers.

My term in Dakar was coming to an end and I got the transfer order for Santiago in Chile. I was delighted. I had visited Chile several times from Buenos Aires. I loved the dry, cool climate of Santiago as well the scenery of the Andes and the sea, and altogether it seemed a delightful place to me with interesting people. When I was in Buenos Aires, I had studied the seniority list of the Indian Foreign service and come to the conclusion that I would never be an Ambassador and would have to retire as Envoy Extraordinary and Minister Plenipotentiary and I hoped that that would be in Chile. The Congress of Vienna in 1815 had recognised four classes of Heads of Mission

1. Ambassador Extraordinary
2. Envoy Extraordinary and Minister Plenipotentiary
3. Minister Resident
4. Charge d'Affaires

Between my tenure in Buenos Aires (1952-56) and my return to South America in 1970 the second and third classes had been eliminated and, with the increase in the number of Indian Missions, I had become Ambassador in Chile with nearly nine years of service left to me! Little did I guess how tragic Santiago would be.

XXV

SANTIAGO 1970-74

We arrived in Santiago towards the end of December 1970 and were welcomed at the airport by the Embassy staff headed by the Second Secretary and Charge d'Affaires, Eudon Lhamu. She was a Sikkimese and had learnt Spanish.

We were taken directly to the Embassy Residence which was a large house rented from a Mrs. Schilling, a woman of German descent. Many people in India including Indira Gandhi who had visited South America the previous year had described the house as 'the most beautiful Indian Embassy'. It was a single storey house in grounds of over an acre. Entering from the main gate which was at the end of a residential street one faced the bottom of an inverted U in which the house was shaped. The main door was secured by an antique German lock with a huge key which I could just about put in my coat pocket. The hall was large and the rear windows were of plate glass showing an old walnut tree and a large lawn surrounded on the other three sides by fruit trees. On the left the hall gave on to a dining room which could seat twelve – rather small for an Embassy residence. However, it was beautifully furnished and had a large picture window with a view of the Andes. There was one particular point from which one could see Mount Aconcagua which I have mentioned earlier. Adjoining the dining room were the pantry and the kitchen below which there was a basement occupied by the central heating plant and a room for storing wine. We did not keep more than a couple of cases of wine so we kept anything of which a shortage could be anticipated – like onions or potatoes. Adjoining the kitchen across a corridor were two servants' rooms; beyond them was a garage for two cars.

On the other side of the hall, corresponding to the dining room, kitchen and pantry was the large, well-furnished drawing room which had a good fireplace. The back of the drawing room gave onto the garden through a French window. In fact all the rooms on that side of the house gave on to the garden through French windows. Adjoining the drawing room was a smaller room whose main feature was a kachelofen which I have described earlier. It also had a card table so perhaps it was meant to be a card room but there was only one card table in it. It is probably best described as a study.

A corridor led to six bedrooms, three bathrooms and a room meant as a dressing room for the master bedroom from which it was separated by the master bathroom. I used it as my library.

The political situation in Chile was quite complex. There were a number of parties. The previous President, Frei, had belonged to the Christian Democratic party which was probably still the largest party in the country. However, leagued against it was multitude of parties of the left. They offered all kinds of goodies to the voter. In that sense they were all 'populist' – a tendency I attribute to Juan Peron who wanted power without having any ideology of his own and did not stop to consider how, in economic terms, he would fulfil the promises he made. This has been common in South America for many decades and the result has been galloping inflation. In my experience of South America I have seen Brazilian currency debased to a millionth of its previous value in a little over twenty years. In Chile, between 1953 and 1970, the annual rate of inflation varied between 30% and 50%.

Salvador Allende Gossens (his mother's maiden name) belonged to a landowning family and had qualified as a medical practitioner before joining the Chilean Navy as a medical Officer. Thus he had been a colleague of Juan Marin. He headed the Socialist Party; I had not met him previously.

The candidate of the Communist party for the 1970 election had been Pablo Neruda – a pen-name, his real name was Neftali Ricardo Reyes Basoalto. I had met him in 1954 because Nawab Sahib before departing had advised me to do so and he had invited me to dinner. He was quite a well known poet and had served as Honorary Consul in Rangoon before Burma was separated from India. He was known to be a leftist but I do not think he had any clear plans for converting Chile into a communist state. In any case the Chilean Communist Party did not have any such aspiration and only sought better pay and conditions for the relatively small organised industrial working class which was its constituency. At the appropriate moment he had withdrawn from the election and advised his supporters to vote for Allende.

Apart from these two large parties, there were six others in the coalition which Allende stitched together. I only remember the name of one of them, the Christian Socialist Party which was said to be a bloodthirsty one.

According to the Chilean Constitution, the President was elected directly by the voters. If no candidate got 50% of the vote, the Senate had to choose between the two who got the most votes. All this had happened and Allende had got the most votes while falling short of 50%. The Senate had a small rightist majority and imposed its own terms on Allende before confirming him. One of the conditions was that he would not nationalise the copper mines. At that time copper was Chile's major export commodity – probably Chile was the biggest exporter of copper in the World.

Allende was a much admired figure among non-aligned countries and I expected that I would be presenting my credentials very soon after arrival in Santiago. However, I was told that it was the holiday season and the newly-installed President was touring the country. In fact, he was trying to tell the world that he might not be popular with the plutocrats of Santiago but that the situation was different in the rest of the country where there were few rich people.

Finally I was told that I would present my credentials not in the Moneda Palace in the middle of Santiago but in the Prefectura of Valparaiso – the biggest of Chile's many ports. So I had to go to Valparaiso, book into a hotel and wait to be escorted to the Prefectura. The Chief of Protocol decided that I should first be driven from my hotel to the Naval Club in Valparaiso and then from there in a formal procession to the Presentation of Credentials. I suspect that this was to show me the Naval Club which was more impressive than the Prefecture. The Chilean

Navy was founded by Lord Cochrane and generally follows the traditions of the Royal Navy.

The ceremony was brief and unimpressive. Afterwards, I was able to have a conversation with the President. I knew already that he was facing economic problems because he was unpopular with the Nixon government. At that time, all Latin Americans, whether of the Right or of the Left, were convinced that their political and economic survival depended on the United States of America. I told the President that the time had come for Third World countries to deal directly with each other rather than through intermediaries and that India was in a position to help. I had found that some of the equipment used in Chilean mines was coming from India but that many people in Chile did not know this because they were buying it in London or in the U.S.A. where much of the money remained. He replied,

'Ah, it does me so much good to hear this from you, Ambassador. That is the way to talk to me.'

That day our conversation ended there but I followed up this subject with our own Ministry of Industry; an Engineer came from India to Santiago and worked out a scheme for setting up a drawing office in Chile where our draughtsmen would see the piece involved, make detailed plans and send them to India to have it manufactured. When I took the project report to the Ministry of Foreign Affairs in the Moneda Palace, it was shot down immediately,

'Oh, that will never do. Already people are saying that we have sold the country to the Russians because they see Soviet technicians here. If they see Indian Engineers who will be more noticeable here, it will be much worse.'

As I have mentioned earlier, Kiran had been left in India from the age of 11 to study at school and college. He lived very happily with his grandmother, Mataji. He also had Mataji's car and driver at his disposal for much of the day which was really quite a luxury. When I was in Manila, I bought a motorised bicycle (Velosolex) with a forty-nine cc. motor and was able to take it into India thinking that he would appreciate the independence it gave him but he despised it as being inappropriate for a 'young man of his size' – he was 17 years old. At this stage in his life, he was very friendly with his maternal uncle Harinder.

Harinder had qualified as a lawyer but was not prepared to wait the years that it takes a lawyer to acquire a good practice. He took over a club where members could learn foreign languages and set up a café in it. Even this did not enable him to earn the sort of income that he wanted although he was quite talented in foreign languages. He was living with his parents. He took up some business ventures and left home because of his losses.

By this time, his father was living in Poona where he managed to buy a large house built by a Parsi at the beginning of the century. He could afford the price because the house had been requisitioned during the World War and was occupied by an Army Officer who was not willing to vacate it. Mr. Jiwan Singh had bought the house before he retired while he was still in service and living in a government bungalow. When he retired from the post of Chief Conservator of Forests of Maharashtra he wanted to move into his own house but the occupant refused to move. Mr.Singh had lived in Poona for a good part of his service, especially towards the end and was well known and respected by all officials civil and military. The General Officer Commanding Southern Command finally got the Brigadier who had been occupying the house to get out.

This house and his standing in official circles made Mr. Jiwan Singh known to the business community as well and they dealt with his son, Harinder, accordingly. When he disappeared leaving his debts unpaid, they approached his father who paid off his debts; this happened three times.

In the course of one of these disappearances, Harinder went to Perugia to follow a course in Italian. There he met an English girl, Ann a student at Oxford, whom he married. She was not at all keen to stay with her in-laws so she persuaded Harinder to take a job and he managed to get a job as a salesman for B.O.A.C. stationed in Assam where there were still a number of British tea garden managers who were potential clients for B.O.A.C.; this happened while I was posted in Singapore.

When I returned to India in 1963, Harinder was working for the B.O.A.C. office in New Delhi. He and Ann came to see us quite often. They were living in a flat in Defence Colony. We got to know Ann quite well and she explained to us that they had not been happy in Assam because they were meeting tea garden managers and, on Harinder's salary, they could not afford that life style. In Delhi, she said, they could live comfortably on Harinder's salary and socialise with a number of families with whom they felt some affinity.

She had underestimated Harinder's financial ambition. He wanted to earn much more. He gave up his job, took over a failed travel agency and started doing business. His contacts with B.O.A.C. and his knowledge of languages gave him some hope of success. His cheerful personality, hospitality and his size endeared him to many people – among them our son Kiran. Finally, he won Kiran over by presenting him with a large second hand motorcycle. I was not happy about the clothes that he gave Kiran from some of his business ventures; however, Kiran had a strong character, complete integrity and was hard working so I was not really worried.

With all these qualities, Kiran had one serious shortcoming as far as studies were concerned. He panicked before an examination if his mother was not there to give him moral support. When we left for Dakar he had not yet finished his college course and the government would pay his air fares for joining us during his vacations once a year. We had decided that he should be a Chartered Accountant. In India, an English qualification in this profession was better respected than an Indian one. I asked Geordie (the Earl of Selkirk) if he could help and he arranged for Kiran to be an articled clerk in the London office of the Scottish accounting firm of Thomson McLintock. In 1970, Kiran arrived in England and settled down quite quickly.

A little earlier Harinder felt that he could make much more money if he could charter ships and he had some success. At this time, there were not too many people in India who knew much about international shipping. For some reason that I have never understood, most Hindus in the nineteenth century who sailed over the 'black water' thought that they would end up in hell. Of course, there were emancipated souls who did go to England. Raja Ram Mohan Roy was in Cape Town on his way to England when he heard about the taking of the Bastille. Only a little later, Rabindranath Tagore's grandfather made a very profitable voyage to England. However, Mahatma Gandhi had to do penance when he returned from his studies in England. The British were keen to retain the monopoly of shipping between England and India as long as they could do so. It was therefore credible that if Harinder ventured into this field it might prove very profitable.

So Harinder set out on a round-the-world trip to find ships leaving his travel agency in the hands of his employees. In fact, the reality was much worse. He had taken money from farmers in Punjab promising them tickets and visas for England and then used the money for his own travels. When the farmers came to know of this, some of them arrived in Delhi determined to get their money back or to kill him in spite of his large size! The employees of course fled. This had happened around the time when we were in Delhi waiting to go to Dakar. All we could do was to save his books and some other belongings.

Harinder had travelled several times to England in the course of his ventures and because of Ann. He now settled down there but took care not to buy a flat or a house or even take accommodation on long lease. Of course, when Kiran arrived in London Harinder saw a great deal of him.

I have mentioned arriving in Santiago at the end of December 1970. Arun was of course with us. He had missed several months of school because the Dakar Academy only had classes up to Grade VIII and these had ended in June. Kirat had gone to the school and asked them to get the textbooks from U.S.A. for Grade IX. This they did and he studied them pretty diligently entirely on his own except for Algebra in which I helped him. In Santiago we found that there was a reputed American High School called NIDO DE AGUILAS (Nest of Eagles) but that the vacations had already started and classes would not open till March. Arun was going to miss a whole scholastic year because of the difference in school calendars between the Northern and Southern hemispheres. Of course, we were prepared for this, hence the books. Kirat went to see the Headmaster and it was agreed that he would join Grade X. When Arun heard about this, he panicked just like Kiran and said he could not possibly skip a whole year. Finally, he was taken 'kicking and screaming' for the test.

When he started on the algebra paper, the examiner – a woman – said,

'How are you doing this? There is no algebra in Grade VIII.'
'Oh, I had the Grade IX books.'

'You can't learn algebra from books.'

'My father helped me.'

'Is your father an engineer?'

'No, he is a diplomat.'

To which all that the examiner could comment, in Spanish, to her Chilean friend was,

'Este joven es muy inteligente.' (this boy is very intelligent)

Which, of course, after nearly three months in Chile was quite comprehensible to Arun. This restored his self confidence and he had a very good time in the Nido de Aguilas.

In Santiago we found old friends. I have mentioned Rafael and Lola Urzua. I have also mentioned Juan and Milena Marin. Juan had passed away before 1970 but Milena was a very helpful friend and introduced us to her Catholic Arab friends Eugenio Hirmas and his wife. They were rich and lived in a large house with menservants – something that few professionals could afford, they had make do with a maid or two. The couple we felt closest to were John and Nelly Blydenstein. Nelly had appeared rather non-descript to me when John had brought her to our flat for dinner in Buenos Aires but by 1970 she had blossomed into a real beauty. She was the same size and only a little younger than Kirat. They had three children, a boy and two girls. The boy Johnny was the same age as Arun and they were in the same class at the Nido de Aguilas. They would take turns to stand first in the class.

The Blydensteins were the only family in Chile with whom we would go together on trips. One such trip was to the South. We found there in the city of Valdivia that there were many families of German origin so there were signs in the shops saying that German was spoken. Nearby there were beautiful lakes and volcanoes. One of these erupted while we were in Santiago and our trip was to see the results. We found a comfortable little hotel in the vicinity and found that the volcano still glowed at night. The lava had found its way into a stream which, of course, dried up. We went to see the solidified lava and found it was still warm. Earlier, some lava had reached the lake into which the stream used to pour and poisoned most of the fish in the water.

In 1972, John complained of pain in his abdomen after meals. He was working for F.A.O. (he had taken a degree in agriculture in the United States) and received a salary which went very far in Chile because it was paid in U.S.Dollars which he could change as and how he liked. Of course, he got the best treatment for his ailment and was examined by a number of doctors. One day Kirat said Nelly wanted to speak to me. I went to see her while John was not there. She said,

'Gunwant, I am not getting a diagnosis for John. I think Dr.X (a surgeon) knows something but will not tell me but I think he will tell you. Will you speak to him?'

When I saw the surgeon, he said,

'Ambassador, I suspect cancer of the pancreas. It is not showing up in X-rays because it is masked by the spinal column.'

'Doctor, that sounds horrible. What can be done?'

'I want permission for exploratory surgery.'

Of course, he performed the operation; his diagnosis was correct and there was no cure. John never knew that he had cancer. He was told he had pancreaititis and should take pills for a few months. The pills were painkillers. He died six months later. His father was living in Switzerland with his third wife. We went to see him in Lausanne in 1973. He told us that his first wife, John's mother, had died of cancer at the same age as John. He felt that Nelly's U.N. pension was quite enough for her and she needed no help from him – he was not wrong. Years later, he died and Johnny inherited his fortune.

I have got far ahead (more than two years) of the narrative in order to deal with these three friends with whom I maintained a lifelong correspondence.

In a few months I was entitled to leave and we decided that we would stop over on the Continent, rent a car and spend some time in Switzerland on our way to India, and then stop over in England on our way back to Chile. I had never rented a car so this would be a new experience.

We landed in Geneva where my cousin Preet Malik was posted in the Indian Delegation to the European Office of the United Nations. We stayed in his house and next day he advised us about renting a Volkswagen Beetle from Hertz. As it had very little luggage space, Arun had to share the rear seat with the luggage. I had arranged for a flat in Davos. This was again a new experience; we learnt that European investors buy these flats and an estate agent sees about arranging rentals. It is the janitor of the block of flats who keeps the keys and so on. The only time I saw any one from the estate agency was when somebody knocked on the door and two men came in and spoke German. Seeing me, they asked if I spoke French. They explained that they had heard that one of the runners of a curtain had come unstitched. We had not even noticed it because we kept the curtains open to enjoy the scenery and the light. The repairs were soon done but I was very impressed by the attention to detail. Of course, it meant that we were expected to keep the flat spotless.

From Davos we were able to visit Austria and we drove through a spot near the frontier where there was a castle converted into a hotel called Schloss Fernstein. This building was not what impressed us but the lake on the bank of which the castle was situated called, of course, Fernsteinsee. Not only was the water blue but it was obviously fed by the snowmelt from a large glacier we could see against the background of a clear blue sky. I can not recall seeing a more beautiful sight in the high mountains anywhere.

On another day, I noticed a signpost in Austria indicating 'Grossglockner'. I remembered this name from 1938 when it indicated a high mountain road only cleared of snow for a few days a year. I decided to explore and Arun in particular was in an adventurous mood. The road was quite winding and not very broad but there was very little traffic and the Beetle proved to be a good climber. As we climbed higher, we noticed that there was snow on the side of the road. At one point the road, which had been meticulously cleared, passed through a snowfield higher than our eye level. At the top of the pass there were restaurants and hotels. We got a good dinner and observed that prices were half of those in Switzerland although we had expected everything to be more expensive at this altitude. So we took rooms and decided to bed down for the night.

Altogether the European motoring holiday had been delightful and we were sorry when it ended. Air India took us from Geneva and made a stop at Tehran. We took off fairly late in the evening and Kirat noticed that one of the propellers was not turning. The pilot announced that there was a technical problem and we would be returning to Tehran. Of course, when we got down everybody complained. I do not know what happened to the others but the local manager was quite good to First Class passengers. He was particularly solicitous of us and a tall beautiful woman whom he introduced to us as the Maharani of Jetpur. She was quite friendly and told us she had been visiting her son who had a job in England. She said she had left her butler with him but doubted that he would be able to afford to keep him.

The night was hot and the air conditioning in the hotel left much to be desired but it was worse next day when we found that a heat wave had struck Tehran and the weather was not only hot but also very humid. We were put on a day's bus tour of the city during which we saw a mausoleum in a park and the Central Bank. We were allowed into the strong room where there was a collection of diamonds in what looked like dinner plates. Diamonds without settings do not look very different from the components of crystal chandeliers! Anyway we had seen Tehran where I have never been before or since.

The holiday in India was not very interesting because of the weather. We spent some time in Poona with Kirat's parents and then went on to New Delhi where I had business with the Ministry.

My cousin Bhuvan Jeet Singh was the least ambitious of three brothers. His elder brother Adhyatam Singh –whom I always thought of as being twenty years older than me - had had a brilliant academic career and became a professor of English at a time when there were few professors and many of them were British. However he was a midget not much more than four feet tall and never married. He died of tuberculosis about the time of Partition. The youngest brother Harimohan Singh, three years older than I, was of normal size and appearance and was bright and hardworking. He had got into what was then the Imperial Secretariat Service early in the World War and was rising rapidly when he died suddenly of a brain tumour without being married. After I came back from England in 1946 I only saw my aunt Kundan Kaur and Bhuvan Jeet who had got a job as a clerk in the Ministry of Defence. Later on, he became a cypher assistant which is a job in which there is hardly any chance for promotion.

He came to see me the day after I arrived and said,

'You must help me. You know the Defence Secretary, K.B.Lall. I am due to retire next year and there are a dozen of us who have applied for promotion as Cypher Officer. It is the only such post in the Cypher Office and it is for one year only. If I get it, my pension will be that much higher. Can you speak to K. B.Lall? The file is on his desk.'

I had known K.B.Lall since 1947 and had seen a good deal of him when I was Commercial Counsellor in Singapore and later when I was in the Ministry of Commerce. I got the appointment quite quickly and he told me that my cousin's information was excellent and he would get his promotion. Then I asked him,

'When are we going to war?'

'What war?

'The war against Pakistan, of course, to break it up.'

He laughed and said no one had talked to him about this topic. Remembering his conversation with Dr.Zakir Hussain in 1947 I became convinced that the war would not be long in coming.

We went off on our way back to London. Kiran and Harinder were there but Harinder's marriage had broken down. As I have mentioned, Ann had been living in London for some time in short

1978 Spain With the Earl and Countess of Selkirk

lets. Harinder's business ventures had their ups and downs and in one of the bad patches, he returned home for lunch one day only to be told by Ann that she had no food for him. That night he slept on the floor of Kiran's room in Gloucester Place near Baker Street.

A while later when Kiran had moved to another bedsit, he came back to the one in Gloucester Place and met a new female occupant of that bedsit. They got on very well and were happy in each other's company.

We knew nothing of all this. We were met by Harinder and Kiran at the airport and were driven to a house near Regent's Park and invited to stay in a 'garden flat' – euphemism for a basement. It was while we were looking round to see where everything would go that Kiran told me this was Harinder's flat and he would be sleeping in the kitchen!

We (Kirat, Kiran, Arun and I) had been invited by the Selkirks to their country house in Dorset for the weekend. It was now the month of August and the peak of the holiday season but we managed to rent a Beetle and go to Wimborne. There was a long drive from the gate to the house itself and it was not very wide. As we were going in another car was coming out; it was no bigger than the Beetle and the driver who was alone in it said they were expecting us. The house was quite old and had a thatched roof. The Selkirks gave us the master bedroom while Geordie moved into his dressing room and Wendy moved to another room. The Selkirks' hospitality was fantastic. Next morning Wendy brought us breakfast in bed! I had stayed in country houses in Belgium but that had been more than twenty years earlier when there had been maidservants living in and we had lived as we were accustomed to in India.

Wendy explained to me that theirs was not really a country house but a 'dower' house meant to be occupied by the widow of a gentleman when her son had taken over the country house. They had no living-in servants but a gardener, an occasional cook and a charwoman came in from time to time. To me it was amazing how much Geordie had to do himself, in the trees, the garden, looking after the dog and so on – things that I could not see myself doing at all. It looked as if Blandings Castle had disappeared from the face of the earth. I think the grounds covered about six acres. At the edge of the property there was high ground from which one could see the surrounding countryside and the village of Wimborne. Geordie explained to me that he was worried about plans for a motorway which was due to be constructed in the neighbourhood and which would be noisy. He had got together with some of the other landowners to try and stop it. I made several visits to the Selkirks in the next twenty years but never saw any motorway.

The Selkirks gave a cocktail party for us. One man mentioned that the daughter of a cousin of his had married a Malik but that the marriage had broken down. It took me some time to realise that the girl was Diana Maclehose who had been married briefly to my second cousin once removed, Baljit Singh Malik (born 1939), grandson of Sir Teja Singh Malik. Many years later I met Diana in Delhi. She was a good-looking woman, taller than Baljit. Baljit is a man of many talents but his social behaviour is not altogether balanced.

When we went back to London, Harinder showed me an album of his photographs. I have been a keen photographer since the age of 11. My albums do contain photographs of people but mostly there is scenery and pictures of buildings. Harinder's album showed women of different ages. When I saw it I was aghast. There was only one of whom I could say,

'She looks all right.'

We returned to Santiago where I was told that Minister Raj Bahadur was coming on a tour of South America to talk to the Governments about the problems we were facing with millions of refugees from East Pakistan where the Pakistani army was carrying out a massacre. He got sympathetic hearings from the Foreign Ministers of Chile, Peru and Colombia. I told him that there was a new Foreign Minister in Ecuador with whom I had been able to establish a rapport when he had been Ambassador in Peru. He agreed and we made a detour to Quito where the Minister told us that Ecuador had no Mission in Islamabad and no Pakistani Ambassador was accredited in Quito. Of course, Ecuadorian and Pakistani Ambassadors did meet at United Nations and in other capitals. A request had been conveyed to him for a visit by a high-powered Pakistani delegation which wanted to meet him and he had agreed to do so but told them they could not have a cocktail party or a press conference during

1973-B Quito, Ecuador At the Equator near Quito with Minister Raj Bahadur

their stay in Quito. He would tell me on my next visit how things had gone.

Soon after the visit by Minister Raj Bahadur, the Bangladesh War took place and a resolution of the United Nations General Assembly condemned India by an overwhelming vote at the behest of the United States of America. The Soviet Bloc voted against the resolution while Great Britain, France, Chile and a few other countries abstained. In Latin America only Cuba had supported India. All this was expected and a few weeks later Bangladesh was welcomed into the United Nations by all those who had condemned India!

Shortly after this, the Ministry of External Affairs sent me the confidential report on me for the previous year. It had been written by Kewal Singh, the only Secretary who had seen me during the year. I have never seen a more vicious confidential report. He said that I had not been able to arrange for him to meet any Senegalese Officer. But he waxed lyrical about my incompetence on the point that I had not given a party for him; what use was there in having an Ambassador who could not do this much for a Secretary to the Government of India?

Considering all the trouble and personal expenditure I had incurred on his visit, I was very upset. I fired off a letter immediately drawing attention to the numerous changes in Kewal Singh's programme, the appointments and party I had arranged and cancelled and his final decision to come for the weekend. I wrote that I was asking my successor in Dakar Hari Krishan Singh to send me the file.

It is not always that one can expect one's successor to be helpful. I had only met Hari Krishan Singh once. Going home on leave in June I had written to him that I would be spending several hours in Dakar between planes and would like to meet him. He had found out that Kirat and I were mad-keen bridge players and had arranged a bridge-lunch to which he had invited a number of our friends which was a delightful gesture especially as neither he nor his wife played bridge.

This time he sent me not only the file relating to Kewal Singh's visit but also the one about the inspection (which included the bills) which had preceded it. I sent them with a brief covering letter to Avtar Singh. A few months later I was promoted from Grade III to Grade II. Avtar Singh's comment was that if Kewal Singh's trip had been more successful, he would not have written such an unfavourable report.

I went on a tour of my concurrent accreditations and saw the Foreign Minister of Ecuador. He told me that the Pakistani delegation mentioned previously had come and had brought enormous lists – apparently census accounts of villages – to prove to him that the number of people who had left Bangladesh was only three million odd and not 'ten million as is being mentioned in some quarters'. At this stage, said the Minister, 'I said to their leader who was apparently their Ambassador in Buenos Aires,

'Mr. Ambassador, if one Ecuadorian were to leave our country because he felt that his life or honour was not safe here, all of us right up to the President of the Republic would feel most upset and ashamed. Are you sitting here and telling me that millions of your fellow citizens have left Pakistan because they do not feel safe?'

'That ended the interview' said the Foreign Minister.

Subsequently I found out that the Pakistani Ambassador in Buenos Aires was, in fact, a Bengali who, a few weeks after this meeting opted for Bangladesh and became for many months the only Bangladeshi Ambassador in South America. I had occasion to meet him.

This journey was not only for my personal satisfaction but also to go to Lima where there was to be a meeting of 'The Group of Seventy Seven' of which India is an important member and which deals mainly with economic matters but they do sometimes have political significance also.

I had presented my credentials in Lima shortly after doing so in Valparaiso. We had a very good arrangement in Lima. A First Secretary, Pascal Alan Nazareth from Bangalore – he is the Roman Catholic friend mentioned earlier – had been appointed Charge d'Affaires in Lima some months before my arrival. He and his charming wife Isobel had won the hearts of Peruvians immediately by organising a charity recital of Indian music and dance for the benefit of victims of a major earthquake which had taken place in Peru at about that time. That they had been able to do this with members of the small Embassy staff and the not very numerous Indian community says much for their resourcefulness

1971 Lima, Peru Presentation of credentials to President of Peru in the presence of the Foreign Minister and Aides-de-Camp.

and enterprise. The Nazareths were also popular because, as he said, 'They call me Hindu Romano Catholico.' It is not easy to explain to people in Latin America that all Hindus are not Indians and all Indians are not Hindus.

The Nazareths were a popular couple and Alan was a very competent diplomat but the Indian Minster of Commerce (Lalit Narain Mishra) and other high officials would be most critical and unhappy if the Ambassador were not there to dance attendance on them.

Lalit Narain Mishra continued as a Minister until he was assassinated on a railway platform in his own State of Bihar. In particular he led the Indian delegation to UNCTAD II. However I am constrained to say that he was a non-executive Chairman. He obviously knew how to get votes but of the matters under discussion at the conference he knew nothing. He did not even seem to know that Lima was in South America. His interest was in night clubs and travelling first class by Lufthansa. Fortunately, a very successful businessman of Indian origin, Swaraj Paul arrived from London to take care of the Minister and another Member of Parliament who was accompanying him.

The effective leader of the Delegation was the Commerce Secretary, Harivansh Lall. He used to hold a meeting of the Delegation every evening in the sitting room of my suite. My job was to provide drinks and snacks for this meeting. I had brought a sufficient supply of duty-free alcoholic drinks with me from Santiago as excess luggage. Occasionally, I would be asked to sit in on a meeting to take care of any political matter which came up.

One evening as I was in my sitting room checking the glasses and ice before the meeting, a delegate whom I had never met before came in. He was a Keshadhari Sikh and I knew that he was a brilliant economist who had studied or taught at Oxford, Cambridge and Harvard and that he was Economic Adviser to the Minister of Finance. His name was Manmohan Singh. We started talking about Indian politics and he said to me,

'Are you not a Socialist?'

'Certainly not, I am a civil servant and by law I am not allowed to join any political party. In fact I am not even allowed to tell anybody how I have voted in an election; As it happens, I have never voted in an election. My political views are my own and I am under no obligation to embrace those of the Government in power.'

'You are a very brave man.'

We have never discussed politics since then.

He is today (2008) the Prime Minister of India.

The economic situation in Chile was deteriorating day by day. The reasons were obvious. Eudon Lhamu had given a cocktail party for me a few days after my arrival and even before my presentation of credentials. At this party I had met, to my surprise, an Indian who identified himself as Vardarajan, Professor of Political Science at York University, England, on an exchange programme with the University of Santiago. I said this was quite remarkable because the very small Indian Community in Santiago consisted of businessmen none of whom had had a college education. He said that he considered himself very fortunate professionally to be in Chile at this time.

'I think Chile is a beautiful country with a lovely climate but how are you fortunate professionally?'

'In York, I could talk to my students about farm nationalisation. Here I can go and do it.'

'What? How do you nationalise a farm?'

'On Saturday morning we discuss the subject in class and in the afternoon we go and take over a farm.'

'Does anybody in your class know how to milk a cow?'

'One can find all that in books.'

Verily, socialism is the philosophy 'What is yours is mine; what is mine is my own.'

We did not discuss politics after that but Varadarajan was a delightful conversationalist and good company and we met again in England and in India after my retirement. He came of a Tamil Brahmin family and told me that he was a relative of Ramanujan, the mathematical genius who he said came from a poor and practically illiterate background rather like his own.

The agricultural situation was indeed disastrous. Some years earlier a team of European agronomists had visited Chile and announced that the Central Valley could feed twenty million persons on European standards of nourishment. The population of Chile during my time was estimated at eleven million. Chile had been quite rich in beef and traditionally the manual labourer expected to grill a fillet on his own spade for lunch. By 1972, the only beef was ground meat some of which would be put in a dish for flavouring. Fish was fairly freely available but it is not part of the national diet. We also learnt that in that year Chile had spent a billion dollars on food imports thus reducing the foreign exchange left by the previous government by half. Where had the dollars gone?

The industrial situation was as bad. In 1971, the Government imposed price controls on 'essential items' a list of which was published. At the time this meant nothing to me but later I found out the inconsistencies created by this. Stacking chairs were price-controlled but the plywood, paint and steel pipes from which they were made were not 'essential items'. Their prices shot up and manufacture was no longer economically viable. Stacking chairs which were in stock were sold at the legal price in the slums thus creating a black market. An ingenious Anglo-Chilean I met said that he had been a manufacturer of cooking ranges which weighed eleven kilos each. With the price of cooking ranges being controlled and galloping inflation, he could no longer afford to make them; he survived by making electric torches which weighed seven hundred grams and which he could sell at the same price as his previous product!

A new initiative was 'Sunday Voluntary Labour'. Ministers and high officials went out to do manual labour in the slums. This was good in the sense that it gave the upper classes an opportunity to see how the poor lived. However, it was combined with 'supply of essential items at affordable prices' at the same time in the slums. This necessarily meant creation of black markets. 'Essential items' included domestic electrical appliances which the poor did not want and also cars which became even scarcer than they had been previously.

I have been asked if the Allende regime was industrially incompetent. My answer is that the only product of which there was no shortage was the currency note.

So much for the economy; I had no fault to find on the political side. The laws were respected; there were no concentration camps and the Chief Justice who came more than once to play bridge had no complaints. In an English magazine an article about Czechoslovakia said the writer had had a conversation with a socialist in that country who had complained about conditions in his own country and when asked which country had the best socialist government had answered 'Chile'.

My own experience was similar. At a lunch party I gave for some East European Ambassadors, the question of capital punishment came up. I said I was glad to say that we still had capital punishment although it was not used very often and asked the Czechoslovak Ambassador about the situation in his country. He replied,

'Well, you see we have adopted a socialist economy. This creates economic crimes which can only be curbed by capital punishment.'

There were no such economic crimes in Allende's Chile.

One of Chile's diplomatic successes was the award of the Nobel prize to Pablo Neruda. India gave its full support for this. He was only the second Chilean to get a Nobel Prize in literature – the previous one had been Gabriela Mistral in 1945.

The Chilean Socialist Experiment attracted leftists from all over the Americas and even from Europe. One French 'intellectual' was recruited by Allende in his economic team. He survived 1973 and tried out his ideas many years later in both France and India. Fortunately he was given short shrift in both countries.

What concerned me was the arrival of Krishna Menon for a communist International Peace Committee. He was no longer a Minister but he was still an influential politician and I could not afford to ignore him. Whenever he had free time, he would turn up at the Embassy Residence – He liked to see good-looking women. Finally he asked me to give a party for his Committee. I told him that my table could accommodate twelve and offered him lunch for twelve or a cocktail for twenty-five. He said twelve was no good and chose the cocktail. Kirat and the servants prepared for that.

When the evening arrived, we waited – the invitation was for 6 P.M. – but no one came till 8 P.M. Then over a hundred of them turned up. They were ravenously hungry. The meeting had started in the morning and gone on through lunch and tea-time without a bite to eat or a drop to drink. They wanted dinner. The snacks which Moorthy had prepared were soon exhausted. He emptied his larder and then went to the basement where potatoes and onions were stored. We breathed a sigh of relief when thy left near midnight.

I had managed to establish quite good relations with the left-wing government in spite of the fact that the society in which I moved had conservative views. The closeness to President Allende was Kirat's work. She had gone to pay her formal call on the President's wife 'Tencha' (Hortensia Bussi de Allende) at the Moneda palace when the President appeared and said that he had heard of the beauty of the Indian Ambassadress and had come to see for himself.

In the middle of 1972, the third U.N.C.T.A.D. (United Nations Conference on Trade and Development was held in Santiago) as I have mentioned earlier. India was obviously going to play an important part at this Conference – the previous one had been held in New Delhi – and it was suggested that an evening of Indian music and dance could be organised.

The problem with organising such functions is, of course, finance. It is only on special occasions that the Government of India will provide an extra entertainment allowance. If there is an important Indian multinational (e.g. Air India) or a wealthy Indian business community as in Tokyo or Singapore they can be persuaded to contribute. We had no such Maecenas to fall back on. There was only one long-standing Indian businessman in Santiago. I had met him in 1954 when he had come to see me at the Carrera hotel where I was staying. He had explained that he was from Goa and had travelled to Chile on a Portuguese passport in which his name was spelt VISHNUM CAROICAR. I had been cautious about meeting him because we had just broken off relations with Portugal!

Since that time he had acquired Chilean citizenship and an upper middle-class Chilean wife. He had demonstrated his attachment for India by having a cross-roads named 'Plaza de la India' to which he had contributed statues of Mahatma Gandhi, Pandit Nehru and Rabindranath Tagore. He helped to finance our evening to which Mrs. Allende was invited.

The Indian delegation to the U.N.C.T.A.D. was a high-powered one containing several high civil servants and four Members of Parliament. When Minister Raj Bahadur had come to Santiago I had introduced Lola Jadeja de Urzua to him. He had noted her name and said that there was a Jadeja who was a Member of Parliament and he would arrange for him to visit Santiago. He had kept his word and Daulatsinhji P.Jadeja was one of the four M.P.s in the delegation. With this connection, Raphael and Lola invited the whole Indian delegation to lunch at their farm some sixty kilometres South of Santiago. The lunch was excellent and went on for some time. It was winter and beginning to get dark when we set off to return. There is high ground at one point in the sixty kilometres and even a short tunnel.

Hardly had we started when, to my horror, it started to snow. Hans, the Embassy driver had no experience of driving on snow. But that did not make any difference because there was a traffic jam. The car was stuck but we kept the engine running so as to stay warm in the car. Very soon the battery of the Chevrolet packed up and the engine gave up. We got out of the car and climbed into the nearest bus. Fortunately, it was only half full so it was able to accommodate the whole delegation which was in three cars. The genuine passengers were school teachers. Of course, most of the delegation could not speak Spanish but they rose to the occasion and started reading palms, telling fortunes and so on to pass the time.

It soon became obvious that we would have to spend the night in the bus. Of course, it was time for dinner and there was neither food nor drink on the bus. I got out to talk to other people from other vehicles – I think there were over a hundred vehicles held up by the blockage of the tunnel as we learnt afterwards. Some of the men felt that we should have a barbecue because we could hear the mooing of cattle from one of the trucks but there was no firewood in sight!

To cut a long story short, we got to the bus station after two P.M. and took a taxi to get home at 3 A.M. Our servants Moorthy and Nainar were exulting in their first sight of snow. Snow does not fall every winter in Santiago.

The Government of India decided about this time that it had enough foreign exchange to buy houses for its Embassies rather than pay rent for ever. One of the obvious places to do so was Santiago because all visitors had praised the house and Chilean currency's black market value was falling catastrophically. We started negotiating with Mrs.Schilling but she finally broke off the negotiations when she realised that she would get virtually nothing for her property. Amusingly enough, we got a telegram from the Ministry a few hours later asking us not to buy the house. They were not happy about the money having to be paid in two countries in three currencies!

The holiday passages for Kiran to join us for his vacations were no longer available because he was too old. He managed to arrange a cheap return fare by British Airways but that would only get him to Lima. I decided that I should make the journey by car to Lima. The distance is over two thousand kilometres but there was a very good Pan-American highway starting from Valparaiso so we (Kirat, Arun, the Chauffeur Hans and I) set off in the Chevrolet Caprice. It was the southern winter and we had to cross the coastal range of the Andes (separated by the Central Valley from the Cordillera) so we found ourselves driving on snow which Hans was not used to. I took over the steering wheel and drove most of the way myself.

One of our stops was Antofagasta which is an important port. A good deal of copper is exported from there. It is also situated near the southern edge of the Atacama Desert. This is the most arid desert in the world. It rains in Antofagasta roughly once every twenty-two years. Further inland – we did not go there – is the village of San Pedro de Atacama where white men had been living for four hundred years and it had never rained. You may well ask how they could live without water. There is a spring which is fed underground from the melting snow in the higher Andes.

The next stop was Arica, the last town in Chile. After that we entered Peru and then there was a petrol pump which had a sign FILL UP HERE YOU WILL NOT FIND ANOTHER PUMP FOR THREE HUNDRED KILOMETRES. The road runs near the coast but we were warned that we must carry drinking water and rugs because if the car breaks down, one can get dehydrated in the daytime (temperature up to 40 degrees Celsius) or frozen at night (temperature down to -40 degrees) if there is a wind. We were booked to stop that night at Arica but when we got there at teatime Kirat went to inspect the kitchen and said it was dirty we could not possibly stay there so we got back into the car and the night fell ten kilometres later as the road left the coast and climbed into the coastal range – the latitude was 15 degrees South.

Usually, a good highway is either asphalt or concrete both of which are a different colour from the surrounding countryside. The Panamericana was concrete but the gravel used for mixing the concrete was local so, at night, one could not see where the concrete ended and the gravel – on which one could easily skid at speed – began. We reached Nazca where we had a booking for the following night at 3 A.M. I had been driving for fifteen hours with breaks only for meals. When the hotel night watchman made a difficulty about the room I insisted that the date was right!

My practice on my visits to Peru was to ask Alan Nazareth what problems he was having which required an approach at a higher level and he would arrange meetings with the Minister or Secretary General concerned. I also gave a dinner every time I went to Lima. Of course, for me the most important event was meeting the plane on which Kiran arrived.

Both Kiran and Arun were keen to see Lake Titicaca which lies between Bolivia and Peru at an altitude of about twelve thousand feet in the middle of the Altiplano - the table-land which the two countries share. It is more than a hundred kilometres long and is crossed by ferries one of which carries railway trains so it is possible to travel by train from Lima to La Paz. I knew some one who brought his car on the train with him and drove away from the railway station in La Paz.

On the return journey, we decided to stop for the night at Arequipa and leave the Panamericana to drive to Puno by a gravel road. This road goes up and down attaining seventeen thousand feet at some points. At one of these places, there was a small lake with aquatic birds on it. Kiran was, as I have mentioned earlier, a very keen ornithologist. He recognised a bird which he had seen on Najafgarh Lake in the Delhi winter. The lake was partly in shade and partly lit by the sun. The part in the shade had a thin layer of ice on it.

Kiran was very excited by what he had seen. He wanted to know the Spanish name of the bird so he asked me to stop when I saw the first pedestrian. I did so and, to my surprise both boys jumped out of the car! Arun was quite sure that the Aymara would not be able to understand Kiran's Argentine-accented Spanish and that his own Chilean accent would be more comprehensible. We have a similar problem in India where practically everybody speaks Hindi but the Hindi of Delhi is not easily understood by a Maharashtrian from Mumbai. However Kiran's question was simple enough,

'What is this bird (*pajaro*) called?'

'We call that a little bird (*pajarito*).'

So much for ornithology. Actually, the bird belonged to the duck family so it could hardly be called 'little'.

By this time I was beginning to feel sick and two of the cars tires were punctured – thanks to the gravel. We stopped a van and Arun and I got into it with two wheels and were driven to the nearest tyre mechanic. As he worked on the punctures, Arun asked me,

'Daddy, why don't we see such poverty in Chile?'

'The short answer, Arun, although it is racist is that the Chilean population is predominantly white.'

Car tyres are seldom seen on the Altiplano where the vehicles are buses, trucks and jeeps. We had to get to Chile to buy new tyres.

As I have said, I was feeling quite sick and when we got to Puno and found a decent hotel, we called for a doctor. The one who came was U.S.-trained and spoke English fluently. I think he welcomed the opportunity to hold a conversation in English. He told me I had 'altitude sickness' gave me some pills and advised me to stay in bed for two days and then fly to Arequipa where the car and the others could join me.

In the course of conversation, he said that he was an Aymara and that geneticists had studied the genes of his tribe and said that due to the small size of the gene-pool, the race would die out in a few generations unless they received 'genetic assistance'. I asked him what that meant. He answered,

'Marriage with people from outside the tribe. I tried to help and married a North American but she could not stand the culture shock of living among Aymaras.'

At this stage, Kiran spoke up,

'Doctor, I am probably going to marry an English girl.'

'Well, it might work out for you; you are the son of an Ambassador and will probably have a different life style.'

We had already found out that Kiran was in love with Susan Melton – the girl who had taken over the tenancy of Kiran's bedsit room in Gloucester Place in London, and who appeared in Harinder's photograph collection – the only one I had found unobjectionable. Kirat was quite unhappy with this situation mainly I think because she wanted, like most Indian mothers, to choose her daughter-in-law herself. She was not alone in her objection. At the turn of the century (twenty-eight years later), Kiran and Susan were here, and I showed them a letter from Geordie Selkirk written after Kiran and Susan had spent a weekend with them in Wimborne. He wrote that after Wendy and he had met Susan they did not think that such a marriage could work out. I told them that Kirat had entirely agreed with this without ever having seen Susan. Susan's comment was,

'Well my marriage has lasted longer than hers.'

In fact the marriage has been an unqualified success. In the words of Chekhov in THE CAPTAIN'S DAUGHTER, 'To know her was to love her' applies to Susan. Kiran is also a very dependable and responsible person. Even in his career, Kiran has only stumbled once and that was owing to Harinder.

That Kirat's objection was not on racial, religious or cultural grounds became obvious a fortnight later when we gave a dinner in Santiago. Among others we had invited the Secretary of the Council of Chilean University Rectors and his family. This charming and witty man was an Oxonian who spoke English as well as any Englishman and had a very good-looking wife and four beautiful nubile daughters. Kirat said to one of them with whom Kiran had been dancing,

'I would be very happy if Kiran would marry one of you girls.'
She laughed and replied,

'I think you are going to have an English daughter-in-law.'

The Chilean socialist experiment was becoming more and more unpopular with the upper and middle classes. European and American (this includes North and South Americans) diplomats were also commenting on the economic failures of the regime so that Allende found himself rather isolated except for what I would call the countries of the Soviet bloc whether in Europe, America or Asia.

A hint was dropped to us that the President was keen to try Indian food. Heads of state usually do not go to Embassies except when the Head of State of the country whose Embassy it is invites them which can only happen if he is there on a State Visit. It was an unusual honour for India that President Allende had asked for a dinner at the Indian Embassy. Of course, on such an occasion he had to be asked to give us a list of names of people that he wanted invited. This was done. We also gave a list of names of people that we wanted to invite. Since our dining table could only hold twelve, it had to be a buffet dinner.

I have been able to find my Visitor's Book for 1973 and I see that there were two dinners. The first was on 9th February and among the guests were the Foreign Minister of Chile – both the President and the Foreign Minister were accompanied by their wives - and the Ambassadors of Ecuador, Peru and Sweden. This was a success and there was a demand for a repetition. This took place on 18th June.

By this time, it was becoming obvious that the Armed Forces were determined to topple the Government. In fact an attempt was made later that month and tanks came to the Moneda Palace but their communications failed, some of the tanks were caught up in a traffic jam, there was no support from the Air Force and the Navy so the Army came out of it looking rather foolish.

1973-A Santiago, Chile Dinner for President Allende at the Indian Embassy in Santiago. From left to right President Allende, Milena Luksic de Marin, Hortensia Busi de Allende, wife of Chief of Army Staff, myself.

At the dinner I mentioned to the President that I was going home on leave soon for a couple of months. Allende said he was keen to visit India, combining it with his attendance at a Conference of Non-Aligned Nations scheduled to be held in Algiers in the month of September. His problem was that he needed permission from Congress if he was away for more than two weeks and it was doubtful if that would be forthcoming. He asked me if the two weeks could be stretched by going round the world the 'wrong way'! It was difficult for me to conceal my amazement at his ignorance but I managed to do so and I told him that I did not think it would make any difference.

From me he went on to talk to Kirat saying,

'The Ambassador tells me you are going to home and won't be back till mid-September. I may not be alive by then.'

At which, Kirat had difficulty in holding back her tears.

As I have mentioned, talk of an impending coup was widespread at all levels of Chilean society and the President had said in a public speech,

'They will take me out of the Moneda in wooden pyjamas.'

The conversation between Allende and Kirat had gone unnoticed and our dinner went on as usual. After everybody else had left, one of his friends whom I had never met before, Senator Volodia Teitelboim asked to stay back to talk to us. He said,

'As you know the big problem is the economy. We have done our utmost to get the best economic advice. We even found a British expert to install a computerised control room so we know every day how much wheat or towels have been produced till that day in the current year. Last year, the President called his economic advisers and said to them,

"Last year, soon after we came to office, we froze the prices of essential commodities because we could see that people unfriendly to us were promoting inflation to make us unpopular. Inflation has not been a problem but the frozen prices are creating difficulties for producers. If we free prices, how much inflation do you think we will have next year?'

'There answer was that there would be about forty-five per cent inflation this year if prices were freed. In the Chilean context inflation of 45% has not been unusual in the past and the President agreed to free prices. You must have seen that inflation is currently running at 300%. Unfortunately, we cannot even shoot those economic advisers.'

Teitelboim belonged to the Communist party and was a Jew of Russian origin. He was about fifty years old at the time, had married late and had a daughter aged three. After the coup he and his wife managed to get away but the daughter became separated. I had to help her to get out of the country.

Shortly after our dinner there was the failed coup and Kirat advised me to go and see the President. I found him rather dejected,

'The problem is that in Chile there are too many disparate elements, people of different national and racial origins and it is difficult to hold them together.'

'Mr. President, we have far more differences in the vast population of our country and there are differences of language, of religion and of other factors that I can not even explain to you, but whenever the country is in danger and there is an external enemy, the patriotic reaction has been wonderful to behold. I am sure it would be the same in Chile under your leadership.'

'Ah! Ambassador, there is one element in our country whose loyalty lies outside our borders.'

'How can that be, Mr.President? And which is this element?'

'The Armed Forces. They are all trained in the United States and those people buy their loyalty.'

It was the last conversation I was destined to have with the President.

While these events of considerable diplomatic importance to the world were taking place in Chile, others of greater importance to me and my family were taking place in London. We had seen Kiran late in 1972 and soon after that he told us that he and Susan were living together. Shortly after that Harinder – whose business seemed to be prospering - invited his parents to England. They seemed not to like the idea of Kiran marrying an English girl, no doubt because of their experience with Ann. Anyhow, early in 1973, about the time of the first dinner for the Allendes, Kiran and Susan got married with the concurrence of both families but in the absence of Kirat and myself.

We saw Susan for the first time at the railway station in Geneva. We (Kirat, Arun and I) had flown there from Santiago and Kiran and Susan arrived more economically by train from London. We all got into the rented Renault and drove off to Davos where we had booked a room in another block of flats for the young couple. We had a very nice holiday and Kirat and Susan got on well together. Later, when we asked Kiran what had been Susan's reaction to us he said that she thought we treated him like a son but did not treat her as a daughter. I explained that I had no idea how to treat a daughter, never having had one.

After Switzerland, we flew to London where Susan and Kiran had rented a small first floor flat. They moved to their study giving up the bedroom to us. I think Arun slept on the dining table! I had been in touch with the Deputy High Commissioner and he had agreed that I could give a party in one of the rooms in India House in Aldwych. The party was held on 8th August at cocktail time but only champagne and biscuits were served. The guests included Susan's parents, half a dozen of their friends, the Selkirks, half a dozen of Kiran's friends and a number of my English friends or Indians resident in England. Altogether I don't think there were more than fifty people. In India in December 2005, a cousin of mine, a retired Air Force Officer had to give a dinner for five hundred persons for his daughter's wedding! *Autre temps autre moeurs,* as the French say.

When I finally got to Delhi, I found that for the first time the Ministry was interested in Chile. One reason was that the Inter-parliamentary Union was holding its conference in South America and several of these politicians were interested in the Chilean experiment; they would like to see Chile for themselves. I was asked to forecast if this would be possible. The Chinese say that forecasting is hard work especially if it concerns the future. Finally, pushed against the wall, I estimated the chances at 50%.

I saw Prime Minister Indira Gandhi also and to her I said the coup would probably take place when Allende would be in Algiers for the Conference. Her comment,

'Then he should not go to Algiers.'

I did not say anything but I felt that South American coups d'etat are not usually violent but that this one would be bloody if it was resisted. Besides most men of Spanish blood remembered the Spanish Civil War four decades earlier which had cost a million lives and would not want to repeat that experience.

Colleagues in the Ministry said,

'There is always a complaint that whenever a revolution or a coup takes place, the Indian Ambassador is absent. Do go back on time so that there may be no complaint this time.'

We got back in time for the North Korean National Day which is 9th September. That day in 1973 was a Sunday so the party was probably held the following evening. I have not known many North Korean diplomats because they do not seem keen to make friends and seldom speak languages other than their own. However, I remember that this party was lavish enough. What was striking and unusual was a large alcove containing a statue of Kim Il Sung; people were bowing before it as if it were the idol of a Hindu god. The statue was surrounded by books. The atmosphere at the party felt very tense.

On the 11th I got up as usual at 7 A.M. and immediately went for my shower. When I came back Kirat was in tears. She said,

'The phone rang so I picked it up to hear Allende's voice. He said, 'I am calling you on the most difficult day of my life. We shall fight all day.' Then he must have put the phone down.'

I felt that 7.30 A.M. was not a good time to ring up anybody. The only unusual sound I heard was of planes flying overhead. Whom should I ask? I decided to go to office as usual and make phone calls. The problem was that my diplomatic colleagues would be divided and would only have news favouring whichever side of the iron curtain they were on. There was no Indian involved in politics. My Chilean friends although generally opposed to Allende were non-political and would know nothing. It did not seem a good day to call Chilean officials or politicians.

When I got to office my Indian and Chilean staff were all there. There was an unusual presence of the Army in the streets.

A crowd of a dozen young men rushed into the Chancery. I asked them who they were and what they wanted. They said they were 'Tupamaros' seeking asylum. Tupamaros was the name assumed by left-wing terrorists in Uruguay in memory of the last Inca, Tupac Amaro, to have opposed the Spanish conquest of his country. I told these young men that India did not recognise the right of diplomatic asylum and they should get out. They said the police would arrest them as soon as they got out; I pointed out that there was not a policeman in sight but that I would call the police if they did not get out. They left.

Reports were coming in of firing around the Moneda palace and of attacks on the building by Chilean Air Force planes firing rockets. At last I decided to call up the Papal Nuncio. I expected him to be both neutral and knowledgeable. Nuncios are generally Italians although I had once come across an Irishman. Unusually, in this case Monsignor Palma was Chilean by birth and a member of a large family – I think nineteen brothers and sisters. In the course of the conversation – in Spanish – he referred to the 'late President'. Radio broadcasts and gossip had been saying for an hour that the President was dead but I had not believed it because, of course, the middle class wanted him out of the way and the radio and television stations are always the first objectives of rebels in any revolution. There was an announcement that telegraph services had been 'suspended'.

The first duty of an Ambassador in these circumstances is to inform his government of the fate of the Indian community. I called up Nathaniel Davis, the U.S. Ambassador, whose children were classmates of Arun's and asked him if he would send a cipher telegram to Delhi from me. He immediately agreed. My telegram conveyed the information about the telephone call and the non-involvement of the Indian community.

I have no personal knowledge of the events of that fateful day. There were conflicting reports of the events. I have seen a press report of a long interview with Fidel Castro in which he says that Allende fought to the bitter end, even after he was wounded, and succumbed to a stray bullet. We listened a lot to Moscow radio for a month after the event and got all sorts of pro-Allende propaganda including a song which said ' Allende is alive'.

My considered belief is that the first plane probably flew over the palace well before 7 A.M. Allende who lived openly in another house in a suburb, treating the Moneda as his Office, rushed there as soon as he got the news. So did most of his Ministers , his daughters, his wife and several of his friends who were armed with small arms and bazookas. His three A.D.C.s, one from each Service, asked for permission to go away because they did not want to fight against their comrades-in-arms, and were allowed to go. One of them gave him a letter-head with my telephone number on it. The palace was under fire from infantry and from the air force which had rockets in addition to machine-guns. In the Moneda they only had infantry weapons. Snipers friendly to Allende occupied some buildings in the neighbourhood and fired on the Chilean Army.

The Moneda was built of stone but the roof was supported by wooden beams which soon caught fire. The rebels probably did not expect such a determined resistance. When they learnt that there were women and non-combatants in the building, they suspended fire and invited them by loud-hailers to leave. The principal women were Tencha and the three daughters – the Allendes had no son. The non-combatants included the Minister of Foreign Affairs Clodomiro Almeyda and Allende's personal physician. The latter stated to the press that while leaving he had seen the President sitting in an armchair with a silver-plated assault rifle – presented to him by Fidel Castro - between his knees with the muzzle under his chin. I see no reason to disbelieve this and therefore think that the President committed suicide.

The Embassy continued to function fairly normally after the coup d'etat. The unusual occurrences were at the Residence. The right of diplomatic asylum ceased, in fact, at some undetermined time in the nineteenth century. The only exception I can think of during my active diplomatic service was the case of Cardinal Mindszenthy in a Western Embassy in Budapest.

However, the situation in Latin America is different. There were two International Conventions on the Right of Diplomatic Asylum in Latin America which were in force in 1973. They laid down elaborate terms for such asylum. The sheltering Mission had to declare the identity of the persons it had harboured to the Ministry of Foreign Affairs and request exit permits – these may not be unreasonably delayed. When the exit permit has been received, a day and time for departure had to be agreed on as also the name of the 'vessel' by which they were to depart.

Quite soon after the coup, a note was issued by the Ministry of Foreign Affairs extending the right of Asylum to all Embassies. The principal 'beneficiary' of this concession was the Italian Embassy. The building was large and empty – the Ambassador and his wife had gone to Rome to attend to their son who was dying of cancer. When the building was cleared there were more than seven hundred persons in it. Even the British Embassy – the British are normally very strict about such things - harboured people although Ambassador Seconde had little sympathy for the Allende regime. One evening I was invited to dinner by the French Ambassador and he told me that there were 'asylees' normally sleeping every night on the stairs which came down into the dining room but that evening they were lying down on the floor of his bedroom!

What was the position of the Chilean Government in international law? I must begin by dealing with the question of who had led the coup and become the de facto Head of State and Government. The Chief of the Army was the only one of the three Chiefs who was loyal to Allende. I can not remember his name. His loyalty was so well-known that early in the month of June while he was being driven in his official car, other cars hemmed him in creating a traffic jam (I was, against my will, caught up in this jam). He got out of his car and fired his pistol in the air. Slogans were then shouted. I remember one, 'We are doing this for our children and the future of our country.' After this the crowd of cars dispersed. It was obvious from then on that he was a spent force but I had no contacts in the Army and did not know what was happening. The name of Augusto Pinochet was not known to the general public until after the coup and it was only then that we realised that the Army Chief must have been kept prisoner since this traffic jam because he could not have been a party to the failed June coup.

By the 13th September all the diplomatic Missions had received a note from the de facto Government informing them of the death of President Allende and the assumption of power by General Pinochet and the composition of his new cabinet, almost all high Officers of the three Armed Forces. The Vice President was a Naval Officer. I sent off a translation of this note to Delhi from where there was no response. India did not wish to recognise this de facto Government. For my part, I continued to deal with the Officers I knew in the Ministry of Foreign Affairs. I did not call on the new Minister of Foreign Affairs – a General - or meet him. I never shook his hand. When I went to a party in another Embassy and he was present I avoided him.

I felt it wise to fly the flag on my car although it had not been the practice in Chile to do so except on formal occasions – for attendance at a Government function or a formal call on another

Ambassador. One afternoon as I was being driven in the city, the car was stopped by a policeman who asked,

'Why are you not flying a Chilean flag?'

'An Ambassador only flies the flag of his own country on his car.'

'But in these times?'

'If you do not like universal diplomatic practice, ask your Government to declare me *persona non grata* and I shall not hesitate to leave.'

I never had any such experience again.

A curfew was imposed – I think at 10 P.M. – after which time one could hear stray shots being fired. I never found out who was firing at whom and there were no reports in the press or on television of any violent incidents. None of my colleagues or Chilean friends or acquaintances knew anything either. Throughout my stay in Chile after the coup there was only one night – which I shall relate later - when I did not hear gunfire.

The first persons to ask for asylum were two young men speaking quite good English who said they were brothers, born in Calcutta, of a Czech father (a Bata Executive) and an 'Indian mother'. We suspected from their appearance that the mother must have been an Anglo-Indian. Their documents bore a Slavonic name. Their parents never came to see them and we were never able to verify their story. They said they were liable to be arrested and tortured if not shot if the police were to see them on the street. They appeared sincere and well-mannered and we believed their story and took them in.

The person who really brought seekers of asylum into the Embassy Residence was Irma the wife of Clodomiro Almeyda, the Foreign Minister. I had found Almeyda inaccessible and unhelpful. He seemed to be totally uninterested in human problems. Some Indian merchants in Punta Arenas (the southernmost city in the world) had fallen foul of the Allende administration and their properties had been seized. The officials in the Ministry were unable to do anything and I had asked for an interview with the Foreign Minister. All he could say was,

'I shall convey your request to the President.'

He had been a guest in the Embassy; in fact I had even given a cocktail in his honour when he had chaired the UNCTAD meeting and, of course, he and his wife had accompanied the President for both dinners. His wife had been more sociable. With the death of Allende and the arrest of her husband – confined in a prison camp near Punta Arenas – she made an all-out effort to build better relations with Kirat, and I ended up addressing her as 'Tu.' She was a well-educated and capable woman with managerial talents. She was in charge of the UNCTAD building which had been built in the style of the U.N. Headquarters in New York. It had the highest tower in Santiago which housed the offices and a large low building commonly known as 'La Placa' which contained the assembly, conference and committee rooms. From her office she had watched the events at the Moneda palace. When the palace was finally taken she thought her husband had died only to get a phone call from him saying he was being carried off into captivity.

One of the first persons she brought in was a woman who according to Irma was the sister of Allende's mistress whom I had never met. This sister was supposed to have been stitching armed forces uniforms for the new guerrillas. She kept to the room we gave her and did not have her meals with us. She must have been four weeks in the house during which time I only saw her a couple of times.

I think I should explain that Allende's socialism was non-violent like Nehru's and totally unlike the National Socialism of Hitler or the Soviet Socialism of Stalin. I did not hear of a single political death or instance of terrorism during the Allende years. Pinochet's rule was quite different. The prisoners that the Police and the Army took were routinely tortured. The Leftists were totally disunited and some of the groups were armed and made full use of their weapons. One man named Miguel, the son of a University Rector, specialised in inventing new weapons. One of his inventions called 'Miguelito' after him was a steel quadripod which had a spike pointing straight up whichever way it fell to the ground. He would drive round in a car and, when he was chased his companions would sprinkle them out of the rear windows to puncture the tyres of his pursuers.

The guerrillas often wore uniforms to be able to mingle with the troops – there was compulsory military service in Chile so all adult males knew how to march, shoot and behave like soldiers.

The Army therefore started wearing distinctive armbands which were changed every day and the greatest secrecy was observed about the armband to be worn on the following day. The Army had orders to shoot anyone in uniform who did not have an armband or was seen wearing the wrong armband.

Three men, claiming to be brothers, turned up asking for asylum. I did not like their appearance and asked them why they needed asylum. Instead of answering me they produced their identity cards which, of course, mentioned their first names which were 'Vladimir', 'Ilyitch' and 'Lenin'. Their father had been a fanatical communist!

I have gone ahead of the story. The new regime quickly broke off relations with Cuba and the Swedish Ambassador Harald Edelstamm took charge of the Cuban Embassy which was situated across the street from his own. To my surprise, I received orders from Delhi to take over protection of the Russian and Czech Embassies. I rang up the Russian Ambassador and he said, yes, the Soviet Union was 'suspending' its relations with Chile. I sent a telegram to Delhi protesting that I did not have enough staff to look after the enormous property and belongings of these two large Missions. A Second Secretary was detached from the Embassy in Brazil and arrived accompanied by his wife. He was a Malayali and proved most helpful. I installed him in the Chancery of the large Soviet Embassy. A few weeks later there was an attempt to break into the building – whether by common criminals or by the agents of the de facto government I shall never know - and he very courageously drove off the intruders with the help of the Chilean night watchman, both of them unarmed. When I reported the event to Delhi, I was told that it was not my responsibility to provide physical protection to the Soviet and Czech Embassies. In fact the Czech Embassy was burgled a little later.

I am going into all these details because it is unusual for an Ambassador to become 'protector' of another Embassy; it was a new experience for me and the details may be interesting for the reader.

Normal diplomatic life resumed fairly quickly but my work increased substantially. The first major operation was the evacuation of the Russians. All the Russian Embassy staff had to leave. The Russians realised that the hundreds of engineers, technicians and specialists they had provided – mainly to replace foreigners working in the mines and multinational enterprises who had left as they found their salaries unviable – must also leave. The Soviet government sent a number of planes in the course of a fortnight to evacuate them. The North Korean government apparently did not have suitable planes so they asked the Russians to carry them out also. The problem was that they insisted on carrying away five tons of the books of Kim Il Sung – apparently they could neither be burnt nor allowed to fall into the hands of 'unbelievers'.

I felt sorry for the Russians who were allowed to take away only one suitcase per person. If any of them had private cars – as diplomats usually do – they had to be abandoned as also extra clothes, furniture, furnishings etc. When the Rumanian Ambassador and his wife, whom we knew rather well, had to leave, he had to go by air and leave belongings worth hundreds perhaps thousands of dollars.

As I have mentioned the Embassy only had one car, a Chevrolet. I suddenly 'acquired' nearly a hundred motor vehicles ranging from motorcycles to an air-conditioned Mercedes-Benz bus belonging to the Soviet Embassy. Between the two Embassies there were a dozen Mercedes-Benz cars of varying ages and sizes. Socialism is obviously good for socialist diplomats.

There was also the question of property. Between the two Embassies they owned a dozen buildings or flats. These did not present a problem because the Chilean employees continued in service and reported directly to Moscow and Prague and presumably continued to get their salaries somehow. The problem was with the thirty or forty rented apartments. They had all to be returned to their owners. I did not inquire whether they were let furnished or unfurnished. The contents were left in the apartments rather than thrown away. I visited one or two of these apartments and noticed that all had been occupied by at least two families. The second kitchen was installed in one of the bathrooms. I could only speculate on the reasons for this policy whether it was economy or security.

A couple of days after the coup, we got a phone call in the evening from the Mexican Embassy. Tencha (Mrs. Allende) had taken refuge in the Mexican Embassy after she was allowed to leave the Moneda. She had now been told that her husband's body had been prepared for burial and she was invited to accompany it to the graveyard with any friends she wanted to accompany her. She was asking us if we wanted to go. Of course, we went. Tencha was in the hearse while a number of Ambassadors and their wives followed in a bus. Later Kirat asked her if she had seen the body. She replied in the negative.

Kirat asked,

'Were you at least allowed to see a hand? If not, how can you know that the body was the President's'

'I believe it was.'

More than twenty years later I received a phone call in Delhi. It was an Officer of the Ministry of External Affairs asking if I had been Ambassador of India in Chile. When I replied in the affirmative, he said there was an invitation for me to go to Chile for the formal reburial of the body of President Allende. Since there was no ticket with the invitation, the question of my paying for a return ticket to Santiago did not arise.

It must have been ten days after the coup that a weekly publication mentioned that when Allende's body was undressed, a quarter of a sheet letter headed 'A.D.C. to the President of Chile' was found in one of his pockets with a six figure number written on it. The magazine speculated that it must have been the number of his Swiss bank account. This was obviously nonsense. Why should a man preparing to die be interested in a Swiss bank account? The next issue of the magazine said that they had found that it was the telephone number of the Indian Ambassador. It went on to say that as the Indian Ambassador had taken over the protection of the Russian Embassy, Allende must have been trying to get Russian help against the Chilean Army. This conjecture was no better than the previous one.

When I returned home from the office that evening, I found Kirat in tears. There had been a number of telephone calls asking,

'Is Salvador there?' or

'Are you expecting Allende?'

Faced with all the requests for asylum, I wrote to the Ministry that we should perhaps recognise the de facto government so as to be able to help these unfortunate victims of the military dictatorship. In reply I got a copy of the note that the Ministry had sent to all Missions in New Delhi, on the occasion of the Svetlana episode, stating that the Government of India did not recognise the right of diplomatic asylum.

This was, of course, the correct answer to my recommendation but it put me in a very difficult situation. By now I had over a dozen 'asylees' in the Embassy. It would be inhuman to turn them over to the police to be tortured. How did I know that they would be tortured or killed? There were plenty of reports, not in the Chilean press, but on foreign television and radio. I was also in daily touch with the reporter of the Toronto STAR, a man called Timothy Ross who had come over from another South American capital where he normally resided to cover the situation in Chile and who was collecting horrible stories. Finally, I got direct evidence.

One of the Russian Embassy vehicles under my 'protection' was being used for carrying stray Russians to Santiago for repatriation. They stopped on the way for the night and were listening to a Russian radio broadcast when the police heard about them and arrested them. Listening to foreign broadcasts was not a serious offence – broadcasting invited immediate execution – but the circumstances appeared suspicious to a zealous policeman. The authorities had no wish to delay the repatriation of Russian technicians but a Chilean working for them could be a dangerous revolutionary and needed to be 'interrogated'. He was taken to a torture camp where he was in the queue for torture – others who had arrived before him were being 'interrogated' when he and several others with him were suddenly released. He came and told me this. They were released to make room for over a hundred newcomers. I learnt from other sources that the army had succeeded in killing 'Miguel' mentioned three pages earlier. In his pocket they found the names, addresses and telephone numbers of over two hundred persons. They were rounded up and taken to the camp where this driver was being held.

It seems strange that an intelligent man like Miguel should have kept such an important list where it was bound to fall into the hands of the police – he must have thought he was immortal.

My problem was that I had to feed all these people and I could not keep them on a diet of bread and water although I did not give them wine because I did not drink it myself. Since I could not tell my Government that they existed I could not ask for extra funds to look after them. Then, again, I could not tell the Chilean Government that I had refugees and ask for exit permits for them. I found that the Ecuadorean Embassy had a low back wall about a hundred meters from my front gate so I started letting my 'guests' out of my front gate at night and helping them climb into the Ecuadorean Embassy. Of course, the Ecuadorean Ambassador soon put barbed wire on his back wall! In this way I was able to help some forty persons – a few of them were quite prominent people. Some of them had stayed under my roof (eaten my salt) for over a month, all at my personal expense. I had 'cast my bread upon the water' and it was only returned to me in 1985, thanks to Kiran.

What proof is there that prisoners were being tortured? One of the victims was a British woman medical practitioner named, I think, Kennedy. She gave specific medical details of what was done to her. These details appeared in English newspapers in most countries.

Many interesting events were taking place almost simultaneously and I cannot remember the dates on which they occurred. One of these was the death of Pablo Neruda, the Nobel Prize-winning poet who had been the Communist candidate in the first round of the Presidential election of 1970. I had met him twice, once in 1954 when he had invited me to dinner in an apartment in Santiago and then in 1971 when he had come to have tea at the Embassy. On the second occasion I had noticed his enormous ankles. Rumour had indicated that he was suffering from cancer of the prostate. He seemed to be well off and I was told that he had been very clever about selling his books in a country in which poets usually starve in garrets as in eighteenth century England.

He lived most of the time on an 'estate' called Isla Negra (Black Island) where he did not have a telephone. My attempts to get to this estate had failed. Once I had got hold of his 'contact number' and had to wait an inordinate time for him to come to the phone. When he did, he would not give me a time and a place for meeting him or accept an invitation to the Embassy. As I got the report of his death, I also heard that a crowd had entered his house in Santiago and ransacked it. It was the first time I heard of his having a house in Santiago and I went there immediately. The house was open and there was a man who let me in when I identified myself. Books and papers were strewn all over but I could not see any physical damage.

I had occasion to go to the Ministry of Foreign Affairs in the Moneda to meet an official whom I had known for some time and I mentioned that the house of the world-famous Chilean poet had been ransacked. I was trying to tell him that the coup had been a disgrace and he was trying to tell me that it followed a hallowed South American tradition and that the Chile famous for its literacy, wealth and culture was unchanged. He invited my attention to an American film currently being shown called ZORBA THE GREEK in which when a man dies, his belongings are looted because he is not of the same Christian sect as the local population. He pointed out that Isla Negra had not been disturbed.

Some Chilean foreign service Officers had been sent home but others continued in office. Generally, the professional and middle classes were happy that the Government had changed but few liked the violence which had accompanied the change. Others were unhappy to have Chilean democracy kept in abeyance by the military rulers.

That had certainly happened. There had been intervals of military rule in Chile before but the 'Congreso' had boasted of over a hundred years of continuous existence and it had now been dissolved.

The men arrested by the new Government (and there were over a thousand of them kept openly in a stadium where they could be met by relations and by the cleverer journalists like Timothy Ross) were tried by military tribunals and subject to military penalties which were announced. Those kept in the prison camps were not acknowledged and I only knew of them through unofficial sources which were probably less reliable than the official ones.

This brings us to the question of how many men and women were killed by the Pinochet Government. I have not seen any acknowledgment by Pinochet of 'executions' much less killings of anybody in the course of or as a result of what the regime called the 'pronunciamento'. My unofficial sources gave me figures between ten thousand and thirty thousand. After the restoration of democracy and during the twenty-first century rule of the Socialist Party – Allende's party – the figure mentioned has been three thousand which can not possibly be an understatement. This illustrates how undependable were my sources including Timothy Ross who, with his wife Sarah, was my house-guest for a week or so.

The meeting of the Inter-Parliamentary Union mentioned earlier duly took place and, in its aftermath, the Speaker of the Lok Sabha wanted to see Cuzco (the last capital of the Incas) and Machu Pichu. I got a respite from the disaster of Chile by flying to Lima. The Speaker was a Keshadhari Sikh named Dhillon (a Jat), a very cultured landowner who had submitted honestly to land reform.

At this stage let me mention an earlier visit to Lima where a Muslim ex-M.P. (A.M.Tariq) who had become Chairman of the Motion Picture Export Corporation had arrived with thirty-odd trailers. Alan Nazareth arranged a private showing on a Sunday morning to which he invited the owners or managers of all the cinemas in Lima.

The success was incredible – I still find it difficult to believe it over thirty years later. Tariq sold a hundred films. Two cinemas in Lima showed only Indian films for a year. Alan, Isobel and the tiny Embassy staff kept busy listening to the Hindi soundtrack and translating it into Spanish. The translations and the films were sent to Beirut where they were sub-titled in Spanish, a facility not available at that time in India.

To return to Speaker Dhillon, Alan Nazareth arranged a full programme for him to meet various Peruvian personalities. One of these made a change in his programme so we were at a loose end for a couple of hours and Alan took us to see the 'Inquisition Museum'. This had models of the various kinds of torture used by the 'Holy Inquisition' to 'persuade' its victims to 'confess to their heresies' after which they were 'handed over to the civil arm' to perform their 'act of faith' i.e. be burnt at the stake. I told Alan and the Speaker that these ancient practices had not been lost but refined with the help of electricity to make them quicker and more efficient in neighbouring Chile. I could see from his expression that Alan at least did not believe me.

Speaker Dhillon and I flew to Cuzco which is at a height of about eight thousand feet and went to our hotel. Next day, when I woke up I found it was drizzling. I went out onto the balcony – we had adjoining first floor rooms – and looking down saw a hundred yards away an effigy of Raj Kapur in his clown's dress and above it a signboard 'BAR JOKER'. I showed it to the Speaker who was delighted with the success of his political colleague Tariq.

To go to Machu Pichu we had to take a narrow gauge train which had to negotiate a switchback on the steep mountain which separated Cuzco from Machu Pichu. Alongside the track were some buildings which were obviously the quarters of the railway workers. Dhillon told me that he had been Minister of Railways and said,

'We cannot give such quarters to our workers any longer. They insist on electricity and running water.'

The social system of Peru is interesting. The coastal plain is a desert like Egypt or Sind with the difference that instead of one huge river, it has over a dozen coming down from the Andes to the Pacific Ocean. The deltas of these rivers have been settled by the white man. The altiplano mentioned earlier is inhabited by Amerindians; the slopes are lived in by 'mestizos' (half-breeds). The Amerindian who receives the full rays of the tropical sun unfiltered by the polluted air of the lower atmosphere is quite dark-skinned. If he wants to find a job instead of living by subsistence farming, the 'Indio' comes down to get unskilled work in a workshop or factory – probably sweeping it out. At this stage, he cannot read or write or even speak Spanish.

Depending on his talent and ambition he may take a year or five to learn to speak Spanish, to sign his name and to wear shoes. He is then known as a Mestizo. If he is really talented, wins the lottery or makes a fortune by selling peanuts, he may acquire a car and a white woman when he then becomes a 'Blanco'.

It is only the Indio who is willing to live in the railway quarters which had surprised Mr. Dhillon.

At that time, the Peruvian Establishment was not very interested in the Indio. At the conference which I had attended in La Paz in 1954, the question had been raised whether the Indio could vote in Peru. The answer was,

'All literate Peruvians have the right to vote.'

We were not told that there were no schools in the Altiplano! Things have changed since then. I gather that the President of Peru in the twenty-first century is of unmixed Amerindian descent. The same has happened in Bolivia and Venezuela although the world press writes more about their political alignment (left) than their ethnic roots.

I find this very interesting. In the foregoing pages I have used the word 'white' where the word used by most European and North American writers is 'European'. When there are riots in these countries, the rabble does shout 'blanco' (white) to indicate its alienation from the ruling class in terms of race rather than politics.

There is another anomaly. In the sixteenth century conquest of what we now call Hispano-America, the 'conquistadores' were not accompanied by women from Europe. The emigration of women took place much later. I can only suppose that the 'Council of the Indies' presided over by the Spanish King in person expected the surviving conquerors to return home and settle down just as the East India Company did in London. The 'fishing fleet' of unmarried Englishwomen only started after the Suez Canal came into operation.

The Spanish occupation of land in the New World was governed by Spanish law which recognised the land rights of the aboriginal occupants. Many Spaniards married the local women – after killing off their husbands or fathers for rebellion! In this way some of them became legal owners of vast tracts of land. In La Paz, some of the great landowners – constituting the landed aristocracy I was introduced to - definitely had Amerindian features.

Harald Edelstamm, the recently arrived Swedish Ambassador, definitely had leftist views. He had become the protector of the Cuban Embassy, the only one to be expelled by Pinochet. The First Secretary of the Cuban Embassy had married Allende's second daughter. It so happened that the Cuban Embassy was situated across the road from the Swedish one. Harald invited us to dinner one evening. We knew that he did not have a wife.

When we got there he showed us a statue of his 'second wife'. He asked us to study it carefully because 'One side of the face is kind and the other is cruel.' Then he asked us whether we would mind crossing the road for dinner.

We duly went across - it was the southern summer by this time so it was still light - and he explained that he was living in the Cuban Embassy the better to protect the scores of asylees that he had taken in. He pointed to bullet hits in the walls of the building and said it was fired on at night by the troops which surrounded it.

Naturally, the Cuban Embassy was not furnished like the Swedish one. The dinner was served by some of the asylees while others sat down at table with us. It was not a very good dinner. Since there was a curfew at 10 P.M., we prepared to leave after coffee. Harald said,

'As soon as you leave, the shooting will start. I expect them to storm this building tonight because I have an asylee whom they particularly want.'

My answer was,

'If that is so, Harald, we won't leave.'

Harald was overjoyed and started making intercontinental telephone calls to journalists he knew in Europe telling them of the shooting against the Embassy and the 'protection I am getting from the Indian Ambassador and his wife.' (In Spanish and French, the expression is 'the Indian Ambassadors'). We prepared to bed down on couches in the library under quilts which were provided to us. The only phone call we made was to our own servants telling them not to wait for us.

That was the most peaceful night we spent in Santiago under the Pinochet regime - not a shot did we hear. However, I am a creature of habit and I was not in a good temper having slept in a lounge suit rather than in pyjamas, not having cleaned my teeth and so on. Next morning having woken up at my usual time we put on our shoes and prepared to leave , without waiting to thank Harald - there was, of course, no toilet attached to the library - and I got into the car. I always used to drive myself in the evenings because of the problem of the curfew for the driver who lived far from the Embassy residence. As soon as we came to the Embassy gate, I saw half-a-dozen men in uniform standing in front. I stopped the car and asked them what they wanted – as I have said I was not in a good temper. They asked me to open the boot. I pointed out that I was the Indian Ambassador and pointed to the Ambassadorial number-plate on the car. They replied that they wanted to know if there was anybody in the boot. This they were entitled to do. The Latin American conventions referred to earlier specifically forbade the carriage of asylees in Embassy vehicles. Of course, there was nobody in the boot.

I got to office fairly late that day and found a long telegram waiting from Delhi. Apparently, the Indian Charge d'Affaires in Stockholm had been summoned to the Swedish Ministry of Foreign Affairs to be formally thanked for the 'protection which the Indian Ambassador has given to Ambassador Edelstamm'. At The Hague the Swedish Ambassador had spoken to our Ambassador (Maharaja Yadvendra Singh of Patiala) to express his appreciation of my action. The Foreign Secretary expressed his displeasure at my involving myself in activities which were none of my concern.

Some years later, after I had retired, I found that the Swedish Ambassador in New Delhi was Harald Edelstamm's brother. I mentioned to him that I had known Harald in Santiago. Harald was declared persona non grata some time after the events I have described but his Government supported him, he continued in the Swedish Foreign Service and went on to hold other posts. In the course of his travels, he stayed at the Embassy in New Delhi and I was invited to dinner. It was the Christmas season and he was looking forward to a midnight swim in the Embassy's swimming pool.

That same morning, I was asked on the telephone by an official at the Ministry of Foreign Affairs what had happened. I said that the Swedish Ambassador's dinner had gone on longer than I had expected and, to avoid the problem of the curfew, my wife and I had slept over at our host's.

'But, Mr. Ambassador, you should have a curfew pass. Please apply for one.'

I thanked him but I did not apply for a curfew pass. They had to be renewed every five days and the process was quite long-winded. In any case, I was not getting many invitations for dinners at Embassies because my hosts would have found my presence embarrassing if I was at the same table with Chilean Ministers or other diplomats.

In the latter half of 1974, a Bengali turned up in the Chancery. He was received by Kashi Chakravarty, the Second Secretary who had just arrived to take the place of a First Secretary who had proved uninterested in working.

Kashi came and told me that a Bengali Muslim had come asking for asylum since there was no Bangladeshi Embassy. His story was that he was a leftist professor of mathematics, famous in his own field, who had come to Chile like many other leftists in Allende's time and was living in a flat when, one day, the police turned up to arrest him. On being asked the reason they said they had found a radio transmitter in a locker under the staircase. This was very serious because using a radio transmitter was punishable by death. He had a brainwave and handed them the bunch of keys from his pocket, saying,

'Here are all the keys I possess – you can search my flat if you like – please see if any of them fits the locker you are talking about.'

Fortunately none of the keys fitted and he was let off after a few questions. He had come because the police might make further enquiries about him now that they knew his name. We sent off an open (not coded) telegram to the Bangladeshi Embassy in Buenos Aires asking if they knew of Professor .... who had come to us asking for shelter. In the meantime, Kashi agreed to keep the man as a house guest. After a couple of days, the Bangladeshi Embassy replied that there was no such famous Bangladeshi mathematician. We were in a quandary. However, Kashi reported, now that he and Meera (his wife) had had this man living in their house for two days, that he appeared to be a dangerous communist and a brilliant intellectual. Their Chilean maid who could not communicate with the guest because they had no common language had given her judgement,

'I would not marry this man, even as a gift.'

I had only one conversation with the Bangladeshi and could not form any opinion about him, not even as a mathematician – as I have mentioned earlier I was trained as a physical scientist. He did appear to be genuine, not a confidence trickster or a sponger. Fortunately, after a couple of days another telegram arrived from the Bangladeshi Embassy apologising for their previous telegram and saying that Professor............ was indeed a famous Bangladeshi mathematician and requesting us to dispatch him to Buenos Aires by air at the Embassy's expense. This ended the ordeal of the Chakravartys.

There were no more requests for asylum but I could still do odd favours for persons who were at risk. My duties had changed. I was seeing less of my European diplomatic colleagues but telephone conversations were continuing so I was spending more time at home.

Arun's studies at Nido de Aguilas were over. He had passed top of his class with *summa cum laude* beating Johnny Blydenstein, unfairly as he thought, by a narrow margin. This was a remarkable achievement. Neither Pitaji nor I nor Kiran could claim any such academic distinction. In fact, the only Malik I know who has such achievement to his/her credit is my cousin Mrinalini Kocchar (nee Malik), daughter of I.S.Malik, the golfer mentioned earlier. Arun was most interested in ecology which was a subject available only in U.S.A. He had sat for the U.S. Common Entrance – I know it has another name but I do not remember what it is – and the result seemed to me good enough for any University but he told me it was not good enough for Princeton which was the University he most admired – Einstein had been there. Finally he was granted admission at Bowdoin of which I had never heard and he went off financed by the sale of the Mercedes Benz which I had now owned for over five years (three of them in Chile) and could sell without paying any duty.

Kirat's first letter to him said that every time she walked past his room she found it 'empty, empty, empty'. One afternoon I was sitting in my dressing room-cum-study - it received the afternoon sun - when I saw a fat, middle-aged middle class woman come hesitantly through the Embassy gate and walk to the door. I did not pay much attention because she would be Kirat's business. A few minutes later Kirat arrived with tears in her eyes. The woman had said that she had a eighteen-year-old son who was going to be executed next morning; Arun was seventeen years old. I went to talk to the woman and after expressing my profound regrets, I said she must understand that I could do nothing to prevent this tragedy so what would she like me to do?

'I have come to request you to make this known to the world.'

'That I think I can do. Please give me the details.' Timothy Ross could do that. He and his wife both belonged to wealthy English Jewish families but were out and out leftists.

My position was becoming known to those who were interested in current political affairs. They all knew that prominent persons had been provided shelter in the Indian Embassy although I vigorously denied it to Chilean officials and journalists. Friends whom I could trust continued to be invited to my parties where they might meet Irma Almeyda. On the other hand, I did not have the reputation of being a leftist. At the height of the Allende period, Fidel Castro had come on an official visit to Santiago – this was when he had presented the silver-plated assault rifle to Allende.

During that visit, the Cuban Ambassador with whom I maintained close relations had given a party for 'non-aligned Heads of Mission'. I had of course attended and found that the other guests belonged to what I considered the Soviet Block. They all embraced Fidel. I contented myself with a formal handshake and a polite greeting in Spanish. This could not go unnoticed. On the other hand, it did not bring me any closer to the new military government either.

What was the effect of the coup on the average non-political Chilean? Inflation had been brought down quite quickly from 300% to normal South American double digits. This was a gain for the upper and middle classes. Many men and women with leftist political affiliations had lost their jobs.

This included the man who, in most Commonwealth countries, would be called the Permanent Under Secretary for Foreign Affairs. He was dismissed and advised not to meet the wrong people. Financially, this proved a benefit for him because he was a qualified lawyer and resumed his practice. He told me that his income had gone up five-fold!

Of course this was not the case of the working class. Their freebies – the purchase of luxury goods at the 'official' price - had ceased. Wages were not being revised periodically to compensate for inflation. A minimum wage was announced. I calculated that it was equivalent to twelve chickens a month and I said so in a cocktail party. The phrase was widely accepted and circulated. The man or woman on the minimum wage was paying for the economic reforms.

These reforms were remarkably successful. Stabilisation of the currency brings enormous benefits to a hard-working people in a market economy. The Chileans had no great reputation for hard work but the low minimum wage was an incentive to work hard especially as food of all kinds and other goods appeared on the shelves. I have no hesitation in saying that Pinochet's economic policies were sound and have continued (with the changes dictated by a changing world) ever since even under the socialist governments of the twenty-first century. The only question is – did these economic policies have to cost three thousand lives?

My normal tenure of my post - three years – had long expired. I had been kept on because of the responsibility for the Soviet and Czechoslovak Missions and because India could not appoint a new Ambassador without recognising the Military Government.

This last problem had already presented itself. Pinochet had recalled the Chilean Ambassador in New Delhi and this gentleman was in Santiago without a job. The Ministry of Foreign Affairs had asked me for an agreement for the man they had selected for New Delhi – I did not know him – some nine months earlier. I had promptly transmitted the request to New Delhi from where there was no response. The Officer in the Moneda with whom I normally dealt mentioned it to me and said that he knew what that meant. I did not make any comment.

Kashi Chakravarty, unlike his predecessor whose main interest in life had been watching tennis on television, was fully competent for handling the routine work of the Embassy and looking after the needs of the Soviet and Czechoslovak Missions. It was not a surprise, therefore, when I got a telegram posting me to Bangkok. My first reaction was adverse because the idea of living in the hot and humid climate of Thailand after the delights of Santiago's cool, dry climate did not appeal to me. However, I soon realised that the 'farthest transfer in the world' gave me unprecedented opportunities for seeing the world. Finally I was missing Arun who had left us a couple of months earlier.

Arun's letters from Brunswick, Maine were depressing. He had always lived with us or, for short periods, with his grandparents in Poona. This was his first experience of living on his own. Normally, one goes to a College with classmates from school. This was not the case in Bowdoin. His letters did not say all this. He was complaining about the weather, it was raining too much. There was also a suggestion that of four colleges in Canada and an equal number in U.S.A. which he had been offered he had chosen the wrong one. I could do nothing about U.S.A. but I did have an old friend who was a Professor of Physics at a Canadian University who might be able to help.

XXVI

THE TRANSFER - SANTIAGO-BANGKOK 1974

The old rule about transfers being always by sea had been changed and we were expected to travel by Air India wherever it was available. The nearest Air India station was New York and, in the case of Chile we were allowed to travel by any airline to New York because there were few passenger ships between Valparaiso and New York. Now there were only Kirat and I to fly.

We flew all night, made a long stop in Miami and arrived at New York where we rented a car and drove off depending on the excellent signposting and the maps provided by the car hire company. It was my first experience of driving in the U.S.A. and Kirat was delighted with the quality of the roads. But more enjoyable than anything else were the 'fall' colours. We had arrived at the best season. We had started too late to get to Brunswick before nightfall so we stopped at a motel – another first – for the night and were delighted with the facilities it afforded us. Breakfast was not available at the motel but we were shown a restaurant where we got a sumptuous breakfast and reached Brunswick in time to find Arun before lunch and book in at a motel of his choice.

The weather was bright with the sun shining all day and Arun had to admit that his complaints on that score had been hasty. We spent a couple of days in Brunswick during which time I was able to meet some of his faculty members with whom I discussed his problems. They said they had no problem with

481

him and his problems would disappear when he got used to the new conditions. Somewhat to my surprise, there were no Indian students on the campus. Some holidays were coming up so we planned a trip to Ottawa to see the Hoopers and on to Frederickton, New Brunswick to meet my old friend Derek Livesey.

Getting from New Brunswick to Ottawa was quite complicated and meant a cross-country journey by rather minor roads, but I found myself driving past Bretton Woods where the decisions about creating the World Bank and the International Monetary Fund had been taken by Lord (John Maynard) Keynes and his U.S. counterpart after very heated discussions. That was the only day of our North American trip when it rained a lot.

The result was that it was very late when we got to Ottawa but the Hoopers' hospitality was fantastic. They gave us their bed to sleep in, moving to another room and there was a separate room for Arun – their three adopted children were away at boarding schools. Patricia and I had a leisurely breakfast while Bill, Kirat and Arun went off shopping. They bought a paper knife with the four Canadian coins set inside a Perspex handle. It is lying besides the laptop on which I am typing.

After that they took us to their country house on the edge of a lake. To my surprise the kitchen and bathrooms drained through a plastic pipe laid on the surface down into the lake. This system did not work when it froze because the exposed plastic pipe froze up and it was just about to do so! The adjoining village had beautiful stone houses quite unlike most of those we saw in Canada which were made of wood. Bill explained that during the Napoleonic wars, Britain had recruited a lot of Highlanders for its Army. The landowners had taken advantage of the absence of the men to demolish their houses. When the war ended, the War Office resettled the surviving ex-servicemen in Canada. Many of them had been stonemasons in civilian life, hence the beautiful stone houses in this village which had a Scottish name.

We had arrived too late in Canada to see its beautiful maples. In fact, the countryside looked mostly grey and dismal while waiting for the snow. Arun decided that Brunswick, Maine was more beautiful than anything he had seen in Canada. However, I still wanted to see my friend Derek Livesey and his wife Lois whom I had last met when they had come for tea to the National

Liberal Club in London before emigrating to North America. We also wanted to see our French friends Henri and Francoise Dumont with whom we had been quite close in Buenos Aires. He was posted at the French Consulate General in Montreal so we bid good bye to the Hoopers and set out for Montreal.

We had not counted on politics. President de Gaulle had visited Canada only a little earlier. He had made speeches about 'Le Quebec Libre'. This had incited the pre-existing but not very important Quebec separatist movement and infuriated the unionist majority both French- and English-speaking. The French Consulate General and all its staff had had to go into hiding! Neither the police nor the telephone enquiries would tell us where to find the Dumonts so after a couple of hours lost in these vain enquiries we set off for Quebec city. We had dinner in Quebec city but decided to carry on. Finally, we spent the night in a motel in the village of St. Anne de la Pocatiere on the right bank of the mighty St.Lawrence river.

Our route by the excellent motorway next morning lay through Trois Rivieres to a place with the strange-sounding name of St. LOUIS DU HA! HA! where we had to leave the motorway and turn right for New Brunswick. We got there and found that snow had fallen in the night but there was brilliant sunshine again. Kirat and I had been wondering about the name and she conjectured that St. Louis was a very big and important city and for a village to have aspired to the same name must have provoked hilarity.

The reality was different. When we got to the middle of the village, I noticed a large building on the left some distance away but there was something unusual about the well-kept lawn in between. I got out of the car and walked towards the house and noticed a deep ditch in front of me. It was quite dry and at the bottom was a well-kept hedge. The ditch and the hedge made the house quite inaccessible from the road but did not interfere with the view. According to the New Oxford Dictionary of English the English spelling of such a barrier is ha-ha. The French spelling is as above.

When planning the day's journey we had not been aware that New Brunswick is in a different time zone from Quebec and when we got to Frederickton we realised that it was too late to go to the Liveseys for lunch so we went to a McDonald's. Arun had introduced us to such an establishment in Brunswick, Maine and we had found the food tasty, wholesome and very economical – only one U.S.$ in those days for a hamburger, a salad and a coke.

After this, of course, we went and had a substantial tea with the Liveseys. Since our last meeting they had had four children. Derek was complaining of a 'frozen' right shoulder for which he had still not found a cure although he had tried several. I never saw him again but we kept on exchanging letters in our annual greetings cards. Two or three decades later the reply to my letter was from Lois who did not remember my name. She said Derek and one of her sons had both died of cancer in the same year. The frozen shoulder had turned into a cancer.

Motels were really very convenient and economical. I had first heard of them in the Philippines. The Philippino wife of an American who had settled in Manila and made a successful career as a broadcaster told me that they were building a motel on the road to Baguio. I told her that I would like to know where it was so that I might stay there on my next trip. She seemed horrified at the idea and said, 'No, no, it is not for you, Mr. Ambassador.' I realised later that, in the Philippines, motels are used for illegitimate and even criminal purposes.

It may be so in North America also but, in my brief experience, I saw plenty of obviously decent tourist families like ourselves using them. On this occasion, after tea in Frederickton we stopped in what I would call a village but, in North America is called a town. After we had occupied our rooms, we asked where we could have dinner and the receptionist pointed to a bar across the road. We went in and I thought we were in a film because we saw all the characters one sees in an American movie, the sheriff, the bar owner, the police chief and so on. They were very friendly and made us feel at home. We also had a satisfying meal.

Of course the next day we were in Brunswick and Arun took us to a good restaurant which specialised in beef which was served to us from a tea trolley (chuck wagon) by a waiter who cut slices from a large joint. Compared to a McDonald's it was expensive. Still, we saw what an American restaurant is, apart from a hotel.

We were sad leaving Arun but it had to be. We drove down to New York, returned the hired car, and went to the hotel found for us by the Consulate General. We walked a good deal in New York because the taxis were too expensive. The only shops we could afford to go into were the large department stores. In any case, we could not buy very much because of the limitations imposed by air travel.

We were excited about getting to London because we were going to see our grandson. He had been born in August and it was now the middle of November. Kiran and Susan were living in very cramped accommodation in a house belonging to a Sri Lankan. They had bought a second hand Volkswagen Beetle which turned out to be a very good buy.

Harinder had done very well for himself. He had rented a large basement flat near Paddington and bought a Ro-80. This car went out of production shortly afterwards and very few were ever made so I should describe it. It was large for an English car and did not have cylinders. It had what was called a rotary engine hence the Ro in the name. It was quite expensive – only a little cheaper than a Jaguar - and not economical to run but the performance was fantastic. Harinder said he had reached a speed of 130 m.p.h. I never drove it but I could see that the acceleration was tremendous. We stayed with Harinder and Kiran and his family spent most of the day there also. There was a little grocery shop across the road from the block of flats which I would pop into all the time to buy bread or milk or whatever was immediately needed because the kitchen was small and the refrigerator was tiny. The basement flat had not been designed to hold six people.

The baby, named Arjun, had been born on 25th August and he was, of course, the centre of everybody's attention. There had been a lot of discussion over the name. At one time, Kiran and Susan had been very keen that one of the names should be English, – and finally he was registered under the name ARJUN BIR PAUL SINGH keeping up with family traditions. I have often had difficulty, when talking to foreigners, in explaining that he is not his uncle Arun. They have always been very good friends but that is not identity.

For myself, I found it difficult to take much interest in a three-month-old baby – I never could. I could not foresee that one day he would be my closest friend and favourite travelling companion. It has been said that there is a generation gap between parents and children but grandparents and grand-children are natural allies! Anyway, we continue to be good friends even now in the twenty-first century when he has his own wife and child to love and look after. Something we have in common is that we are both only children. This could not be foreseen at the time of his birth. Kiran and Susan were both keen to have another child but for various medical reasons they never had one. Kiran saw to it that he was not spoilt in consequence of being an only child just as Pitaji had made sure that I was not spoilt. Only children are generally spoilt which does not help them in life.

My own interests at that time were different. It was wonderful to be in the London that I loved. I could take the entire family for lunch at the National Liberal Club. I could go shopping for accessories in Jermyn street and we had a good time going to Regent's Park. How could I go shopping in London and not in New York which, at that time, was cheaper? I have mentioned the problem of carrying goods when travelling by air. Well, I realised in London that Air India would let me carry a hundred kilos per head on transfer – we bought a trunk because the rest of the journey up to Bangkok would all be by Air India.

There was no getting away from the fact that England had changed. The 'deferential society' mentioned by Louis Heren had disappeared much earlier. Now, near Paddington I noticed crowds of dark-skinned West Indian children which were, for me, a new phenomenon. It seemed that there was a school in the neighbourhood which only had black children; this was strange because the flat in which Harinder lived (I think St. Mary's Terrace) appeared to be typically middle class. Harinder himself was not averse to *non-U* work. He had had a stall in a weekly market, he told me, which had been quite profitable. Of course, he was a born salesman even if the goods he sold were not his to sell.

At that moment, things seemed to be going well for Harinder. He had an office in another basement in a residential locality where I had occasionally stayed myself in my student days and there was a good-looking young Gujrati Muslim woman helping him in the office. He told me that some inspector had turned up and asked why he was not paying social security contribution for her. He had replied that she was his 'sales force' working on a commission basis. He was importing textiles from India by air and selling them to retailers in London. Kiran was helping him with his books so that part of the business was irreproachable.

We left London after a fortnight satisfied that everybody was all right.

The stay in Delhi was uneventful. My predecessor in Bangkok was my old friend Romesh Bhandari who had already left for another post. I was told that a new First Secretary (Press) named Usha Nath was going out at the same time and I met her. She had grey eyes which is unusual in India and was only a year or so younger than I. She was to have the local rank of Counsellor. She had been taken into the Indian Foreign Service from the defunct Information Service of India. In addition to being Ambassador to Thailand I was to be the Permanent Representative to the United Nations in Bangkok.

Bangkok was the hub for the various U.N. bodies in South East Asia. It was also the seat of the Economic Commission for Asia and the Far East. This large and important body had a legislative session every year held alternately in Bangkok and in other capitals. One was due to be held in New Delhi shortly. For taking care of the U.N. affairs there was a senior First Secretary with the local rank of Counsellor. His name was Amar Nath Ram. He was an Andhra married to the good looking daughter of a former President of India. I had met him during the UNCTAD session in Santiago when he had been introduced to me as a member of the Bhutanese delegation. I had stared in surprise because Andhras do not look at all like Bhutanese. He had laughed and explained that he was a member of the Indian Foreign Service on deputation to Bhutan with the object of forming and training the infant Bhutanese Foreign Service. Since then he had returned to us with the valuable experience he had acquired of U.N. problems and procedures.

I called on the Prime Minister. She had forgotten or, more likely, lost interest in Chile. India was in no hurry to send another Ambassador to Santiago which would constitute formal recognition of the military government.

BANGKOK 1974-77

We arrived in Bangkok to find a spacious two storey house situated in a pleasant garden with a lotus pond adjoining the verandah which surrounded the large drawing-dining room. This space had raw silk curtains and upholstery. A curtain of the same material separated the dining area from the drawing room. There were four large bedrooms and a library upstairs with bathrooms attached. All these rooms were provided with air conditioners by the landlord – a middle-aged woman who spoke very little English and created no problems for us. Connected to the house by an open, covered parking space for two cars was another structure which contained the kitchen and several servants' quarters with arrangements for bathing, flush toilets and washing. We had our two Indian servants and we found a couple of Nepalese maids already in place whom we engaged immediately.

The government provided two doormen/watchmen who lived on the premises. The driver – an Indian from Gorakhpur in U.P. - also lived there but he had a Thai Muslim wife and children who lived elsewhere and she appeared from time to time.

Before I arrived in Bangkok I knew that there were communities of Gorakhpuris in Burma and Thailand. I think it is generally known that in Asia there is a dividing line between milk drinkers and those who traditionally do not know milk. Kirat had noticed in Japan that there was a word *gyunyu* for mother's milk but any other milk was only known by its English name. In the Philippines

1975 Bangkok, Thailand The Embassy Residence.

a draft animal called 'carabao' could be interbred with the Indian milch buffalo and the Indian government had donated buffalo bulls with high 'dam lactations' to enable milk to be produced in that country.

The Thais had felt the need for milk, milch cattle and milkmen before Indian Independence and had imported them from Gorakhpur. So numerous was the Gorakhpuri community in Thailand and Burma that the Bharat Overseas Bank which had an important presence in South East Asia had opened a branch in Gorakhpur. Hence my Gorakhpuri chauffeur in Bangkok and his son in the Indian consulate in Chiengmai.

To get back to the house, the lotus pond had interesting hydrology. The level of water in it rose and fell with the level of the Chao Phray river which was nowhere in sight. Bangkok is built on alluvial soil brought down by the river in historical time. The construction of any building of more than a single storey is only possible on piles. The municipal water supply is quite insufficient for multi-storeyed buildings so they all have tubewells with the result that the whole building sinks and the footpaths in areas which have such buildings break up. The cheddi (tower) of Wat

Arun (Temple of the Sun) is of solid masonry, stands as high as a six storey building, was built over two hundred years ago on the right bank of the river and has not shifted! The architects of those days understood these problems like the architect of the Taj Mahal, built appropriately and the Kings did not allow the builders to cheat on pain of death.

In practice, the garden so lovingly maintained by the gardener could not be used in the evening because of mosquitoes and our life was lived in the air conditioned house, the air conditioned car and the air conditioned office. The air conditioned car had its own story. My predecessor had bought it without waiting for sanction because 'the old car has broken down and this is the only Mercedes available at present'. He was destined to have a great career because the Ministry was not authorising air conditioning of cars.

Considering the price of electric power –chargeable to me – we decided not to use the drawing and dining rooms except when entertaining and to live upstairs in the library.

In fact, we did not really settle down immediately because our lift-van had not arrived from Santiago and I had to return to Delhi for the E.S.C.A.P. session while Kirat took the opportunity to spend some time with her parents.

There was not much I could contribute to the E.S.C.A.P. session because New Delhi had all the experts who had experience of these sessions. I remember giving a lunch in my own home for Maramis, the Secretary General and another for Swaraj Paul.

I took the opportunity to go for a 'Bharat Darshan' – a tour of India – because many years had passed since I had last been on one and the links of Thailand were mostly with South India of which I had little experience. In the course of a flight from Cochin to Madras I sat beside a senior I.A.S. Officer who soon became Commerce Secretary in which capacity he made several visits to Bangkok. His name was Alexander and he had a great career in the I.A.S. before taking to politics.

Returning to Bangkok I decided to join the Alliance Francaise. I have always been interested in French literature and in Thailand I met a French Ambassador who seemed more interested in books than in parties and helped me to get French books from which I had been cut off for some years. At the Alliance we could see French films which I had not been able to see in previous postings.

This connection with the French Embassy proved very useful. On 1st April, the Khmer Rouge entered Phnom Penh. A few days later I got a phone call from the French Embassy saying that the French Embassy in Phnom Penh was still functioning – ours had been withdrawn shortly after King Norodom Sihanouk had left Cambodia – and that several Indian citizens had taken refuge in it. The French Embassy was transporting them to the frontier and would we like to take charge of them at a point they indicated?

This created a problem for me. Although Indian Embassies are meant to help Indian citizens in distress within the country of accreditation, spending money on them is another question. Fortunately the Indian community in Thailand proved to be wonderful. I compared notes later with some European Ambassadors and they told me that they had never been able to get such co-operation from their people. I also had come across Indian communities in other countries of which I had not been proud. This time I just had to tell one of my Indian friends about the problem. They paid for the refugees to be transported to one of the two Hindu temples and they were fully taken care of.

An amusing situation arose when a Muslim turned up. There were plenty of mosques in Bangkok but they were for the use of the Malay-speaking Muslims from the southern provinces. We had no means of communicating with them. I had only met one long-resident Indian Muslim in Bangkok. He was a prosperous stationer from Bombay who was married to a Parsi – just as Jinnah had been. He was a very secular Muslim as I am a secular Sikh. I spoke to him and he put up the sole Muslim refugee, but when I talked to him later he seemed to be rather embarrassed by the incident. He spoke English and Gujrati whereas the refugee only knew Urdu!

Some of the refugees came to see me. They were all Sindhi Hindu Bhaibands and it seemed that they had foreseen the arrival of the Khmer Rouge and sent their families away while they earned a little more money and disposed of their stocks. What had taken them by surprise was the violence of the Khmer Rouge. One man gave me a very graphic description of his expulsion from his shop,

'I was alone in my shop as usual when a group of armed men with fixed bayonets entered. They signalled to me to get out. I had hidden a few dollars in the regulator of the ceiling fan against such an eventuality; I made a move to go towards the wall but they made it quite clear to me by their gestures and their body language – they never spoke a word although I understand and speak Khmer - that they would stab me if I did not go straight out to the street.'

I reported this and other similar incidents in a telegram to the Ministry. For a change I got an answer saying that this was a refugee's statement and the stories of refugees are seldom to be believed. The Khmer Rouge were socialists and friends of India and would not harm our citizens. This was in accordance with Nehruvian tradition. Panditji believed in his socialist ideology and was not interested in facts which might go against it. When on a visit to our northern frontier, he had been told by a Section Officer that the Chinese had occupied Aksai Chin – which we considered to be our territory – the Officer was immediately transferred to another post.

Thailand was for many months the only source of information about Cambodia and I kept on sending reports but there was no further comment.

I had, of course, presented my credentials to the King but the ceremony did not give me an opportunity to have a conversation with him. I was told that that access to the King was easier the further one was from Bangkok. For some of the hottest months the Court would move to the hills near Chiengmai. Of course, the Court comprised over a hundred persons and there was appropriate accommodation for all of them but there was no hotel nearer than Chiengmai some forty kilometres away. It was time for me to go to Chiengmai, 'inspect' our Consulate and meet the Indian community.

Apart from the Gorakhpuris, the Indian community in Bangkok was largely composed of Punjabi businessmen. As I have mentioned, there were few prominent Muslims. The majority were Hindus organised around two large and very prominent temples known as 'Vishnu Mandir' and 'Shiv Mandir' irrespective of the mother tongue of the worshippers. Unlike Singapore and Manila, the Punjabis outnumbered the Sindhis.

There were also two Gurudwaras. One of these was in the heart of the town, large and old, in a congested locality. The 'Granthi' (reader of the book) was a talented teacher who ran a very successful school situated in the same building. His alumni occupied prominent positions in the Sikh community all over Thailand. The community which worshipped in this temple was what I would call 'Orthodox'. In Bangkok, it was called 'Akali'.

There was another Gurudwara, situated in a more modern, more fashionable area. It was called the Namdhari Gurudwara. I was never invited to it so I never saw it. There had been a stepson of a paternal aunt of Mataji known to everybody as 'Atma Singh Namdhari'. I had met him. In 1952, he had been a member of the first Lok Sabha (Lower House of the Indian Parliament), was rich and had three wives which was legal at that time. After his death one of his widows was acknowledged and respected by the Namdhari community. I heard people in Bangkok talking about her visit to Thailand some years earlier. Otherwise, I knew nothing about the Namdharis.

Mataji came and visited us in Bangkok. She told me that the Namdhari sect had been founded by a man known as Baba Balak Singh who had been a disciple of Sain Sahib, her great-grandfather and that she had the original letter from Balak Singh to Sain Sahib in Punjabi in Gurmukhi script acknowledging that whatever scriptural knowledge he had he had learnt from Sain Sahib. This document is now in my possession.

The Namdharis were easily distinguishable from other Sikhs by the fact that they were always dressed in white and tied a turban of unusual form exposing both ears. Some of them were very rich but they all had an austere lifestyle. They were vegetarians and teetotallers. I was once invited to a Namdhari wedding. It was distinguishable from a Sikh wedding by the fact that there is a fire lit in front of but some feet away from the Granth Sahib and the couple walk around the fire instead of the Granth Sahib. There are some very admirable features about the ceremony. The groom and the bride are both dressed in white without any jewellery. Some Sikh families ruin themselves for a daughter's wedding. This cannot happen with a Namdhari. If he is too poor even to afford what I have described – fee of the granthi, cost of the fire, hire of the premises – he can approach a rich man who is organising his daughter's marriage and ask to avail of the arrangements he has made and the request is usually cheerfully granted.

I did meet several Namdharis but never got to be really friendly with any of them. Kirat befriended a Namdhari girl who revolted, married the man of her own choice and emigrated to England with him.

Of course such austerity provokes rebellion. In certain restaurants one could order a 'Namdhari Coca-Cola' which was laced with rum – apparently the bottler knew how to cater to his clientele! I do not see many Namdharis in Delhi. I am told there is a wealthy Namdhari community in Nairobi, Kenya.

To return to Chiengmai. The Indian community was not as rich as the one in Bangkok. Later I learnt that a Thai author had written a book in which he said that the European powers had not been able to colonise Siam like the rest of South East Asia but that there had been 'internal colonisation' and the Establishment in Bangkok had established its economic and political domination of the provinces drawing the wealth out of them. He appeared to have been right. We were very well entertained by the Indian community but they seemed to be mainly vegetarians (although few were Namdharis) and I suffered the consequences. They told me that my predecessor, Romesh Bhandari, had persuaded them to pay for the building of a school in the hills for the children of the hill tribes and this was under construction.

This was a remarkable achievement by Romesh. Indian communities are charitable and generous but the beneficiaries of their charity are generally the communities themselves and that too some section which has made the donation. Thus the Gurudwara and the associated school in Bangkok were mainly used by Sikhs of Indian origin or descent, and there were few Thai boys and girls in the school or Buddhists among the worshippers although no respectful, orderly person was turned away from a gududwara.

My predecessor had made the Indian community donate money for a school which would not be attended by any child of Indian ancestry. Land could only be bought in the hills by tribesmen. There were only tribesmen around for miles. No one was more appreciative of this generosity than the King who took a special interest in the tribals. I would benefit by Romesh's action when the school started functioning. In the meantime, I was invited for dinner to the palace when I made my presence known to a Prince in his entourage.

It is time to explain the Thai nobility. There are, and there have always been, old families in Thailand owning land. Members of these families and other well-to-do and/or educated persons can attain high positions in the administration or the armed forces and be known by their offices, Minister, Governor, General, etc. Titles of nobility are only used by descendants of Kings in the tail male. These titles are not hereditary as they are in India or the United Kingdom but come down by one degree with each generation until, after four generations they are extinguished and the descendants only retain the right to add *na ayuthya* after their surnames which they seldom do. As the Royal Family and others practised polygamy for many centuries, there are numerous persons entitled to use the four titles I have referred to but in English they are generally referred to as Prince.

There were several Princes in Chiengmai including one I had known as Ambassador in the Philippines. However, there was one (he had a house in Bangkok also and carried the title – third grade – of Mom Rajawongse) who by his closeness to the King was assigned all kinds of duties like observing the construction of the school referred to above. In conversation, when people in Chiengmai said 'The Prince', they referred to him. He had called on me in Bangkok and he was the one I contacted on arrival in Chiengmai.

I will continue the story of the school which covers a couple of years. My next visit was on the occasion of the opening of the school. This was done by Queen Sirikit who is famous for her beauty and charm. All the prominent Indians of Chiengmai were present for the occasion. One man, who had donated generously was not proficient in English and said to the Queen,

'Sir, we are in paradise.'

The Queen was not upset by the form of address and understood that this man of humble origin was expressing gratitude for the fortune he had been able to make in Chiengmai. She said to me,

'We are happy to have these people here. By their activity they contribute to our prosperity.'

I noticed that the tribal children looked beautiful with their light skins and rosy cheeks but men and particularly women in their late twenties looked much older than their age. I discussed this with the King and the local authorities and the consensus was that they did not get good medical facilities and that the traditional huts in which they lived were full of smoke because they had only one room and no adequate chimneys to let out the smoke from the fire. Attempts at providing chimneys had not been successful because the smoke kept the mosquitoes out and when it was eliminated the incidence of malaria went up!

While the first generation of Indian immigrants in Thailand had little education, their children could get Indian government scholarships with the result that there were two medical practitioners in the Indian community. I asked then if they would like to help the hill tribes particularly the children in the school. They were willing but the problem was transportation. In the city they could get around by public transport or their cars but to get to the tribes required off the road vehicles. A Japanese utility vehicle was identified but the customs duty on such vehicles was high. Finally, the vehicle was paid for by generous businessmen in Bangkok and presented to His Majesty, thus avoiding duty.

In the course of my travels, speaking to Thais in various parts of the country I had heard or sensed a complaint that Indians were not sociable. They did business with the local people but did not join their social organisations or, to use Xenophon's phrase, 'set up an intercourse of hospitality' with them. At one city, I gave a talk on the Parsi community saying that they had come to India over a thousand years ago and done so well that the Chairman of Air India, the Chief of the Army Staff and the head of the largest Industrial company were Parsis. The answer was,

'But they do not get assimilated; we had Parsis in Thailand in the seventeenth century and they controlled the rice exports at that time but their descendants intermarried with the local people so that they can no longer be identified.'

I reflected on this and when somebody complained to me in Chiengmai that I had created a perpetual burden on the Indian community by obliging the Indian doctors to look after the hill tribes, I replied,

'Not perpetual, only as long as there is an Indian community.'

'What do you mean?'

'When the Indians get assimilated with the local population, there will not be an 'Indian community''.

I could see that my remark was not appreciated. Indians do not like to marry outside their own baradari. In January 2006, an English language newspaper the HINDUSTAN TIMES has carried out a survey and found that a majority of young men and women prefer an arranged marriage. I remember reading an article sixty years earlier by an English woman journalist who travelled to India by ship and got to know an Indian girl returning from a long period of studies in England where she had been held up by the war. She asked her how she expected to get married and got the reply,

'I am not bad looking. I know several young men I met in England who are not married. In this post-war society there should be no problem in marrying a man of my choice.' She met her again in India six months later and asked if she was engaged. The girl appeared to be embarrassed by the question and answered,

'It is strange. The men I mentioned to you last time and several others are happy to invite me to lunch in restaurants, but about marriage they do not wish to talk. I have the feeling that they would prefer a bride chosen by their mother with an appropriate dowry.'

Dowry is a problem. Dowry as a condition *sine qua non* for a marriage is now illegal and asking for or accepting it is a criminal offence but, in fact, it still exists. However, there are, and there have always been plenty of marriages without a dowry. I have not come across a case of dowry in my own baradri. And, of course, there have been for a hundred years 'love' marriages which parents have refused to attend. I know couples across castes, even across religions and some where the only common language between husband and wife is English.

In India, Indira Gandhi had declared an Emergency because her own election to the Lok Sabha had been disputed and the opposition to some of the activities of her son Sanjay had become very serious. I did not know Sanjay but his reputation had been bad for a long time.

He had been a friend and classmate of Adil, the son of my colleague and friend Mohammed Yunus. Adil was a juvenile delinquent and had created unending problems for his father. I should explain that Yunus was one of the scores of sons of the Wali of Swat – a princely state in the North West Frontier Province – of course a part of Pakistan after Independence. Yunus was a little older than me. He had taken some part – probably as a lark – in the Independence movement but there he had met Pandit Nehru. Yunus's own father had not taken much notice of this particular son who did not have much interest in the Wali's pastimes. Pandit Nehru took a liking to this young man and he became the son the Pandit never had. Yunus's loyalty to the Nehru family became legendary. He opted for India after Independence and was appointed to the Indian Foreign Service, as far as any one could make out, only for this reason. Later, when Pandit Nehru became Prime Minister and his daughter became his hostess, it became clear that Indira and her aunt, Vijaylakshmi Pandit could not stand each other, Yunus would not tolerate any criticism of either of them.

Apart from the talk in Delhi society I knew of Sanjay Gandhi's activities from Yunus who would talk of his son's car accident - after which he was so badly injured that he had to spend several weeks in hospital - and his brushes with the police without at all criticising the behaviour of his associate in his pranks.

To return to the Emergency, it was very unpopular with everybody I knew. I, of course, avoided talking about it even in the company of close relations and friends and I was surprised to hear it criticised by a friend of mine, Ajit Mozumdar – a Secretary to the Government of India - in an official party.

I did write to the Ministry saying that the Emergency was no concern of mine but I had to say that Press Censorship was being criticised by Thai journalists although in Thailand I did not consider the Press to be very free. Of course, there was no response.

As I have mentioned, there were a lot of international meetings, big and small, in Bangkok. A regular feature was the annual 'legislative' session of ESCAP. Two years running the Indian delegation was led by Vishwanath Pratap Singh, at that time Minister of State. On the first of these occasions I gave a cocktail party for him. At the end of the party, to my surprise, Kirat brought out a small silver sugar bowl and gave it to him. The following year, on the same occasion, I went to the airport to receive him. This meant spending an hour in the then horrible traffic of Bangkok and another hour in his company on the way from the airport to the hotel where he was staying. I accompanied him to his room when he asked me if we could go for a walk. I explained to him that there were no parks in Bangkok where one could walk and all we would be able to do was to walk on the footpath in front of the shops since the hotel was in a shopping area. He said that would do. We walked into a small jewellery shop where the shopkeeper was busy with some customers. V.P.Singh took me to the other end of the shop, pretended to look at some of the showcases and took the little silver bowl out of his trouser pocket and said,

'Last year your wife gave me this present and I accepted it because it was a sincere gift given out of friendship and affection without any ulterior motive. However, when I got back to Delhi, I consulted the rules and I find that I can not accept it. Would you please take it back and explain the position to your wife?'

Kirat gave many presents to Ministers and others but, in all my career, this as the only such experience of ministerial integrity that I came across. As everybody knows, V.P.Singh went on to become Prime Minister of India but was not a success in that capacity. An honest man can hardly expect to be popular with politicians.

Another visitor whom I saw a great deal of was Pranab Mukherjee, at present (February 2006) Minister of Defence. He came to Bangkok leading a delegation from the Ministry of Finance in which he was Deputy Minister. The occasion was a meeting on Regional Economic policies. I had been asked to arrange meetings with various Ministers and I had done so. The delegation was holding its strategy meeting at the other end of my rather large office but I had not been asked to join it. I was, however, listening to their discussions. Finally, they invited me to join. I said,

'You have been talking about what you will discuss with the Thai Minister of Finance. You can not discuss these specific matters with him because he is a pure politician and knows nothing about international economic policy; besides he speaks no English.'

'Then, with whom will we discuss these important topics?'

'With the Minister of Commerce whom you are meeting the following day. He speaks English, is quite knowledgeable and will be accompanied by his Secretary General whom you will probably recognise because he is a veteran of many such meetings.'

And so it turned out.

On another occasion a 'workshop' was organised relating to labour problems. India sent a delegation headed by a junior Minister. He was looked after by Amar Nath Ram who dealt with all U.N. matters and seldom bothered me about them. Halfway through the workshop the Minister came to see me. He said that he was unhappy about what he was reading in the English-language Thai papers about the Indian Emergency which was not all bad and he felt he should like to talk to the Thai Minister of Labour about it. I replied,

'I will show you what I wrote to our Ministry on this topic about which I cannot do anything. There is no Labour Minister in Thailand, the department is looked after by the Minister of the Interior. I will try and get you an interview.'

I got the interview two days later. Of course I accompanied the Minister. In the car I said to him,

'Mr. Minister, the Minister of the Interior speaks no English but there will be an interpreter and you will have no difficulty.'

'What exactly do you mean?'

'You will see.'

When we entered the Office of the Minister of the Interior, he got up, smiled, bowed, shook our hands and immediately turned to the interpreter and made a fairly long speech of which we understood nothing at all until he had finished and the Interpreter said,

'Your Excellency, before you say anything, I would like to take this opportunity to request you to convey to your Prime Minister my felicitations on the declaration of the Emergency. Democracies like ours and yours are taken advantage of by irresponsible and unpatriotic persons to indulge in anti-social activities. I cannot sufficiently say how much we are beset by such miscreants who would like to undo our developmental and other social programmes and destabilize our societies. Prime Minister Indira Gandhi has taken a very statesmanlike decision which will be of lasting benefit to your great country.'

I will say for Indira Gandhi that she realised Ajit Mozumdar's unhappiness with the Emergency and instead of scolding or penalising him for his openly expressed views, she posted him to the Asian Development where he got a salary several times higher than that of a Secretary to the Government of India. I have known Ajit since 1947 and his career has proved his outstanding ability. On his way to Manila he stopped over in Bangkok rather than in Hong Kong where the shopping was much better. A few weeks later, his beautiful and charming wife Maya also stayed with us.

Again I will say for Ajit that when the Emergency ended, there was an election which the Congress party lost and H.M.Patel became Minister of Finance, Ajit immediately wrote to him and asked for his job back in the Ministry of Finance and got it, throwing away the 'fortune' he had been making entirely legally in the Asian Development Bank. It was from him and his wife that I got this story.

To return to the Emergency, it is obvious that I am not particularly interested in political theories but have taken to heart the advice given by Talleyrand to an Ambassador he was briefing,

'Keep a good table and look after the women.'

I found on going through the Embassy records that no Prime Minister of Thailand had ever had dinner at the Embassy – the records may have been defective which I had no means of knowing. I set to work to rectify this situation and invite Prime Minister Kukrit Pramoj to dinner. This was, of course, a long and complicated process and took several months. During this period the Emergency was imposed!

When the Prime Minister came for dinner, the table was excellent but when we got up, the guest of honour came to me from the other end of the table where he had been sitting on Kirat's right and asked me if he could have a word with me. I replied, 'Of course, Your Excellency' and took him to a corner where he asked,

'As you know I have been in the Opposition for most of my political life so my friends have been opposition politicians. Tell me, with this Emergency that your Prime Minister has declared, are all my friends in prison?'

It was just as well that his Cabinet colleague the Minister of the Interior did not share his views.

It was some time after this that I was told that two couples wanted to spend three days in Bangkok. I offered to put them up at the Embassy for the very good reason that they were Rajiv and Sonia Gandhi and Ajitabh Bacchan and his wife.

I did not know any of them. Of course, I knew that Ajitabh was the younger brother of Amitabh whom I had recently seen in the film SHOLAY (sparks) which the Indian community had got for a special showing. He was considerably shorter in stature than his elder brother and his wife was a Sindhi with an exceptionally light complexion – she could have passed for a beautiful young white woman.

I had met Harivansh Bacchan, the father of my guest, when he was Officer on Special Duty (Hindi) a score of years earlier in the Ministry of External Affairs. He had the reputation of being the greatest living Hindi poet but, owing to our bureaucratic ways, this appointment was the only way that the Government of India could show its appreciation of his eminence. I had met him in 1956 in the office of the Under Secretary (Foreign Service Personnel), M.K.Rasagotra who was destined to become the Foreign Secretary and to hold some of the most prestigious posts under the Government of India. The fact that he was entertaining the Hindi poet to a cup of tea was evidence of the variety and breadth of his interests. To my surprise, Bacchan had asked the man who brought the tea, 'Tumhari health kaisi hai?' and I voiced my surprise. Bacchan said that there was a word, *tandrusti,* for health but it was less well-known even to Hindi speakers than the English word!

Sonia Gandhi, seen close up, was much prettier than in the newspaper photographs I had seen of her. They had breakfast with us but they spent most of their time sightseeing. Sonia hardly ever spoke; it was hard to get a word out of her. Rajiv's conversation related mostly to sight-seeing topics. It was quite obvious that there was no political motive to their visit. I had been informed verbally that they did not want to meet anybody and I was not to arrange any party for them.

I had some concern about the security of the elder son of the Prime Minister of India in a country with a large and well-to-do India community some of whom might not harbour the best feelings for the Government – particularly after the Emergency. However, the Counsellor dealing with passports and visas was, in fact, an Officer from the Home Ministry and he told me that he had been authorised to take care of the security aspect in collaboration with the Thai government.

From all that I had heard of Sanjay Gandhi, I was feeling rather apprehensive about dealing with his elder brother and sister-in-law. To my delight, no one could have been more polite, well-bred and better behaved. I only regretted that I could not introduce them to Thai royalty and society. A few days after they left, Kirat and I received a very nice letter and a gift of an Italian crystal objet d'art.

Many men who have the opportunity of entertaining the future Prime Minister of India as a houseguest would be able to use it to make a political career for themselves. It is obvious that I am completely devoid of political ability because I never got any appointment after my retirement. However, Sonia Gandhi and her husband, until his tragic assassination have always recognised me on the rare occasions when we have met.

Bangkok had turned out to be a fascinating and challenging post. The bad climate was amply compensated by the charm of the people and the interest and variety of the work I had had to do. I recall going to a party given by an Indian merchant where I saw a Sikh of about my own age. I asked him,

'What is your line if business?'

'Sir, I am not a businessman, I am an I.A.S.Officer, my name is Avtar Singh Bawa. I am from the Orissa cadre. In Cuttack I have met your uncle, Mr.Gajinder Singh Malik.'

'Don't call me 'Sir', you must be of the same age and rank as I am. What on earth are you doing here?'

'I am on deputation to the Food and Agriculture Organisation. My last post was in Delhi. I was a Joint Secretary in the Ministry of Food and Agriculture. I hope to return to that post after my six months deputation here.'

A few months later I met him again so I asked him,

'I thought your deputation was only for six months?'

'I am the prisoner of my greed.'

'What on earth do you mean?'

'In Delhi our problem was that I could not buy my wife a new sari every month and if we broke a teacup, it was a problem to replace it. Now my wife has enough saris to last her the rest of her life and there is no space in the flat for any more crockery so we are going home soon.'

'What is wrong with having enough money?'

'It is the work. As a Joint Secretary in Delhi, a new project would arrive on my desk every day, sometimes there was a second project in the afternoon. I would examine the project and if I liked it, it would usually be authorised. I could have the satisfaction of monitoring the project and each project would change the lives of a thousand persons. Here, in nearly a year, I have only had one project to study which I originated myself and I know it has collapsed because it was for Cambodia and that country is now in chaos.'

Unfortunately, I learnt from my cousin Preet (Gajinder Singh's son) that Avtar Singh did not live long.

The time was coming for me to be transferred to my last post and I was called to Delhi for some work. While there, I was told that the National Defence College was going on a study tour which would include three days in Thailand. I went to the war College and found that its students were Officers of the three Armed Forces of the rank of Brigadier. The Directing Staff told me that the group would be looked after by the Thai Ministry of Defence under a reciprocal arrangement but they would like me to give a party. I told them that I was under orders of transfer and I would combine the party with my own farewell party so they would meet a lot of top people. They were happy with the arrangement.

Kirat had already left for Poona and most of our luggage was packed up to go by sea to Spain. I decided to give the party in the Royal Bangkok Sports Club. I should explain that since Thailand was never colonised by a European power, it had 'grown like Topsy' without an overall plan. Individual landowners when developing their land as the growing city approached it could lay out streets to give access to the housing plots which they sold to house builders but without much consideration for the ever-enlarging city as a whole. The result was that there were no parks or large open spaces like sports fields or stadiums. I did not make any attempt to study the history of the city but I suppose that European and American sportsmen in the latter half of the nineteenth century decided to invest in a racecourse and bought a very large plot for this purpose. On this, they not only built a track and stands for horse races but they were also able to have a golf course – within the perimeter of the racetrack. I was even able to start a cricket match between Indian and Thai teams. One diplomat joined the club just so as to do his morning jogging!

I therefore held my farewell cocktail party on a wet monsoon evening. In 1977, traffic in Bangkok was very bad and one could usually attend only one party in an evening. The rain that day was so heavy that some shopping streets were more accessible by boat – like the shikaras in Srinagar – than by car. The guests at my party were only half of what I expected and they arrived late. One Indian Air Force Officer seeing me standing alone near the door to welcome the guests who had not come, asked if he could have a word with me. Of course, he could,

'Sir, we have been twenty-four hours in Bangkok of which we have spent more than ten in the bus, owing to the traffic. This has given me an unparalleled opportunity to study the people on the footpaths. I have observed how they walk, how they talk to each other, how they greet friends they meet by chance and how they manage to deal with the pedestrian traffic. It seems to me that Indians and Thais started from the same place. Where have we gone wrong?'

The question though completely unexpected made perfect sense. Thailand is known as the 'Land of Smiles'. I once saw a calendar with the subject of 'Brides of India'. Half the brides were 'tribal' while the other six represented the 'settled population' of different states. All the tribal brides were smiling; the others were not. Why are we so serious? Anyway I had to give a prompt answer so I said,

'We made the mistake of having a geographical situation which was accessible to invaders of an alien culture.'

Even as I gave this facile answer, I knew that it was not truthful but I am too slow-witted to think out a brief and correct answer. Even nearly thirty years later, I do not have a brief answer. It is true that with the several invasions between the eleventh and eighteenth centuries which we were unable to repulse militarily, Hindu civilisation ceased to grow and could only survive in a fossilised condition by becoming totally conservative and ritualistic. But there was another side to the medal. Afghans, Turks and especially Iranians had very advanced civilisations – two-and-a-half centuries ago Edward Gibbon could refer to the 'polite and peaceful nations of India, China and Persia' – and they have enriched India greatly but the attempts to fuse them together like Sufi-ism and the Emperor Akbar's 'Deen Illahi' have had very little success. It is only after the Europeans in Bengal in the eighteenth century were able to penetrate the hard shell of Hindu conservatism that the majority community could think of a renaissance.

Again, that is not the whole story. There is something to be said for the national character of the Thais. Not only do they smile a lot but I think they created the original 'permissive society.' Nearly a thousand years ago, King Ramkamheng whose capital was in the North – the Thais had only recently arrived from Yunnan in China where there is still a Thai ethnic minority – carved a stone edict which says, 'This Sukhothai is a good place. There is fish in the water, there is rice in the field. Whosoever wishes to dance, dances. Whosoever wishes to trade in horses so trades...'

We in India do not have this attitude. I think we resemble the Jews in creating and maintaining all kinds of restrictions, dietary and otherwise. We often attach more importance to these taboos than to our fellow-men. Our attitude is best summed up by the mother shouting to her pre-teen daughter, 'See what baby is doing and stop him doing it.' This was, of course, the Victorian attitude which ended in May 1968 with the Parisian slogan, 'It is forbidden to forbid.'

THE TRANSFER: BANGKOK- MADRID 1977

I knew very well that I was going to my last post because the age of compulsory superannuation was 58 and I would attain that on 29th May 1979. I was anxious to get there as early as possible because my linguistic and cultural interests were European and I had not had a posting in Europe since Brussels in 1950. Of course, I could not arrive in Madrid till my predecessor had left. Who was my predecessor? It was V.M.M.Nair who had been chosen for the I.C.S. by the India Office in 1942 in preference to me – He had stood second in the selection while I had got the fourth rank and only two were appointed. I had seldom met him but I knew that he belonged to a very prominent Nair family from Kerala which had several members in the higher civil services. He had been High Commissioner in Kuala Lumpur shortly before I arrived in Singapore in 1959. I had enquired before leaving Bangkok if he was taking 'leave preparatory to retirement and received a negative answer. Obviously he was as keen to stay on in Madrid as I was to get there.

The political situation in India was good for me. The defeat of the Congress in the election had brought to power a coalition of non-Congress parties including a completely new entity which called itself the CONCORD OF INDIA composed mainly of princely families who were furious with Indira Gandhi for taking away the titles and privy purses which Vallabhai Patel had allowed them to keep. The Concord's leader was H.M.Patel because he was the only one with administrative and political experience. The Prime Minister was Morarji Desai, jokingly known as 'Moralji' because of his tendency to preach to the public. He was a Gujrati but he had not been very successful in Gujrat politics because of his idiosyncrasies like prohibition. One of the conditions that other members of the coalition had insisted on for making him Prime Minister was that there would be no attempt to impose prohibition. The fact that H.M.Patel was a Gujrati brought him closer to the Prime Minister than other politicians of longer political experience like Ashok Vajpayee who was destined to serve later as Prime Minister for a long time. I saw a good deal of H.M.Patel during my short stay in New Delhi. I was also lucky that Jagat Mehta who was my batchmate and friend was Foreign Secretary.

Since I was gong to Spain I made a point to go and see the Spanish Ambassador in New Delhi. Fortunately, Leopoldo, Count of Santovenia was an old friend of mine. He had been Ambassador in Dakar and we had often played golf there on the horrible golf course which had 'browns' instead of greens. We had kept in touch in the intervening years and I had met him during some of my visits to New Delhi from Bangkok. His father had died in the meantime and he was entitled to call himself Duque de la Torre instead of Conde de Santovenia. He explained to me that he had not yet gone through the formalities of assuming the title because it was the custom to let some months elapse before doing so. He explained that if the direct heir (son, daughter or grandson) did not claim the title within a year, a collateral (brother, nephew, etc.) could claim. If nobody claimed it within two years of the demise, an ally (brother-in-law, etc.) could do so. This opened the field for many persons. The result is that it is very rare for a Spanish title to become extinct.

Leopoldo invited us for lunch and told me that, if I could afford it, I should go to Madras and call on ex-Queen Frederica of Greece who lived there most of the year. She was the mother-in-law of the King of Spain. I had already realised that the recently-elected Spanish government was not very interested in India and a contact with the Court would be valuable. It was easy for me to apply for a 'Bharat Darshan' (tour of India) before going to a new post and Madras could be fitted into it. Leopoldo gave me the address and telephone number. He also told me that the Manager of Ralli

Brothers in Madras was the Honorary Sheriff of Madras and took care of Queen Frederica because the original Ralli had been Greek.

When I got to Madras, I got in touch with the company and the Manager drove me around in his car which had the sheriff's flag on it. I sent flowers to the Queen and called her on the phone to ask to meet her. She was a charming lady of the average height of an Indian woman and belonged to the Brunswick family. She explained that she lived half the year in Madras because she was interested in the Upanishads which she said were related to the Schroedinger Wave Equation (I know the Schroedinger Wave Equation but any connection between that and Hindu philosophy escapes me completely) and that the greatest exponent of the Upanishads lived in Madras and she attended his lectures. She also said that her grandchildren (the Spanish Infantes) spent part of the winter with her in Madras.

While this conversation was going on, my flowers arrived and produced the desired effect. She invited me for lunch at her club where I also met her daughter Princess Irene who was unmarried and interested in some other aspect of India which she pursued very diligently. Irene showed me her Greek Royal Passport which, somewhat to my surprise, the Republican government had not cancelled and was of 'perpetual validity'! The Queen gave me three of Professor Mahadevan's books which I have since read but to no purpose – I am no wiser than I was before. This acquaintanceship with Queen Sofia's mother was useful to me in Spain.

Returning to New Delhi I felt that a coalition of such disparate elements could not be expected to last very long. The voters took only a few years to forget the harm done by Indira Gandhi's 'kitchen cabinet', mainly Sanjay Gandhi but also my colleague Yunus. I felt that I should move quickly to take advantage of the situation and get my final promotion (to Grade I) before retirement. It would substantially increase my pension and give me other advantages. I spoke to H.M.Patel, he spoke to Jagat Mehta and I got my Grade I.

Since this was to be my last post, I decided to take Mataji with us to Madrid. Of all my postings, she had only accompanied me to Tokyo, Singapore and Bangkok. A passage to Buenos Aires or Santiago would have been too expensive.

The Ministry's rule was that we were to travel by Air India where flights existed and otherwise by surface route which meant by train from Geneva to Madrid. The holidays we had enjoyed in Europe in 1971 and 73 convinced me that travel by car in Europe was much more enjoyable than travel by train and I worked out that travel by rented car for three people staying for three nights in hotels on the way would not cost more than first class rail fares for two. Kiran was living in London and could no longer be described as a dependent and Arun was at Bowdoin.

We arrived in Geneva and the Gharekhans, Rita and her teenage daughter – Chinmaya was our Permanent Representative to the United Nations in Europe but he was not in Geneva just then – very kindly vacated two of the three bedrooms in their flat to accommodate us and Mataji. (Tragically, we learnt some months later that the daughter had succumbed to an asthma attack in New York.)

We rented a car and set off through the mountains of Savoy, down the Rhone Valley, carefully avoiding large cities like Lyon and Marseille to arrive very late in the evening at Carcasonne where all the hotels were full and we got three rooms in a private house after a very unsatisfactory supper. Fortunately, we had had a very good lunch.

Next morning, as soon as it was light we looked around the fairy tale little city with its high walls, romantic towers and view of the countryside surrounding the walled city on the hill. I felt that my choice of a stopover had been fully justified; I don't think either Mataji or Kirat shared this view. The three rooms we had got did not include a bathroom and we had to perform our ablutions with cold water in an open courtyard and had to take a continental breakfast at a pavement café! Fortunately, I found in the Guide Michelin I had bought in Geneva a moderately priced restaurant which we reached at lunchtime to have the best meal of the trip. That night we stayed in an ultra modern NOVOTEL where service was minimal but was otherwise satisfactory.

As we entered Spain on the third day of our trip we bid good-bye to the few motorways we had driven on in France. I must say that the 'routes nationales' in France were also very good. Our first lunch in Spain – Spanish omelette – did not compare with the lunches we had eaten in France. However our arrival in the evening at Segovia was an excellent first night in Spain. The hotel was situated in the main street of Segovia practically in the shadow of the Roman aqueduct which passes over that street. Of course, the aqueduct is no longer in use because the present day Spaniard uses more water than his ancestor twenty centuries earlier and today there are pumps such as the Romans did not have to make the delivery of water to the home that much easier. To cap it all, the dinner that night was the best we had eaten during the whole of the trip.

Something that impressed us was the method the Spanish government has adopted to protect its beautiful old cities. Half a dozen of the best monuments in each city are maintained by converting them into museums or public offices. The rest are allowed to be used by the owners as shops, homes, etc. as long as the façade is not changed or neglected. In fact these old cities are not very convenient for today's much larger needs so new modern living quarters are built outside the walls of the medieval cities. Thus the population is housed in modern cities with all the amenities for present-day living and the beautiful old cities are available to the millions of tourists that Spain welcomes each year.

After this, we arrived in Madrid the following day late in the morning in very good spirits.

MADRID 1977-79

My predecessor was due to retire on 31st October 1977 and I arranged to arrive in Madrid in the middle of the morning, well before lunch on 1st November. I drove up to the Chancery which was situated on the first floor of an office building in a street in the commercial centre. I arrived there, left the family in the car and took the lift to the first floor. When I opened the door of the office flat I was surprised to see two uniformed members of the Guardia Civil – the national police. Anyway, I went up to the middle-aged woman at the reception desk and said, in Spanish,

'My name is Malik, I am the new Ambassador.'

'Yes, Mr. Ambassador, I am the receptionist and am called Zara – it is a Basque name.'

Zara spoke good English and was a useful member of the team. Occasionally, she took a fortnight's leave to conduct a tour group to India. I liked that because it gave her knowledge and experience of India without costing the Embassy a penny. While I was there, she got engaged to a non-diplomatic official of the British Embassy. They are both retired now, live mostly in Eastern Spain, and we exchange New Year cards every year.

Of course, I went into my office and all the staff came in to greet me. The only Diplomatic Officer was the Second Secretary, Parthasarathy Ray. He is now (February 2006) Ambassador in Copenhagen. He and his wife Sujata were very helpful. I enquired about our servants, Nainar and Sri Ram. They were supposed to have arrived by train from Geneva with the 200 kilos of luggage which Air India had carried for us from Delhi to Geneva. Apparently there had been some problem about accommodating them for the two nights they had been there.

In the course of this conversation I got the impression that V.M.M.Nair had been in the office that morning. One of the staff seemed to be making frantic phone calls to the Embassy Residence to get him out of there!

I gave the rented car back, we transferred to the Ambassadorial Mercedes and were driven to the residence which turned out to be a seven-bedroom flat in a residential development in the midst of open fields fourteen kilometres away!

We took the lift and when we got to the landing, there was a strong smell of curry powder. We were told that a consignment had arrived from India some weeks ago and the package had split open. It took several weeks to get rid of the smell.

The flat was large, well-heated – it was already November – and comfortable. However, its location was unfortunate. There was no custom in Spain of newspapers being delivered early

1977 Madrid, Spain Seated from left: Susan, Arun, Sujata (a friend of Arun's), Kiran, Arjun, Kirat, and me. Standing: The servants, Nainar and Sri Ram..

in the morning. The result was that one newspaper arrived by post a day late, generally after I had left for the Chancery. The other papers – I particularly appreciated the International Herald Tribune - I only received in the Chancery. This upset me greatly because I was not accustomed to this practice. There were no shops nearer than five kilometres away; if we wanted aspirin or a toothpaste, we had to get into the car and go to the nearest village. And fourteen kilometres was a long way to office. The advantages were the clean air and the open fields round about. I decided that if I achieved nothing else in my nineteen months in Madrid I must change the Embassy Residence.

The mystery of the policemen in the Chancery was explained to me as being due to an anonymous threat received earlier that year which had caused the Ambassador to ask the Spanish Government for protection. Of course, much depended on the character and personality of the policemen. While generally they were well-behaved, occasionally the individuals were noisy and unsuitable for an Embassy. The following year I got rid of them. It was only after I retired that the Government of India cracked down on the 'Anand Marg' a terrorist organisation claiming to be of Bengali Hindu origin. Two of the men arrested said they had wanted to attack the Indian Embassy in Madrid but found it 'too well protected'. My predecessor had been wise and I had been lucky.

I was able to present my credentials within a fortnight after my arrival. In this, my last Embassy, I was able for the only time in my life to travel in a coach drawn by six horses. A nineteenth century German scholar had written his doctoral thesis on the 'Right of an Ambassador to drive in a six-horse carriage'. In Tokyo as a First Secretary I had followed C.S.Jha's coach in one with two horses. Very few people in the twenty-first century travel in horse drawn vehicles and the hallowed phrase, 'The postillion has been struck by lightning' is hard to understand. Equally incomprehensible is the importance of Ambassadorial coaches in diplomatic histories. There was an incident involving the coach of the Russian Ambassador in London in the early eighteenth century. Queen Anne wrote a letter of apology to Peter the Great and promised to rectify the 'defect in our laws'. The result was the 'Act of the eleventh of Anne' which governed the protocol rules of Commonwealth countries until the middle of the twentieth century.

Why had V.M.M. Nair rented a flat so far away for his Chancery? He has told me it was because of the good heating arrangements. Another factor may have been that this whole development belonged to a co-operative of Spanish diplomats who had chosen to invest their pension fund in this housing estate in the 'green fields.'

For some years the Ministry of External Affairs had been wanting to acquire property abroad rather than to go on paying ever-increasing rents. It has been the practice of the Government of India not to pay large lump sums to its personnel abroad and leave them to fend for themselves as is the case of many Latin American countries. The salaries of Indian Government servants are necessarily related to the Indian economy. If they are to live in Manhattan, they would probably need fifty times as much. I have heard of a Latin American Consul having his Office in a hotel and sleeping on his desk! Our practice was of providing free furnished accommodation and then giving allowances which can only be spent on the facility required e.g. leave passages.

About buying property, I had met with failure in Chile as I have described. To obviate such an eventuality, I had consulted the officials dealing with these problems in the Ministry on my way to Madrid. The Deputy Secretary (Establishment) would deal with the mechanics but, of course, the final decision would be taken at a higher level. I had met her – she was a Kannadiga (from the State of Karnataka) as far as I can remember. She must have been in her thirties and I was told she had divorced more than one husband. My recollection is that she was quite a large woman very smartly dressed in an impeccably starched and ironed cotton sari.

In Madrid I found that the oldest Embassy residencies were in the centre of the city but the British Ambassador was moving out to a twentieth century area which had become fashionable. Madrid is situated to the south of a very large forest in which only Spanish Kings could hunt and much of this forest is at present inaccessible to the public. General Franco was very fond of hunting and continued the old Royal prohibitions. The access to that part of the forest which the public may visit is through a square in the middle of which there is a small iron gate – PUERTA DE HIERRO in Spanish. Some of General Franco's friends persuaded him to let them buy an area near this gate and build houses there. This area is called by the name Puerta de Hierro and some of its houses had, by the time I arrived in Spain, been bought or rented by foreign Embassies. In fact, Nair's predecessor had lived in one of these houses which was now on sale but it was quite uncomfortable to live in.

After seeing several houses, I found one which seemed suitable. The owner wanted nine-tenths of the price paid to him in Sterling as 'finder's fee' but our legal adviser said such a procedure would not be legal. Then, the owner came up with proposal that he should be paid by four cheques only one of which he would take to the Registry Office. The legal adviser approved the scheme and I sent it with plans etc. to the Ministry saying that if the money arrived in the Embassy account, I would take it that the scheme was approved.

Naturally, all this correspondence and the payment in four instalments took several months but, in the latter part of 1978, we moved in. One fine day a few weeks before I was to retire, a letter arrived from the Deputy Secretary (Establishment) pointing out that the property had been registered for a quarter of the money disbursed by the Embassy and asking what I had done with the rest.

Naturally, I was incensed. I got hold of the papers and typed out a one-page letter to the Foreign Secretary giving the numbers and dates of the diplomatic bags by which my earlier letter and four signed and stamped receipts had been sent to the Ministry as also the details of the receipts of these bags in the Ministry. My letter ended with the question, ' Would it not be better to have someone at that desk who can read?' I heard no more about it. When I arrived in Delhi, one of my friends in the Ministry said he had seen the deputy Secretary's letter and been shocked by it. He told me she had gone on leave. Later I learnt that she never rejoined duty. The last I know of her was an item in a newspaper that she had died from an overdose of a drug she was taking for her asthma.

There was in the Embassy a local recruit who was in fact an Indian. Such employees exist in many of our Embassies. He was a Punjabi who must have come to Madrid to study, married a local girl and not gone back home. He spoke Spanish fluently but his syntax was imperfect. On the other hand, he was brash and pushing so he was good at dealing with artisans and tradesmen. I would ask him to accompany visitors from India who wanted to go shopping or see the night life of a 'city which never sleeps'. The visitors were delighted with him and thought that he should be promoted to a better job. I even got an enquiry from the Ministry about this. My predecessor, who did not speak Spanish, had found him indispensable. He possessed a new Mercedes Benz which had a TOURIST number plate which meant that it had been imported without paying customs duty for a period of less than a year. How he paid for it I never found out. I myself purchased a second hand Volkswagen Passat from a Hungarian Embassy employee who was not a diplomat.

One day an Indian politician arrived whose interests were cultural and aesthetic and I decided to take him myself to the Prado Palace – one of the most famous picture galleries in Europe. As they were informed of our coming, we were received by a very young, pretty, English-speaking guide. She showed us round including the room which contained eight rather frightening Goyas. Then we came to a large room in which there was a round table made of dark red marble with an inlaid top and the girl said,

'This table was built to commemorate the battle of Lepanto.'

'Battle of Lepanto, when was that?' asked my guest. The guide seemed at a loss so I volunteered,

'It was at the end of August, beginning of September. It lasted rather a long time because Don John of Austria who was in overall command insisted that all the Turkish ships should be destroyed and the Marques de Santa Cruz who was the Admiral of the Spanish squadrons had to chase them into several creeks where they had taken shelter and capture or burn them. I can't put it more precisely than that.'

'What year?' asked the politician.

'Oh! 1572.' (In fact I was wrong; the battle took place in 1571 and the news reached the Philippines the following year when the Governor General named the largest copper mine after this historic event.)

'How is it that you know so much about it and she doesn't?'

'How could she possibly? It was before her time.'

When I had arrived in Madrid, I recollected that I had known two men there in earlier postings. The first evening I settled down I picked up the telephone directory and dialled the number of the 'Marquez de Villalobar y Guimarhaez'. The gentleman answered the phone himself and I asked him if he remembered giving me lunch in his flat in Geneva in 1948 when I was escorting his sister-in-law Yolande de Ligne to India. He sounded quite mystified but finally remembered me. When we met (his first name was Pedro) he said,

'But surely we did not speak Spanish to each other in Geneva?'

'No, Kirat and I learnt Spanish during our postings in Argentina and Chile and I find that my South American Spanish is fully comprehensible to people here; nor have we had any difficulty in understanding what everybody here says to us.'

Pedro always gave me sound advice about people he knew. I had known his wife, Margot in Brussels. She considered herself prettier than her younger sister but obviously it was Yola who had made the better marriage in any conventional terms. Pedro and Margot had three sons whom I met at various times but I never saw the two together. Margot was living on the South Coast (the 'coast of the sun') where she had a large shop selling Indian garments. I called on her when I went there and she told me over lunch that she could not stand the climate of Madrid where 'one freezes in winter and roasts in summer.' I must confess that the climate of Delhi is only slightly warmer than Madrid but otherwise similar. On the other hand when I visited that part of Spain I definitely needed heating in the winter which I found rather damp.

The other person I knew was Pelayo Olay. In a previous chapter I mentioned Urmila Sen, the daughter of my Ambassador in Tokyo. Everybody in the Spanish-speaking diplomatic community had told me that she and the Spanish Ambassador (a widower some forty years older than her) were visibly in love with each other. They used to meet at a swimming pool frequented by many foreign diplomats. I don't remember who told Kirat,

'When either of them arrives at the pool and does not see the other, he/she looks as if the Sun had disappeared.'

This remark was familiar to me. I had heard it from my Tayaji describing my parents when he had visited them in Ahmedabad in 1920 before my birth. I was therefore not surprised when, the following year (1957), shortly after C.S.Jha arrived, another Spanish diplomat said to me, 'You are going to fall over backwards when you hear the news I have got for you!' I told him I was expecting to hear that Urmila had married Pelayo Olay.

Pelayo's next posting was New Delhi. I called on him when I happened to be home and Kirat and I were invited for lunch. The other guests included Urmila's mother – of course I never knew her first name – and an Austrian woman who had married an Englishman. The conversation turned to the subject of international marriages. The Austrian said that when she had met her mother after living in England for a dozen years, the latter had said,

'You don't move at all!' referring to the fact that, unlike most Continentals, English people don't gesticulate when they talk. Urmila said that she was wearing a dress which her husband wanted her to do whereas her mother would have liked her to wear a sari.

In Madrid, Pelayo came more than once for lunch – he said that he did not like to drive in the dark – but always alone on the pretext that Urmila was not well. Once, I dialled their number at a time when I knew Pelayo was not there and she answered but refused to come for a meal on the same pretext. They had a son and Pelayo said he wanted him to join the diplomatic service. In the twenty-first century I learnt that Pelayo had passed away and Urmila had returned to India but I have not seen her since that lunch at the Spanish Embassy in New Delhi more than three decades ago.

Air India did not fly to Madrid but there was an off-line booking office with a very active Spanish manager in charge. One afternoon in March 1979 I got an urgent phone call from him that Queen Frederica was leaving in an hour for India and I should go to the airport if I wanted to see her off. We had met Queen Frederica several times in Madrid. As I have mentioned, my visit to Madras and the bouquet I had sent had paid off. The King of Spain was in the habit of giving small receptions for new Ambassadors in the Palacio Real where I had presented my credentials. At one of these receptions Queen Sofia had said to me,

'I hear from my mother that you were good to her in Madras.'

'No, Your Majesty, it was the Queen your mother who was kind to me.'

The King and Queen did not live in the Palacio Real but in a much smaller mansion further away from the centre of the city known as the Moncloa Palace where Queen Frederica invited us for tea; there was some misunderstanding and finally she came to the Embassy residence for tea when Kiran and his little family were visiting us. She loved children – she generally had one or other of her numerous grandchildren with her in Madras – and spent most of her time playing with Arjun, then four years old.

On this afternoon in March 1979, I saw Queen Frederica among several other people I had never seen. The Air India Manager told me that she was being accompanied by her daughter's sister-in-law the Infanta Margarita. I looked around and saw a couple clinging very closely to each other. The Infanta Margarita is blind

1979 Madrid, Spain. Oxford and Cambridge Society Dinner in April, mentioned on the last page of my book.

and married to a medical practitioner who, at that time, had no title. When she heard me speak, she said,

'Ah! An Argentine!'

All the books on etiquette say that one should not speak to Royalty but wait to be introduced and be spoken to. However, I did not stand on ceremony but spoke up.

'Your Royal Highness, I am the Indian Ambassador here to wish you a pleasant journey and happy landing in my country which I understand you are honouring with your visit. It is true that I learnt my Spanish in Buenos Aires so what I speak is more *porteno* than *castillano*.'

Then we had a conversation about population politics and I found that she was a staunch Roman Catholic as opposed to family planning as Mahatma Gandhi. I have never been able to understand how in Italy, where the Pope resides, the native population is decreasing faster than in Protestant Northern Europe.

My last formal function in Madrid was attendance at the annual Boat Race dinner of the Oxford and Cambridge Society of Madrid. I was asked to speak on behalf of Cambridge while the British Ambassador, Sir Anthony Acland was to speak for Oxford.

Of course, I knew Sir Anthony well. He was in Madrid when I arrived so I had called on him. I had remarked that in the Diplomatic List published by the Spanish Government, the letters R.C.V.O. appeared after his name. I knew that the degrees in the Royal Victorian Order are: G.C.V.O., K.C.V.O.........I asked if he was a Knight Grand Cross.

'No, no, it is a misprint. I am a K.C.V.O. because I covered a Royal visit. The G.C.V.O. is only given to Heads of Mission who cover three Royal visits.' Sir Anthony had a brilliant career going on to be Ambassador in Washington and Permanent Under Secretary.

In my speech I said, *inter alia*,

'I am going to retire at the end of next month and this has come as a great surprise to me. Retirement for an Ambassador can be traumatic because his income decreases overnight by ninety per cent or more. This has never worried me because I learnt statistical probability at school and I have known for many years that my great-grandfather died at the age of eighty-six, my grandfather at seventy-eight and my father at sixty-two. Plotting these three figures on graph paper a curve emerged which I have extrapolated with a 'French curve' and the result provided conclusive proof that I could never survive till the age of fifty-eight which is the age of compulsory superannuation in the Indian Foreign Service.

'Last month, on a fine Spring day it suddenly dawned on me that retirement was only a few weeks away and if I was enjoying the Spring I must be alive. Thinking a little further I realised that literature is rather deficient in autobiographical accounts of death and I may have absent-mindedly crossed the Styx. If this is so my friends and acquaintances, colleagues and fellow-workers must have noticed it but they have been too polite to tell me that my Excellency is dead. Even the Embassy Doctor is hardly likely to say, 'Mr. Ambassador, you are dead; why don't you get yourself cremated?' However, I thought that I could ask him to prescribe a brain-scan for the decline in hearing in my left ear and I am sure the medical computer cannot have been programmed to be polite to Heads of Diplomatic Missions.

'To my horror, the computerised tomogram gave no indication of brain death. What is wrong with these new-fangled gadgets?'

◆ ◆ ◆

INDEX

Tokyo

Manila

Delhi

Bangkok

Singapore

Cambridge

Hamburg

Belgium

Birmingham

London

Madrid

Addis Ababa

Dakar

The Gambia

Upper Volta

Bogota

Quito

Santiago

Buenos Aires

HAMBURG

CPSIA information can be obtained at www.ICGtesting.com
Printed in the USA
LVOW030003041211

257380LV00006B/3/P